Interpreting Wagner

Interpreting Wagner

James Treadwell

Yale University Press
New Haven and London

For information about this and other Yale University Press
publications, please contact
U.S. Office: sales.press@yale.edu   yalebooks.com
Europe Office: sales@yaleup.co.uk   www.yaleup.co.uk

Set in Bembo by SNP Best-set Typesetter, Hong Kong
Printed in the United Kingdom at the University Press, Cambridge

ISBN 0-300-09815-4 (hbk.)

Library of Congress Control Number 2003101946

A catalogue record for this book is available from the British
Library

10 9 8 7 6 5 4 3 2 1

for Meredith
sine qua non

and in memory of William Beckmann
1968–2002

Contents

PART IV   *Religion*

Illustrations

Preface

This book is not intended as an interpretation of Wagner, nor as a guide to how Wagner ought to be interpreted. It's an attempt to think out a different set of questions: What is it like to interpret Wagner? What kind of possibilities for interpretation does Wagner's work offer? What is it about that body of work which makes interpretation such a complex and challenging matter? Books on Wagner often begin with some form of slightly apologetic justification for presuming to add another title to one of the most bloated bibliographies in the sphere of the arts. My self-defence might be that although I can't presume to add any significant new answers to the question of what these works mean, I hope that I have set out some better ways of asking the question – or (retreating further into apologia) that I have at least shown the question to be more complicated than it is sometimes taken to be.

Admitting an urge to complicate matters may sound forbidding. In fact, what follows is intended for anyone who has found themselves compelled to think about Wagner's work, whether out of love, loathing, or just an inability to stave off the fascination of an entirely unique phenomenon. I have tried not to presume any specialist knowledge. Readers who have a general familiarity with the operas – stories and music – will find that nothing further is expected. Because this is an effort to grasp Wagner's work in all its forms, a good deal of attention is paid to his prose writings, but the claims made about them do not depend on a complete knowledge of his various theories in the fields of aesthetics, politics and philosophy. In them, as in the operas, what interests me most is their habits of thought – their character, as it were.

There are no musical examples in this book. Printed music is a language that not everyone – not even all Wagner enthusiasts – can read; I have tried instead to use a descriptive terminology to refer to passages from the scores. Inevitably, this invites imprecision (like any act of translation from one language into another). My choice of adjectives will sound wrong to some readers, and without the strict technical accuracy of musical analysis the descriptions of what is happening in the music cannot claim to be authoritative. The risks seem worth taking. Music, after all, sounds differently to different listeners, and it's the sound of Wagner's scores – rather than their formal structures, the subject of technical analysis – which mostly occupies me here.

Nor does this book have much to say about the contexts that shaped Wagner's work. With the exception of the first chapter, which fills in a rough background for the ideas about art (especially the art of music) that determined Wagner's understanding of what opera was, there is very little reference to historical, political or philosophical influence. Only when those contexts are refracted through the operas themselves, as with the obvious nationalism of *Die Meistersinger* or the equally obvious Schopenhauerian vocabulary of *Tristan und Isolde*, are they treated in any detail; and even in those cases, my aim is not to look at Wagner's work through the lens of external influences, but to consider the contexts as seen through the (always distorting) lens of the operas. My aim has been to keep the interpretative eye fixed steadily on the works themselves, to see what they have to say about themselves and their contexts, rather than to explore what outside forces have to tell us about them.

Interpreting Wagner is a matter of thinking about a body of work, not exhuming a biographical corpse or psychoanalysing a consciousness that was switched off more than a hundred years ago. Which is not to say that personal history or psychoanalysis is not a valid means of interpretation: merely that exploring the character of the operas is an entirely different act from writing a biography of Wagner the man (that notoriously compelling and intriguing distraction). I am not concerned with what Wagner himself may or may not have thought about his works, nor with how the books he read or the people he encountered shaped their creation. When I discuss biographical material (the distraction is very hard to resist), it is as a way of illustrating the play of themes within the operas or prose writings. There is no doubt that Wagner the revolutionary had everything to do with the kind of work the *Ring* became, that Wagner the anti-Semite had a great deal to do with how *Parsifal* turned out, that Wagner the incurable fantasist was responsible for the visionary and escapist yearnings expressed in *Der fliegende Holländer*, *Tannhäuser* and *Lohengrin*. Nevertheless, what concerns me is what the *Ring* has to say about revolution, how racism works in *Parsifal*, what kind of vision and what kind of escape are sought by *Tannhäuser* or *Tristan*.

The book proceeds in roughly chronological fashion, beginning with the aesthetic atmosphere out of which Wagner's first works emerged and ending with their posthumous legacy in the form of the Bayreuth festivals. Again, this is not meant to imply that the course of Wagner's life determines the progress of his works. No line of continuous development is traced here.

Instead I have aimed to provide a series of themes, most of which are evident across the range of Wagner's work from *Die Feen* to *Parsifal* and from the lightly ironic short fiction 'Eine Pilgerfahrt zu Beethoven' (1840) to the densely earnest essay in musical aesthetics and nationalist politics *Beethoven* (1870). The chronological arrangement is meant only to show how these themes gain in complexity and depth as Wagner's art matures.

The chapters are gathered under four general headings: Romance, Revolution, Exile, Religion. Each corresponds to a period in Wagner's career, and focusses mainly on a set of works dating from that period: first – 'Romance' – the years up to 1848 (the three self-described 'romantic' operas and the Paris journalism); second – 'Revolution' – the period 1848–54 (the major theoretical writings and the *Ring* poem); third – 'Exile'– the chaotic years 1855–71 (*Tristan*, *Meistersinger*, some essays on musical form, the political writings of the 1860s, and the effect of Schopenhauer and of Ludwig II of Bavaria); fourth – 'Religion' – the final phase 1872–83 (*Parsifal*, Bayreuth, and the late essays). The headings are in no sense meant to be definitive or mutually exclusive. Some important parts of Wagner's work are under-represented, mostly for the sake of maintaining a focus on my main themes; thus – with regret – nothing is said here about the 1869 essay 'Über das Dirigiren' ('On Conducting'), and next to nothing about *Rienzi* or the essay *Beethoven* or the 1861 Paris production of *Tannhäuser*. The *Ring* is treated mainly in Part II, despite the fact that it was completed after *Meistersinger*. The headings are not meant as labels for stages in his life or his work: 'Exile' comprises both the wandering years 1858–64 and the physical, emotional and political return to Germany of the later 1860s, while I argue in Part II that in relation to Wagner, 'Revolution' means more or less the exact opposite of what is ordinarily understood by the term. In any case it is the conflicting interrelations among the different parts of Wagner's work that are of most interest here, not the development of distinct phases in his career. The words are intended to suggest no more than four fundamental dimensions of Wagner's art, four shifting compass points with which to orient our thinking about interpretation.

Writing on Wagner always incurs debts to the critical and scholarly work that has gone before (incurring debts being an aptly Wagnerian process). Because this book is not intended as an academic exercise, it may give the impression of refusing to pay those debts (also appropriate to the subject, perhaps). In the course of my argument I have generally not acknowledged the direct inspiration or provocation of existing work on Wagner. The focus is meant to stay on confronting Wagner's art itself. At the back of the book, in the 'Notes and further reading' section, I have supplied a short general note to each chapter listing some volumes (and the occasional article) which have stimulated my own thinking on the relevant topics, or which would help anyone looking for more detailed scholarly treatment. (The lists are restricted to works in English.) However, there are some obligations so deep and pervasive that they need to be mentioned before I begin. My thinking about Wagner has been influenced by two books in particular in so many ways that it would be impossible to acknowledge separately each occasion when I am aware of developing suggestions first discovered in them: Theodor Adorno's *In Search of Wagner* and Jean-Jacques Nattiez's *Wagner Androgyne* (for bibliographical details, see the aforementioned notes to chapters 10 and 5 respectively). The former is a thoroughly political and ideological exercise, the latter primarily concerned with theories of interpretation: it will quickly become obvious that this book has less specific and exacting aims. Nevertheless, the portraits of Wagner's aesthetic character drawn by Adorno and Nattiez have shaped my own experience of Wagner's operas very deeply. My sense of Wagner's personal and historical character owes everything to Ernest Newman's wonderful *Life of Richard Wagner*, crustily opinionated and enlivened by cheery prejudice as it is. Newman's facts have been corrected and his biases exposed, but no one has yet done a better job of capturing what one feels is the authentic flavour of Wagner's life and personality, nor does any other book bear such eloquent witness to what it is like to be both repelled and entranced by the composer.

The chiaroscuro of Wagner's genius makes him a volatile subject still. This book has not been written as a declaration of allegiance in any of the apparently permanent wars being fought in the field of Wagner studies (the battle over what to do with the composer's anti-Semitism being only the noisiest of them, and the one where the stakes seem highest). That said, there is a point around the middle of the book where the argument recognizes a need to make certain basic choices. Experience suggests that at this point, if not before, some readers will feel a compulsion to take up arms to 'defend' Wagner against a perceived siege. The book should be left to speak on its own behalf; all I would want to say at this stage is that everything that follows rests on the almost incomparably rich resources of Wagner's works themselves, and therefore that whatever one may find to criticize in his art, it is still the case that the tools for the criticism are also supplied by those works. If Wagner comes under attack here (which I would in any case deny), the assault is from within. Chiaroscuro is after all an art in which opposites are conjoined within the same frame, so that their contrast becomes mutual illumination. Light and dark, as Wotan (in his guise as the Wanderer) knows, are aspects of each other.

Acknowledgments

The process that led to this book began with a great and generous gift, a gift of a *Ring*; it is dedicated to the giver, with all gratitude and love.

Without the interventions of Roger Parker and Malcolm Gerratt, the opportunity to gather these thoughts together would never have arisen. Writing about Wagner is almost an indulgence, however rarely it feels like one, and I owe an enormous debt to them for making this book possible, as well as for their faith that it was a worthwhile effort. The tolerance and generosity of the Governing Body of Christ Church, Oxford, created room for the early stages of my work on Wagner. I am also grateful to the Faculty of Graduate Studies and Research of McGill University for supporting the project.

The ideas developed in this book derive more from reflecting on Wagner's works than from scholarly or archival research. Correspondingly, I have benefited incalculably from conversations with teachers, colleagues, students and friends. Peter Conrad encouraged me, both directly and by example, to think critically about opera. My experiences at Bayreuth would not have led to wider considerations of the Wagnerian aesthetic without the chance to discuss those experiences in the shadow of the Festspielhaus, and I am particularly grateful to Jonathan Osser and Vance Johnson in this respect; also to Sandra Leva for some inspiring and rewarding conversations. At McGill University, I am indebted to Professors Maggie Kilgour and Peter Ohlin for the opportunity to intrude Wagner into a syllabus of literary and cultural study, and to Ross Bonnell, Daphné Brunelle, Erica Buehner, Laure Cañadas, Louis Choquette, Mark Diachyshyn, Joanne Matson, Michael Maurushat, Carrie Schoemer, Cynthia Taylor, Andrea Valenta and Janie Yoon for weeks of intense Wagnerian discussions. My parents, Tom Treadwell and Tanya Barker, have been patient and encouraging victims of that intensity, and it is a pleasure to thank them, along with Colin Senior, for an early induction into Wagner's worlds.

Roger Allen's expert comments on parts of the manuscript have been an invaluable resource. His wide knowledge of matters Wagnerian and Bayreuthian has been indispensable to the writing of this book, and it has also made his support for the project very encouraging. (Needless to say, no one but myself is to blame for any remaining errors.) Dr Sven Friedrich and Gudrun Föttinger of the National Archive of the Richard Wagner Foundation at Bayreuth were very generous with their time and expertise, as were Cécile Verguin and the rest of the librarians at BIFI Iconothèque in Paris; I am indebted to them all for their assistance in collecting material for the illustrations, and to Stewart McCombie and Anita Cotic at McGill, and (especially) to Arthur Ka Wai Jenkins in London, for technical help with the reproductions. The staff of the Marvin Duchow Music Library at McGill have also provided patient and generous assistance. John Bell's advice guided me through the beginning of the publication process; and I owe thanks to Robert Baldock at Yale University Press for his encouraging supervision. At a crucial stage in the writing of the book, the project would have been impossible to complete without the help of Linda Borden, Bev Davis, Elissa DeFalco (*prima inter pares*), Ian Degroff, Chris Holmes, Jennifer Koopman, Jaime Shepard and Ursula Shepard; my thanks to all of them for their labours.

William Beckmann taught me so much about what music can mean and how to talk about those meanings that it's impossible to say where my thanks to him should begin. His untimely death prevented them from being given in person. Here at least I can record that he is the one reader I would most like to have had.

The characters of Elsa and Kundry figure very prominently in this book; to Justin and Kit Treadwell I owe a deepened insight into Kundry's words 'Schlafen − schlafen: − ich muß', but also into Elsa's: 'euch muß ich dankend sagen,/ wie sich mein Glück enthüllt'. My acknowledgments end where they began: Meredith Hyde has inspired, encouraged, corrected and cajoled from beginning to end. My debts to her are too mountainous to be repaid, and my thanks to her go much further than can be said here.

A Note on Citations and Translations

Citations from Wagner's prose writings in English are followed by a reference to the volume and page number of William Ashton Ellis's translation, *Richard Wagner's Prose Works*, 8 vols (London: Kegan Paul & Co., 1892–9). This edition has recently been reprinted by the University of Nebraska Press in the form of eight separate paperback volumes. Their published titles correspond to the order of volumes in the original edition as follows:

Vol. I   *The Art-Work of the Future, and Other Works*
Vol. II   *Opera and Drama*
Vol. III *Judaism in Music, and Other Essays*
Vol. IV   *Art and Politics*
Vol. V   *Actors and Singers*
Vol. VI   *Religion and Art*
Vol. VII *A Pilgrimage to Beethoven, and Other Essays*
Vol. VIII *Jesus of Nazareth, and Other Writings*

Other abbreviations used in citations are as follows:

L   *Selected Letters of Richard Wagner*, ed. and trans. Stewart Spencer and Barry Millington (London: J.M. Dent, 1987)
ML   Richard Wagner, *My Life*, ed. Mary Whittall, trans. Andrew Gray (Cambridge: Cambridge University Press, 1983)
WR   Stewart Spencer, ed., *Wagner Remembered* (London: Faber and Faber, 2000)

All further references are given in endnotes at the back of the book.

Working on Wagner in English means losing a lot of sleep over the issue of translation. In the absence of reliable standard English versions of all his

significant writing – libretti, prose works, letters, autobiography and diaries –
the only absolutely ideal solution is to translate all necessary material afresh,
giving the original German text in parallel so that any idiosyncrasies in the
rendering can be taken into account by the informed reader. This would have
resulted in a very cumbersome read – not to mention two further objections:
firstly, my lack of the expertise required for accurate rendering of all Wagner's
different rhetorical styles and registers, and secondly, the threat of losing not
just sleep but every waking hour as well to the extra labour.

I have therefore adopted different solutions depending on which texts
are at hand. Wherever possible I have tried to use fairly recent, well-translated
editions of Wagner's work, as long as those editions have some claim to
being authoritative, or at least standard for English readers. Thus for Wagner's
correspondence the superb selection made by Barry Millington and Stewart
Spencer is equally admirably served by Spencer's translations; the autobiography *Mein Leben* (*My Life*) is also widely available in an adequate version.

The texts of the operas present difficulties all of their own. There is no
authoritative edition of the whole canon even in German. The versions
appearing in the standard Geman editions of Wagner's writings – the ten-
volume *Gesammelte Schriften* of 1871–83, prepared by the composer, and the
sixteen-volume *Sämtliche Schriften und Dichtungen* (1911–14), incorporating
material not included by Wagner – are not always the same as those eventually published in the first editions of the scores: Wagner often made changes
to his libretti as he prepared the operas for print. English translations, meanwhile, vary widely in usefulness and availability. A series like the excellent
Opera Guides of English National Opera/Royal Opera (originally edited
by Nicholas John) has the advantage of full translations of each separate
opera in accessible paperback format. However, the translations were made
for performance; they are 'singable' versions, and therefore necessarily sacrifice accuracy to the rhythm and overall phrasing of the music (and in some
cases they aim to rhyme in English as well, producing further constraints on
a faithful rendering of the original libretto). Andrew Porter's translations of
the four *Ring* operas for this series resolve these challenges unusually
successfully; they have been separately published in a single paperback (Faber,
1976). The tetralogy is served by a more recent version, also excellent and
accessible: another Spencer/Millington collaboration (Thames and Hudson,
1993, with interesting annotation and some brief introductory essays). This
edition has the added advantage of printing what the editors claim as an
authoritative German text. Beyond the *Ring*, though, there are no satisfactory
English versions.

All citations of the German *Ring* libretti in this book refer to Spencer and
Millington's text. Otherwise, for the sake of consistency, I have used the
1911–14 *Sämtliche Schriften* as the copy text for all references to Wagner's

writings, libretti and prose works included (with one exception noted in chapter 15). The Spencer/Millington *Ring* preserves the nineteenth-century orthography of German forms like *Muth* and *thun* (rather than *Mut* or *tun*), as of course does the *Sämtliche Schriften*; since this is an accurate quotation of Wagner's usage I have seen no reason to modernize it.

Because the words of the libretti are inextricably entangled with the music to which the words are set, any English reader at all familiar with Wagner's operas is likely to 'hear' them in German. It would look and sound strange to refer to the moment when Tristan and Isolde join voices and sing 'O sink down, night of love'; but as soon as one reads the words 'O sink' hernieder,/ Nacht der Liebe', the hushed rapture of the phrases fills one's aural memory. When citing the texts of the operas, therefore, I have given parallel versions in German and English. The presence of the original text obviates any worries about the standard of the translation, so in the absence of any single reliable English version of all the operas, I have simply given my own colour-less, more-or-less literal renderings. Wagner's poetic eccentricities present many challenges to the translator, a further reason to keep the English versions as banal as possible and allow readers to look to the parallel German text for the authentic Wagnerian tone. (It was very tempting to use Spencer's vivid render-ing of the *Ring*, which reflects the stilted, craggy artificiality of Wagner's pseudo-antiquarian *Stabreim* – alliterative verse – and his condensed grammar, but no translations of similar value are readily available for the other operas, so the result would have been an unfair bias in favour of the tetralogy.)

Which brings us to the apparently unslayable bugbear of Wagner in English, Ellis's translation of the *Prose Writings*. It is hard to exaggerate the wrenching badness of Ellis's version, produced at a time when Carlyle's knotty style (itself strongly influenced by German models) was still considered the exemplar of sublime English prose, and by an author whose reverence for all things German clearly extended to a sneaking desire to Teutonicize his own native language. (At one point, Ellis refers with evident satisfaction to the fact that the untranslatable German word *Stimmung* appears in his view to be well on its way to becoming a part of English usage, as *Zeitgeist* has – a misap-prehension which gives a rather frightening insight into the nature of general conversation in the circles he must have moved in.) All that can be said in defence of his translation of Wagner is that it is inspired by a dogged servil-ity. It at least *tries* to be a completely faithful rendering, preserving as far as possible the sentence structure of the original, and looking for direct equivalents in English for compound German words. However badly the result reads, it perhaps conveys something of the strangeness of Wagner's own prose. Nevertheless, there are occasions – many of them – where Ellis's version is so contorted as to be almost unreadable; and at times, inexplicably, he fails even to be accurate to the sense of the original.

The problem is that there is no other English version of *all* Wagner's prose (at least, all the writing the composer himself gathered for publication). Until such time as some brave publishing house commissions a new translation – 'Will this Prince be found?' – Ellis is the standard edition. Even this might not be such an obstacle had it not been for the University of Nebraska Press's recent reissue of his eight volumes in convenient paperbacks, an act which put Ellis on the shelves of Wagner enthusiasts all over the English-speaking world. Blessings rarely come so mixed. To have an affordable complete edition of Wagner's works in English at last is wonderful; to have it include the line 'How's hight the hero?' (from Ellis's translation of Wagner's 1850 sketch *Wieland the Smith*) makes one ask if it was worth the wait. Still, the fact is that English-speaking readers who choose to delve into Wagner's writings will do so via the stiff poeticisms and ungainly contortions of Ellis's idea of fine prose.

With a rather heavy heart, then, I have chosen to cite all those writings in Ellis's translations. When his versions seem seriously to obscure the meaning of what Wagner wrote, or when they use a vocabulary barely recognizable as English, I have given short passages of the original German text (from the *Sämtliche Schriften*) in square brackets. On a few occasions, though too many for comfort, I have been unable to find any excuse at all for Ellis's style, and have resorted to small alterations in the phrasing, also signalled by square brackets. For example, where Ellis has 'for reason that . . .', I have been unable to stomach his faux-German contraction, instead writing 'for [the] reason that . . .'. Needless to say, the term [*sic*] has not been used; readers can assume that however bizarre the passage in front of them looks, Ellis actually wrote it. As so often happens with annoying eccentricities, after long exposure one actually ends up feeling a guiltily submerged affection for his translation. I hope this pernicious effect has not led me to leave too many of his grotesqueries as they are, thus further obscuring Wagner's already less than pellucid thought.

The titles of the operas have been left untranslated ('The Mastersingers of Nuremberg' somehow doesn't sound like a Wagner opera). I refer to the individual prose writings by their German titles when they are cited for the first time (or after a long interval), followed by a translation; thereafter, English titles are used. For the sake of consistency, I have again employed Ellis's renderings of the titles, so that readers can easily refer to their own copies of his translation. This means quite a few infuriating sillinesses – Wagner's late essay 'Heldenthum und Christenthum', 'Heroism and Christianity', becomes 'Hero-dom and Christendom'. It also has one seriously controversial result. The notorious, appalling 'Das Judenthum in der Musik' becomes 'Judaism in Music', an altogether too dignified-sounding piece of phrasing. Most writers in English now prefer to capture the bitter taste of the title by rendering it as 'Jewishness in Music' or 'Jews in Music'. Having chosen to live by Ellis, though, one has to be prepared to die by Ellis as well.

'Parzifal has preoccupied me very much: in particular, there is a curious creature, a strangely world-demonic woman (the messenger of the grail) who strikes me with increasing vitality and fascination.'

Wagner to Mathilde Wesendonck, December 1858 (*L* 434)

PART I

Romance

CHAPTER ONE

The Romance of Opera

The theatre Wagner built for himself is a surprisingly unprepossessing building. By the standards of an artist whose tendency is always towards intensification and exaggeration, the Festspielhaus ('festival-theatre') in Bayreuth radiates humility. True, it is perched on a hilltop at the end of a long straight avenue, like some grandiose manor or castle, but the hill is small, and the building sits squatly there, hardly dominating the approach. It has a formal entrance, colonnaded and galleried, but this decorative façade occupies only about a half of the front of the building, and the most casual glance reveals that it has obviously been stuck on; it doesn't belong. The rest is bare brick. The structure seems to have made a half-hearted attempt to live up to the self-importance of its creator, before giving up to devote itself to more important things.

It isn't immediately obvious what those things are when one enters the building, either. First impressions fail to live up to the monumental quality usually exuded by everything Wagner touched. Most theatregoers expect their palaces of art to have a certain grandeur, whatever the architectural language used to communicate that impression – the red and gold and marble of the later nineteenth century, the shapely sweeps and curves of the Baroque, the impressively airy scale of more recent buildings. The Festspielhaus has no foyer. A few short, blunt corridors offer unglamorously functional conveniences: cloakrooms, lavatories. In many opera houses, the key interior effects are communicated by staircases, offering appropriate visions of elevation, or of hierarchy, in cases where they invite wealthier patrons to the boxes while leaving the rabble in the pit. In the Bayreuth theatre, though, visitors are conducted almost apologetically to their place, with the minimum of fuss and display. The Opéra Garnier in Paris, roughly contemporary with Wagner's building, positively invites you to pause and gape in the midst of your ascent; climbing the stairs is part of the show. Not so the Festspielhaus. Some entrances to the auditorium are gained almost as if one were using a stepladder.

The auditorium itself is attractive, but not impressive: a pleasingly shaped box. There are no aisles. The seats look as if they might have been raided secondhand from a salvage yard, and feel surprisingly like that too. One of the most titillatingly bizarre facts about Wagner was his predilection for furnishing his homes and costuming himself in outlandish swathes of texture and colour, but visitors to his theatre get no intimations of such excesses; the austerity of this interior verges on being punitive.

It is only after you have entered and found your place and waited for everyone else to find theirs that you discover how the Bayreuth Festspielhaus captures and communicates the essential nature of Wagner's art. What happens is simply that the lights go down; but because the orchestra pit is hooded from the eyes of the audience, concealing the light needed by musicians and conductor, there is a moment of total darkness, before your pupils dilate enough to take in the dim glow being cast by those hidden lights on the silvery-grey curtain. Briefly but startlingly, the whole environment disappears. You feel yourself to be suspended in emptiness, your attention totally absorbed by the faint glimmer in the space where Wagner's world will shortly appear.

Then the sound begins. The effect works best with the opera that was written for this theatre, and which describes itself as a ritual consecration of that building, the *Bühnenweihfestspiel* ('stage-consecrating festival play') *Parsifal*. But the elemental E flat in the basses that unveils the *Ring* would be nearly as good, as would the shimmering, distant breath on high violins that is the first sound of *Lohengrin*, or even the stately wind and horn chords of *Tannhäuser's* pilgrimage hymn. In the first few seconds, the actual music being played isn't really relevant. You are riveted instead by the way you are hearing it, the scene music has placed itself in. Sound arises with no visible sign and from no apparent source, conspiring with the near-total darkness to make you believe that it is some kind of purely spiritual emanation, rather than the product of musicians and instruments. Nothing is more characteristic of Wagner's genius than this effect. A blend of simple technologies creates for you a moment which distils everything most fundamental to his art: its intensification of aesthetic experience, its almost physical engagement with the audience, its desire to captivate the attention. Everything one expects and fails to find in the building itself is contained more subtly, and a thousand times more potently, in the otherworldly emergence of music from the invisible orchestra. The experience itself is not overwhelming or exaggerated or monumental; on the contrary, the arch of sound that begins *Parsifal* is austere, almost bare. The Wagnerian excess comes entirely from the sheer brilliance of the effect, the completeness of the composer's power over his listeners at that startling moment.

This book is an investigation of the character of that power. It asks what it is that Wagner's work – operatic and literary – thinks it is doing to us. It also explores the possibilities of resistance to power which those works hold out to us, because without those possibilities we are left merely gaping in awe at the stage. I start with the auditorium of the Festspielhaus in order to emphasize the aspect of Wagner that matters most to this effort. The book is not primarily about Wagner's music, or his poetry, or the intellectual sources and contexts that inform his work. It looks elsewhere for the root of the Wagner phenomenon. The starting-point is suggested by Nietzsche, the most eloquent witness of what it is like to come under Wagner's spell – the magic glimpsed at its clearest in that fraction of time in the darkened theatre. In May 1888, seven months before his complete breakdown, Nietzsche published his morbid, desperately comical pamphlet *Der Fall Wagner* (*The Case of Wagner*), in which he claims finally to have unmasked his antagonist. His true domain, Nietzsche says, is neither music, nor poetry, nor drama in the classicized sense Nietzsche understands the term, but the stage.

> Was Wagner a musician at all? At any rate, there was something else that he was more: namely, an incomparable *histrio* [actor], the greatest mime, the most amazing genius of the theatre ever among our Germans, our *scenic artist par excellence*. . . .
>
> . . . Wagner never calculates as a musician, from some sort of musician's conscience: what he wants is effect, nothing but effect. And he knows on whom he wants to achieve his effects. . . .
>
> . . . One is an actor by being ahead of the rest of mankind in one insight: what is meant to have the effect of truth must not be true.[1]

This is of course meant as a triumphant exposure of Wagner's fraudulence, an insight that allows us as it were to look through the screens Wagner's art throws before us and to see the machinery he (as at Bayreuth) hides from view. The accusation that Wagner finally achieves only 'effect' drips with contempt; even more hostile is the accusation that 'effect' is innately mendacious, because it is by definition a process of making lies appear true. It is not surprising, therefore, that serious defenders of Wagner have often started by denying Nietzsche's accusation outright and arguing not only that he is a musician, but that his genius is fundamentally musical.

Yet any attempt to get to grips with the Wagnerian aesthetic as a whole must recognize the hard-won accuracy of Nietzsche's verdict. Wagner was always a man of the theatre, and his art is in every sense (including the best) 'stagy', characterized by an instinct for astonishing *coups de théâtre*. He spent much of his life in search of stages, finally achieving the almost absurdly hubristic ambition of building his own, and decreeing that no one else's work could ever be performed there (and even, in the case of *Parsifal*, decreeing that his own work could be performed nowhere else). He observed, worked in and wrote about theatres again and again in his life. He exploits the nature

of theatrical experience to fill his operas with effects that have no immediate dramatic function but nevertheless make you catch your breath in
live performance. Everyone will have their own favourites among these;
mine is the introduction of the offstage voice to begin the first act of
Tristan und Isolde, when after the agonized turbulence of the prelude, the
sailor's song drifts over the quiet stage, an eerily invisible and disorienting
aural effect.

First of all, though, theatre − and, in particular, opera − was the world
Wagner grew up in. His father, whom he never knew, was a civil servant with
an amateur's passion for the theatre. His stepfather Ludwig Geyer, who may
or may not have been his biological parent, was an actor and playwright. His
oldest brother was a singer and theatre manager, and that brother's oldest
daughter would become the first Elisabeth in *Tannhäuser*. Three of his sisters
became actresses or singers. He married an actress. Dresden, where he spent
his early years, had a German opera company founded and maintained by
Weber, whose opera *Der Freischütz* epitomized the vernacular romantic style
that inspired Wagner's initial understanding of the genre; Weber employed
Geyer and was an acquaintance of the family. Under the influence of
Beethoven, he produced some symphonic works in his youth, but overtures
and incidental music − music with a plot − are more typical. Wagner's first
and last employments were in theatres (after 1848 he was never paid for his
labour, only for his genius). He was nineteen years old when he became
chorus-master of the small provincial theatre company in Würzburg. At this
stage in his life, the position looks like the culmination of a theatrical apprenticeship, not the first step in the career of a great composer.

Wagner's generation inherited a dignified notion of the stage as a central
element in German cultural life. However much this dignity was attenuated
at the level of badly-run local theatres with poor resources and unreliable
audiences, such places could still see themselves as part of a national resource
that had been re-energized by Goethe and Schiller in the previous decades.
In this conception, the popular art of drama was a place where artistic ideals
could be transmitted directly to the people. Schiller's drama turns the stage
into a medium for presenting political and psychological themes with tremendous intensity and seriousness. Goethe's conception of the institution had
been more august still; as manager of the theatre at Weimar, his project was
to unite civic virtue with the moral life of the individual, seeing the state-
sponsored stage as the point where citizens and rulers discovered and represented to themselves their common purpose.

Goethe also knew about the more elemental pleasures − and dangers −
of performance. The eponymous hero of his 1795−6 novel *Wilhelm Meisters
Lehrjahre* (*Wilhelm Meister's Apprenticeship*) grows up seduced by the captivating imaginative liberation of make-believe. Over the course of the novel, he

has to learn a more disciplined discrimination between imagination and simple deception. Nietzsche rails against Wagner for failing to educate himself out of the same confusion, and pursuing instead an increasingly decadent indulgence in theatre's exhilarating falsehoods. It is certainly true that Wagner's operas show no inclination to be suspicious of the magic of the stage. Indeed, for all the sober and serious purposes Goethe and his contemporaries imagined for the theatre, Wagner describes himself as having been attracted first and most powerfully to the purely fantastic element. Dictating *Mein Leben* (*My Life*) in the summer of 1865, he recounts the almost erotic thrill of his family's habitual world:

> What attracted me so strongly to the theatre, in which I include the stage itself, the compartments behind the scenes, and the dressing-rooms, was . . . a tingling delight in finding myself in an atmosphere that represented such a contrast to normal life by its purely fantastic and almost appallingly attractive quality. Thus a set, or even a flat . . . or a costume or even only a characteristic piece of one, appeared to me to emanate from another world, and be in a certain sense interesting as apparitions, and contact with all this would serve as a lever to lift me out of a monotonous everyday reality into that fascinating demoniacal realm. Everything connected with the theatre had for me the charm of mystery, an attraction amounting to intoxication. . . . (*ML* 13)

Although written long after the fact, the language of this recollection is very like some of Wagner's articles of the late 1830s and early 1840s. The tone in *My Life* may be tinged with gentle self-mockery, but it still captures the absorbing seductions of a marvellous and exotic world. For the young Wagner, this aspect of the theatre came to be associated with one particular dramatic genre. The great playwrights of the preceding generations had bequeathed to Germany a serious and elevated mode of drama, but the proper medium for 'mystery' and 'intoxication' was an altogether different kind of native theatre: romantic opera.

  The phenomenal popularity of Weber's *Der Freischütz* after its appearance in 1821 allowed Germans once again to claim this kind of opera as their own characteristic achievement. Although the repertory was and would remain dominated by Italian and French works, Weber's atmospheric piece demonstrated a distinctly different set of aesthetic possibilities, based on neither Italianate melodiousness nor Parisian heroic grandeur. Music was here being allied with drama in order to create a mood, to inundate the audience with thrillingly obscure sensations. *Der Freischütz* was also famous for a few popular set-piece songs, but its most striking passage – the 'Wolf's Glen' scene in Act II – evokes a coherent musico-dramatic character based on the atmospheric powers of harmony and orchestral sonority rather than the self-contained appeal of a tune. This is essentially an aesthetic of effect. The purpose of melody, in late eighteenth- and early nineteenth-century opera at least, is to express human emotion; it appeals to us by inviting us to sympathize or identify with the feelings from which it springs. By contrast, Weber's scene relegates the human characters to the position of observers, and allows the stage to be filled instead with supernatural sights and sounds. The audience cannot feel itself to be part of this world: hence the captivating 'mystery' Wagner remembers in the passage from *Mein Leben*, which goes on to describe how he and his friends tried 'to imitate performances of *Freischütz*' (ML 13). Instead of presenting particularly affecting scenes of human behaviour, operatic scenes like these give the impression of having opened up some new, alien, exotic domain.

At least potentially, German romantic opera provides a theatrical experience which corresponds to an idea of the stage as a magical space. This approach to the audience is very different from the ennobling ideals advocated by theorists of the drama; in *Wilhelm Meister* it appears as a childish (or adolescent) fantasy. Other operatic genres paid lip-service at least to more elevated conceptions of the role of theatre. The stock in trade of the most successful operas in northern Europe in the 1800s and 1810s was an impassioned heroism. Characters had larger-than-life motives, especially love and patriotism, and they acted out the consequences of these idealized impulses in grandly conceived historical situations. By the 1820s, these conventions had become identifiable as 'grand opera', the hugely popular, spectacularly overblown genre particularly associated with the Paris Opéra (a theatre whose technical resources allowed appropriately sumptuous stagings). Such works might imagine that they roused their audience's most solemn and worthy passions. Setting aside the question of whether the operas of Spontini, Auber and Meyerbeer are justified in claiming this sort of effect, it is possible at least to see the basis on which the claim is made. The essential factors are character and narrative. The genre, that is, bases itself on depictions of inspiring people in inspiring situations.

German stages mostly had to import this kind of opera, but one masterly native example was available to them in the years of Wagner's childhood and youth: *Fidelio*. Beethoven's work exemplifies the kind of effect 'grand opera' would come to rely on (although its own generic roots are in the more melodramatic, less sweeping narratives of 'rescue opera', the typical mode of revolutionary and Napoleonic France). The heroine is impelled by extraordinary courage, selfless devotion, and dauntless persistence. Nor are these only private virtues. The plot of *Fidelio* turns them into explicitly political qualities; her noble love for her imprisoned husband translates effortlessly into an equally passionate devotion to the idea of freedom in the abstract. Hence the opera's exuberant final chorus celebrates her as a model of both domestic and civic virtue. As she and Florestan stand centre stage, the chorus surrounds them with praise for their heroism. Here the audience is implicitly invited to join in: the chorus speaks for us. The opera is a rite celebrating revolutionary values through the elevation of its central character and the narrative progression from imprisonment and tyranny to freedom and justice.

Instead of asking the audience to identify with (or at least admire) heroic action, romantic opera stresses the detached position of the spectator. Its favourite passions are wonder and fear, both of which imply an awareness on the spectators' part that they do not belong in the world portrayed on stage. Its narratives tend towards tragedy, or else towards resolutions achieved by magical intervention rather than the noble heroism of the central characters. The characters themselves often labour under the weight of forces they cannot control or resist. Where *Fidelio* gives its heroine the power to choose her own actions, and therefore to do the right thing, operas like *Der Freischütz* or Spohr's *Faust* (1816) or Marschner's *Hans Heiling* (1833) and *Der Vampyr* (1828) hinge on fateful conditions and curses that restrict such agency. Under these circumstances, character and narrative cannot serve as inspiring models. The interest of the work must be sought elsewhere.

An aesthetic of effect had begun to be formulated in Germany as early as the 1750s, and around the turn of the nineteenth century it would become closely associated with purely instrumental music. Two features of music are particularly relevant here. Because of its non-mimetic nature – its lack of any reference to the world of actions and objects – its appeal could not be based on character or narrative. More obviously, it was also claimed as a specifically German achievement, thanks mostly to Beethoven. As early as 1761, though, the influential historian and essayist Justus Möser claimed that the idea of music as 'an autonomous world of imagination' was essentially German; its expressive or quasi-pictorial function appeared only in France.[2] Opera seems an unlikely candidate for representing such a view of music. After all, it appears to press music into the service of telling stories and portraying feelings, rather than allowing it to express its 'autonomous' effects. Nevertheless, Christoph Martin Wieland proposed in 1775 the creation of a genre of opera (again specific to Germany) which would radically simplify the *Handlung* – the actions, situations, plot: the *content* – in order to emphasize the overall mood.[3] Instrumental sound thus gains the ascendancy over more dramatic elements. For the audience, sympathetic identification with, or admiration for, the characters is superseded by the inarticulate sensations produced by sheer sound. A later generation would make this aim the defining characteristic of German romantic opera.

One of the striking features of the genre is that it was always pursued in theory at least as ardently as, and perhaps more successfully than, in practice. Wagner was far from being the only person to combine writing operas with writing about them. E.T.A. Hoffmann, whose various writings articulate most fully the idea of romantic opera, was also the composer of the hugely popular *Undine* (1816) among other stage works. Weber's 1817 review of *Undine*, incorporating fragments of his unfinished semi-autobiographical novel *Künstlerleben* (*An Artist's Life*), contains interesting comments about the kind of qualities that would later impress Wagner (and others) in his own *Freischütz*. He writes of 'the opera which the German desires', implying that he and Hoffmann and others are engaged in creating something founded on fundamentally different principles from the dominant styles of Italy or France.[4] Spohr, too, published a brief manifesto for the future of German opera in 1823. Although its popularity was relatively short-lived, the romantic style bears with it a disproportionate weight of desire, of aspiration. It envisions itself laying open new realms of aesthetic experience. One of Hoffmann's characters declares that

> genuinely romantic opera . . . can bring to life the wondrous phenomena of the spirit world; on [its] wings we are lifted over the chasm which otherwise divides us from it, and, grown accustomed to the strange country, we believe in the marvels which, as inevitable effects of the action of higher natures on our being, take place visibly and bring about all the strong, powerfully affecting situations which fill us, now with awe and horror, now with the highest bliss.[5]

It may well have been the gap between such lyrical theories and the actual nature of the operas produced in Germany at the time which caused the 'Young Germany' movement to turn away from romantic philosophizing in the wake of the Parisian revolution of July 1830. Wagner joined in the temporary enthusiasm for the 'warm south' and its unencumbered sensuality. His opera *Das Liebesverbot* (1836) allies itself to this movement by imitating Rossini's musical style, and (taking over the plot of *Measure for Measure*) telling the story of a coldly ascetic German hypocrite battling with, and being defeated by, exuberant Sicilian amorousness. Yet in theory at least, the hoped-for German opera would not be passionless. What Wagner and others objected to was the idealism in which German aspirations were always clothed, a spiritual tendency which seemed like mere shadow-play in comparison with the July revolution or the more tangible pleasures of the culture of the south. Nevertheless, Weber could claim in his *Undine* review that 'what love is to man, music is to the arts and to mankind, for it is actually love itself . . .'.[6] The romantic theorists imagined their music overwhelming its audience with intense and potent sensation. For all Wagner's Young German cynicism about the practical possibilities of such an aesthetic (and of course he spent much of the 1830s discovering what German operatic audiences were really like), his various accounts of the effect of *Der Freischütz* demonstrate how naturally it came to him.

The mysterious and exalted theatrical sensations he describes certainly tally with the romantic theorists' deep interest in opera audiences. This again contrasts with prevailing concerns outside Germany. Eighteenth-century writers in Italy and France filled most of their discussions of opera with debates about the nature and legitimacy of the genre itself, and consequently about how it ought to be practised by composers and poets. These were ultimately arguments over style, couched in abstract terms. The relative value to be placed on music or poetry, for example – the longest-running cliché of writing about opera – was a philosophical matter, or, if the writer appealed to classical standards, a question of the correct interpretation of ancient Greek drama. The audience's experience is relevant only insofar as a critic wants opera to express natural feeling. Such expression is still a matter for the composer; it is his job to know how human nature is touched and moved. For the Berlin writer C.G. Krause in 1752, however, the importance of opera is not that it corresponds to some essential existing quality of humans in general, but that it provides a unique, irresistibly fascinating experience for the particular people assembled in the theatre. His *Von der musikalischen Poesie* (*On Musical Poetry*) says that 'the soul and the fantasy [*Das Herz und die Phantasie*] of a person who enters the opera house are prepared to surrender themselves to the deception of imagination and the outbreaks of passion'.[7] Such an open appeal to undignified and irrational enthusiasm would have been unthinkable to most serious writers of the mid-eighteenth century. Their general attitude was that opera could only be taken seriously if it could justify itself on sound (that is, Aristotelian) intellectual principles, with no inherent appeal to the passions of the mob. Even such an anti-classicist as Rousseau recoiled with embarrassment from the public's taste for opera's theatricality.

Yet for Hoffmann the felt encounter with music is what matters most. He wants sound to 'surround mankind in luminous sparkling circles and, enkindling its imagination, its innermost soul, . . . bear it in rapid flight into the faraway spirit realm'.[8] This is the language of that staple of romance plots, abduction. Opera audiences are most vulnerable of all to being surrounded and carried off, because a theatre is a more potent machine for abduction than a drawing-room or concert hall (witness the Bayreuth Festspielhaus). In Hoffmann's dialogue 'Der Dichter und der Komponist' ('The Poet and the Composer', 1819–21), the musician Ludwig – he has Beethoven's name, naturally – establishes as the criterion of all opera its power to 'take hold of us and transport us . . . forcefully'. The poet Ferdinand is easily converted to this view. 'Only in the genuine romantic', he effuses, does opera fulfil its aim of 'laying hold of the feelings of the audience in a wonderful way'.[9]

By devoting so much attention to the effect of music, romantic theorizing exposes its fascination with art's theatricality. The experience Wagner describes in *Mein Leben* is typical, and exemplary. Opera's fundamental purpose is to abduct those gathered to watch it. From the vantage-point of 1888, amid a Europe infected with pandemic Wagnerism, Nietzsche thought that his adversary had achieved this secret aim with appalling success. At the other end of the nineteenth century, most sceptical observers would have been able to dismiss the romantic aesthetic more comfortably. For critics in England and France, the adjective 'German' could be used to signify melodramatic sensationalism, whether in music, drama or poetry. Even some German observers were uncomfortable with the fervent romantic embrace of illusion and fantasy; hence the 'Young Germany' movement, and hence also the brilliantly ironic eye Heinrich Heine casts over his artistic fellow-countrymen. The sceptics' concern is that an aesthetic of effect is at best irresponsible, at worst dangerous. As Wilhelm Meister has to learn, theatre encourages a naïve idealism which can only sustain itself in the glow of stage fire. Hoffmann's 'flight into the faraway spirit realm' is from this perspective just escapism. Take away the mystical vocabulary, and the spirit realm is indistinguishable from the confines of the stage, a space marvellous in its fictions but – when the curtain is dropped and the lights are off – just bare boards and greasepaint after all.

In such a view, what seems so alarming about romantic thinking is that it cares less about what is actually performed than about the mere sensation of performance. Sensationalist and clumsily melodramatic it may be, but at least *Fidelio* offers inspiring ideas: it communicates its content. In the world of German romantic opera (so the sceptical critic might proceed), the specific dramatic content is all but superfluous. The work is dedicated simply to arousing and intensifying the feeling of being in an illusory world, no matter what that world contains. Hence the fascination with instrumental music, which has no explicit content. Romanticism's abductions don't take the audience anywhere. The pleasure is contained entirely in the sensation of being rapt away. Such gratuitous aesthetic thrills can only be based on the sheer falsehood of theatre; the experience of fantasy becomes an end in itself. Audiences may think that they are being given sublime and visionary revelations, but in fact all romantic opera has to offer is the pleasant but empty sensation of imagining that such revelations are taking place.

The arguments are not so simple, needless to say. German thinkers of the early nineteenth century were acutely aware of the ironic perspective which might expose their aspirations as mere fiction. Nevertheless, the criticisms to which a romantic aesthetic lies vulnerable help explain what the basis of that aesthetic really is. In the light of a responsible and rather cynical pragmatism, we can see that the new world promised for opera by Hoffmann and others is inseparably connected to the character of theatrical performance. Hoffmann would have been delighted by the Festspielhaus. When he writes of music transporting its audience 'over the chasm which otherwise divides us from' the spirit world, his language anticipates the actual architecture of Wagner's theatre, where the gap between viewer and stage is made invisible, and sound emerges from the 'mystic abyss' (Wagner's phrase) to fill the whole darkened space. The creation of these perfectly romantic conditions would be the work of a lifetime for a composer dedicated to the art of affecting his audience.

Like all his contemporaries, though, Wagner had to admit the disparity between the idealized theatricality prophesied for romantic opera by its theorists and the actual state of performance in his own world. Growing up in a thespian family, he knew the tawdry mechanics of the stage as well as the fantastic possibilities of *Der Freischütz*. If we are to believe *My Life* – not always a good idea – then in his youth at least it was the juxtaposition of the two that held such intoxicating enchantment for him. Costumes and scenery were so thrilling because they exemplified theatrical transubstantiation, the way ordinary substances (clothing and painted flats) became windows into an extraordinary world. The journeyman chorus-master and musical director of the 1830s could not see things so numinously. When Wagner became Kapellmeister in Dresden in 1843, after the phenomenal success of the Frenchified *Rienzi*, his disillusionment was complete. Romantic idealization of the theatre could never be compatible with the pragmatic details of professional theatrical administration. Likewise, opera's claim to transfigure its audience is hardly plausible outside the domain of theory. From a practical point of view, romantic opera, like other genres, is a form of entertainment. The audience is there to be gratified, not exalted – if, that is, an audience is there at all: Wagner's first opera *Die Feen* was not staged in his lifetime, while the first run of *Das Liebesverbot* consisted of one performance. Even the success of *Der Freischütz* probably had more to do with a few memorable tunes than the glimmer of a romantic aesthetic in Act II. When Wagner filled a whole opera – *Der fliegende Holländer* – with atmospheric and mysterious tonal colouring, contemporary audiences appear to have been displeased by the relentless gloom.

In reality, then, romantic opera was as much a set of conventions as any other form. Its immediately significant characteristics were not those conjured up in the fantasies of Hoffmann, W.H. Wackenroder and others. They are to be found in certain technical and formal advances: 'scene complexes, recurring themes and orchestral sonority', in Barry Millington's summary.[10] The overall effect of these developments may have been to imbue opera with a more sustained and unified mood, which in turn translated into a different kind of aesthetic. The genre itself, though, was in decline by the 1830s, put to flight by the international triumph of Meyerbeer's first sensationally popular grand opera, *Robert le diable* (1831; a month after its premiere, another blockbuster, Bellini's *Norma*, opened in Milan). Idealized fantasies of a magical theatre could not compete with audiences' more straightforward desire to be diverted and impressed. Wagner's early enthusiasm for romantic opera might in this light be seen simply as a sign of his susceptibility to reigning trends. His three earliest stage works are all exercises in generic conventions. *Die Feen* (completed January 1834) is a supernatural tale saturated with exotic stage effects and passionate monologues, along the lines of Weber's *Oberon* (1826). *Das Liebesverbot* (1836) imitates Italian and French comic opera; *Rienzi* (1842) is grand opera in the Parisian mould. In one way, this confirms Nietzsche's verdict. Like Wagner himself, many of his biographers talk about his juvenilia in terms of his internal development as an artist, as if his early works represented stages in the secret maturation of his genius. It is hard not to look at these three operas in more pragmatic terms, as experiments in reigning theatrical taste, responding most readily to the state of contemporary audiences rather than to some interior creative impulse. Is Wagner's investment in the aesthetics of romantic opera merely to be dismissed as a fad, though?

Faced with the recalcitrant ordinariness of the actual theatrical world, many enthusiastic theorists of the period end up admitting defeat, with an ironic or sentimental flourish. Joseph Berglinger, the fictional composer who populates many of W.H. Wackenroder's writings, is eventually martyred to his exalted notion of music: 'Is then its mysterious pleasure for me alone – is it to all other men mere sensual pleasure and agreeable amusement?'[11] It would require a colossal idealism to avoid this final ironic recognition that the other world glimpsed by romanticism is no more than a fantasy. For all his sardonic wit and occasionally appealing black humour, Wagner (as an artist, at least) lacked an ironic bone in his body. Without in any way mythologizing his personal struggles of the 1840s, when he attempted to create the conditions for his new conception of drama to be performed, it is nevertheless true that his idealized – or perhaps fantasized – vision of theatre as a place of abduction and transformation remains very much in evidence. That is, he goes on taking the romantic aesthetic seriously. Bayreuth stands witness to this consistent pursuit of theatrical goals, but we need not look so far away from the world of Hoffmann and *Der Freischütz*. *Tannhäuser* and *Lohengrin* can be, and were, described as demonstrations of romantic theory in action.

A young music critic in Vienna wrote after the premiere of *Tannhäuser*:

It is not a composition in which I could find pleasure merely by understanding how nicely this or that has been accomplished. It was, rather, a musical experience, carrying the listener irresistibly with it, in such a way that what occurred in the orchestra and on the stage became part of his own life.[12]

The abductee here is Eduard Hanslick, later to become the most articulate and cogent anti-Wagnerian before Nietzsche. His language is thoroughly romantic, at least here (the review goes on to conduct a detailed analysis of the score). Initially, Hanslick wants to emphasize the empirical impact of the opera. He describes it in terms of sheer unprecedented effect. If this seems slightly surprising to us now, familiar as we are with the incomparably more powerful musical resources of later work by Wagner and others, it is worth remembering that a critic as sensitive as Hanslick could describe the 1845 version of *Tannhäuser* as a uniquely captivating theatrical experience. With hindsight, Nietzsche located the breakthrough a little later, but in the same kind of terminology (though his comment is bitter rather than admiring): 'the *Lohengrin* prelude furnished the first example, only too insidious, only too successful, of hypnotism by means of music'.[13] While the prelude is an entirely musical rather than theatrical phenomenon, the effect Nietzsche describes – and which anyone who has heard it can understand – corresponds to the power over the audience central to romantic aesthetics, and fundamentally rooted in the stage. Faced with the obdurate nature of existing theatrical conditions, Wagner's operas seem to have responded by exerting a greater effort against them. The colossal idealism required of the romantic theorist is incarnated in the media of performance – Hanslick's 'orchestra' and 'stage'.

Perhaps we should describe this as seduction rather than abduction. Up to a point, the artist can imagine a forcible transportation of his audience to Hoffmann's 'faraway spirit realm', but this sort of attempt tends ultimately more towards bombast than mystery. The overture to *Rienzi*, for example, is extremely effective – until quite recently it maintained a place as a concert piece – but the effect is a crude one, based on the principle that contemporary theatregoers are more likely to be enthralled by deafening militarism than by the spiritual intimations beloved of romantic theory. What Wagner's operas slowly discover is a way to enthral their public by the seductive display of their potent fantasy. Nietzsche's word for this – 'hypnotism' – is close to the mark, as is the parenthetical swipe that follows: 'I do not like whatever music has no ambition beyond persuasion of the nerves'.[14] He overestimates the ease of this persuasion, though. Wagner experienced the resistance of the public at first hand. The degree to which he surpasses *Der Freischütz* is also the extent of his reconfiguration of the romantic aesthetic, from an art which points towards transcendence to an art which instead deploys all its resources to display its enraptured visions to the audience. Instead of fantasizing about an audience of Hoffmanns to respond to opera's effect, he dedicates himself to an enormous intensification of those effects, in the face of which even the most obdurately dilettantish theatregoers will be enticed into the visionary stage world.

No one knew more instinctively than Wagner that the theatre is a place of seduction. His art conjures up this image of itself again and again, with astonishing fertility of invention. It starts innocuously enough: no one can really be surprised that Senta in *Der fliegende Holländer* is in love with a legend, since her romantic fixations are not all that unusual among operatic heroines of her day. The Venusberg is perhaps a different matter; the opening scenes of *Tannhäuser* seem alarmingly eager to give the stage over to erotic self-indulgence. By the time of the second act of *Tristan und Isolde*, previously unimaginable musical resources are being employed to dramatize two lovers' delayed gratification, and the delay itself is prolonged to such extraordinary lengths that time seems to stop, allowing the pair an infinity of the bliss of longing without ever having to fall prey to the disappointment of consummation. In Act II of *Parsifal*, we do at last witness a kiss, but only after a seduction scene of bewildering tortuousness and complexity, starting with the naïve blandishments of the flower maidens before leading us into Kundry's maze of regression, disillusionment and guilt.

Romance, of course, is an operatic staple. Implausibly ardent heroes and impossibly devoted heroines have sung their way through the history of opera from its earliest times to the beginning of the twentieth century, and occasionally beyond. As with so many other facets of his art, though, Wagner intensifies the conventions of his genre to an extraordinary degree. To other nineteenth-century composers, love in all its varieties might simply be an endlessly convenient plot-device, suitable for grand or passionate or heroic or comic treatment as the case demands. In Wagner's hands, the perfunctory device comes to look more like an obsession. Opera is no longer just happy to adopt love as its favourite story. It seems instead to be inseparably entwined with stories of fantastically exaggerated passion. These tales of romance represent something more fundamentally 'romantic': a relationship of intense desire which is aesthetic rather than erotic. Art itself arouses longing. It holds out the promise of otherworldly delights, whether as pure as Elisabeth or as sensual as Venus.

Seductive theatre reconciles the pragmatic idea of opera as entertainment with more idealized romantic theories. It attempts to change the audience's desire for pleasure into a deeper longing, rather than seeing these two responses as polar opposites (as does Wackenroder's Berglinger). What gets sacrificed here is the spiritual nature of the deeper aesthetic experience. There seems to be no common ground at all between the quasi-religious ecstasies that appear in the theoretical writings and the actual conditions of performance. Romantic opera is therefore never going to be able to bring its audience into the 'spirit realm'; whatever its achievements are, they are going to remain within the confines of the theatre. So Wagner's art chooses to remain complicit with the illusions and fantasies of the stage, instead of aiming for the purely ideal realm of instrumental music. Again, Bayreuth is the consummation of this tendency. As we shall see, its sacred pretensions are a mask for aesthetic sensations; it is a temple of earthly, not heavenly, delights. The first steps on the road to Wagner's palace of art are directed by the genre of romantic opera, which exerts itself to draw the public into its world, by offering them mysterious and thrilling visions incarnated in stage action and orchestral sonority.

In German romantic theory, the artist is often cast as a victim. His (or, rarely, her) devotion to the otherworldly dreams of his inspiration results in tragically inevitable punishment. He chooses to exile himself from the ordinary sphere of existence, and so that sphere treats him with hostility, or with equally murderous incomprehension, indifference or neglect. He is sacrificed to the fissure between reality and the ideal. For the composer of operas, as we have seen, the myth of victimization takes a specific form. The villain's role is played by the theatrical public, whose degraded and trivial taste condemns the artist to failure in the eyes of the world. Wagner's early work is particularly interested in this characteristic myth. At the same time, however, he is unwilling to embrace it wholeheartedly; as I have been suggesting, he clings on to the hope that he can present his art in such a way that it will successfully abduct or seduce its audience. To see how he steers his way between a romantic aesthetic and an acknowledgment of theatrical conditions, we need to turn to his early essays and operas, and look at how they return repeatedly to themes of the artist's role and music's power. Never good at admitting defeat, Wagner refuses to present himself merely as a victim. His most characteristic narrative is what has become known as 'redemption', which means a tragedy that turns out not to be tragic, an apparent defeat or death that is in fact a triumph or a resurrection. Through this structure, the artist implies his power to overcome the conditions that appear to defeat him. In the case of romantic opera, the tragic conditions are represented by the audience. The purpose of Wagner's romantic art is to redeem this tragedy, to turn the theatre from a place where the composer admits defeat into the scene of his ultimate triumph.

CHAPTER TWO

Myths of the Artist

Here are two romanticized fables about art's relationship with the public.

A musician and poet is the hero of the first. He lives in a place of glorious imaginative abundance, where all his enraptured visions turn to flesh and perform before his eyes. Unfortunately, though, this fantasy-world is only a kind of dream, played out for his benefit alone. He longs to show his music and poetry to a wider public. So, with a great effort of self-denial, he casts himself out of his private Eden and takes his art to an open venue, a grand hall filled with audiences, critics and competing poet-musicians. This public, alas, finds his work offensive and hateful. From then on, wherever he goes, the wider world passes judgment on him, and its reviews are always damning. After a while he gives up on it altogether, opting for a visionary death.

The outlines of the second story are much the same. Its hero isn't an artist, but might as well be: he is an emissary from a celestial sanctuary, who arrives in the real world surrounded by a radiant aura of sublimity and enchantment. His every word causes wonder and astonishment in his hearers. What, his audience asks, is this magical power he has? But it is not for them to know: his gift is too marvellous to suffer the inquisitive probings of the mundane. However, the public insists on looking this gift horse in the mouth, tormenting the hero with its petty doubts and criticisms until finally he is forced back to the supernatural regions whence he came. His audience is left ruing its failure to accommodate itself to the demands of his genius.

These two variants on the myth of the tragically solitary romantic artist supply the plots of (respectively) *Tannhäuser* and *Lohengrin*, but other, less familiar versions of the same story abound in Wagner's work of his Paris and Dresden decade (1839–49). The myth is a particularly congenial one for a composer struggling to establish himself in the world. It is no surprise to find it everywhere in the articles Wagner wrote to support himself during his disastrous attempt to have his operas performed in Paris. In the best of these journalistic fragments, Wagner invents an alter ego, 'R.', a German musician devoted to exalted romantic conceptions of his art but starved and finally killed by the degraded Parisian public's neglect. Even after the success of *Rienzi*, though, the characteristic story survives, its hero transmuted from a poverty-bitten unappreciated genius into an artist whose audience (like Lohengrin's) adulates him for the wrong reasons and misunderstands the sacred nature of his vocation. The mythic hero is as indifferent to success as to neglect, since his gift is not to be measured in worldly terms. Isolation and alienation are his glories.

'R.', the protagonist and/or supposed author of four of Wagner's articles for the Paris *Gazette musicale*, is a very thin disguise for Wagner himself. All that separates him from his creator is the higher perfection of his martyrdom. Wagner's own sufferings in Paris were grimly tawdry: financial desperation, marital squabbles, misfortunes and disappointments at the hands of the theatre directors whose patronage he sought. The figure of R. clothes these quotidian miseries in the sacramentalized vocabulary of romanticism. He expends his funds on making a pilgrimage to Vienna to see Beethoven, is driven to madness by the triviality of Parisian opera, and finally – in the essay 'Ein Ende in Paris' ('An End in Paris') – expires in a garret in Montmartre (the 'mount of martyrs'), bidding the world farewell with an operatic deathbed *credo*:

> I believe in God, Mozart and Beethoven, and likewise their disciples and apostles; – I believe in the Holy Spirit and the truth of the one, indivisible Art; – I believe that this art proceeds from God, and lives within the hearts of all illumined men [*aller erleuchteten Menschen*]; – I believe that he who once has bathed in the sublime delights of this high Art, is consecrate to Her for ever, and never can deny Her; – I believe that through this Art all men are saved, and therefore each may die for Her of hunger; – I believe that death will give me highest happiness; – I believe that on earth I was a jarring discord, which will at once be perfectly resolved by death. (VII 66–7)

R.'s story transfigures Wagner's journeyman frustrations into this Christ-like myth. Spurned by operatic administrators and audiences, he becomes the stone the builders rejected, whose beliefs will be the cornerstone of a new and more perfect dispensation in the world of opera.

In this sense, there is a direct connection between R. (in the essays of 1840–1) and Lohengrin (whose story was first drafted in 1845). Both are the rejected evangelists of a higher faith, a creed that would come to be formulated in the closing chorus of *Die Meistersinger von Nürnberg* in language which (as with R.'s monologue) borrows from religion in order to surpass it:

| zerging' in Dunst | should the Holy Roman Empire |
| das heil'ge röm'sche Reich, | dissolve into mist, |

uns bliebe gleich	there would still remain for us
die heil'ge deutsche Kunst!	holy German art!

The kind of sanctity Lohengrin possesses is derived from a religion in which – as R. puts it – God shares his trinity with Mozart and Beethoven. As in *Tannhäuser*, the swan knight's story is as much about art as religion. The sacred nature of the artist's vocation allows for this constant overlapping of 'German art' with Christian symbolism. In 1849, Wagner went so far as to sketch out a lengthy draft for a drama about Jesus. Art and religion are the two domains of spirituality, and thus come to be symbolically interchangeable in Wagner's romantic myth, two terms for the same fundamental idea. (Their equivalence is articulated far more intensely and complicatedly in *Parsifal* and that opera's special relationship with the Bayreuth festival.) At the heart of this myth lies the notion that the artist is a prophet of spiritual experience, and that such experience is never really compatible with the mundane world. The difference between failure in Paris (the story of R.) and success in Germany (the story of Lohengrin) is irrelevant; both equally are forms of the artist's sacrifice on behalf of an uncomprehending world. Indeed, Wagner's myth is almost unhealthily eager to adopt the vocabulary of martyrdom and salvation for its own purposes. Without it, the story of his career is merely a dreary and unexceptional instance of a musician's struggles to win an audience for his work and a salary for his household.

The case of R. is therefore also the case of Lohengrin and Tannhäuser, and indeed of Rienzi as well. While R. is an obvious journalistic substitute for Wagner himself, the heroes of the operas are also figures who symbolize not only artists in general, but one particular devotee of 'holy German art'. The most characteristic feature of Wagner's oeuvre in the 1840s is that the artist is the hero of his own work. Operas and prose works dedicate themselves to an exhaustive representation of Wagner's vocation, heroically or sublimely transfigured. The Dutchman also, doomed as he is to tragic solitude and desperate to find an 'audience' that will dedicate itself to him, represents another version of the theme. *Rienzi* is concerned with the politics of civil life, but it reaches its tragic conclusion by presenting its hero as the victim of a deluded public whose best interests he has at heart, and so converges ultimately with the essential plot of *Tannhäuser, Lohengrin* and the Paris essays. *Die Feen* follows a similar trajectory. For most of the opera, we see its hero Arindal in his role as the political and military leader of his people, and yet he achieves his final triumph through 'der holden Töne Macht,/ der Gottheit, die der Sterbliche besitzt!' ('the power of glorious music, the divinity which mortals possess'). All these variations on the central theme are barely less transparent than the flimsy fiction of R. Their heroes don't echo the actual circumstances of Wagner's life as R. does, but then the specific details of R.'s life in Paris are not what matter about him. Only at the moment of his martyrdom does he become a significant symbolic substitute for Wagner himself, rather than merely a pen-name. His dying speech reveals the transcendental purpose of the German musician's vocation, and it is this higher myth of the artist that appears again in the operas.

It has always been recognized that Wagner is a potent maker (or remaker) of myths. In the early 1840s, he was able to exploit the previous generation's antiquarian and bibliographic energy; he was particularly absorbed by Jacob Grimm's *Deutsche Mythologie* (*German Mythology*), which had appeared in 1835. His best subject-matter was mined from ancient, elemental stories: the sagas, the Eddas, the densely allegorical world of medieval romance. In his hands – especially in the mature operas, the ones usually dignified by the title of 'music-drama' – these stories retain their concentrated symbolic potency, and so provide fertile ground for continuing myth-making: myths of redemption, myths of German national destiny, myths of Aryan supremacy. The most enduringly powerful of his mythic creations, however, is the figure of Wagner himself, a colossal presence bestriding the cultural landscape of the nineteenth and twentieth centuries, a sun of originality and genius irresistibly drawing Europe's artistic and political life into its orbit. No dispassionate observer would dispute Wagner's immense importance in the history of music, and indeed the phenomenon of Wagnerism has had a widespread influence, for better or worse, in a number of different areas. Dispassionate observers, though, are not encouraged in the myths propagated by Wagner, his family and his followers. Whatever conclusions an independently-minded critic might come to, the striking feature of Wagnerism is the hyperinflated scale of its claims and its judgments, all dedicated to transforming the image of an important artist into a myth of the incomparable genius. Over and over again, Wagner's work – implicitly or explicitly – adopts this myth as its central subject. In *Oper und Drama* (*Opera and Drama*, 1851), for example, it is clear where we are supposed to start looking for the new and authentic form of drama theorized in the work: the creator of the Nibelung tetralogy lurks between the lines as the answer to all the book's questions. It doesn't take much effort to identify the real name of Walther von Stolzing, the poet-musician who rejects stuffy rules for a natural, inspired and utterly persuasive art form. This character was conceived in 1845, alongside work on *Lohengrin*; the first draft of the *Meistersinger* scenario dates from the summer of that year, at which stage the hero is a nameless 'young man'. By the time of the Bayreuth circle and its printed arm the *Bayreuther Blätter* in the 1870s and 80s, the instinctive tendency to mythologize the artist has turned into a fully-formed propaganda machine. To read Rienzi, the Dutchman, Tannhäuser and Lohengrin as instances of self-imaging equivalent to the obvious R. is simply to recognize an early stage of a habitual Wagnerian procedure.

The distinctive form of the myth of the artist in the 1840s is his conflict with the public. (By the 1870s, this will have mutated into a more hieratic, prophetic role, where the artist is priest rather than victim.) The idea is a cliché of the romantic aesthetic in which Wagner was steeped. Earlier in the century, readers all over Europe had been entranced by Byron's prolific variations on the theme – 'I have not loved the world, nor the world me', says one of his narrators, speaking for almost all of them – and many German artists had found the pose of isolation equally effective, from the sentimental, suicidal hero of Goethe's *Werther* through to the mystic solitudes of Novalis's poetry and of Caspar David Friedrich's paintings. Wagner's R. wears his isolation on his sleeve as if it were the artist's badge of honour, as if the mark of Cain were also the mark of genius. Similarly, the Dutchman's burden is what makes him sublime: he is repeatedly juxtaposed with the trivial figures of Daland and Erik in order to highlight the splendour of his utter remoteness from human affairs. Striving for an exalted position, the artist defines himself against the rest of the world, and especially against those who hold him to their own debased expectations. He takes his sense of his own worth from the intensity of his struggle against the frivolous public. In his 1843 'Autobiographische Skizze' ('Autobiographical Sketch'), published to satisfy the Dresden public's curiosity about the composer of *Rienzi*, he declares that the 'very notion of being consciously weak or trivial – even in a single bar – was appalling to me' (I 13). Everything suffered for the sake of this refusal helps to confirm the heroism of the artist's uncompromising integrity. In the 'utter childishness' (I 12) of German audiences, and in Paris, where 'Renown is everything' (I 15), Wagner finds the negative scale against which to measure his own sacramental conception of the value of his work. Their incomprehension (or disapproval) is a necessary validation of its worth. R. salutes the ideal of a 'Victory, gained by our higher sense over the worthlessness of the vulgar!' (VII 81).

The artist's vocation is thus a secret and private one. If he enters into collusion with the public, he betrays himself, and what he produces is no longer art, but commerce. For Wagner in the early 1840s, Paris becomes a kind of *paysage moralisé* in which the artist-hero wanders, tempted and threatened by this danger. Over the next few years, the enemy would change shape: the commercial world would no longer be represented by Paris in general, but by Meyerbeer in particular (the type of the successful, worldly composer), a shift that demonstrates how Wagner's romantic myth becomes the basis of his anti-Semitism. (Popular nineteenth-century anti-Semitism frequently associated Jews with the sordid realm of commerce, creating a scapegoat for the evident triumph of capitalism over religious and spiritual conceptions of value in western Europe.) Demonizing the economic and social structures on which opera, like other arts, actually depended, the artist imagines instead that his labour is being carried on at some invisible, spiritual level. This is the scene set at the beginning of an 1841 essay, 'Der Künstler und die Öffentlichkeit' ('The Artist and Publicity'), presented as an extract from R.'s journal. 'When I am alone . . . the musical strings begin to stir within me', he writes, and goes on to wonder why he feels compelled to expose the outcome of this secret bliss to the outside world: 'What can the most brilliant welcome of this public give thee worth a hundredth fraction of that hallowed joy which wells from thine own heart?' (VII 134). Out of this sense of an absolute disparity between the inner and outer worlds comes the theme of isolation and alienation that pervades Wagner's myth.

In many ways, of course, this myth is deeply self-serving, or at least self-interested, as is clear enough from the sacramental language it tends to adopt. The most cursory attention to R.'s essays shows that although the composer presents himself as a victim of his isolation, it is really meant as a sign of his superiority to all other men. That's how martyrdom operates, converting what looks like a defeat into a mark of ultimate triumph. Later incarnations of Wagner's myth of the artist show all too transparently how it becomes a tool for aggrandizing his stature, over all petty external considerations. Think of Tristan and Isolde, enabled by the magic of the potion to dismiss the domain of *Sitte* ('custom', 'manners') as an envious antagonist of their desires, or of Walther and Sachs staging an open display of their contempt for inhibiting conventions. In *Tannhäuser* too the artist-hero shocks his audiences by following only the law of his own inspirations; in each act of the opera he expels himself from his environment (Venusberg, Wartburg, Rome), though he is far less confident of the authority of his inner life than later versions of the same figure will be. The prose writings are less ambiguous. However ironic the treatment of R., there is never any doubt in the essays that he knows a higher truth than other men have access to. His deathbed proclamation is meant seriously.

In this light, a penniless German composer trying to make his way in Paris can see himself as the prophet of the true religion of art, and the Kapellmeister of a Saxon court theatre can imagine himself as the spiritual leader of the German nation. Wagner's myth serves to breathe an atmosphere of mystery around the business of being a professional musician. He himself becomes the object of the kind of transformations desired by the romantic aesthetic; his career is moved onto the stage, lit by an unearthly glow and exotically costumed. (It is hard not to see Wagner's notorious later penchant for luxurious interior decoration and sensuous clothing as a weirdly literal extension of something his work had been doing for years.) Without the effort to mythologize itself, that career would look very different. The unornamented facts are that in the 1840s Wagner was first a failure and then an employee. Moreover, the professional life he had committed himself to could hardly be interpreted along rapturous Hoffmannesque lines, as he knew well enough. Not only was opera a business, it was (in northern Europe) a business transacted among a fairly distinct social group. The scale of Wagner's imagination narrowed that group still further. One only has to read the lengthy stage directions that open *Tannhäuser*, which call for a series of complex and crowded tableaux in a space of eight minutes or so, to realize that Wagnerian opera could only be accommodated by the large theatres that catered to the prosperous metropolitan classes and the aristocracy. Wagner's orchestration belonged in the same institutions, despite the efforts of provincial theatres to perform his scores with what seem to us like absurdly limited resources. So far from being a quasi-religious rite, opera of this sort had a well-established place in secular society. It existed because of the patronage of the wealthy leisured classes, who saw it as one among many instruments of their leisure. Like performers and theatre managers, composers of large-scale operas were part of this inescapable set of social relations. The Wagnerian myth is dedicated to concealing or denying this all too obvious fact. By veiling the socio-economic situation of the most expensive of arts under layers of romantic idealism, it allows the artist to appear as the undisputed master of his own territory (the Montsalvat where art and religion are identical) rather than as a salaried functionary in a domain ruled by financial and administrative forces over which he has no power. The logical consequence of this denial of opera's existing social contexts is the anarchist rhetoric of Wagner's revolutionary writings from the late 1840s, in which art and society simply cannot coexist at all, and Wagnerian opera is therefore interpreted as a prophecy of the imminent destruction of civil order. The contradiction between the myth and the real state of affairs can only be solved by some apocalyptic upheaval.

As this increasingly radicalized attitude demonstrates, though, the self-aggrandizing myth comes at a cost. However fervently the artist believes in his own superiority, he is compelled to admit that his conflict with the public is one that he is likely to lose. At this stage in his career, Wagner's versions of the story are all tragedies. Although the tragic conclusions are presented as martyrdom (R.) or redemption (Tannhäuser), in order to convert actual failure into mythic triumph, these disguises mask but do not conceal the central fact of the hero's defeat. The myth, that is, recognizes that it is a story which will always be contradicted by the facts (hence, ultimately, the demand for a revolutionary conflagration followed by an entirely new start). It is a dangerously double-edged weapon. At the same time as it promises a sublimely exalted version of the artist and his art, it reveals the absolute hopelessness of his position.

Because Wagner himself had such an alarming talent for self-aggrandizement, it is easy to forget that his myth-making contains this flaw. Indeed, his later works deploy their extraordinary resources in an effort to make us forget; their presentations of tragedy as martyrdom (Brünnhilde), bliss (Isolde) or redemption (Parsifal) are, superficially, so fully formed and comprehensive that any trace of a recognition of defeat seems to have disappeared from them. (We shall wrestle with this problem in Parts III and IV.) Yet if we are not to swallow the Wagnerian myth whole – and history suggests plenty of reasons why we should not – then it is vital to realize the doubts and anxieties contained *within* the story. Doing so involves recognizing the genuinely disruptive force of the conflict the myth generates, the antagonism between the isolated hero and his world. As I have suggested, Wagner's work attempts to arrange this opposition in such a way that it validates the transcendental mission of the artist. That is, there is a correlation between victimization and value: the more the hero suffers at the hands of his world, the more heroic he becomes. The highest pitch of this interpretation is achieved with the hero's death: he suffers the greatest punishment, and at that moment is confirmed as a spiritual hero. The same formula governs the Dresden Kapellmeister's idea of his profession, in that the less appreciated he is by administrators and public, the truer he secretly knows his vocation to be. Yet this self-serving correlation invites alternative interpretations. Can negative experience be so glibly converted into positive value? Might it not be the case that the battle between the artist and his world results in a genuine defeat, that the embrace of isolation ironically produces a real anxiety about the artist's relationship with his audience? In the last chapter, I argued that romantic opera defines itself by its claim to possess and abduct the audience. Wagner's romantic myth cannot entirely forget this need. Consequently, the isolation it glorifies remains potentially troubling, however much it serves to define the artist-hero's sense of his own worth. Signs of this tension can be traced throughout the work of the 1840s.

The first of the sequence of essays involving R. is 'Eine Pilgerfahrt zu Beethoven' ('A Pilgrimage to Beethoven'). It originally appeared in French in the *Gazette musicale* in late 1840, under the title 'Une visite à Beethoven: épisode de la vie d'un musicien allemand'; the story is told in the first person, and the 'German musician' is never named (there was no signature to the article). The title it is now known by was given for its first German publication, in the Dresden *Abend-Zeitung* (July–August 1841). At this stage, a subtitle was added, linking it to the later essays in which the protagonist is named 'R.': 'From the papers of an actually deceased musician'. The hero, then, is identical with the martyr of 'An End in Paris'. If the latter story describes his martyrdom, 'A Pilgrimage to Beethoven' is – as the adopted title indicates – an earlier stage in the same spiritual quest. It describes how R. spends the money he has earned from musical hackwork in Paris on a journey to Vienna, with the sole aim of meeting his idol. On the road he encounters a wealthy and philistine Englishman, who stands in the story as a representative of the triviality and stupidity of the public. The Englishman is also going to see Beethoven, though his motives are no higher than dilettantish cultural tourism. Discovering that R.'s mission is the same, he plagues the hero by persistently following him in the hope of being led to Beethoven. R. manages at last to shake off this and other obstacles, and is rewarded at the end of his pilgrimage by the revelation of a meeting with the composer, who has just finished his ninth symphony. The story ends with R., 'uplifted . . . and ennobled' (VII 45), turning north on the road back to Paris.

The language of 'A Pilgrimage to Beethoven' preserves a delicate balance between seriousness and irony. It is clear that Beethoven is indeed the one true god, possessing the secret of music in its highest and holiest form, in contrast to the frivolously popular ephemera prized by the Parisians. On the other hand, by persistently describing his veneration of his idol in exaggerated terms, R. tinges his self-portrait with wry mockery, as if permanently aware that the values he cherishes are not just idealistic but hopelessly idealistic. Take the moment when he discovers his vocation:

> I'm not quite certain what I really was intended for; I only remember that one night I for the first time heard a symphony of Beethoven's performed, that it set me in a fever, I fell ill, and on my recovery had become a musician. (VII 22)

As conversion narratives go, this is markedly tongue-in-cheek. Throughout the story, R. seems to be aware that his pilgrimage is on one level a faintly absurd diversion; as he says, the more dedicated to Beethoven he becomes, the more he develops into 'what sober people call an idiot' (VII 22). This is because there is no one to share his devotion. He is a pilgrim without a religion. He has to make up his spiritual quest as he goes along, improvising its obligations and rituals in order to persuade himself that his journey to Vienna to meet a composer is in fact a sacred act. The presence of the utterly unspiritual Englishman in the story serves to draw attention to this need by illustrating what a visit to Beethoven might otherwise be like. The Englishman is a grotesque parody of a musician, but R. knows that the only measure of the difference between himself and his unwanted companion is their respective attitudes. In the eyes of the world, they are both simply on a visit to a famous man. R. needs his sacramental postures in order to validate his own pilgrimage, and with the awareness of this need comes the ironic realization that his religion is a fantasy entirely of his own making. It is as if we are watching R. clothe himself in his myth, shuffling a little uncomfortably as he tries to make it fit.

Shortly after crossing paths with the English 'wealthy coxcomb [*Gentleman*]' (VII 28), R. is offered a ride in his carriage. Despite – or, more accurately, because of – the cost in fatigue and expenses, R. insists on walking the rest of the way to Vienna. It is a typical moment of conscious self-definition, where he chooses to interpret his own actions and obligations in the necessary light:

> My Englishman interested me; but I avow I little envied him his equipage. To me it seemed as though my weary pilgrimage afoot were holier and more devout, and that its goal must bless me more than this proud gentleman who drove there in full state. (VII 26)

In part, the decision is made in order for R. to avoid being tainted by the odour of the polite world which the Englishman carries about him. Nevertheless, it is an intriguing moment. Why does he feel he has to walk? He must imitate a proper pilgrimage, of course: those travelling to Rome or Santiago have to go on foot. Yet this choice also recalls the essential nature of those institutionalized journeys that R. is wryly copying. Pilgrims are penitents. Suffering is not incidental to their journey, but essential to it; the journey itself is an expiation. It is only this which distinguishes it from an act of tourism (like the Englishman's). Hence the 'weary' trip to Vienna is not so much a way of (temporarily) escaping the trivialities of mundane existence as a conscious decision to expose oneself to the world's vexations.

In this case, the question arises as to what sin R. has committed, what he is doing penance *for*. As always in this story, it is an act that is only a sin in his own eyes, according to the articles of his private faith. As far as the public is concerned, the deed he has to expiate is just the conduct of a professional musician. His publisher in Paris suggests that he should establish his name as a composer by writing 'galops and pot-pourris' – adaptations of popular opera tunes for the mass market. R. calls these 'sacrifices of my innocence', but grimly admits that only such compromises with public taste can earn him the money for his trip to Vienna.

> I shuddered; but my yearning to see Beethoven gained the victory; I composed galops and pot-pourris [*Galopps und Potpourris*], but for very shame I could never bring myself to cast one glance on Beethoven in all that time, for fear it should defile him. (VII 23)

The compromise achieves its end; R. achieves some renown as a composer. Here he interjects his most openly penitential remark, which – it is no coincidence – is also the story's most explicit pastiche of Christian vocabulary: 'Saint Beethoven, forgive me that [fame]; 'twas earned that I might see thee!' (VII 24). That may be so, but it also follows that the journey is a means of absolving the sin as well as a justification for it. The saint will both inspire and heal the penitent.

R.'s offence lies in his willingness to bring his music before the Parisian public. Beethoven is therefore the only person who can grant him forgiveness, because he is the patron saint of privacy as well as music. Reclusive and utterly indifferent to the world, he has acquired a fame that (unlike R.'s) is somehow bought without the cost of degrading compromise. His deafness provides an even more striking sign of his intense isolation. His music is fundamentally instrumental, appealing to the listener's inward experience, as opposed to R.'s operatic ambitions which necessarily taint music with the externalizing force of language and the socialized sphere of theatre. Wagner has Beethoven grumpily dismiss even his own *Fidelio*: 'I am no opera-composer; at least, I know no theatre in the world for which I should care to write another opera!' (VII 40). This is an art that does not belong in front of audiences. On the road to Vienna, R. encounters a group of travelling musicians who play Beethoven's E flat septet – 'but only for ourselves; not for gentlefolk' (VII 24). The little episode sharply indicates the impurity of R.'s ambitions, and his need to be absolved by an encounter with the perfectly spiritual musician.

The climax of a pilgrimage, and the final act of contrite penitence, is to make a confession. This is a prerequisite for absolution. In R.'s personal religion, however, confession takes a slightly unusual form, one which links 'A Pilgrimage to Beethoven' very closely to the rhetoric of Wagner's operas. Instead of simply naming his sin and begging forgiveness, R. performs a comprehensive act of self-exposure. (It has been argued that the Christian practice of confession originally consisted in this complete submission of the whole self to a higher authority, the submission taking place through spoken narrative and the authority represented by the listener.) Finding himself tarred by his association with his unwanted travelling-companion, R. cannot get access to Beethoven: 'he had taken me for an Englishman!' (VII 33). The misidentification contains a secret truth: insofar as the Englishman represents music trivialized and urbanized, R.'s sin has made him liable to be taken for such a musician. The only way to correct the error is to profess his real nature: 'So at last I decided to pour out my heart upon paper' (VII 34). The hinge of the story is thus an impassioned monologue, like 'Die Frist ist um' in Act I of *Holländer*, or Tannhäuser's Rome narration, or 'In fernem Land' at the end of *Lohengrin*, or Wotan's outburst in Act II of *Die Walküre* (the list of examples could easily be extended). Like an operatic hero, R. 'pour[s] out' his history in his confessional letter to Beethoven, recounting who he is, what he desires and what he has suffered:

> . . . narrating the history of my life, how I had become a musician, how I worshipped him, how I once had come by the wish to know him in person, how I had spent two years in making my name as a galop-composer, how I had begun and ended my pilgrimage, what sufferings the

Englishman had brought upon me, and what a terrible plight my present was. (VII 34)

With 'a silent prayer', this confessional monologue is delivered to Beethoven. It wins R. an invitation into the presence of the master.

The conversation between the supplicant R. and 'Saint Beethoven' is the concluding scene of the story. As befits an act of absolution, the saint does most of the talking, giving R. encouragement, instruction and forgiveness – the last contained in his parting benediction: 'think of me, and let that console you in all your troubles' (VII 44). Interestingly, though, the doctrine Beethoven propounds is suggestively weighted towards R.'s world rather than his own (and here Wagner's stake in the story becomes most obvious). He continues to dismiss opera as 'that nonsense', and yet the secret he reveals to the pilgrim is how opera ought ideally to be written. Rather than being initiated into the mysteries of instrumental music, R. is sent back out in the world with the master's instructions about how to bring 'the wild, unfettered elemental feelings, represented by the instruments, in contact with the clear and definite emotion of the human heart, as represented by the voice of man' (VII 42). The recently-completed choral symphony is interpreted in the story not as the culmination of Beethoven's own achievement, but as the originating model of a new kind of vocal writing. This recipe for Wagnerian music-drama demonstrates that R.'s vocation is different from his idol's. The latter exists in his private domain – his Montsalvat, the fantasy of Wagner's myth – but R. seems implicitly to recognize his obligation to go back into the world and offer his music to audiences. Beethoven dismisses these operatic aspirations:

> Whoever wrote a true musical drama, would be taken for a fool; and so indeed he would be, if he didn't keep such a thing to himself, but wanted to set it before these people. (VII 40)

This is precisely the folly R. is guilty of, and which his pilgrimage atones for; and yet R. takes Beethoven's message back to Paris, presumably with the intention of becoming a composer of operas, and therefore engaging again with the theatrical public. The story supports Wagner's myth of the artist by glorifying and sanctifying Beethoven's isolated genius. For R., however, the myth remains just that: an ideal, a holy vision. His pilgrimage (again like orthodox religious ones) is a spiritual incident inserted into a thoroughly secular life. The story does not turn Wagner's alter ego into a Beethovenian genius. Instead, it offers him a momentary encounter with this ideal, and then leaves him to return to his commerce with the world. R.'s sin is a necessary one. Having been absolved of it, he sets out to commit it again.

'A Pilgrimage to Beethoven' thus recognizes the contradiction in the Wagnerian myth. It shows that the embrace of this ideal is a deliberate and temporary fiction which must ultimately come to terms with pragmatic, compromised reality. In this light, the apparently self-serving myth proves to be far more ambiguous than it at first seems, with its commingling of exaltation and penitence, exhilaration and irony, holiness and folly. Once we realize this, many other Wagnerian images of the artist-hero may seem equally ambivalent. The fact that what the world sees as folly is part of Beethoven's sacred doctrine recalls the holy fool Parsifal, the last and most acutely divided incarnation of Wagner's myth. However, the most direct analogy with 'A Pilgrimage to Beethoven' is much nearer at hand, in the story of another penitent musician whose absolution works in unexpected ways.

Like R., Tannhäuser is a poet-musician who commits a sin by misuse of his art and undertakes a long and painful journey in search of expiation. His pilgrimage is also a sacred event dramatically interrupting an otherwise profane career, and meant to validate it (the Pope's forgiveness would restore Tannhäuser's standing among his resolutely Christian fellow-minstrels). Where R.'s pilgrimage ends ambiguously, though, Tannhäuser's ends in absolute failure. The visionary rapture he has achieved thanks to his sojourn in the Venusberg turns out to be unforgivable. At this point in the opera, Wagner's myth rescues itself by providing an alternative – and, as the miracle of the staff confirms, higher – absolution for Tannhäuser through the sacrificial death of Elisabeth. This final stroke enables the opera to certify the artist Tannhäuser's essential holiness, despite the malediction of Pope Urban. His rejection – by the Landgrave and his court, as well as by the church – becomes his glory, thanks to Elisabeth's intercession. Nevertheless, this contest over whether the inspired musician is hero or sinner reveals the extreme uncertainty contained within Wagner's representation of the artist. Most interestingly, this uncertainty is expressed in Tannhäuser's own confessional monologue, his long narration in Act III.

This remarkable passage exposes an almost pathological interweaving of holiness and guilt. Tannhäuser finds that he can only express his difference from the other pilgrims, the superiority of his individual spiritual capacity, by taking penitence to its extreme:

Wie neben mir der schwerstbedrückte Pilger die Straße wallt', erschien mir allzuleicht: betrat sein Fuß den weichen Grund der Wiesen, der nackten Sohle sucht' ich	The way the most heavily burdened pilgrim took to the road beside me, seemed far too easy to me: when his feet travelled the soft ground of the meadows, my bare soles sought out

Dorn und Stein;	thorns and stones;
ließ Labung er am Quell den Mund genießen,	when he refreshed his thirst at a spring,
sog ich der Sonne heißes Glühen ein;	I drank in the hot glow of the sun;
wenn fromm zum Himmel er *Gebete* schickte,	if he sent ready *prayers* to heaven,
vergoß mein *Blut* ich zu des Höchsten Preis;	I offered up my *blood* as the highest sacrifice;
als das Hospiz die Wanderer erquickte,	as the hospice refreshed the traveller,
die Gliede bettet' ich in Schnee und Eis. . . .	I laid my limbs in snow and ice. . . .

Here the artist glories in his suffering, as the myth requires; but he does so through a hysterically exaggerated sense of worthlessness. There is no uncomplicated assumption that his alienation is the mark of a higher destiny. His striving for exceptional holiness has become inextricably associated with the sense that his sufferings are real and deserved. The Pope's refusal to forgive his sin marks a temporary but ghastly failure of the expected redemption-plot. Because Tannhäuser is recounting these events in a retrospective narration (the forerunner of the great retrospective scenes that occupy so much of the *Ring*), we understand that the pilgrimage he describes has *already* failed, and the narration itself therefore becomes a confession with no possibility of absolution, a re-enactment of a guilt which apparently cannot be expiated. Correspondingly, the music of the passage oscillates abruptly between the sounds of holiness (the Dresden Amen, the bell-like chords) and guilt (the heavy, dragging figure dominating the opening, the persistent string fragment that sounds like a brief groan of pain). These alternatives are never resolved, remaining in bitterly ironic conjunction. The music of the narration is famous for its free dramatic development, using the orchestra to evoke the contradictory aspects of the journey rather than binding the scene in closed melodic and harmonic structures. The effect is to confound any idea that the narration represents a move towards a thematic conclusion of the opera (this will have to be provided from an entirely separate source, Elisabeth). The monologue is not a heroic declaration of defiance in the face of the church's cruel authority – unlike, say, Tannhäuser's earlier outburst in the Hall of Song, where he proclaims his own passionate genius against the pious conformity of Wolfram. It is, instead, a despairing account of the unresolvable contradiction inherent in the artist's position. The music recognizes that spiritual passion and spiritual guilt cannot be separated. After being refused the Pope's absolution, Tannhäuser describes how he heard again the pilgrim's 'frohe

Gnadenlieder' ('joyful songs of grace'), but was now disgusted by the 'lügneri-schem Klang', 'lying sound'. The orchestra quotes the bell-like sound again. At this point, the music of holiness seems only ironic: the sound that signi-fies the sanctity of Rome is heard by Tannhäuser as an exact opposite, a false music. At this point, the score contains two opposite meanings at the same time. The same is true of the narration as a whole. Penitence and damnation are as real and as vital as holiness and redemption.

Again, what this means is that the conflict between artist and world on which the Wagnerian myth is based turns out to be more genuinely damag-ing than it appears at first to allow for. If Wagner's heroes of the 1840s are exalted by their alienation, it is nevertheless also true that this isolation is often represented as a heavy curse, one which cannot be romanticized into pleasurably melodramatic self-indulgence. Hence the earlier operas' fascina-tion with the idea of penitence. As early as *Die Feen* and as late as *Parsifal*, Wagner's work focusses intently and acutely on processes of expiation, with their corresponding implication that the characters' sufferings are genuinely punitive rather than mythically heroic. Ada and Arindal, the main figures of *Die Feen*, both suffer heavy punishments for actions that are not really crimes. The opera's two most effective scenes are the monologues in which they express their terror (and, in Arindal's case, madness) at the curses they neces-sarily suffer under. *Der fliegende Holländer* derives great dramatic weight from the idea of the doomed hero. Largely, of course, we see the Dutchman's curse through the sentimental eyes of Senta herself. She idolizes his suffering exactly as the myth demands, defining his isolation as the mark of his sublime grandeur. Nevertheless, his own narration of a failed absolution – the mono-logue in Act I – suggests the disproportionate curse laid on the hero. He is doing endless penance for one rather trivial crime, engaged on a pilgrimage for absolution whose destination appears to be unattainable. Significantly, the Dutchman's particular pilgrimage consists of a search for an audience. He needs to find someone who will listen to him faithfully and allow herself to be abducted by him, consenting to fall under the same curse that burdens him. Here again the myth threatens to gravitate towards suffering rather than heroism. The remoteness from audiences, which is the artist-hero's glory, has turned into a guilty and penitential doom. Wagner will go on working and reworking the theme of the curse, and it always turns out to be more than just an excuse to bring about plots of triumph and redemption. Look at the curses that are *not* broken: Alberich's ring does indeed end up destroying everything, and even in his moment of triumph Parsifal knows he is caught in the maze of error to which Kundry condemns him.

For all one's suspicions about the myth of the artist being merely self-aggrandizing fantasy, there is a dangerous element contained in it which not only cannot be disguised, but becomes increasingly visible as Wagner's operas develop and mature. Isolation turns out to be a recalcitrant (and artistically fertile) problem, precisely because it cannot be translated into heroism as glibly as the self-serving power of the myth hopes. The figure in whom these anxieties are most powerfully expressed is Wotan. Like R., the Dutchman and Tannhäuser, he too is given a grand confessional monologue. What he confesses in Act II of *Die Walküre* is that there is no escape from the curse he has discovered, and moreover that it is he himself who is ultimately responsible for that curse. There is no heroic posturing in the style of the Dutchman's 'Die Frist ist um' as he makes this confession. He is virtually whispering as he begins, the basses holding an almost inaudibly low A flat; his guilt is too real to be shouted, and the speech proceeds in bitter, muttering music. When it does rise to a theatrical climax, at the shout of 'Das Ende!' ('the end!'), Wotan immediately retracts this moment of melodrama, repeating the words softly, to the accompaniment of an eerily muted chord. 'Das Ende' is first a bang, then a whimper. Its potential grandeur is swiftly cancelled, replaced with something stranger and far less certain. Likewise, the end that Wotan foresees here – the end of the tetralogy, the conflagration that closes *Götterdämmerung* – is hard to be certain about, as we'll see later. Is it redemption, which is the end the myth always hopes for, or is it merely annihilation, wiping away all the myths and leaving us right where we started?

In the Paris and Dresden period of Wagner's career, the stakes are not so high. The operas don't claim to present the history of everything, and the prose works don't claim absolute authority. *Holländer*, *Tannhäuser* and *Lohengrin* have more conventional plots, populated by mysterious supernatural figures and damsels in distress. Nevertheless, amid all this rather predictably romantic material, damaging curses still figure strongly, resisting the pull of happy endings. The central figures are pressured and hurt by the roles Wagner casts them in and the forces he makes them subject to. All three operas are pervaded by the power of enchantment. Instead of simply imaging the glorious magic of the stage, though, these powers reveal the world of romantic opera to be more complex, and more troubled, than it looks.

CHAPTER THREE

Enchantment

Nowadays, Wagner's three canonical 'romantic operas' are usually treated as progressively longer strides along a road leading beyond that genre. With the evidence of the later works leading us on, we look for signs of the breakdown of traditional forms: the use of motivic material, the expansion of aria and ensemble to accommodate more continuous dramatic presentation, and so on. Musically, the three operas appeal to modern audiences most at those moments when they hint at the composer lying a few years in the future. The wonderful tone-painting of the storm in Act III of *Holländer* or the prelude to Act I of *Lohengrin* seems poised on the brink of the intensely expressive sound of *Tristan*, while the handling of key monologues and dialogues – Tannhäuser's Rome narration, Elsa and Lohengrin's catastrophic wedding night – foreshadows the subtle development of an extended scene like the first act of *Die Walküre*. Concomitantly, some Wagnerian tendencies here appear in their rawest form, particularly the fondness for melodrama and bombast which his later works usually manage to sublimate. The librettist and composer of *Rienzi* obtrudes on all three of the subsequent operas. His technique is echoed most embarrassingly in the way the crowds in *Tannhäuser* and *Lohengrin* like to indulge in mass shouting, shaped by repetitive foursquare rhythms with brass-band harmonies: 'Hail to Landgrave Hermann, leader of Thuringia!' 'Hail, King Henry! King Henry, Hail!'

Questions of interpretation also tend to be influenced by views of the later masterpieces, because all Wagner's work broadly shares a set of recurrent thematic fixations: the questing man, the saving woman, the pure hero, the talismanic object, the fatal compulsion. Nevertheless, the three romantic operas have more in common with each other than with the later works. Even the family kinship between Lohengrin and Parsifal is deceptive, since Lohengrin effectively descends from heaven while Parsifal, despite his 'purity', is all of the earth. The more telling relations are between Elsa and Senta, and between Ortrud and Venus, all shaped by a rather conventionally melodramatic style of presentation. Music above all reveals what the early operas share with each other and not with their successors. This is not to refer to their relative lack of sophistication, which is after all not a thematic issue but merely a normal feature of the creative life of an artist. What links these scores together is a structural idea absolutely implicated in the operas' dramatic and thematic concerns, an idea seen most clearly (because least subtly) in *Tannhäuser*: the musical representation of opposing worlds.

Each of the three works enacts the encounter of the familiar with the strange, and in each case it is exotic orchestral colouring (along with the technology of stage effects) which most clearly marks the presence of the other-worldly. Land and sea in *Holländer*, Wartburg and Venusberg in *Tannhäuser*, earth and heaven in *Lohengrin*: these central dichotomies achieve their force through the shifts in musical language which accompany the passage from one world to the other, or (more threateningly) the temporary juxtaposition of both. In Wagner's later work, the gradations will be finer, the shadings more complex. *Tristan* has its opposition of respectable, civilized *Tag* (day) and transgressive, impassioned *Nacht* (night), but there is no single tonal colour associated with either (the contrast is expressed at a far more fundamental harmonic level), and anyway the borders are unstable: in Act III, Tristan's memory of his daylight history is completely entangled in delirium and fantasy. The split in *Parsifal* between the Grail's castle and Klingsor's realm seems more straightforward, and yet (as we shall see later) the two are not so distant. Kundry lives in both places together, dragged between them in an instant; her potent mix of chaste self-abasement and abandoned sexuality reminds us that Klingsor also was once a knight of the Grail, and that Amfortas is a sinner, his body bearing an incessant reminder of his fall in the garden. Consequently, the music of *Parsifal* has a consistency that crosses the borders between the three acts. The whole score seems to evolve from the opening arch of melody, even when the shape is twisted into the jagged chromatic figure that opens Act II; its binary contrasts are dimensions of an overall symmetry. In Wagner's romantic operas, the alternatives are drawn more starkly, even blatantly. Music is either stable and assured – the hymn-like pilgrims' chorus, the pompous fanfares of *Lohengrin*, Erik's cavatina – or it conjures thrilling, exotic vistas of endless seafaring, erotic excess or visionary sanctity. The abruptness of the contrasts isn't simply a sign of Wagner's compositional immaturity in his earlier years. There is nothing in the early operas as marvellous as the *Lohengrin* prelude, but it is not only fantastical sounds which anticipate the orchestral mastery of *Tristan* or *Götterdämmerung*. In *Tannhäuser*, the solemnity of the pilgrims is more impressively articulated (in the earlier versions) than its antagonist, the bacchanalian abandon of the Venusberg. Unlike Wagner's more subtle later style, music in the romantic operas works by exaggerating such antagonisms. In doing so, it draws attention to its powers of evocation and transformation. It is the force that propels the characters out of their ordinary existence and into the magical terrain of operatic romance.

Music shares the nature of those weird presences, benign or malevolent, which inhabit German romantic opera – Hoffmann's water-spirit, Spohr's diabolic agent, Marschner's vampire, Weber's supernatural huntsman. From the first bars of *Lohengrin*, the opera is under an enchantment far more powerful than the oddly irrelevant plot-device of Ortrud's spell. The prelude evokes an ethereal mood that haunts the rest of the opera, recurring at particular moments to signify that the domestic and international politics of the Duchy of Brabant are about to be subsumed under higher, sacramental influences. Out of sight, beyond the visible action on stage, a supernatural drama is being played out. We aren't allowed to know the story of Montsalvat, merely to sense its nature through the radiant harmonies surrounding its emissary; he narrates the offstage plot only after he has confirmed his retreat into an inaccessible domain. A similar effect obtains in *Der fliegende Holländer*, where the quotidian trivialities of Norway are repeatedly disturbed by the dark sonorities associated with the enchanted Dutchman. *Tannhäuser*, of course, derives its whole action from the idea of a threatening sorcerous power coexisting with the chaste and orderly places where people live. Appropriately enough, when Wagner came to revise the opera for the notoriously catastrophic Paris production of 1861, he depicted this power using the sensuous musical language of *Tristan*, which, by virtue of its utter remoteness from the 1845 score, conveys the otherworldliness of the Venusberg's magic all too effectively.

The three operas derive many of their most telling effects from moments of musical contrast or transition, when the opposition of the sound-worlds is at its most pronounced. This again is not characteristic of Wagner's later works. By the 1850s, his musico-dramatic vocabulary had expanded enough for him no longer to rely on bluntly melodramatic dualisms. Still, the power of contrast is genuinely effective in the earlier operas, precisely because such oppositions are their central thematic concern. Where two worlds are thrown into contact with each other, the premises of romantic opera are sharply illuminated. A civilized society, Norway or Thuringia or Brabant, is suddenly confronted with an eerie, magical visitation. It is as if the situation in the theatre – bourgeois operagoers submitting to the exotic spell of opera – has been mirrored on stage (this mirroring is a characteristic Wagnerian effect, theorized at length in the prose writings of 1848–51 and the Bayreuth plan). Romantic opera invests much of its energy in accentuating the transition from the familiar to the uncanny, or the conjunction of the two. As it tells its stories of enchantment, it is also working to bring the audience under its own spell. Watching one world giving way to another, we are witnessing the power of opera itself in action.

Der fliegende Holländer dramatizes this process, and exposes its possible costs. When we first see Senta, she is in her world but not of it. The spinning chorus that begins Act II is Wagner's most successful portrait of humdrum domesticity, not a field which naturally captured his imagination (all his other representations of human sociability, even in *Meistersinger*, are freighted with some degree of anxiety or threat). Senta's romantic melancholy is evidently worlds away from this charmingly folksy sound. The other girls' singing is, after all, a form of work: it is what they do when they are spinning, and it mimics the sound of the wheel. It captures them neatly in their communal household function. Senta, however, neither works nor sings. The girls are conventional stereotypes of the mundane, but she is an 'operatic' character, extreme in her passions and devoted to her private raptures. Evidently, the scene's move from their world to hers is going to involve effort; this is how we appreciate the scale of the distance travelled. The greater our sense of disjunction, the more territory opera claims for itself, by declaring itself entirely irreconcilable with the world it leaves behind. In this sense, Senta shows us how to take the opera as a whole. Refusing to participate in the commonplace, functional goings-on around her, she is instead staring at a picture of the Dutchman, whose melodramatic agonies we have just witnessed. She is openly choosing the fabulous story over the mundane actions (and songs) of her prescribed existence. The Flying Dutchman has enchanted her, as the conventions of romantic opera demand that he enchant and captivate us.

Gradually, the other characters fall silent, preparing the way for Senta to initiate them and us into the magical world, via the ballad which tells the Dutchman's story – and which, through its combination of the work's salient melodies, also lays out the structure of *Holländer*, like a second overture. Certainly it is central to the opera's dualism; its raw melodic energy could not be in greater contrast to the spinning chorus. This is clearly the song of someone who lives in a romantic otherworld, its vivid vocal line the equivalent of the howling orchestral storm music in Act III. Still more interesting, however, are the five rhythmless bars that Senta sings before she launches into the first piercing note of the ballad's opening challenge. The song is at least in regular stanzas, and to that extent conventional in form; we gather that Senta learned it from Mary, who epitomizes landbound bourgeois respectability. The introductory phrases, by contrast, sound shapeless, weird. Even though they chart out a simple sequence of tonic Gs and dominant Ds, they give the impression of being an exhalation from Senta's soul rather than any sort of structured music. This signals the moment when the scene moves us from one sound-world to another, when the supernatural intrudes on and overwhelms the ordinary. The strength of these few incantatory wordless phrases is in the sense of deliberate effort they communicate. Senta seems to be singing herself

into a trance, or into hysteria; at the end of the ballad, say the stage directions, she collapses in psychosomatic exhaustion. The eerie sounds she begins
with are therefore her way of announcing her allegiance to the aesthetics of
romantic supernaturalism, in which the visionary power of fantasy shows its
disdain for the mundane world it has left behind. This dichotomy is in itself
conventional enough, according to the standard practices of romantic supernaturalism. What makes Senta's unaccompanied moanings significant is that
they equate a musical transition with a more fundamental aesthetic and psychological shift. As the sound of the scene changes from the familiar to the
exotic, Senta visibly and audibly surrenders to opera's enchanted aspect, which
(as the ballad explains) will demand that she finally extinguish herself completely for its sake. Hence her 'Johohoe's are both exciting and frightening.
This is genuine 'transformation music': the sound of operatic fantasy casting
its spell over an individual imagination.

The same compulsion is signalled in Act II of *Tannhäuser* by a ripple in the
orchestral fabric, a momentary eddy in the sonorous stream of pompous music
that builds up steadily after the first distant fanfares heralding the knights and
ladies of the Wartburg. Immediately after the chorus of praise for Wolfram's
hymn to spiritual love, one fortissimo bar of the leaping, shimmering
Venusberg music flashes out against the heavier background. (Throughout this
chapter, I refer to the Dresden version – or versions – of the score, which
are naturally more uniformly within the spirit of 'grand romantic opera' – as
the original subtitle puts it – than the *Tristan*-era revisions.) The brief
disturbance obviously signals the abrupt tug of the first act's sensuality on
Tannhäuser's thoughts. Like Senta, although now without any deliberate exercise of will, he suddenly rediscovers a musical space antithetical to the one
surrounding him. The contrasting sounds encode fairly straightforward thematic meanings: glittering, enervated music indicates eroticism, while martial
fanfares and choruses represent the social and religious orthodoxy, not unlike
that of mid-nineteenth-century bourgeois northern Europe, which the
Landgrave and his retinue uphold (the Wartburg itself, historically associated
with Luther, is an icon of Protestant nationalism). Beyond this simple
dichotomy, though, the moment of Tannhäuser's relapse into fantasy reminds
us of opera's own powers of enchantment. Whatever the thematic meaning
of Venus's music, it interrupts this scene like a ghost. Wolfram's very piety
appears to conjure up its demonic opposite; we have to remember that the
Venus of the medieval legend is a pagan sorceress, not Botticelli's demure and
wispy blonde. Tannhäuser's largely inexplicable fall is therefore really a surrender to the magic of a sound that refuses to be suppressed.

In the various forms of romantic opera, music characteristically claims a
right to disrupt stability and evoke extreme states. In Act II of *Tannhäuser*, we
watch this tendency revenging itself on a society dedicated to restraint and

control, through the apparently helpless figure of the hero, who, as Wagner later noted in the 1852 pamphlet *Über die Aufführung des 'Tannhäuser'* (*On the Performing of 'Tannhäuser'*), always submits to immediate influences (III 198–9). Attempting a summary of the fundamental quality that allows one to speak of 'romantic opera' as if it were a genre, Carl Dahlhaus has written that 'the musical realization of the Romantic aesthetic was based on features such as the characteristic, the striking, and the interesting'.[1] Wagner's habit of exaggeration means that in his hands this aesthetic of the unusual becomes a full-blown embrace of the extreme. His music enacts romantic opera's conflicts between the familiar and the supernatural to the most acute degree. Hence the drama played out between Wartburg and Venusberg begins with not merely a contrast but a rupture, a tiny but startling tonal break as telling in its way as Senta's deliberate incantation. This is no schematic representation of two opposed moral choices (though unfortunately it will become one in the rather clumsy ending to Act III, a dénouement Wagner seems never to have been happy about). Instead, the conjunction of irreconcilable worlds dramatizes music's inherent pull toward the unearthly.

The conflict is staged most explicitly in the first scene of Act III of *Holländer*, where both stage and score split in two. On one side are the sights and sounds of mundane life, at least in their conventional operatic form: a chorus of lusty folk preparing for a communal feast, eating, drinking and joking to a galumphing dance tune. On the other side is a crew of the dead, singing about an invisible storm engulfing their ship. Sociability confronts solitude; the everyday is inverted by the supernatural. Out of this pairing of opposites Wagner summons some of the score's most potent effects. The alternatives are also represented by Erik and the Dutchman, between whom Senta supposedly chooses, but the polarity of these two figures has none of the visceral energy conjured in the choric scene. Only when the two worlds are directly superimposed (as in Act II of *Tannhäuser*) does music discover its power to dramatize the breadth of the gulf which separates them. The space that Senta earlier forced herself across now appears on stage as a battleground, the site of a *Sängerkrieg* (song-contest) far more violent than that of *Tannhäuser*. In the Wartburg all the competitors are at least playing by the same rules; it's what Tannhäuser *says* that is so shocking to his peers. By contrast, words disappear entirely in the maelstrom of *Holländer* Act III. The songs of the Norwegians and the unseen sailors come across only as music in conflict, while the orchestra threatens to drown both with its own fury, epitomizing human beings' vulnerability to the sheer power of sound. There's no reason for Daland's crew to go on with their jokes aimed at the Steersman; they sing only to try to assert their voices against the chorus around them, itself singing words that belong somewhere else, not at anchor but on the open sea. Something much more elemental is at stake here than in the philosophical argument about love between Tannhäuser and Wolfram. Sound itself takes centre stage. The essential aesthetic of romantic opera is being dramatized in the starkest possible way, as the music of the uncanny and the extreme violently contradicts the music of the everyday.

At bottom, then, all these stories of enchantment and supernatural forces are really about how opera works, and especially about the musical element on which (as Dahlhaus's remark suggests) romantic opera grounds itself. This is why in 'Eine Mittheilung an meine Freunde' ('A Communication to My Friends', 1851) and elsewhere Wagner so vehemently denied that *Tannhäuser* was a story of Christian salvation, all the evidence of its plot and libretto to the contrary. ('A Communication' originally appeared as the preface to a volume containing the poems of the three romantic operas.) Though it's always necessary to be extremely wary of Wagner's instructions for interpreting his own work, as I shall be arguing throughout this book, his distinction between the mere 'outward garb' of the opera and its real 'artistic aim' (I 271, 272) is in this case an important one. It is as if the workings of the plot are no more than the conventional superstructure beneath which opera performs its real actions and works out its real meanings, through the abstract processes of the score. No doubt the post-revolutionary Wagner of 'A Communication' would have us believe so. The position allows him to dismiss the obviously derivative aspects of his existing work as irrelevant distractions, and so to ignore his kinship with the musico-dramatic environment whose destruction he had been demanding throughout his writings of the previous three years. But this is to overlook the real resources that the conventions of romantic opera may have supplied. Tales of supernatural wonder provide the arena in which music can transcend its accompanying plots, because they encourage the evocation of an orchestral magic which no amount of conventional piety can restrain.

Take for example the end of *Lohengrin*, an opera which, as Wagner crossly observes in 'A Communication', is also liable to be taken for a story of the triumph of Christianity over evil. In its closing stages, the plot strains at the seams attempting to accommodate two ideas of its hero's function. A tragic mood predominates: Lohengrin and Elsa are doomed to part, and the Brabantines loudly bewail the loss of their new 'Führer' ('leader'). Alongside all this, however, Lohengrin (like Elisabeth in *Tannhäuser*) guarantees the existing political order. He recovers the lost heir to the throne, promises the German king Heinrich victory over the barbaric hordes, and removes any doubts over his own spiritual legitimacy by performing a public miracle sanctified by a hovering dove. It is easy to see why Wagner might have suspected that this plot laid him open to charges of conformity with 'a specifically Christian and impotently pietistic drift [*Tendenz*]' (I 323). Despite the overwhelming impression that we are watching a disaster unfold, this final scene secures the triumph of church and state more emphatically than any of Wagner's other operas (in *Meistersinger* religion and empire are vassals of the new reign of art).

The music tells a rather different tale. As the plot happily wraps up all loose ends, even supplying Elsa with the timely ritual death required of the truly 'pure' heroine, the orchestra perpetuates those magical sounds which belong in what Lohengrin famously calls 'a far-off land' ('In fernem Land . . .'). Next to these otherworldly harmonies, the restoration of Gottfried to his throne and the defeat of the encroaching Huns seem superficial at best. In this sense, Wagner is right to deny the importance of the plot's triumphalist 'drift'. *Lohengrin* is really a tale of loss, organized around the simple rhythm of descent followed by ascent, or revelation followed by withdrawal, which is described in the prelude to Act I (according to Wagner's frothy 1853 programme note for a concert performance of the piece). This loss gains its pathos from our sense of the distance between the two worlds temporarily conjoined in the person of Lohengrin; it is not just a hero but an archangelic emissary who leaves the human world at the end of the opera. This distance is measured by the score. Music is the power that places Lohengrin's holiness beyond our reach, beyond the Teutonic ascendancy of the opera's concluding actions. He explains that Montsalvat is a 'far-off land', its perfection maintained by absolute seclusion from the ordinary world, but it is the unearthly accompaniment to these words which reinforces the Grail's remoteness. Like the storm-music of *Holländer*, the celestial strings are an orchestral passage into supernatural regions defined by their entire incompatibility with mundane human events. So for all the plot's insistence that Lohengrin ends by sorting out everything that needs to be resolved, his role as an agent of political or religious stability can never be confidently asserted. The music surrounding him always seems to have the most tenuous link to reality. Like Lohengrin himself, it is perpetually on the point of disappearing, ascending into aural regions so refined as to be inaudible – hence the programme note's description of the prelude as representing 'the clearest light of Heaven's æther' (III 233), pure radiance without substance. The real story of this opera, as of its two predecessors, is to do with the precarious balance between the supernatural and the mundane – a relationship whose movements are charted by gradations of melodic character and orchestral colouring.

This is not to say that plot is either an irrelevance or an encumbrance. Because the operas explore music's power to represent magical or otherworldly presences, tales of enchantment, however conventional, are entirely appropriate to them. All three are thick with curses, miracles, spells of all sorts. The ubiquitous narrative motif of unearthly compulsion may derive from hoary romantic clichés, but in Wagner's work it turns into the aesthetic crux of the operas. Enchantment is what they are all about, because enchantment is what happens when music's magic exerts itself on the human world. In the important 1842 essay 'Halévy and "La Reine de Chypre"', omitted from Wagner's edition of his collected writings, this aesthetic of rapture is categorically defined:

> . . . for as soon as we are carried away from ourselves, from our sensations and impressions of the hour, from the habitual sphere where our existence passes, and transported to an unknown region, yet with full retention of all our faculties, – from that moment we are under the spell of what [people] call Romantic poetry. (VIII 181)

It is interesting that Wagner only praises Halévy's grand historical romance, a characteristic product of Parisian grand opera, once he has made it sound like an exercise in German supernaturalism. No such contortions are required with *Der Freischütz* in Wagner's reports on the 1841 Paris production of Weber's work:

> Ah! thou adorable German reverie; thou *Schwärmerei* of woods and gloaming, of stars, of moon, of village-bells when chiming seven at eve! Happy he who understands you, can feel, believe, can dream and lose himself with you! (VII 183)

Wagner rapturously embraces the *Schwärmerei* (the word connotes passion, fanaticism and delusion) of the quintessential German romantic opera, just as in the companion essay addressed to the sceptical French public he begs them to enter 'par la pensée au milieu du monde merveilleux qui se révèle dans *le Freischütz*' (VII 182), to move in thought into *Freischütz*'s magical world. Throughout the journalism of his Paris years (1839–42), he reserves his praise for those operas possessed of the power to reveal a 'marvellous world' or an 'unknown region'. Opera's purpose and value, he asserts, lie in its enchanted transformations, suffusing the 'habitual sphere' with magic.

Such tales of enchantment depend on an antithesis between nature and the supernatural, and this basic structure can in itself be seen as a reflection on the way opera functions, as Wagner imagines it. In his early writing, music in general and opera in particular are often described in terms of an opposition between transcendental ecstasy and trivial everyday experience. His first essay for the *Revue et Gazette musicale* aggressively confronts the urbane, sociable Parisian readership with an image of 'the earnest, deep and visionary German' (VII 91):

> . . . nothing is more natural than that he should include music in his thought and feeling, and, far from looking on its practice as an empty entertainment, religiously approach it as the holiest precinct in his life. He

accordingly becomes a fanatic, and this devout and fervent *Schwärmerei*, with which he conceives and executes his music, is the chief characteristic of German Music. (VII 90)

To a greater or lesser degree, almost all the subsequent essays contrast this sacramental German concept of art with a debased French (or, in 'A Pilgrimage to Beethoven', English) version in which music has been reduced to a habitual activity. The dichotomy is not restricted to the field of opera, although Wagner often attempts to satirize what he thinks of as the superficial attitudes of the operagoing public. Instrumental music, particularly the symphony, provides a still more perfect model, especially because it is the art in which Germans are admitted to excel. The gift of the symphonist, contends one of the characters in 'Ein glücklicher Abend' ('A Happy Evening', 1841), is his access to 'the kingdom of the supramundane [*Überirdischen*]', where he dwells among purely ideal conceptions. The language here is strongly reminiscent of the story of Lohengrin, though Wagner did not begin work on the opera until 1845:

> It would be to drag the musician from this high estate, if one tried to make him fit his inspiration to the semblance of that daily world; and still more would that instrumental composer disown his mission, or expose his weakness, who should aim at carrying the cramped proportions of purely worldly things into the province of his art. (VII 76)

Like the swan knight, music must remain aloof from the world in order to retain its power. Ideally, therefore, its effect is to lift its hearers into some approximation of the Montsalvat where it has its being, 'that high altitude which is true Music's sole domain' (VII 77). Later, in 'A Communication to My Friends', Wagner will define the aesthetic moment of true artistic inspiration as 'ecstatic excess' (I 286). The audience's proper attitude is that of Senta, so entirely enraptured by imaginative conceptions that she eventually demands to live in its world rather than her own – which is the choice of the romantic hero of 'An End in Paris'. Opposed to this are the Dalands of French theatres and concert-halls, impressed only by the gaudy exterior ('here nothing pays but *virtuosity*', VIII 173). Wagner's Paris writing returns over and over again to these polarized alternatives, constantly reminding itself of the stark choice between sacramental art and mere trivial bourgeois entertainment.

His operas recast this theoretical argument into the symbolic shapes of romance. The antitheses set out in the journalism of this period are exactly those dramatized everywhere in the operas: our world against the otherworld, the mundane against the fantastic. Once we identify this plot-structure as a way of exploring opera's enchantments, the rather conventional romantic trap-

pings of *Holländer*, *Tannhäuser* and *Lohengrin* no longer seem irrelevant. Moreover, looking at them more closely, it becomes apparent that the operas present
a rather more subtle and complex treatment of the notion of enchantment
than the hot-headed (not to say heavy-handed) rhetoric of the journalism.

This is because Wagner's early writing, with that characteristic one-
sidedness which will harden into gross tyranny as his career goes on, describes
music's rapture as altogether a valuable thing. The martyr of 'An End in Paris'
may die for it, but it's a glorious death. Despite the essay's attractive hints of
Heine-like satire, there is no question but that its hero is a great spirit
destroyed by the petty soullessness of ordinary experience. The equation is
simple: Germany, symphonic music, poetic idealism and the *Schwärmerei* of the
inner life are positive, while France, artistic virtuosity, money and bourgeois
society supply the negatives. Music's role is to confer value on the individual, drawing him by its ecstatic power from one side to the other, preferably
so far that return is impossible and (as for Wagner's fantasized alter ego in
'An End') he dies rather compromising his ideal with economic or pragmatic
considerations. By enchanting the hearer, music gathers him into the
supernatural terrain antithetical to ordinary existence.

In the operas, enchantment is a far more ambiguous effect. *Tannhäuser* looks
as if it ought to mirror the situation established in the prose writings quite
closely, in that its hero is a musician faced with a choice between sacred and
profane ideals. But which is which? In Act I, Tannhäuser declares that the
erotic excess of the Venusberg is stifling his art. Ordinary reality, so despised
in the writings, turns out to be precisely what he desires. A longing for nature
in its everyday, pastoral aspect is contrasted with a description of Venus's realm
couched in the very terminology usually associated with the transcendental
enchantment of music:

Entzückend sind die Wunder deines Reiches,	Enchanting are the marvels of your realm,
den Zauber aller Wonnen athm' ich hier;	here I breathe every bliss's magic,
kein Land der weiten Erde bietet Gleiches,	nowhere in the wide world offers its like;
was sie besitzt, scheint leicht entbehrlich dir.	all it contains seems petty without you.

More familiar is the position in Act II, where Venus's magic appears as an
impassioned alternative to the sterility of art as practised in the Wartburg.
Even here, though, Tannhäuser is aghast at himself almost as soon as he has
surrendered to the spell, calling himself a sinner and begging for absolution.
The magic ('Zauber') of the Venusberg is authoritatively redefined by
Elisabeth as an overmastering delusion. She describes Tannhäuser as

Der Unglücksel'ge, den gefangen	The ill-starred man, held captive
ein furchtbar mächt'ger Zauber hält. . . .	by a fearfully potent spell. . . .

In her eyes he's a victim of black magic; yet her description uses the kind of language associated with the exalted *Schwärmerei* which music is supposed to induce in its hearers. Which are we to believe: his description of enchantment as a wonderful power, or her conviction that it is sinful? How are we expected to evaluate the competing claims of the opera's two worlds? Compared with the polemical consistency of the journalism, *Tannhäuser's* signals are strangely mixed.

The opera finds it increasingly difficult to distinguish between erotic desire, consistently regarded as an evil, and passion in general, the intensity of feeling which marks Tannhäuser as a hero more elevated and inspired than his peers. Insofar as Venus's enchantment is merely sexual, the plot is able to present it in a religious context, as the inverse of the Christian world of the chaste Elisabeth, the Pope, and the Virgin Mary who miraculously saves Tannhäuser from the Venusberg in Act I. But this is not the whole story. Act III requires us to sympathize with the sinners as much as the saints. The Pope's refusal to grant Tannhäuser absolution turns Christianity into tyranny; at this point, the insistence on chastity can no longer be taken as the moral and spiritual benchmark which everyone in Act II assumes it to be. Tannhäuser's Rome narration brings us instead perilously close to the values of *Die Walküre* or *Tristan*, where individual passion is elevated over the moral consensus. His desire to re-enter the Venusberg might now be an embrace of his human nature, not a sinful erotic fixation. There is an authenticity to this feverish rapture lacking from his protestations of guilt and religious fervour in Act II. Desire seems to be more potent than faith, despite the plot's final vindication of God's saving power through the miracle of the Pope's staff. So although all the characters agree that the Venusberg is the gateway to hell, if not hell itself, the opera is hesitant about interpreting its two opposed worlds in this way. It recognizes its affinity with the impassioned sensibility that only Venus can arouse, what 'A Communication' calls art's 'ecstatic excess' (*entzückenden Übermaße*: Venus's magic was called *entzückend*) (I 286). *Tannhäuser* is unable altogether to condemn the Venusberg's enchantments.

The key figure in these confusions is Elisabeth. On the surface, her role appears unambiguous. Rome and the Wartburg court are equally ineffectual counterweights to the Venusberg, but Elisabeth is a genuine saint – the character is based on the historical daughter-in-law of Hermann of Thuringia, canonized a few years after her early death – and her direct intercession proves to be the means of Tannhäuser's final salvation. She is consistently described as chaste, pure and angelic, which of course means in turn that Venus can confidently be identified as a diabolic temptress. However, Elisabeth's virtue is oddly inconsistent. Though the plot relies for its conclusiveness on her sanctity, the opera prefers to emphasize her secular nature, especially in Act II where a stage direction surprisingly refers to her approval of Tannhäuser's first riposte to Wolfram (this exchange is cut from the 'Paris' version of the opera). Whence this instinctive sympathy with the sinner? It belongs to the same side of her character that is portrayed in her exhilarated address to the hall of song at the beginning of Act II, and in the pulsing wind figures and agitated melody of the preceding orchestral introduction. For all her orthodox saintliness, Elisabeth is moved by passionate love. Her music may be fresh and joyful where Venus's is languorous and decadent, but the contrasting styles disguise a similarity of expressive content. The opera sexualizes Elisabeth despite her sainthood; she never sounds austerely pure in the way Lohengrin does. Her sacrifice in Act III is therefore open to slightly divergent interpretations, which *Tannhäuser* leaves unresolved. Her final prayer, the young pilgrims' chorus, Tannhäuser's last words, the miracle of the staff, all suggest that she has taken on the role of the Virgin and miraculously saved a sinner from damnation. But it is equally true that she has given her life for her beloved just as Senta does, as a heroine of profane romance, that is, rather than as a sacred martyr. The act of sainthood is also a deed of love.

Desire and its enchantments are not so easily suppressed in *Tannhäuser* as the direction of the plot seems to indicate. It is tempting to see in these confusions an anticipation of the extraordinarily complex relation between sex and sanctity in *Parsifal*, but the comparison, though interesting, is unnecessary at this stage; the earlier work is ambiguous enough in itself to hint at how opera disturbs an explicitly Christian framework with its delightful (*entzückend*) raptures. Elisabeth is not both Madonna and whore as Kundry is, but her role wavers uneasily between desire and renunciation. If she is finally the one who breaks the spell of the Venusberg, she is equally under a spell of her own: 'Im Traum bin ich', 'I am in a dream', she says when reunited with Tannhäuser. In fact, her entanglement in the theme of enchantment exactly mirrors Senta's, who also breaks a curse through the force of her own desire. The parallel confirms Wagner's otherwise rather disingenuous assertions that a secular (what he would later call 'purely human', *reinmenschlich*) drama lies beneath the pious surface of *Tannhäuser*, though we can't dismiss the implications of the religious structures as easily as he was willing to do. At stake here is that overused and abused Wagnerian cliché, redemption through love. *Tannhäuser* makes us ask what one is redeemed from, and what kind of love does the work of redemption. Love seems potentially to refer either to the world of the Venusberg or to the martyrdom of the pure heroine.

The ambiguity is starker in *Der fliegende Holländer*, because the distance between love and enchantment is powerfully reduced. Senta breaks Satan's spell not by angelic intercession, although the Dutchman calls her *Engel*, but by submitting to the same magic herself. She is at least as enchanted as the cursed sailor. Her enthusiasm for self-sacrifice, which horrifies Mary and Erik, has the ring of true fanaticism about it; evidently she is possessed by the *Schwärmerei* defined in Wagner's writings of this period as the essential character of music. Although the opera's plot appears to be about an escape from enchantment, the means to salvation are inseparable from delusion and desire. This is the most unequivocally 'romantic' of Wagner's canonical works, in that it most enthusiastically adopts specific conventional elements. It accords closely with the Paris writings in setting supernatural romance against everyday life. Nevertheless, there are questions to be asked here about the effects of opera's magic – the same questions raised more urgently in *Tristan*, where the lovers' rapture borders on dementia. In terms of the conventions, or of Wagner's writings, *Holländer* simply dramatizes the redemptive power of a grand passion. But it also begins to explore the contradictions that might be involved if one began to take this theme seriously, as the proximity of magic to music suggests we should. It shows us that the surrender to an enchanted world – the surrender demanded by opera – is a dangerous one. Far more obviously than Elisabeth, Senta is caught between two roles, redemptrix and victim of enchantment. Romantic models of female virtue require that she sacrifice all to break the spell, but Wagner's portrait shows that the impulse to self-destruction must come from an equally powerful compulsion. Salvation is manifestly a struggle in *Holländer*; the obsessiveness of Senta's love for the Dutchman turns it into a form of mania.

These contradictory pressures are explored again in the figure of Elsa. Like the two operas before it, *Lohengrin* is saturated with enchantment and disenchantment, and again like them it is uncertain about how to interpret the relation between them. Elsa is the victim sacrificed to these uncertainties. After her death, Wagner will no longer be in the regions of romantic opera, where generic conventions can accommodate the supernatural forces of music and translate them into fantasized stories of salvation. Elsa's problem is that she asks questions: where does this magic come from? How can we be sure that it is heavenly rather than demonic? What is its secret? In the enchanted terrain of romance, music can find a way of dramatizing its pull beyond the world of lived experience, while at the same time accompanying plots that end in resolution. The Venusberg or the phantom ship can be conjured up in order to act out opera's power, only to be dispelled by myths of salvation. There is no such salvation in *Lohengrin*. Elsa is asked to submit to a mysterious enchantment, but finds herself unable to do so; her failure forces Lohengrin back to the fantasyland whence he came, and the possibility of enduring magical redemption is denied. Romantic opera cannot survive the forbidden questions with its power intact. It should not be a surprise that

Wagner spent the years following the completion of *Lohengrin* tortuously retheorizing the nature of his art.

The story of Elsa disrupts what might otherwise be a relatively straight-forward contest between holy and pagan magic, not unlike the one in *Tannhäuser*. Ortrud's malevolent witchery is confined to destabilizing the world of Brabant, and when Lohengrin arrives, he undoes her magic, but only to impose a higher one of his own – higher because the source of his power is distant and inaccessible. His first appearance is described by the gathered crowd as an 'unerhörtes, nie geseh'nes Wunder!' ('an unheard-of, never-seen miracle'). Later in Act I, King Heinrich and his people still feel that they are under some new enchantment:

Welch' holde Wunder muß ich seh'n?	What glorious marvel do I see?
Ist's Zauber, der mir angethan?	Is it magic that has been cast on me?

Elsa has already been captivated by this same magic in her dream. When she first appears before her accusers and judge, the crowd murmur 'Ist sie entrückt?' ('is she bewitched?'). Lohengrin's arrival confirms their impression rather than proving them wrong, since Elsa has indeed – again like Senta – been touched by the presence of the otherworldly. Ortrud is right to insinuate in the first scene of Act II that Lohengrin's victory in single combat is the result of his enchantment rather than Telramund's falsity, and to say that he is 'durch Zauber stark', made strong by magic. Throughout the opera, the word *Zauber* attaches itself more easily to Lohengrin than his pagan enemies, and indeed his music conveys a sense of pervasive magic, while Ortrud's expresses the malevolent brooding of an individual rather than the presence of some demonic force.

On this level, the story accords entirely with Wagner's writings by celebrating the transcendent glory of opera's mysterious presences. Uncertainty enters with the prohibition accompanying this power. By declaring his essentially unknowable nature, Lohengrin exposes the impossible conditions of his authority. Romantic opera works by clothing itself in fantasy. Its supernatural incursions are always in conflict with the human world because it must always present itself as deriving from some source we cannot master. It demands that we acknowledge its illusory power, in order to be exalted by the *Schwärmerei* it dramatizes for us. The forbidden question in Lohengrin is banned because it might disenchant romance itself, exposing opera's affinity with magic as either a mere theatrical trick or (more significantly) a disturbing delusion. And yet, as Ortrud cleverly appreciates, the question cannot be dispelled once it is raised. Her promptings catch Elsa in an impossible paradox. Either she must give way to an inexplicable and unknown enchantment, or she must try to accommodate the magic to herself by determining its real nature, so ceasing to allow it to continue as magic at all. Like Tannhäuser, she finds herself enraptured by a delusion which is incomparably exhilarating as long as it seems real, but loses its power as soon as it is known to be something different from reality. But whereas *Tannhäuser* bewilders itself attempting to decide whether the spell of the Venusberg is hellish or not, *Lohengrin* brilliantly suggests that enchantment carries ambivalence with it, as its condition. The power of the Grail is effective enough – the music makes that clear – but it resists appropriation or resolution; nothing can be done with it. It retreats from Elsa's questions because they are impossible to answer without breaking the spell. Opera's magic must maintain itself in purely imaginary space, leaving those who try to take hold of it – Senta, Tannhäuser, Elsa – dead on the stage.

Each of these three operas ends with a disenchantment, a broken power. Beyond these resolutions, though, all acknowledge to some degree that enchantment is what they celebrate; enchantment, as figured by music, is what enables them to exist at all. Opera is a place where magic is raised, exulting in music's captivating and transfiguring command over human feelings and experience. At the same time, opera is an arena of delusion, where people are afflicted with supernatural temptations and submitted to music's extreme and otherworldly force. With his usual ability to articulate a problem in its most extreme condition, Wagner takes this gentle uncertainty endemic to German romantic opera and works it into a vital thematic crux. As the three stories oscillate between enchantment and disenchantment, they reveal their ambivalent attitude to their own workings. Opera's siren song resounds through them all –

Naht euch dem Strande,	Draw near this shore,
naht euch dem Lande. . . .	draw near this realm. . . .

The distant voices, promising seduction, bliss and destruction all at once, summon the characters to worlds they can never enter, but also can never resist. Whether the domain is Venusberg or Montsalvat is irrelevant: the stories always both indulge and fear the temptations of fantasy.

The question of what one's proper relation to opera's magic should be persists – and in fact becomes increasingly urgent – throughout Wagner's work. Enchantment grows in potency and becomes more extreme in its effects, whether in the plots (the curse on Alberich's ring, which destroys the world), the score (the sound of *Tristan*) or the theatre (Bayreuth, a place dedicated to enthralling its audience). As anyone at all familiar with the Wagner phenomenon knows, the problem lives on. Enthusiasts for his work often give the impression of being bewitched, like Senta or Elsa; the same is true for a number of scholars and critics, from the fervid Bayreuthians of the decades following Wagner's death to writers of the present day. It is important to recognize that this response is authentically Wagnerian, since even the early operas thematize magic, its powers and its limits. But it is still more vital to see that these works probe their own conditions rather than simply imposing them. By paying attention to their rather conventional stories, rather than gratefully tracing the emergence of a more distinctively impressive 'Wagnerian' style, we can begin to ask the central question they deal with, the question whose complexities trap Elsa: is it right to break opera's spell?

CHAPTER FOUR

Disenchantment

Elsa's forbidden questions – the doubt which banishes romantic magic – are ones that still need asking. We shall return to them again and again, as talismans protecting us from the increasingly overwhelming mastery of Wagner's musical wizardry: where does it come from, and what is its real nature? It is, however, worth remembering how much Wagner's own attitude towards the romance of opera, especially in the later 1840s, is pervaded by Elsa's scepticism. One source of his greatness as an artist lies in the way his work restlessly struggles with the limitations it encounters within itself. This ability to see fundamental problems where contemporaries might just have accepted conventions is one aspect of his monumental originality. Dissatisfaction generates innovation; and only a powerful doubt about the whole nature of the operatic enterprise could have impelled Wagner's unlikely alternatives (tetralogy, Schopenhauerian opera, Bayreuth). Despite his work's thorough exploitation of romantic opera and its characteristics, Wagner looks hard at the genre, and asks it questions which it finally cannot answer.

His personal disenchantment with institutional opera is a constant theme of the Dresden years (1843–9). His daily professional life as co-Kapellmeister at the Saxon court brought home the disparity between his idealized conception of a magical art and the pragmatic business of rehearsing all-too-mundane musicians and carrying out official duties. Nevertheless, the problem is not only a personal one. What matters for our purposes is how this disenchantment is woven into the fabric of opera itself, an art which (in the hands of Wagner and many of his earlier contemporaries, at least) often concerns itself with precisely this disparity between the ordinary and the supernatural. We have seen that Wagner imagines theatre as a place where the artist's fantasy exerts power over its audience, and that this relationship between fantasy and reality becomes an intensely conflicted struggle. Confessing a disenchantment *with* opera, then, is also a kind of disenchantment *in* opera, a breaking of its spell, an admission that its magical power doesn't work.

Wagner thus shares in the defeat suffered by the enchantresses Venus and Ortrud (although in both cases, of course, the operas appeal to a higher supernatural power, and both end with miracles – the Pope's staff and the swan prince). For the increasingly disillusioned Kapellmeister, the stage might itself come to look like a place where illusions are destroyed, not created.

Any composer of the time other than Wagner (and the equally ambitious Berlioz) would probably have been content to live with the fact that their operas were subject to practical considerations – the economics of patronage, for example, or existing stage technologies. Meyerbeer was almost as famous for his acute understanding of these conditions as for his work; as many contemporary commentators observed, his art was a brilliant expression of the spirit of the age, as least insofar as the age was defined by the ascendancy of the capitalist leisured classes. For Wagner, though, the pressure exerted by reality on the aesthetics of romance threatened to undermine opera at a fundamental level. This is not – as Wagner himself would have us believe, a claim still repeated today – because his art has a deep spiritual integrity that could never compromise with opera's institutional situation, as he thought Meyerbeer had done. Nor is it because opera had been deprived of its proper environment and taken over instead by the wrong kind of controlling forces – the aristocrats, the French, the Jews. The problem is to do with the nature of romance itself. However much Wagner liked to lay the blame on external factors, his work comes to realize that the ambivalence of romantic magic itself is ultimately insupportable. Claiming power over its audience while constantly discovering the limits of that power, opera ends up as an anomaly. For Meyerbeer this situation does not present a problem, because his operas display the interests of the audience, rather than hoping to exert an exotic power over them (at least after the supernatural chiller *Robert le diable*, which premiered in 1831). While their splendid settings and gratifyingly self-sacrificing heroines are clearly fantasies, they speak directly to bourgeois nationalism and humanism, representing orthodox patriotic and domestic virtues. Again, Wagner would later argue that this was precisely what was wrong with Meyerbeer: his operas were the parade-ground of decadent bourgeois values. In fact, though, *Les Huguenots* (1836) and *Le prophète* (1849) could be seen as models for a disenchanted opera. Their claim to historical and social seriousness, however distorted by the overblown tastes of European audiences, suggests the possibility of a sustainable relation between reality and the stage. Ciceri, the designer at the Paris Opéra from 1816 to 1848, was famously attentive to scrupulous historical detail. His illusionistic sets were designed to give the fullest possible impression that the stage area actually was seventeenth-century Naples, or pre-Columbian America, or wherever the libretto required. Instead of creating an otherworldly space, this type of theatre located itself specifically in the audience's world, however geographically or chronologically remote.

Admittedly, the dividing lines between romance and history are nothing like as starkly drawn as this contrast suggests. Though the worlds of *Tannhäuser* and *Lohengrin* are saturated by supernatural forces, they do still have explicit political and historical meaning for German audiences as well. Similarly, the exotic settings favoured by Halévy, Meyerbeer, Bellini and others rely for their effect on the flavour of mystery permeating such places, as well as their historical specificity. Still, in Wagnerian terms the difference is a telling one, because it is not just a question of what sort of subject-matter operas should have. It bears on the whole issue of what happens in the theatre, what the stage does. Each of the three 'romantic' operas ends with a sign of transcendence. Senta and the Dutchman are seen ascending into the sunrise, 'transfigured' ('verklärten') as the stage direction has it. At the close of the *Tannhäuser* score, the pilgrims are singing 'Halleluja' as they welcome the news of the hero's escape from damnation. Despite the tragic end of *Lohengrin*, the stage is blessed by the appearance of 'the white dove of the Grail' hovering over the waters. All of these events are, obviously enough, instances of salvation. What if salvation is merely a romance? What if it exists only under the proscenium arch, dispelled as soon as the curtain falls? Tannhäuser makes the whole fantastical grotto of Venus disappear with a simple appeal to a higher power; but what if the whole world of opera is itself a Venusberg, its transcendental aspirations evaporating on contact with reality?

Wagner's interest in national history in the later 1840s can be seen as an attempt to reconnect his disenchanted art with its environment. Though legendary, the subjects which began to interest him were stories of rebellion and conquest, situated in the distant Germanic past. There are already clear signs of this politicized turn in Act I of *Lohengrin*, although Henry the Fowler's appeal for German unification is rapidly marginalized by the romance plot. (Musically and dramatically, this shift occurs with the appearance of Elsa, whose mysterious dream interrupts the martial, authoritarian tenor of scene one.) Towards the end of 1846 – during the composition of *Lohengrin* – Wagner outlined an idea for an opera on Friedrich Barbarossa, the twelfth-century emperor said in popular legend to be sleeping under a mountain, ready to emerge again in support of the fatherland. The *Meistersinger* draft of 1845 also indicates an interest in more socialized subjects. For all its romanticized view of the Middle Ages, it tells a story of artists as members of a civic community, rather than (as in *Tannhäuser*) focusing on the psychology of the musician's inner life. However, the richest lode of historical material was the Teutonic myths. Wagner mined the sagas and Eddas throughout his time in Dresden, and at the end of 1848 completed the libretto of *Siegfrieds Tod* (*Siegfried's Death*), the forerunner of *Götterdämmerung*.

In this drama, as in *Lohengrin*, magic is a tool of deceit, used by the wicked. The supernatural elements are the magic potion which causes Siegfried's infatuation with Gudrune (as she is called at this stage), and the Tarnhelm, which makes possible the betrayal of Brünnhilde. Unlike in *Lohengrin*, these powers are not overcome by the intervention of a greater supernatural force. Instead of a contest between white and black magic, the early version of the Nibelung drama is a mythologized political battle, with Siegfried and Brünnhilde representing the so-called Young Hegelian ideals of human freedom. In striking contrast to the three earlier operas, the heroes of the planned mythohistorical dramas – Barbarossa, Siegfried, and (in a sketch of 1849) Wieland the Smith – are actively involved in struggles over resistance and power. This would be impossible in romance. Its enchanted terrain is controlled by irresistible, invisible forces; like the audience, the characters are subject to opera's spell. This accounts for the strange passivity one encounters in all of them. Arindal and Ada (in *Die Feen*) despair at the impossibility of escaping the malicious magical conditions imposed by the Fairy King, and the eventual victory is won only thanks to the entirely unsought aid of the wizard Groma, whose offstage voice gives Arindal the necessary instructions at every critical moment. The Dutchman is held completely captive by his curse. Senta is equally spellbound, and the choice she appears to make is really a submission to this compulsion. Tannhäuser always reacts to the immediacy of each 'passing incident' (III 198), as Wagner himself commented in *On the Performing of 'Tannhäuser'*. He is tossed on the surface of the plot, responding to a series of bewilderingly contradictory impulses, internal and external, as if he has no will of his own to assert. His escape from the Venusberg might look like an act of defiance, but in Act II he confesses that it was 'ein unbegreiflich hohes Wunder!', 'an inexplicable, high miracle', not something of his own doing. Despite his roles as Elsa's defendant and leader of the Brabantines, Lohengrin seems to be immobilized by the aura of *gravitas* surrounding him. He wins his victories without exerting himself, and suffers his expulsion without the power to intervene. In all four operas, the main characters are vehicles through which unearthly powers work.

By contrast, the mythic dramas place power within the reach of individuals. The heroes and heroines are not enchanted beings but more or less free agents, with at least some ability to intervene in the forces that govern the stage. Indeed, this redefinition of heroism is central to *Siegfrieds Tod*. The main difference between the version of 1848 and the familiar libretto of *Götterdämmerung* is in the cosmological meaning of what happens to Siegfried. In the simplest terms, *Siegfrieds Tod* allows the curse on the ring to be broken and the gods to return to power, whereas in the tetralogy the curse destroys the whole world. (There will be much more to say about this difference in Part II.) Hence the earlier version of the opening Norns' scene, though structurally similar, is completely different in mood. Hard as it is to imagine the scene without the aural memory of *Götterdämmerung*'s first chord, that musical cry of warning and despair, one has to read the beginning of *Siegfrieds Tod* as a confident prophecy of triumph. The role of Siegfried is explained clearly. He is the answer to the guilty gods' need, and the Norns pun rather heavy-handedly on his name to confirm his destiny: 'through conquest [*Sieg*] a hero brings peace [*Friede*]'. Their rope doesn't break. The history they weave will come to pass, necessarily: 'what we have spun binds the world'.

How is this different from the supernatural enchantments that bind the characters of the earlier operas? At first sight, the Norns' control over history looks like another example of the overwhelming power of operatic romance, subjecting the world to its spell. Yet they are not enchantresses. The binding certainty they announce is not a power they exert over the characters, but the force of historical necessity itself, of fate. Its intellectual roots are in the Hegelian vision of history as an inevitable, ascending unfolding of spirit, which Wagner encountered in the 1840s through his immersion in the radically progressive thought of the Young Hegelian thinkers, especially Ludwig Feuerbach (a philosopher much given to the concept of necessity). Siegfried and Brünnhilde are not slaves to an external compulsion but agents of world history. Even so, *Siegfrieds Tod* dramatically asserts their independence. In another scene interestingly different from the *Götterdämmerung* version, Siegfried's conversation with the Rhinedaughters in Act III climaxes in his refusal to recognize any destiny outside himself. As in the existing opera, the Rhinedaughters warn him of the curse attached to the ring, which they know is about to slay him. They tell him that the curse is inevitable, woven into fate by the Norns as 'Urgesetz', primeval law. This threat is in *Götterdämmerung*, but Siegfried's reply is not:

Wozu mein Muth mich mahnt,	What my courage urges me to,
das ist mir Urgesetz, –	is primeval law to me, –
und was mein Sinn mir ersieht,	and what my own mind sees
das ist mir so bestimmt.	is destiny to me.

He refuses passive obedience to fate, insisting that he is author of his own history; again, contrast Lohengrin, who knows he has to obey the rules ('Ich muß, ich muß', he sings in answer to Elsa's entreaties: 'I must, I must'). Siegfried goes on to claim that his own heroism transcends the Norns' wisdom:

. . . entbrennt der Kampf, dem die Nornen selbst	. . . a battle is beginning, whose outcome

das Ende nicht wissen zu künden:	the Norns themselves cannot tell:
nach meinem Muth	with my own courage
entschied' ich den Sieg!	I will decide the victory!

Though his defiance of the curse is ironically mistaken, his overall claim is not. According to Brünnhilde's final speech, Siegfried has indeed won a lasting triumph for the gods. Having finally escaped from Hagen's deceptions, she sees that the Norns' prophecy of victory has been achieved: 'Der Nornen Rath vernehm' ich nun auch,/ darf ihren Spruch jetzt deuten' ('now I understand the Norns' wisdom, now their sayings may be fulfilled').

As the Nibelung drama began to coalesce in Wagner's dramatic imagination, it was accompanied by a new conception of opera's nature. The aesthetics of romance are all about drawing the audience in: it is a gravitational force, seducing and abducting the enraptured listeners, pulling them across the border between their world and its own in the same way that Senta's ballad works on the spinning-girls. *Siegfrieds Tod* changes opera into prophecy. Rather than enchanting the public with remote visions and intimations, drama speaks out publicly to them, announcing their own destiny. It is an obvious enough point: the Nibelung drama, like the Barbarossa sketch and the plan for *Wieland der Schmied* (*Wieland the Smith*), is patently revolutionary in a Young Hegelian sense. That is, it stages the victory of a liberated humanity over old delusions and corrupted authorities. The same is true of other operas planned in early 1849, on the subjects of Jesus and Achilles. To a greater or lesser degree, all Wagner's work of this period is inflected by political aspiration, centred around vague ideals of utopian freedom. In mythic form, the planned dramas symbolically present these prophecies to the public. They are, however obliquely, addressed to the historical awareness of their audience. (Or so the theory goes: none of them was ever actually made ready for performance, not even *Siegfrieds Tod*, which is far from being the same opera as *Götterdämmerung*.)

In many ways, though, prophetic opera is no less fantastical than its romantic counterpart. There is not much to choose between visionary dreams of universal liberty and happiness and the frankly imaginary spectacle of Senta and the Dutchman flying up to heaven. The really significant difference is to do with a new conception of how opera articulates itself. As we have seen, the moving force of enchanted opera is music. This is because music does not speak. It appears to be speaking, but the effect of communication is just that: an effect, an illusion of voice where no actual speech occurs. Hence its mesmerizing appeal, so potently exploited by Wagner's gift for orchestration. Music draws us into a world full of intimation without expression, feelings without definition, sensations without objects. This powerful absence of definition dissolves the world, replacing the fixed and visible contours of

ordinary experience with a magically shifting landscape. Music is the spell
with which opera conjures up its romantic terrain.

By contrast, the utopian dream of disenchanted opera is to gain a speaking voice. In order to prophesy to the public, it must address them in a language whose meaning they can understand. Montsalvat's celestial strains can
no longer represent opera's highest visions. Such ideals, like the *Schwärmerei*
of romance, like music itself, are too remote from human affairs. Opera's
emphasis has to shift in the direction represented by the Norns, who weave
a magic that belongs in the arena of human history, or by Siegfried and
Brünnhilde, whose strength is knowledge and action rather than mystery and
suffering.

This shift leads quite straightforwardly to the theoretical position outlined
in *Opera and Drama* (1851), where drama gains ascendancy over music. The
theories of Wagner's lengthy, sprawling tract are, however, intimately connected with his developing work on the Nibelung tetralogy, and need to be
considered later, in close connection with the emergence of the *Ring*. A more
immediate problem presents itself: where does music belong in disenchanted
opera? The question seems all the more pressing because of the conspicuous
absence of music for the Barbarossa drama, *Jesus von Nazareth*, the Achilles
subject, *Wieland der Schmied* or *Siegfrieds Tod*. Some musical sketches exist for
this last libretto, made in the summer of 1850. Compared with the intensity
of Wagner's work on the dramatic substance of these projects, though, these
fragments look like the most abortive of gestures. Lengthy, detailed, partially
versified drafts exist for *Jesus* and *Wieland*, while the Barbarossa legend is
mingled with the Siegfried myth in the extraordinary quasi-anthropological
fantasy *Die Wibelungen: Weltgeschichte aus der Saga* (*The Wibelungen: World-History
as Told in Saga*, published in 1849). These plans show fully worked-out plots
and sometimes brilliantly compressed stories. The narrative material has been
shaped and refined, its political significance concentrated in the particular dramatic form Wagner has chosen. Where is the music?

The obvious (though banal) answer is that Wagner simply found it impossible to concentrate on the laborious business of composition during the pre-
revolutionary turbulence of 1848, the 1849 revolution itself, and his subsequent
migrations in exile. Again, though, something more fundamental is at stake.
The aesthetics of romance imply that music by its very nature is remote
from the mundane world of the public. It suspends reality, or evades it, or
transcends it. Prophetic or political opera requires an altogether different idea
of music, if it is not simply to become fantasy again. As part of a drama
that addresses the public directly, music must somehow be made to speak
intelligibly.

Wagner had found his model for this idea much earlier, in the finale of
Beethoven's ninth symphony (which figures so prominently in 'A Pilgrimage

to Beethoven'). At the beginning of this movement, after the furious opening fanfare, there is a passage of music which is essentially dialogue. Cellos and basses in unison, without accompaniment, play a long line whose inflections and phrasings are clearly modelled on speech. This is periodically interrupted by orchestral quotations of the three earlier movements, after each of which the bass strings make a 'comment'. Eventually, the basses begin the famous melody, which ascends through a number of repetitions into a full orchestral *tutti*; after this, the fanfare is repeated, and then the human voice appears: music speaks. 'This', Wagner writes in *Das Kunstwerk der Zukunft* (*The Art-Work of the Future*), 'was the word which Beethoven set as crown upon the forehead of his tone-creation'. Music is no longer an enchantingly mysterious vision but a clearly speaking voice. Wagner emphasizes the progressive, Young Hegelian significance of the moment: '*this Word* will be the language of the *Art-work of the Future*' (I 126).

Like the revolution itself, though, the music of the future is more easily imagined than achieved. Music's non-verbal character would seem to be an insuperable problem here. More than the other arts, it appears to be confined to the domain of the aesthetic, to perception and pleasure; this merely sensuous appreciation of sound was Wagner's main target in his journalistic railing against contemporary audiences. Writing from Paris at about the same time, Heine related an anecdote which neatly (and, typically, with a lighter touch than Wagner) illustrates the difficulty. Setting himself the question 'What is music?', he explains how arguments between supporters of Rossini and Meyerbeer end with the two sides 'trilling several particularly beautiful airs' at each other.[1] Unable to find any substantial content on which to base a comparison, they can only appeal to helplessly unspecific standards of beauty and subjective pleasure. Even in opera, where text and plot are superadded to aural pleasure, music threatens to exert what the Young Hegelian Wagner might see as a regressive influence. In fact, as the example of Auber's *La muette de Portici* (1828) shows, the intensifying effect of music could concentrate and emphasize a work's historical meaning for its audience. A performance in Brussels in 1830 ended in a riot, and the same night there was a popular uprising that led eventually to Belgian independence. Violent protests were not uncommon in Parisian theatres in the 1840s. Nevertheless, the disenchanted Wagner was at least partially right in thinking that attractive melodies and grand orchestral pomp drained opera of its capacity for meaning and contributed to making it mere empty theatre. Luxurious sonority smothers the articulate voice.

In this light, Wagner's drastic musical and structural innovations appear as an effort to bring the art of music closer to the state of language. By the time the first clear instances of 'music-drama' actually appear (Act I of *Die Walküre*, begun in June 1854, is the real point of no return), many other factors had intervened, and the promise of prophetic opera was no longer relevant. The goal of an articulate music was always provisional, and largely theoretical. Nevertheless, it exerts a strong influence on some of the technical advances of the 1840s, in particular the gradual dissolution of self-contained operatic 'numbers' in favour of more fluid musico-dramatic sequences. This most fundamental instance of Wagner's originality has been extensively discussed. For our purposes, its crucial significance lies in its subversion of melody. 'Number' opera, whether through-composed or punctuated by some form of recitative, proceeds in a series of individual musical structures, each of which stands as a self-contained unit. This is what Heine means when he writes of the partisans of Meyerbeer and Rossini warbling at each other. The musical quality of the individual 'number' (aria, duet, or whatever) is what makes it interesting and appealing; its melody is the most obvious vehicle of the appeal. Hearing opera thus becomes an experience made up of isolated musical pleasures, strung together along the line of the plot. As Wagnerian opera moves towards its mature form, these self-contained musical structures begin to disappear, leaving the listener unable to latch on to melody as an end in itself. Music instead follows the line of the drama. Rather than providing a beautiful form through which words are spoken, it helps to articulate the unfolding progress of the story.

In the first scene of Act II of *Lohengrin*, for example, the evocatively sinister sounds permeating the conversation between Ortrud and Telramund never form themselves into a shape which overrides the actual dialogue. It is impossible to imagine a Wagner enthusiast attempting to prove the composer's genius by humming the music, as Heine's anecdote has it. Only Telramund's first outburst, versified in rhyming quatrains, is recognizably an aria (specifically, a conventional 'rage aria'). Here the musical setting offers itself (however ineffectively) to the audience as a melodic representation of Telramund's anger, with appropriate accompaniment. In doing so, it arrests the action; the dialogue stops in order for the opera to display his rage, and then starts again after the crashing chords which signal the end of the display. Elsewhere in the scene, music refuses to obtrude its own formal demands. The malevolent restlessness of Ortrud's F sharp minor themes belongs *in* her character, and *in* this moment of the story, in a way that the rage aria does not. Her characteristic sonorities are a means to inflect and express her nature; by contrast, the rage aria is simply an instance of anger in music, which one can easily imagine being transferred to any other operatic scene where it might be required. Telramund's outburst shows off music's capacity to perform rage, but in the rest of the scene the score is bound in to the specific demands of the dramatic moment. By its very nature, an aria (or a similar 'number') draws attention towards itself, and therefore away from its surroundings. Yet the most striking things about Ortrud's music are its elusiveness and its pervasiveness.

It lurks and insinuates, like Ortrud herself; it infiltrates the scene without ever coming to the forefront.

Tannhäuser's Rome narration – another scene much cited as an instance of advanced techniques in the earlier operas – also rejects traditional aria structure in favour of dramatically sensitive music, in this case more obviously striving for quasi-linguistic status. Wagner's innovation here is to make the score eloquently descriptive. Again, there is a strong contrast with melodic form. An aria-like setting of this scene – melodic and strophic – would make the music convey the hero's feelings in an affecting way (one can see Wagner attempting this in the notoriously lame cavatina given to Erik in Act III of *Holländer*). The Rome narration instead denies us the satisfaction of expressive melody. It enacts the story itself, through vivid musical pictures: the limping, dragging themes in the bass at the beginning; the long, flowing quavers in the violins, suggesting the steady progress of a long journey; the 'Dresden Amen' for the holy city; the tremolo strings of Tannhäuser's anxiety as he approaches the throne, and the stark monotone of the Pope's curse; the disintegrating tonality as Tannhäuser finally collapses into desperate hysteria. Breaking with traditional operatic structures, Wagner turns to a musical language with the power to tell stories.

There is a less obviously radical but similarly effective instance of musical description earlier in *Tannhäuser*. The short third scene of Act I is in some ways quite conventional. Miraculously transported from the Venusberg to a pastoral valley below the Wartburg, Tannhäuser awakes to the sound of sheep-bells. The young shepherd plays and sings; then the pilgrims cross the stage, hymning as they go. What is interesting here, as Carolyn Abbate has observed, is that all the sounds of the scene supposedly emerge from the stage: the bells, the shepherd's pipe and voice, the pilgrims' voices.[2] For a few minutes, the score is entirely contained within the action. Wagner achieves very beautiful effects – the alternation and overlapping of the pilgrims' slow, steady, regular phrases with the dancing figures of the shepherd's pipe is a marvellous instance of his aural imagination – but without the use of 'music' in the conventional sense. We are still a very long way from the exquisite symbiosis of orchestra and speech-like vocal line in Act I of *Die Walküre*, yet the scene finds its own way of integrating music with the action, rather than presenting it as an independent source of pleasure for the audience.

In many nineteenth-century operas, music is used as a quasi-narrative device through the association of distinct themes with particular characters or ideas. The stronger the association, the more obvious the semiotic function of the theme: that is, it audibly refers to something, as if it were a word. While no one claims that Wagner invented this technique, it is certainly true that his operas are the first to grasp the possibility of using motifs as dramatic elements rather than melodic themes. The more conventional usage relies on establishing and then maintaining a connection between a theme and the person or idea it refers to, and the clearest way to make such a connection is via the melodic and harmonic character of the theme. The motif of the 'forbidden question' in *Lohengrin*, for example, works by sounding forbidding. It has a distinct, complete melodic shape, making its later appearances easy to hear and understand. The theme thus functions effectively as a 'word' which can be 'spoken' at appropriate moments. Wagner's development of this technique essentially involves making these words into a flexible language; joining them, developing them, giving them syntactic relations to one another. The resulting musical fabric looks almost like narrative. Instead of relying purely on the *sound* of the isolated motif to suggest its particular association, leitmotivic technique also exploits the *structure* of music. It can do more than utter one word at a time; it strives for something closer to articulate speech.

All this is a long way from the aesthetics of romanticism, according to which music is valued precisely because of its difference from ordinary language. Because it makes no reference to particular things, it can be imagined as the language of the intangible, the invisible, the supernatural: the language of spirit. This idea would go on being vitally important to Wagner, during and following his revolutionary years. After all, there is always a strong element of pure idealism (or, less charitably, fantasy) even in his most pragmatic attitudes; he is never truly disenchanted. His dissatisfaction with romanticized conceptions of his art in the later 1840s is nevertheless an important way of understanding the technical advances that gradually manifest themselves within the three romantic operas. We have looked at them in musical terms so far because music is the arena of romantic magic, and therefore the greatest obstacle to an opera which inhabits the world of its audience. For Wagner, though, the full development of these musical techniques – continuous melodic structure based on leitmotifs – remained in the future. Of more immediate importance was the larger theoretical goal of which they were a part. Rejecting entertainment and pleasure as standards for opera, Wagner imagines instead a far more dignified and serious genre, genuinely meaningful and truthful, communicating realities to the public rather than displaying fantasies. This is the fundamental alternative to romantic enchantment. (Again, we have to set aside for the moment the suspicion that it is itself really another fantasy – a political fantasy this time, a utopian delusion.) The Dresden Kapellmeister saw himself as a man with a social and historical responsibility to his public, co-director of an institution 'which claims, as no other, to be the expression of the higher intellectual activity of the whole nation' (VII 323). As a composer, he felt an equal obligation to the 'higher' spirit of the age. His work ought to participate in the Hegelian ascent of the German national spirit towards self-revelation. This is not just a matter of choosing the appropriate subjects. Whatever the chosen material, opera must be a coherent and forceful presentation of its essential significance.

One gets a glimpse of these ideals in two pamphlets Wagner wrote after being exiled from Germany, *Über die Aufführung des 'Tannhäuser'* ('On the Performing of "Tannhäuser"') and 'Bemerkungen zur Aufführung der Oper "Der fliegende Holländer"' ('Remarks on Performing "The Flying Dutchman"', both 1852). Both were responses to the outbreak of enthusiasm for Wagner's scores all over Germany's theatres after the premiere of *Lohengrin* (under Liszt's direction) in Weimar in 1850. They consist largely of precise instructions for various aspects of the production, including details of musical phrasing, tempo, dynamics, actors' gestures and expressions, and general interpretation of the characters. This precision is motivated throughout by a stress on the meaning of the operas. The first scene of *Holländer*, Wagner says, must be performed in exact accordance with the pamphlet so that 'it becomes possible for [the spectator] to conceive the mysterious figure of the "Flying Dutchman" himself [*die wunderbare Erscheinung . . . selbst zu begreifen*]' (III 209). The final scene must leave 'no more room for misunderstanding' (III 216). It is as if the pamphlets recognize that both operas might otherwise seem to be genre pieces, merely sentimental or rousing. Instead, Wagner insists that each element of the work – libretto, stage directions and score – is part of a unified whole. Hence his extraordinary insistence on perfectly synchronizing gesture and movement with music: 'with the first crotchet of the third bar he makes his second step, – always with folded arms and sunken head; his third and fourth steps coincide with the notes of the eighth and tenth bars . . .' (III 210). Nothing is to be seen as accidental. There is no music which is just sound, no stage direction which is just ornament. Even the scene-painter needs 'a close and genuinely artistic acquaintance with my inmost aims' (III 197). Wagner demands exhaustive study of the printed score by conductor and producer, read-throughs for the singers – in effect, all the procedures of today's directors. This enables the performers to discover the correct method of communicating the works' meanings; otherwise they might work on the perfectly normal assumption that opera doesn't really have meanings, and therefore that their job is to play or sing the notes. With a certain amount of desperation, the pamphlets try to convince theatre managers that these particular works cannot succeed unless the audience achieves an instinctive intellectual and emotional grasp of the whole drama. The things that might in other circumstances make an opera popular – appealing music, a strong story, and such – never enter into consideration, unless they are seen as positive dangers. So Wagner warns against tenors trying to produce a brilliant *éclat*:

> Whoever, then, relying on his previous successes in the said operas [i.e. Meyerbeer's], should attempt to play Tannhäuser with merely the same

expenditure on the art of portrayal as has sufficed to make those operas both widely given and universally popular, would turn this rôle into the very opposite of what it is. (III 203)

He is appealing for a properly sensitive understanding of his characters and his drama. More significantly, he is making his demands for the sake of a completely clear presentation of the work to the audience. The pamphlets try to reclaim *Tannhäuser* and *Holländer* from the genre of romantic opera and cast them instead as intensely serious articulations of significant ideas.

In May 1848, Wagner submitted to the Dresden court authorities his 'Entwurf zur Organisation eines deutschen Nationaltheaters für das Königreich Sachsen' ('Plan of Organization of a German National Theatre for the Kingdom of Saxony'). His suggestion for the chorus singers' pension arrangements do not make for the most riveting reading, but it's an intermittently intriguing document. It is predicated again on the idea that the theatre and its public are intimately connected: the state of art and the nation state 'go hand in hand, and act reciprocally upon each other' (VII 355). Even under the direct patronage of the court, Wagner argues, the theatre belongs to the nation as a whole. By supporting it, the king enacts his role as the incarnation of the people's 'higher intellectual [*geistigen*] need' (VII 323). This spiritualized sense of national culture takes the terrain of romance, with its yearnings for transcendence, and transplants it into history and politics; idealism has become revolutionary rather than visionary. Theatre is no longer the 'fascinating demoniacal realm' remembered in *My Life*. What happens on stage is an articulation of 'the nation's faculty [*Fähigkeit*] and will' (VII 333). Opera now speaks to its audience at the institutional level, as well as in its subject-matter and its musical style. The 'Plan' is thus in every sense Wagner's most disenchanted piece of theoretical writing. It arises out of his practical sense of the inadequate conditions in which he has been working, and takes that personal sense of opera's failings as the impulse for a grand project to confirm his art's place in the world. Unusually, it describes the project in thoroughly mundane terms, pensions and all, in full knowledge of the economic and social circumstances which provide the conditions of performance. The numbers might not add up, but the effort at least is a piece of theatrical pragmatism worthy of the despised Meyerbeer and his notorious negotiations with officialdom. At this brief historical moment, on the threshold of revolution, Wagner imagines theatre as a medium for reflecting and enacting the condition of its public, without any of the contempt which such compromises would usually inspire in him.

Evidence suggests that Wagner took his 'Plan' with him on his trip to Vienna in the summer of 1848. During that visit he seems to have been in contact with a number of figures active in the revolutionary movement, which had spread rapidly into Austria in the wake of the expulsion of Louis Philippe from Paris that February. He produced two more inflammatory articles on theatre reform early in 1849; not long before, the court authorities had refused to mount a production of the recently completed *Lohengrin*. In May 1849, Dresden was in revolt, led by the intellectual professional classes which included Wagner and many of his closest associates. The politics of disenchantment had decisively overtaken aesthetic concerns. In Wagner's eyes, though, the relation between them was clear. Rejecting the procedures of romantic opera, he was to create a radically new form of musical theatre. The fruits of disenchantment are revolution, in aesthetics as well as in history. If the utopian vision of fully articulate, meaningful, prophetic opera was always to be chimerical, Wagner's doubts about the failure of operatic magic would nevertheless result in an astonishingly relentless expansion of the borders of his art.

PART II

Revolution

CHAPTER FIVE

Writing the Future

At the beginning of the *Ring*, everything begins again. The world builds itself out of nothing. Hearing the prelude to *Das Rheingold* is like watching speeded-up film of a seed sprouting and flowering: first there is bare earth, then a tiny shoot appears and grows and branches and unfurls into full life. The first sound of the *Ring* is as close to silence as sound can be, as if introducing the unadorned vibration of air. With the entry of the bassoons, the sound warms, deepens, fills out, gradually finding its voice, becoming music, but only by amplifying and extending itself, without seeming actually to change. Then the first horn uncoils the sound into an arpeggio, giving it the simplest shape and breadth. The arpeggio begins to echo itself with the overlapping horns, filling more space, though still nebulous, almost formless, more like the raw material of music than the finished art. With the entry of the strings, the material discovers articulation, form, rhythm. Sound achieves movement and flow, the arpeggio flexes itself into scales and discovers higher and lower registers, rippling up and down this new-created musical space. Then the clarinets and oboes take up the scale again, but now accelerated, purposeful, a shape and movement with melodic definition. The melody is propelled faster and higher until the contours of the scale gain dizzying rapidity and breadth, a welter of ascents and descents traversing strings and wind and brass; but this teeming ocean of sound still feels as if it has germinated itself from inside the first bare note. More magically, it feels as if it has grown out of absolute silence itself, as if the *Ring* has made itself a musical version of matter's creation from the void.

On 8 April 1849, just weeks before the outbreak of armed revolt in Dresden, a radical Saxon journal published a prose rhapsody celebrating the imminent arrival of the 'lofty goddess **Revolution**' coming 'rustling on the wings of storm' (VIII 232). To the cheers of the oppressed masses and the distress of aristocrats and financiers, she delivers a fiery statement of intent, announcing 'I bring to nothing [*vernichte*] what exists, and whither I turn there wells fresh life from the dead rock' (VIII 235). Whether or not the anonymous outburst was written by Wagner, this goddess is the muse inspiring the conception in late 1848 of what would decades later become *Der Ring des Nibelungen*. Revolution is a new beginning, or so she imagines (anything less is just reform). On 1 June, a Dresden friend recorded a political argument with Wagner in his diary: 'He wants to destroy in order to rebuild' (*WR* 59). Well after the disappointingly undestructive Dresden revolution, around the time he made an abortive start on the music of *Siegfrieds Tod*, Wagner was still imagining a European apocalypse in a private letter:

> . . . how shall it seem to us if the monster that is Paris is burned to the ground, if the conflagration spreads from town to town, and if we ourselves, in our wild enthusiasm, finally set fire to these uncleansable Augean stables for the sake of a breath of fresh air? . . . I assure you that I no longer believe in any other revolution save that which begins with the burning down of Paris. . . .
>
> . . . Look, just as we need a water-cure to heal our bodies, so we need a fire-cure to remedy (i.e. destroy) the cause of our illness – a cause that is all around us. (*L* 219)

The *Ring* is the child of these fantasies. In all sorts of more familiar ways it is a 'revolutionary' work; any history of opera or of Western music is likely to comment that Wagner's mature style, which is first marked by the leap from the romantic opera *Lohengrin* to the so-called 'music-drama' of the tetralogy, 'revolutionized' the stage and the musical resources and techniques used to tell stories there. Its ambitions are astonishing, unprecedented. Its narrative scope is vast, its themes encompass the political and moral order of the world, and given that its technical demands put off many opera houses even today, it is hard to imagine just how insanely Olympian they must have seemed to the steam-age world of mid-nineteenth-century theatre. But, as the *Rheingold* prelude quietly hints, the *Ring* is 'revolutionary' in a more literal sense too. It was born in dreams of a world wiped as clean as a blank slate, ready to receive the imprint of what Wagner's 1849 essay called 'The Art-Work of the Future'; one that the goddess Revolution had turned to 'nothing', to 'dead rock', so that 'fresh life' could well from it as the watery scales of the prelude spring up from utter silence and give birth to Wagner's monumental new drama.

A few weeks after the letter quoted above, Wagner wrote to Liszt that 'between the musical composition of my Lohengrin and that of my Siegfried there lies a world of tumult' (*L* 220). He was referring to his development as an artist, but the statement reflects his personal history as well. The score of *Lohengrin* was completed in April 1848, that of *Rheingold* begun in November 1853. In that span of months Wagner went from being a respectable salaried professional best known as the composer of the utterly conventional and wildly successful *Rienzi* to an exiled revolutionary busily publishing utopian treatises proclaiming work on unperformable operas. During the same period, the project he calls 'my Siegfried' grew from *Der Nibelungen-Mythus. Als Entwurf zu einem Drama* (*The Nibelung Myth as Sketch for a Drama*), a short and concentrated prose redaction of the legend, to four complete libretti. Revolution and the *Ring* go hand in hand, parallel versions of the same dream: to create something utterly new out of the annihilation of everything that came before.

Dreams of this sort are the hallmark of the real fanatic. Did Wagner seriously imagine Paris going up in flames, taking the whole political and civil structure of Europe with it? The prophecy of the goddess Revolution in the 1849 essay is a product of the same imagination, leaping beyond the bounds of political possibility into purely visionary rapture:

> Down to its memory will I destroy each trace of this mad state of things, compact of [*die zusammengefügt ist aus*] violence, lies, care, hypocrisy, want, sorrow, suffering, tears, trickery and crime, with seldom a breath of even impure air to quicken it, and all but never a ray of pure joy. Destroyed be all that weighs on you and makes you suffer, and from the ruins of this ancient world let rise a *new*, instinct [*voll*] with happiness undreamt! (VIII 237–8)

Europe was thick with revolutionary thought and action. *The Communist Manifesto* had appeared the previous year, and there had been popular uprisings in Paris, Vienna and Berlin. Marx and Engels were materialist radicals, though, seeing revolution as the consequence of economic and historical necessity. For Wagner, starting again means making a clean break with the existing 'state of things'. An all-or-nothing thinker as always, his revolutionary writing pitches itself around the idea of an absolute, apocalyptic ending followed by an entirely new beginning, a chasm in history on the far side of which is something completely unlike the world that was destroyed to make way for it. The revolution cannot be a product of history, in his extremist imagination; it can only be the end of history and the beginning of something else. To his wife Minna he wrote in April 1850:

> You think of the past only with longing and regret, – I abandon it and think only of the future. All your desires are directed at a reconciliation with what is old, at compromise and conformism, and at re-establishing old ties, – I have broken with all that is old, and fight against it with every ounce of my strength. (*L* 196)

This is true enough, at a mundane level. Between 1848 and 1853 he effectively expelled himself from his prior life (to which Minna was understandably attached). By actively involving himself in the Dresden uprising he ensured the end of his social existence as well as his professional career in Germany, and his plan for the Nibelung drama guaranteed equally effectively that he would no longer be a composer of repertory operas. His break with the past happens at a more fundamental level too. He ceases to recognize the legitimacy of any of the social and cultural institutions of his own world: he decides that as an artist he is no longer beholden to the 'state of things' in which everyone else lives (thus allowing him to live off other people's money, and perhaps other people's wives as well, as the Jessie Laussot and Mathilde Wesendonck affairs of the 1850s suggest). He commits himself entirely to a visionary future. By definition, this means living in a world that does not (yet) exist, which is not so much a sign of fanaticism as of delusional insanity – no doubt that is how it must have looked to Minna, for whom the epithet 'long-suffering' might have been invented. There is certainly something almost comically visionary about his revolutionary ambitions of the late 1840s. In his autobiography, the critic Hanslick remembered meeting him in Vienna in July 1848: 'Wagner was all politics: with the victory of the Revolution, he was convinced, would come a total rebirth of art, society and religion and a new type of theatre and music' (*WR* 61). What is harder to remember today is that his ambitions for the *Ring* in those years must have struck contemporaries as equally demented. From the vantage-point of 1852, when the poem of the tetralogy was finished (in its first version), can his utopian political fantasies have seemed all that much more absurd than his plan for a four-part opera with no conventional structure, beginning under water and ending in celestial conflagration? Only the fact that the *Ring* actually came into being, albeit not until 1876, persuades us that what we are dealing with here is not insanity, but a visionary imagination so stupendously stubborn and energetic that – thanks ultimately to the intervention of an authentically deluded visionary, Ludwig II of Bavaria – it dragged its fantasies at least partially into life.

At the period we are dealing with now, though, the events that culminated in the first Bayreuth festival of 1876 were unthinkably distant. His turn to the future, both political and artistic, was purely utopian, a rejection of everything that existed in favour of entirely imaginary ideals. Needless to say, this presents certain problems. At the moment of revolution – the word means 'turning around'– the visionary finds himself suspended in limbo. He has (unilaterally) declared the end of the old order of things; his eyes are now fixed on a future that has not yet arrived. It is the same predicament summarized by Matthew Arnold's famous lines from 'Stanzas from the Grande Chartreuse' (1855): 'Wandering between two worlds, one dead,/ The other powerless to be born'. Or, as Wagner more clumsily puts it in *Die Kunst und die Revolution* (*Art and Revolution*, 1849):

The perfect Art-work, the great united utterance of a free and lovely public life . . . is not yet born again: for reason that it cannot be *re-born*, but must be *born anew*.

Only the great *Revolution of Mankind* . . . can win for us this Art-work. . . .

. . . But whence shall we derive this force, in our present state of utmost weakness? (I 53–4)

In the period of the conception and development of the *Ring*, Wagner situates himself between an end and a beginning. The years 1848–52 are an interval in his musical career. The fantastic, romantic period culminating in *Lohengrin* and Elsa's unanswerable questions is over, while the Wagner of *Die Walküre* and *Tristan*, the Wagner who remade opera, is waiting to be born. Instead of music, the years are filled with frenetic writing, increasingly turbulent and voluminous: the relatively modest *Art and Revolution* in the summer of 1849, the hundred and fifty pages of *Das Kunstwerk der Zukunft* (*The Art-Work of the Future*) written at tremendous speed that winter, the book-length *Opera and Drama* completed in January 1851, and a host of others including 'Das Judenthum in der Musik' ('Judaism in Music'), as well as the *Ring* libretti. All this work is obsessed with endings and beginnings, staring into a future that has not yet arrived, proposing in theory things that are still unimaginable in practice. Only with the first bare, dull E flat of *Das Rheingold* – music which he later claimed came to him in a waking dream – will what Wagner imagines as the 'perfect Art-work' begin to gather itself into existence. Until then, his predicament is exactly that of Wotan in the long, bitter monologue in Act II of *Die Walküre*: unable to complete the plan he has conceived, powerless to make the future he imagines.

Within the theoretical writings of these musically silent years, therefore, there exists a crucial visionary strain. Forests of paper have been expended on the question of how (or indeed whether) the increasingly detailed descriptions of 'the true Art-work', 'the Drama of the Future' (I 155) in *The Art-Work of the Future* and *Opera and Drama* correspond to the actual nature of Wagner's mature operas. In *Opera and Drama*, for example, poetry is given decisive priority over music as the agent of dramatic inspiration and execution, so does this mean that *Die Walküre* should be understood primarily as a poetic achievement? Asking questions of this sort involves emphasizing the theoretical aspect of the long prose works, on the assumption that they are instruction manuals for producing the 'Art-work of the future', outlining in theory what will later be put into artistic practice. And it is certainly true that many of the ideas proposed in them are clearly related to the later execution of the operas, in particular the *Ring* tetralogy. The subordination of purely melodic impulses to a dramatic aim, the principle of *leitmotiv*, the use of alliterative verse, the focus on heroic death, all these characteristically Wagnerian elements are proposed in the writings of 1848–52.

Equally, though, the prose works conjure up entirely imaginary prospects, rather than simply offering a step-by-step theoretical guide to achieving the coming 'Art-work'. The difference is between an attainable future (outlined by theory) and an unattainable one (prophesied in vision). Wagner's imagination fastens vitally on the latter option, for it allows the drama of the future to preserve its utopian quality, entirely untainted by any relationship with 'the filthy dregs of your Culture of to-day' (I 207–8). It seems perverse to idealize an unreachable future state – just as it seems perverse to work on a four-part music-drama which could not possibly be performed in any existing theatre – but this is nevertheless the essence of Wagnerian revolt. Revolution does not signify progress, gradual change in the right direction. It means absolute difference, a future *then* which has nothing at all to do with the present *now*, an apocalyptic break between reality and vision. Outlining the art-work of the future, then, is never simply a matter of issuing pragmatic instructions on how to get there; we shouldn't expect the theoretical works to correspond to Wagner's later practice, or indeed read them in the light of the operas at all. They stand more importantly as testimony to Wagner's strange compulsion to imagine the unimaginable, to locate his art outside the realm of reality in the domain of utopia. Towards the end of *The Art-Work of the Future*, he argues that the only way to think about the future is as the opposite of the present, the exact 'antithesis'. Nothing can be said about it except that it will be the not-now, the not-this. When we think about present reality, he writes, we can analyse it in detail, explain its nature and its historical conditions, and so describe every feature of the art of today with absolute accuracy. But

> the case is exactly opposite, when we desire to portray a future state of things; we have only one scale for such a picture, and that lies . . . in the Past and in the Present; even there where the conditions are still in [existence] which make the longed-for future state impossible to-day, and allow its sheer antithesis to seem an unavoidable necessity. . . . [W]e can only grasp it . . . by a logical induction which tells us that this state will be the very opposite of the evil which we recognise in our system of to-day. All individual features [i.e. all precise details about the visionary future] . . . could only figure as arbitrary assumptions of our phantasy [*Phantasie*], and must constantly [betray] their nature as borrowed from the bad conditions of the present day. (I 205–6)

Wagner is tying himself in knots here (assisted by Ellis's translation), but it's worth tracing the thread of the argument and laying it out in full view, because its paradoxical quality is so fundamental to the revolutionary theme underpinning the story of the *Ring*. The point he is trying to make is that there can be no clear description of the 'individual features' of the drama of the future: he can't say what it is, what it will be. This is because the only language that can be used to describe it is the language of 'to-day', the language of 'evil' reality, whereas the prophesied art-work will belong in an altogether different sphere of human existence, 'the very opposite' of the conditions obtaining in the present. Ultimately, then, there can be no theoretical blueprint of 'the one great, genuine work of Art' (I 46). The passage goes on to conclude that the 'shaping of the Future must be the work of Life itself alone': in other words, the future somehow has to bring itself into existence. 'When this is brought to pass, we shall conceive at the first glance what to-day we could only palm off upon ourselves by the exercise of whim and fancy [*Laune und Willkür*]' (I 206). We'll know it when we see it. Until then, it is only and entirely a vision, awaiting the 'great *Revolution of mankind*'.

To an important degree, then, the whole impassioned, prolix corpus of Wagner's writing in these years is in the same position as the rhapsodical essay 'The Revolution' of 8 April 1849. All of it is a deliriously excited celebration of something that is about to happen – but hasn't yet happened. *Opera and Drama* is by far the most precise and detailed (that is, the most theoretical) prescription for the art-work of the future dating from this period, but it too knows that it is waiting for the apocalypse, rather than (as Marx and Engels had) providing instructions for how to bring the future about. In its last pages, the arrival of the goddess Revolution is still, as it always will be, just out of sight over the horizon: '[w]ho has not felt the leaden murk that hangs above us in the air, foretelling the near advent of an earth-upheaval?' (II 374). In the final scene of *Das Rheingold*, the thunder-god Donner dismisses this 'Schwüles Gedünst' ('sultry mist') with a whirl of his hammer, revealing the rainbow bridge, a path across a chasm into the future. The thunderclap of his hammer-blow is here exactly analogous to Wagnerian revolution: at one stroke it dispels the existing gloom and (as Loge ironically comments) enables the gods to forget the past and stride confidently ahead into the new-reared utopia of Valhalla. This option isn't available in the prose works (and, as it turns out, it isn't available in the *Ring* either: the chasm the gods bridge turns out to have voices in it which issue plangent reminders of the past the gods think they have left behind – an issue to be dealt with later). The best *Opera and Drama* can do is to suggest that artists see over the horizon, anticipating the arrival of revolution thanks to the urgency of their prophetic longing for that future state:

The artist has the power of seeing beforehand a yet unshapen world, of tasting beforehand the joys of a world as yet unborn, through the stress [*Kraft*] of his desire for Growth. (II 375)

His gift is to see what isn't there; but, strikingly, nothing is said about his power actually to shape that world. 'So neither', Wagner goes on, 'can the artist prescribe from his own Will, nor summon into being, that Life of the Future which . . . shall redeem him' (II 376). His imagination seems by definition to have outstripped itself. So far from theorizing his future practice, Wagner's prose works of the revolutionary period often insist that they are in fact a sign of what the artist *cannot* do. The 'Art-work of the future' is literally that: an art-work always *in* the future, always out of sight of the present, an object of desire rather than attainment. The really significant link between *Opera and Drama* and the *Ring* lies in this paradox, not in details such as the use of *Stabreim* or *leitmotiv*, for the problem of wishing for an unachievable future is precisely that confronting Wotan at the decisive moment in the plot of the tetralogy:

Wie schüf' ich den Freien,	How can I create the free man,
den nie ich schirmte,	whom I never sheltered,
der im eig'nen Trotze	who, in his own defiance,
der trauteste mir?	is most faithful to me?
Wie macht' ich den And'ren,	How can I make the other man,
der nicht mehr ich,	the one no longer myself,
und aus sich wirkte	yet who of his own accord does
was ich nur will? . . .	what I alone wish? . . .
Das And're, das ich ersehne,	That other whom I long for,
das And're erseh' ich nie;	that other I never find;
denn selbst muß der Freie sich	for the free man has to create
schaffen. . . .	himself. . . .

'The free man has to create himself': the problem of revolution in a nutshell. A free humanity is the goal of *Art and Revolution* and *The Art-Work of the Future* also: 'The *free Artistic Fellowship* is . . . the foundation, and the first condition, of the Art-work itself' (I 201), and that work in turn will be 'the living utterance of a free, self-conscious community' (I 41). All political revolutions have been undertaken in the name of liberty. As Wotan asks, though, who makes the revolution? How can it come about 'freely', of its own accord? To create that which one imagines is to destroy its freedom, because it is then no longer self-generating, yet Wagner wants his revolution to happen by itself, according to what he repeatedly calls (using Feuerbach's language) 'necessity', rather than via the agency of individuals. We can perhaps begin to grasp now why in the aftermath of the failed uprising in Dresden he began to dedicate himself to artistic works that seemed doomed to be for ever imaginary. The art-work of the future must always be a vision: and what could be more hopelessly visionary than the *Ring*? At the end of 'Eine Mittheilung an meine Freunde' ('A Communication to My Friends'), written in late 1851, he announces the tetralogy and adds: 'with *this* undertaking I have nothing more to do with our Theatre of *to-day*' (I 391). At the same time he wrote to a friend in Dresden:

> A *performance* is something I can conceive of only *after the Revolution*; only the Revolution can offer me the artists and listeners I need. The coming Revolution must necessarily put an end to this whole *theatrical business* of ours: they must all perish, and will certainly do so, it is inevitable. Out of the ruins I shall then summon together what I need: I shall *then* find what I require. I shall then run up a theatre on the Rhine and send out invitations to a great dramatic festival: after a year's preparations I shall then perform my entire work within the space of *four days*: *with it* I shall then make clear to the men of the Revolution the *meaning* of that Revolution, in its noblest sense. *This audience* will understand me: present-day audiences cannot. (L 234)

Everything is contingent on the final arrival of the red goddess and her train of destruction. She will make the *Ring* performable, she will create an audience and a theatre for it, she will make it meaningful; in fact it will turn out to be about her, a kind of retrospective prophecy of the revolution. Until the apocalypse has passed, though, the *Ring* (like the revolution itself) is stuck in a visionary future, powerless to be born. It cannot bring about the new world it describes. It can only reveal its meaning after the fact.

Wagner's efforts to write the future are thus haunted by a curiously inescapable helplessness. However much the prose writings of these years may look like statements of intent – and at first sight they look like nothing else – they are, essentially, something like the opposite: admissions of incapacity, always deferring the future they anticipate so eagerly. Wagner defines himself as a revolutionary by imagining the impossible. He claims in *Opera and Drama* that the artist is possessed by an 'intoxicating joy which drives him on, with all the courage of the drunkard, to undertake the making possible the Impossible' (II 356). Anything lying within the bounds of possibility is beneath his notice, which is why authentic revolutionaries like Bakunin and Marx diagnosed Wagner as a mere fantasist, a bourgeois idealist rather than a true radical. In this situation, the only possibility available to the artist in his own experience – the only thing he can actually *do* – is to put as much distance between himself and reality as possible (as drunkards do). Before the events of May 1849, revolution can be imagined in marginally more pragmatic terms. In both the theatrical and the political arenas – always effectively interchangeable in his thinking of this period – Wagner seems to have striven for effective historical change, a tendency discussed in chapter 4 and manifested simultaneously in his efforts to reform the institutions of the German stage and in his close involvement in the Dresden uprising itself. The failure of revolutionary action in Dresden (and, ultimately, all over Europe) put an end to this striving, far more decisively than Wagner's later discovery of Schopenhauer's philosophy of resignation. The link binding his ideas to the world around him was ruptured on 9 May 1849, and as a result, imagination or vision becomes the compensation for what has been lost. Revolution shifts out of the sphere of politics and into the region of the impossible, leaving the artist with only one course of action: a continuous denial of his actual surroundings. 'Destruction alone is what is now needed', he writes in a letter of late December 1849. The creative act is itself purely revolutionary in this sense: 'even the work that I am writing . . . can only be a single moment in the revolution, a token of affirmation in the process of destruction' (*L* 184). That June he had told Liszt of his 'enormous desire to commit acts of artistic terrorism' (*L* 171). The appropriate act for the new revolutionary artist is to unbuild the world in the name of the visionary imagination, to reduce everything to silence so that the art-work of the future can evolve from its first single sustained note.

It's not always apparent from Wagner's writings that this is how revolution must essentially work. Specific requirements and instructions pour out of the volumes published in the years between the end of *Lohengrin* and the beginning of *Das Rheingold*. Indeed, Wagner shows himself sensitive to the link between art and society or history, always arguing that the drama of the future will be an exact and essential manifestation of the society of the future, just as the commercial, bourgeois-aristocratic drama of the present 'materializes the ruling spirit of our social life' (I 43). For the purposes of this argument, it isn't necessary to summarize his ideas about the nature of utopian art/society. What I want to stress is how his turn to the future works, what it rests on, rather than the precise details of what that future looks like. From this perspective, it is striking that throughout his revolutionary writings the immediate goal is always an act of dismantling. Utopia remains as visionary as Montsalvat. The task for the present, then, is simply continuous negation – a procedure enacted in the grammar of the essay 'The Revolution', whose closing paragraphs ring with the iteration of the phrase 'I will destroy . . .' (VIII 237).

Art and Revolution, the first of the documents describing the future conditions of theatre, is in many ways the most pragmatic. Dashed off a couple of months after the Dresden catastrophe, it perhaps retains lingering traces of the fervour for real revolutionary action that preceded May 1849. It sets itself the eminently clear-sighted goal of explaining 'the meaning of Art as a factor in the life of the State' (I 31), and as a consequence devotes itself to mostly straightforward analysis of the effects of existing social and economic factors on the theatre's role in public life. Its ambitions boil down to one simple (and, for a writer who had spent years as a professional man of the theatre, astonishingly naïve) proposal, the entire separation of art from commerce. Under some unspecified system of patronage, all theatrical activity would be 'free' – that is, unwaged, costing nothing to either performers or audience, and as a result the stage would become 'the standard of all future communal institutions' (I 64). This is communism without a trace of economic or political sophistication. If we think forward a few decades to the period in Wagner's life when he was in essence offered a 'free' theatre, thanks to the seemingly inexhaustible financial resources of King Ludwig, it becomes obvious that *Art and Revolution* conveniently glosses over what the Wagner of the 1860s would discover: someone eventually has to foot the bill. In the end, the 1849 essay knows that this is the case, which is why it has to confess at last that its recipe for a theatrical practice 'from which the idea of wage or gain shall disappear entirely' is conceivable only in tandem with 'the great and inevitably approaching social revolution' (I 64). In other words, the pragmatic, theoretical proposals are conditional on the coming moment of destruction. For most of its length the essay suppresses this admission, concentrating (broadly speaking) on social and historical fact. Only on this final page does it veer into the realm of the visionary, peering over the horizon towards the invisible, fictional revolution which it desperately tries to describe as inevitable.

The Art-Work of the Future, written later the same year, lays more explicit stress on acts of dismantling. Its utopian aspirations towards the 'universal fellowship of all mankind' (I 166) are the same as in the earlier essay, as is its analysis of the corruption of all the arts under contemporary conditions. In recognizing the exact correspondence of modern art to modern society, though, it admits more openly that the 'Drama of the Future' can 'rise up *of itself*' (my emphasis) only when

> the ruling religion of Egoism, which has split the entire domain of Art into crippled, self-seeking art-tendencies and art-varieties, shall have been mercilessly dislodged and torn up root and branch from every moment of the life of man. . . . (I 155)

From architecture to landscape painting to pantomime, each of the arts has to decompose itself, annihilating its independent ambitions to prepare for incorporation into the united drama (what will later be labelled the *Gesamtkunstwerk*, the total work of art). Sculpture, for example – this is typical of the perverse ingenuity of Wagner's argument here – will have to abandon its efforts to reproduce a lost ideal of the human form. It 'desires to be released' (like the Dutchman, the form of this release is of course death) by hoping for 'the disenchantment of the stone into the flesh and blood of man', in other words by ceasing to be sculpture at all and becoming instead the art of living bodies moving on stage (I 172–3). Dramatic poetry, too, longs for 'her own self-abrogation [*Selbstvernichtung*], her dissolution into Life, into the living Art-work of the future' (I 149). The immediate future is conceived as a series of disintegrations, out of which something united and communal will emerge, 'the redemption of the egoistically severed humanistic [*reinmensch-lichen*] arts into the collective Art-work' (I 162). Like all instances of 'redemption' in Wagner's work (except the restoration of the Grail commu-nity at the end of *Parsifal*), this one is predicated on death, in this case the death of all the arts and of the capitalistic, self-interested social structure which supports them and which they reflect. This is why *The Art-Work of the Future* says that the only possible plot of the utopian drama is the story of a hero's death, the final 'renunciation [*Entäusserung*] of his personal egoism, the demonstration of his full ascent into universalism'. 'The celebration of such a Death is the noblest thing that men can enter on' (I 199), Wagner creepily adds, and the story of Siegfried is clearly in his mind here. In the libretto of *Siegfrieds Tod*, unlike that of *Götterdämmerung*, there is a full onstage rite of mourning and praise solemnizing the hero and heroine's ascent to Valhalla. The perfected drama of the future, it appears, will stage a ritual death so that its audience can celebrate their own passage to utopia. The key point here is the essay's focus on the moment of destruction. If a revolution is necessary to bring about the future, as *Art and Revolution* openly says, then the nature of that revolution is 'self-abrogation', 'dissolution', *Entäusserung*, death.

In September 1850 Wagner published the most brutal of his 'acts of artistic terrorism', 'Judaism in Music'. The essay might look as if it stands separate from theoretical-visionary efforts like *The Art-Work of the Future* and *Opera and Drama*, since it has little to say about the future. It is essentially an attack on Meyerbeer, with a few side-swipes at Mendelssohn. According to the habitual logic of nineteenth-century anti-Semitism, though, it equates Judaism with bourgeois mercantilism and capitalism. What *Art and Revolution* calls 'Commerce' (I 41) is in this essay named 'the Jewish nature' (III 79). Each stands for what Wagner sees as the degraded condition of unrevolutionized society. 'Judaism is the evil conscience of our modern Civilization' (III 100), he pronounces. What the Jew Meyerbeer is to art, Judaism is to the state as a whole: the opposite of utopia, the mark of everything revolution has to sweep away. The reason 'Judaism in Music' belongs with the theoretical essays and volumes is that its racist language frees Wagner's imagination to focus exclusively on acts of destruction: in this case, of course, the elimination of the Jews, horrifically anticipated in the final sentence of the essay:

> . . . only one thing can redeem you from the burden of your curse: the redemption of Ahasuerus – *Going under!* [*der Untergang*]. (III 100)

Ellis's literal translation is dangerously coy: *Untergang* could mean 'annihila-tion' (which, unlike any of the more charitable translations such as 'assimilation', is the actual 'redemption of Ahasuerus', the Wandering Jew of legend whose curse, like the Flying Dutchman's, ends only in death). The Jews are here being collectively made into protagonists of a Wagnerian drama. Redemption from a curse by death is what happens to the whole world in the *Ring*, to the hero and heroine of *Der fliegende Holländer* and to Kundry in *Parsifal* (she, like the Dutchman, is also openly compared to Ahasuerus), and to the lovers in *Tristan und Isolde* as well if one understands Brangäne's potion as a curse. But in the anti-Semitic fury of the 1850 article, the redemption part of the equation is barely significant. It's clear that the focus of Wagner's desire is on the death, the annihilation. (One may well ask – and we will keep asking this question – whether this isn't true of those other instances of 'redemption' as well: however much we are asked to believe that what happens to Siegfried or to Kundry is a kind of liberation, what we actually see is just their death – in the case of Kundry, also named as the Jewess Herodias, a humiliation, silencing and death.) 'Judaism in Music' is not an aberration, but rather a display of the essential structure of Wagner's thinking about how the corrupt present might become the utopian future. As Wotan confesses, in the depths of the same crisis:

Auf geb' ich mein Werk;	I give up my work;
nur Eines will' ich noch:	one thing alone I still desire:
das Ende –	the end –
das Ende!	the end!

'We have reached the end', Wagner writes in *Opera and Drama* (II 103), and faced with specific objects of his hatred like the city of Paris or Jewish artists his imagination exults in thoughts of absolute termination.

His acts of artistic terrorism do not spare their own author either. Like Brünnhilde leaping joyfully into the flames, he envisions a purgative destruction of his own career. The introduction to *Opera and Drama* announces '*the open death of Opera*' (II 16), on the face of it a surprising thing for the composer of *Rienzi*, *Der fliegende Holländer*, *Tannhäuser* and *Lohengrin* to proclaim with such evident glee. In fact, when Wagner's book was published in November 1851 those operas were on the brink of achieving real popularity throughout Germany for the first time, and within a year their composer had become one of the most talked-about musicians in northern Europe. In the eyes of both Wagner's partisans and his opponents, some sort of operatic revolution seemed to be under way, the ascendancy of Meyerbeer and Rossini challenged by the upstart fugitive ex-Kapellmeister with his exciting aura of political danger. Wagner himself, though, could not subscribe to this model of revolution after 1849. Unlike the writings of many Wagnerites in the musical press of the 1850s, *Opera and Drama* never envisages *Tannhäuser* and *Lohengrin* storming the theatres, expelling the Meyerbeerian *ancien régime* and proclaiming a new era on the German stage. On the contrary, it begins by declaring that the very notion of opera is incurably infected by an 'error' (*Irrthum*), and every attempt to escape it has been a 'mere way back to the error's starting-point' (II 12). Diagnosing this fatal mistake means 'the exposure of [opera's] nullity [*Nichtigkeit*]' (II 17); by the end of the survey of the history of opera in Part I, not only is the genre 'dead already' (II 103), but 'modern music' in general is condemned to 'barrenness' (II 109), to infertility. Wagner's existing operas clearly do not signpost an escape in this situation, whatever their advocates might think, for nothing new can emerge out of the barren corpse. (Wagner allows for one exception only: the last movement of Beethoven's ninth symphony, in which *Opera and Drama* discerns a real promise of the future marriage of poetry and music in the drama.) Once again, it is not a question of progress, renewal and change. Something much more fundamental is called for, some entirely fresh start once the dead body has been disposed of.

Accordingly, *Opera and Drama* like its predecessors turns its eyes to the utopian future. Unlike *Art and Revolution* and *The Art-Work of the Future*, though, it largely sets aside the political dimension of this utopia. Here, at least, Wagner has given up the idea that the rebirth of art can be anticipated in tandem with the 'inevitably approaching social revolution'. The book concentrates instead on the aesthetic nature of the perfected future drama. Hence its increasingly detailed accounts of how exactly the poetic impulse becomes musical, how words should be set to music, what the proper relationship of melody to harmony is, and so forth. All these technical issues beg one fundamental question, though, the fundamental question of the revolution: how is this future going to come about? More exactly: how does one describe the passage from actuality into impossibility?

The whole discussion of music, poetry and theatre in *Opera and Drama* is governed by a metaphor which draws the clearest possible attention to these questions. 'Music is a woman', Wagner writes, while 'the poetic Aim' is the male 'procreative seed' (II 111, 236). The relation of words to music is a sexual encounter, in which 'Music is the bearing woman, the Poet the begetter' (II 111); and, obviously enough, the anticipated result of this union is a birth. *Opera and Drama* thus becomes a kind of extended epithalamium, celebrating 'the glorious marriage of Poetry's begetting Thought with Music's endless power of Birth' (II 280), and so heralding the conception of this couple's progeny, the art-work of the future. Indeed, the metaphor controls Wagner's whole idea of how anything is achieved at all, how anything can come about, how any birth can occur. The male 'Aim' or intent only exists as a desire, while the female capacity for birth is in itself just an empty womb; their joining is thus the only way any kind of intention can incarnate itself in action. So Wagner's whole problem of the unattainable future is neatly distilled into *Opera and Drama*'s symbolic language. 'Let us now lend ear to this act of Birth', he writes at the end of Part II, as if the entirely new life his revolutionary writings so ardently desire is just about to be brought into being.

Anyone who has fought their way through the convoluted sentences and densely textured thought of Part III would probably agree that it imitates the pain of labour, at least. Nevertheless, it can't itself bring what it has conceived into the world. As much as it exults in the quasi-sexual union of poet with musician, the drama is still powerless to be born. The argument of Part III ties itself in extraordinary knots attempting to insist that the 'realization' (the birth, that is) of the musico-poetic conception is an inherent and necessary aspect of the wedding of the two arts. It is convinced that this particular marriage-bed cannot possibly be barren. The metaphor holds out the promise of a solution to Wagner's recurrent problem about the future: instead of facing the fact that utopia is more or less by definition unrealizable (without some purely imaginary apocalyptic revolution), it suggests that once the sexual act has taken place, the mysteries of gestation mean that a new birth will come about, inevitably and of its own accord. Remember the claim in *Art and Revolution* that the 'perfect Art-work' must be 'born anew'. *Opera and Drama* appears at last to have set this process in motion, reaching out of Wagner's revolutionary limbo towards the *ex nihilo* creation musically enacted in the first bars of the *Ring*.

And yet — in Wagner's revolutionary prophecies of the future there is always an 'and yet' — the book ends not with a birth, but with 'yearning', 'longing [*Sehnsucht*]' (II 376), the conditions not of conception and delivery but of frustrated sexual desire. The last paragraphs of *Opera and Drama* are redolent with the language and tone that will later come to dominate *Tristan und Isolde*, a drama in which the impulse to consummation is continuously, perpetually thwarted, a hymn to endlessly deferred fulfilment. (Many years later, the wheel having turned full circle, *Parsifal* will recommend a potent abstinence.) Having promised an 'act of Birth' a hundred and fifty pages earlier, Wagner finds himself merely restating the unattainability of utopia: 'neither can the artist prescribe from his own Will, nor summon into being, that Life of the Future which once shall redeem him'. At this point, the book suddenly adopts the exact language of Wotan's helplessness in Act II of *Die Walküre*. The sentence continues: '. . . for it is the Other [*das Andere*], the antithesis of himself, for which he yearns' (II 376). Wotan's unanswerable question — 'Wie macht' ich den And'ren', 'How can I make that Other' — rings unmistakably in the background, once again deferring the longed-for birth. There follows in *Opera and Drama* one of the most extraordinary passages in all of Wagner's prose, as he desperately attempts to convert the incapacity of the artist of the present into a necessary prophecy of the art-work of the future, to consummate the 'fecundating seed' of his frustrated desire in the 'mother-element' of futurity. A dizzying series of analogies climaxes with one last furious effort to bring about a birth:

> . . . *just as* [*verse weds itself with the future melody it envisages, so*] *will the prophetic Artwork of the yearning Artist of the Present once wed itself with the ocean of the Life of the Future.* – In that Life of the Future, will this Artwork be what to-day it yearns for but cannot actually be as yet: for that Life of the Future will be entirely what it *can* be, only through its taking up into its womb this Artwork. (II 376)

The reader's head is left spinning here, not so much because of Wagner's notoriously unweeded prose but because the passage is attempting to dissolve the nature of time. The art-work of the 'Artist of the Present' is prophetic because it will wed itself to futurity in order to give birth to the more perfect drama of the future. But at the same time the art-work of the present is waiting for the 'Life of the Future' to arrive in order to achieve its own potential, to fulfil its own creative capacity. And, the final clause states, the future will only happen as a result of the art-work of the present. Which comes first? How can this tangle of reversible causes and effects actually straighten itself out into a linear chronology in which one event follows on from another, as conception follows consummation and birth follows conception? The truest index of Wagner's predicament is in the weird phrasing of that last clause. In direct contravention of the whole body of *Opera and Drama*, his favourite metaphor here reverses itself. Birth goes backwards: instead of being born out of the bearing mother, the art-work is 'taken up' into the womb of the future, and itself somehow gives birth to the 'Life of the Future' which was supposed to bring it about.

Once again, it is a testament to Wagner's dramatic genius that even this bewildering reversal should work itself out in the *Ring*. For Siegfried, imagined in 1848–9 as the man of the future, is born in reverse, appearing on stage as an orphan and discovering his mother only in the final scene of the last act of what is now *Siegfried*: 'O Heil der Mutter,/ die mich gebar' ('hail to the mother who gave me birth'). Famously, the conception of the tetralogy itself repeats the pattern. Beginning with Siegfried's death (*Siegfrieds Tod*), the event described in *The Art-Work of the Future* as the kernel of the perfected drama, Wagner's plan expanded by pursuing the hero's existence in reverse: the events leading to that death in the original drama (finished in its first version in November 1848), his youth in *Der junge Siegfried* (conceived and drafted in the summer of 1851), his parents and the chain of events leading up to Wotan's creation of the Wälsung race in *Das Rheingold* and *Die Walküre* (sketched out in November 1851 and versified in 1852). Each part of the tale seems to call forth its prehistory, as if the drama of the future is indeed constantly being taken back up into its womb. At the very end of this backward history lies a beginning: the transition from silence to sound in the first bars of the score, written in November 1853. With this quiet resumption of Wagner's compositional career, the art-work of the future finally manages to give birth to itself.

What it inherits from the turbulent years of its conception, though, is a severe complication of the idealistic attitudes towards the future which attended its very earliest stirrings in the pre-revolutionary optimism of autumn 1848. In *The Nibelung Myth as Sketch for a Drama*, the first germinal form of the project, Siegfried dies dreaming of his ascent to Valhalla, and Brünnhilde in her final oration announces that she will conduct him there, explaining that his self-sacrifice has freed the Nibelungs from slavery, wiped away the gods' guilt, and restored the triumphant rule of Wotan. Everyone marches boldly together into their bright new utopia (except Hagen, dragged to a well-deserved watery death). The writing of the subsequent years undoes all such representations of a straightforward ascent into futurity. As the dimensions of the story expand and expand, its progressive impulse weakens. Wotan's plan for the future is no longer freely enacted by the revolutionary hero. It becomes an impossible desire, resulting at last in a universal conflagration which makes no promises about what might come afterwards, if indeed anything might. Instead of staging the passage into the future, the *Ring* finds itself asking the Norns' questions: 'weißt du wie das wird?', 'weißt du was daraus wird?'. 'Do you know how it will be? Do you know what will become of that?'

CHAPTER SIX

Staging the Future

Der Ring des Nibelungen took twenty-six years to complete, but its forward-looking revolutionary expectancy only lasted about three months. At the end of *The Nibelung Myth as Sketch for a Drama* (completed in early October 1848), an inspired Brünnhilde slips into a Sibylline future tense: 'One only shall rule, All-father thou in thy glory!' (VII 311). The first versification of these lines as the libretto of *Siegfrieds Tod* was complete by the end of November, and it still rings with the heroine's exhilarated sense of what will come after the curtain falls:

Nur Einer herrsche:	One alone shall rule:
Allvater! Herrlicher du!	All-father! You glorious one!
Freue dich des freiesten Helden!	Rejoice in the freest hero!
Siegfried führ' ich dir zu:	I lead Siegfried to you:
biet' ihm minnlichen Gruß,	offer him a loving greeting,
dem Bürgen ewiger Macht!	the guarantor of eternal might!
Freue dich, Grane: bald sind wir frei!	Rejoice, Grane: soon we will be free!

That last line positively invites a revolutionary interpretation of the scene. (The rather curious fact that Brünnhilde both predicts the absolute rule of Wotan alone and at the same time announces freedom for everyone is in fact in line with Wagner's political thinking in 1848; his speech that June before the Vaterlandsverein – 'fatherland-society' – had attempted to reconcile universal democratic suffrage with the continuation of the monarchy.) 'Soon we will be free' could not sound more like a rallying-cry at the barricades. Translated into prophecy rather than political activism, as it is in the libretto, it suggests an absolute confidence in what will happen after the drama ends.

Within a matter of days that future was gone. The lines quoted above disappeared from the libretto by late December. In their place, Brünnhilde's grammar shifts from a prophetic future tense to an imperative present. Her speech now ends:

Erbleichet in Wonne vor des Menschen That,	Fade in bliss before the deed of mankind,
vor dem Helden, den ach ihr gezeugt!	before the hero whom you fathered!
Aus eurer bangen Furcht	From your anxious fear
verkünd' ich euch selige Todeserlösung!	I proclaim to you blessed redemption in death!

Neither rulership nor freedom now awaits after the fall of the curtain; only a final extinction, a death, which according to the characteristic Wagnerian alchemy is somehow supposed to constitute *Erlösung*, redemption. One might explain the change as a response to the failure of Wagner's revolutionary ambitions in Dresden, were it not for the fact that the revision was made months *before* the abortive uprising. The drama of the future abandoned that future long before its author did. The so-called 'Feuerbach ending', which replaced this second version during further revisions in 1852, restores a kind of foresight to Brünnhilde's speech:

lass' ohne Walter	though I leave behind me
die Welt ich zurück:	a world with no ruler,
meines heiligsten Wissens Hort	my hoard of holiest knowledge
weis' ich der Welt nun zu.	I now bequeath to the world.

But these lines are more retrospective than progressive. Yes, Brünnhilde is talking about what will happen after the end of *Siegfrieds Tod*, but this new world is left 'behind' (*zurück*), waiting to inherit whatever endures after 'Walhall's Ende', Valhalla's end. Whatever future there may be, Brünnhilde has nothing substantial to say about it. She refers to it only in a series of negatives:

Nicht Gut, nicht Gold,	Not property, not gold,
noch göttliche Pracht;	nor godly splendour;
nicht Haus, nicht Hof,	not house, not court,
noch herrischer Prunk . . .	nor lordly pomp . . .

– and so forth. The 'hoard' she bequeaths to it – in orthodox Feuerbachian manner – is simply 'die Liebe', love, which is no doubt the most precious of gifts but nevertheless seems to be defined more by the empty space left after the removal of wealth, pomp and splendour than by any capacity to create a new world. Moreover, in contrast to the first version, Brünnhilde herself will not be in this world (hence 'bequeath'). There is no anticipated freedom here, only a serene knowledge of impending death. What comes afterwards will be an entirely different world.

The 'Schopenhauer ending' of 1856, which in turn replaced the lines just quoted, reverts to an absolute sense of termination, unruffled by the slightest intuition that anything at all will follow the *Ring*. Brünnhilde's language is now dominated by verbs of exit and closure:

Aus Wunschheim zieh' ich fort,	I move on from the home of desire,
Wahnheim flieh' ich auf immer;	I flee forever the home of delusion;
des ew'gen Werdens	the open gates
off'ner Thore	of eternal becoming
schließ' ich hinter mir zu. . . .	I close behind me. . . .

Her triumphant achievement, she says, is 'Alles Ew'gen/ sel'ges Ende', 'the blessed end of all eternal things'. Futurity itself has been foreclosed. The continuity of time is finished at last: 'enden sah ich die Welt', 'I saw the world end'. Nothing, of course, can come after this.

The text of *Götterdämmerung* in its final form shows no interest in the question. Movingly bidding Wotan simply to 'rest', Brünnhilde announces the return of the gold to the Rhinedaughters and the imminent destruction of Valhalla. She then turns her attention entirely to her own enraptured immolation, ending in the 'now' of the present tense: 'Siegfried! Siegfried! Sieh'!/ Selig grüßt dich dein Weib!' ('Siegfried! Siegfried! See! Your wife greets you in blessing!' – perhaps this should be called the 'Cosima ending'?) The stage directions record the inundation of the stage, the collapse of the Gibichungs' Hall, and the obscuring of Valhalla and its gods by the rising flames. And then – what? Wagner's revolutionary writings leave no doubt that *Der Ring des Nibelungen* is, or will be, the art-work of the future; so what happens to the future in the *Ring*?

One of the crucial differences between the project conceived between 1848 and 1853 and the tetralogy as we now know it is the intervention of music. When we think about how the *Ring* ends, Brünnhilde's actual words may well be remembered rather hazily at best, but no one could forget the glowing final pages of the score, filled with the flow of water and the brightness of fire. One melody in particular seems to soar over the scene here, attaching itself to the end of the tetralogy particularly firmly by virtue of having only occurred once before (very briefly, in Act III of *Die Walküre*). The music it floats above has a reasonably clear descriptive or narrative effect. Themes associated with the Rhinedaughters, Loge (fire) and Valhalla form the body of the passage, all of them much-used throughout the tetralogy and easily associated with the visual content of the closing scene (the overflowing river, the conflagration of Wotan's palace). By contrast, the so-called 'redemption' motif doesn't correspond to anything we can see or anything we already know. It seems to be only about *this* moment; it is the tetralogy's true last word, the comment that closes the *Ring*. Which, presumably, is how it gained the label 'redemption', a word denoting the way Wagnerian operas were (and some-times still are) assumed to end, telling us what they are ultimately about. The future, this music says, is 'redeemed'. The whole vast action of the *Ring* has brought us to this last and best revolution. Brünnhilde has broken the curse pronounced by Alberich, solved Wotan's dilemma of *Die Walküre* Act II, and paved the way for the bliss this exceptionally lovely music expresses.

Or so the story goes. As most now admit, though, there is no reason to call this music 'redemption' (whatever weak link the melody has with any concept in the *Ring* would suggest that it is to do with Brünnhilde as heroine, but the fact that it only appears twice means that it cannot have a strong semiotic value: we can't 'translate' it). When Wagner's operas want to announce a redeemed future, they are quite open about it. Senta and the Dutchman ascend in visible transfiguration, Tannhäuser's death is accompanied by hymns and miracles, *Parsifal* closes with invisible voices singing 'Erlösung dem Erlöser' ('the redeemer redeemed'). The end of *Götterdämmerung*, radiant as it is, makes no promises, redemptive or otherwise. Indeed, the appearance of the motif known optimistically as 'redemption' works more like a question than a state-ment, because we don't know what it is about. Wagner's own recorded comment that it means 'glorification of Brünnhilde' would, if taken as author-itative, simply place us back in the present moment much as Brünnhilde's final words do, since it only tells us what is happening on the stage, not what it means or what if anything the events might be prophesying. It makes more sense to understand this melody not as a motif at all, but as an instance of more-or-less 'absolute music', that is, music with no power of denotation, no reference to anything outside itself. Or, perhaps, it should be taken as refer-ring to something unknown, making its final comment on the *Ring*, but in a language we cannot understand. This, Wagner writes in *Opera and Drama*, is how orchestral music works. The language of the orchestra is 'the faculty of uttering the *unspeakable*' (II 316). Music makes reference to that which cannot be grasped or articulated; it starts where verbal language stops:

> . . . it speaks out the very thing which Word-speech in itself can *not* speak out . . . : [t]hat which, looked at from the standpoint of our human intel-lect, is *the Unspeakable* . . . this Unspeakable is not a thing unutterable *per se* [*ein an sich Unaussprechliches*], but merely unutterable through the organ of our Understanding. . . . (II 317)

In other words, music refers to things, but things we cannot know or say any-thing about. This is very much the way the *Ring's* untranslatable last melody works. It seems to be laden with meaning, but (as shown by the long history of its mislabelling) that meaning is not accessible to 'the organ of our Under-standing'. If it refers to a future, then – if it is any indication of what happens at and after the end of the tetralogy – that future is itself unknown and unknowable. Wagner's revolutionary drama once again seems to have hurled itself into the abyss between past and future, rather than bridging the gap as do those confidently optimistic first drafts of the story's end.

In Wagner's stage directions as printed in the score of *Götterdämmerung*, the final tableaux are crowded and busy. The Rhinedaughters are seen 'playing with the ring' below, the whole population of Valhalla – 'gods and heroes assembled as in Waltraute's description' – appears above as the fire rises around them, while at stage level the Gibichung vassals stand and watch the whole panoply. Theatregoers of today will find this throng hard to imagine. The most familiar visual representation of the closing bars today, inspired by the still hugely influential stripped-down style of Wieland Wagner and the 'new Bayreuth', is probably some version of a bare stage. Even in the recent production of the *Ring* at New York's Metropolitan Opera, which set itself the task of faithful adherence to Wagner's presumed intentions as directed by the printed score, the stage was unpopulated at the end. The furthest this version was prepared to go in pursuit of a literal enactment of the stage directions were some clunky mechanical efforts to visualize the flooding and collapse of Gunther's hall. Patrice Chéreau's centenary Bayreuth *Ring* (first seen in 1976) was in this as in so many other respects exceptional: the chorus of Gibichung men and women stayed on stage, facing the audience, as the final diminuendo faded into silence – a gesture which seemed strikingly confrontational, despite being authorized by the published stage directions. The more conventional final emptiness corresponds with the logic of the tetralogy's narrative, which works towards the undoing of its original acts: the renunciation of love, the thefts, and the curse. Wotan's story, as well as Siegfried's, derives from the series of mistakes made in *Das Rheingold*, and in this sense the whole concentrated action of the myth is about how to reverse and atone for everything that happens in its course. It makes sense that the culmination of the story should be cleansing, negation, putting things to rest as Brünnhilde does in her closing oration. In its first seconds, the *Ring* emerges out of an aboriginal silence; a return to nothingness consequently seems like its proper culmination. Certainly, despite the busy stage directions, the impulse driving Wagner's visual imagination in the final scene is one of apocalyptic effacement. Flood and fire are destructive elements, meant to wipe away the world, leaving nothing behind. Think by contrast of the end of Mozart and Schikaneder's *Die Zauberflöte*, where the hero and heroine also have to pass through fire and water. For Tamino and Pamina this is a trial and a rite of purification, a point of entry, that is, into the perfect brotherhood beyond. There is no such implied future at the close of *Götterdämmerung*. Wagner's elemental purge works by cancelling, not purifying, the world.

If the tetralogy ends in an 'unspeakable', ungraspable nothingness, its meaning as a revolutionary drama turns out to be based on the most literal sense of 'revolution': a turning around. It is still often referred to as 'the *Ring* cycle', as if to acknowledge the circularity of its narrative. As rings do, it ends where it begins. This of course is the exact opposite of our more instinctive idea of what 'revolution' means. The word is supposed to be about progress, or at least change – the *difference* between where you started and where you end up. In Wagner's colossal drama, though, the idea of the future always seems to have a regressive tinge. However much the characters imagine and strive for progress, an inexorable pressure works to cancel out their actions, following the law of 'revolutionary' turning which bends the forward direction of straight lines into the inevitable return of circularity.

One of the most memorable circular 'turns' in the *Ring* occurs at one of the moments where the idea of the future is raised and then questioned most powerfully. This is Erda's strange prophecy towards the end of *Das Rheingold*. Strange, because as countless readers have noticed (beginning with Wagner's revolutionary colleague August Röckel right back in 1853), she seems at once to hold out the promise of progress by implying that Wotan can stave off future destruction if he gives up the ring, and also to prophesy an inevitable doom no matter what he does. Either way, her abrupt appearance in the scene represents a sudden turn to futurity. Erda is the voice of what will happen:

Wie alles war, weiß ich;	How all things were, I know;
wie alles wird,	how all things are,
wie alles sein wird,	how all things will be,
seh' ich auch. . . .	I see also. . . .

Her speech is accompanied by eerie ascending minor scales, one after another lifting out of the bass register as if describing the slow, fatalistically inevitable emergence of the future she sings of. That future, she says at last, is empty: what will happen is nothingness: 'Alles was ist, endet', 'All that is, ends'. She goes on to decree (with a finely ambiguous metaphor) that 'Ein düst'rer Tag/ dämmert den Göttern', 'A darker day dawns for the gods'. Dawn implies progress and futurity, a beginning, but this beginning will be an end, the dawn of darkness instead of light. As she sings these words, her ascending scale turns, reversing itself, descending in a new motif which will later resound through the last pages of the *Götterdämmerung* score. This music enacts the literally revolutionary aspect of her prophecy, describing a future in which events are turned full circle to sink back to the point where they began. Her ascending scales are in fact a very close, very dark echo of the first melodic gesture heard in the *Ring*, the horn arpeggios of the *Rheingold* prelude. The descending motif, which refers to the final twilight (or dark dawn) of the gods, is thus a mirror of the tetralogy's opening, reinforcing the irresistible circular motion of the narrative, the convergence of its end with its beginning.

Alberich's ring itself, the engine of the whole plot, provides the most apt symbol of the *Ring's* reigning circularity. Its creation is described throughout *Das Rheingold* as the forging of matter into a circle, 'zum runden/ Reife geschmiedet' ('forged to a rounded ring') as Loge puts it. The musical motif associated with it turns through a descent and ascent that seem to have been forged by breaking down, twisting and tightening the bright, expansive music of the Rhine and its gold. Its effect on the plot also involves the twisting of the future back to the past. The shadow it casts over the story of the *Ring* is not to do with forswearing love (the condition of its making, as Woglinde explains). Despite the often-stated cliché that the tetralogy is about the conflict between power (represented by the ring as instrument of might) and love (the antithesis of the ring, according to Woglinde), this straightforwardly Feuerbachian interpretation bears very little on the drama as a whole; one of the story's strangest features is the way that none of the ring's possessors ever *uses* its power, while the force of love – as always in Wagner – has a psychotic edge that makes it at least partially complicit with dangerous force (think of Sieglinde's hallucinations in Act II of *Die Walküre*, or the ease with which Hagen's stratagems transform Siegfried and Brünnhilde's love into delusion and revenge). The ring's real significance is embedded in the moment Alberich lays his curse on it. From then on it carries a leaden inertia through the narrative, weighing fatefully on the unfolding story. Again, its pressure is not to do with lovelessness: what has love to do with Fafner? Siegfried is even wearing it when he finally discovers what love is. The ring's curse is defined by Alberich's grim prophecies:

. . . nun zeug' sein Zauber	. . . now its magic shall bring
Tod dem – der ihn trägt! . . .	death to the one who bears it! . . .
. . . wer ihn besitzt,	. . . he who owns it,
den sehre die Sorge,	may care torment him,
und wer ihn nicht hat,	and he who does not,
den nage der Neid! . . .	may envy gnaw at him! . . .
. . . ohne Wuche hüt' ihn sein	. . . without gain its lord shall
Herr	guard it,
doch den Würger zieh' er	yet it will tighten its noose on
ihm zu! . . .	him! . . .
. . . bis in meiner Hand	. . . until once again I hold in
	my hand
den geraubten wieder ich halte!	the stolen ring!

The details don't matter here (it's not relevant that Wotan and Siegfried, for example, never experience the 'envy' of desiring the ring). What is important is that the object now becomes the vehicle of a prophecy as inflexibly certain as Erda's. Its guarantee of destruction is in fact a baleful but otherwise exact equivalent to her reminder 'All that is, ends'. Alberich, though, is more explicit about the circularity implied by this doom: the end of the spell, he says, will be when the ring comes back to the moment right before it was pronounced ('bis in meiner Hand . . . '). This curse's effect is at once to determine and to annihilate the future. It ensures that the whole coming course of events will be driven by various characters' desire to possess the ring (and indeed it is Mime and Hagen who keep the plot moving; everyone else is more acted upon than acting). At the same time, it also guarantees that all those desires will end in death, that no one who either strives for or owns the ring will have a future.

More significantly, the curse turns future history into a series of repetitions or cycles; Alberich declares that the story of the ring, or of the *Ring*, will happen the same way over and over again. This is one of the effects of motivic composition. In specific relation to the curse, it is striking how the extremely distinctive motif associated with it comes to function in the score as a reminder of inevitable repetition. The brutal theme, usually scored in darkest brass, tends to rise vividly and prominently out of a pause in the flow of sound: accompanying Alberich's defiance of the gods at the end of the first scene of *Siegfried* Act II, for example, or thundering out over a fortissimo sustained orchestral chord to accompany Hagen's greeting to Siegfried in *Götterdämmerung* Act I. Its own consistency penetrates the musical fabric like a punctuation mark, repeating the melody to which Alberich sings the first lines of his curse and so reminding us that its effect recurs unchangingly no matter where we are in the story. Time after time the motif attends the downfall of the characters. Even Mime, who never actually lays his hands on the cursed gold, has his corpse tossed into Fafner's cave to the accompaniment of its grim rise and fall. It could in fact almost be labelled the motif of real death, so regularly does it appear as a mark of termination without the slightest hint of redemption. As the dragon Fafner breathes his last, it sounds out around his dying words: 'Merk, wie's endet', 'Mark how it ends'. The injunction is lost on Siegfried, who never pays attention to anything anyone says to him (except the woodbird, oddly, but then he had tried to speak to her first), but it foretells his death as well as everyone else's. Again like Erda, Fafner understands that 'it ends', that death draws up all the plots of the tetralogy. The curse motif is the musical sign of this fatefulness, as Alberich's curse itself is its narrative sign, and the ring its onstage symbol.

Fafner's death speech is one of those moments in the action of the *Ring* where the progress of the plot is overwhelmed and temporarily halted by prophetic language. There is no obvious reason why the dragon should suddenly become the mouthpiece of mysterious wisdom here, but Wagner's matchless power to clothe drama in the aura of myth suddenly interjects a

surprising solemnity into what might otherwise be merely a moment of triumphant action (hero slays monster). Scenes like these acount for one of the
most remarkable effects of the *Ring*, its way of seeming to encompass more
– *even* more, perhaps one should say – than it actually does. Despite the relatively small number of incidents and the generally slow pace of the action,
the tetralogy overall produces a plausible impression of covering an entire cosmological cycle from creation to apocalypse. This is to do with the immense
weight that invests many of the scenes, loading the particular incidents of the
drama with the force of myth. Only in some of the central scenes of *Rheingold* do we occasionally feel that we are observing the everyday interaction
of characters, talking and negotiating and fighting over their own immediate
concerns almost as if they belonged in one of Da Ponte's libretti. Donner,
Froh and Freia sound more like bourgeois adolescents than gods, Fricka and
Wotan squabble and make up in banal terms (utterly unlike their monumental
confrontation in Act II of *Die Walküre*), and Loge especially, with his rapid
delivery, his spirit of mockery and his tendency to comment on what is going
on around him, seems to be a figure out of domestic drama rather than
legend. The abrupt intervention of Erda changes the mood entirely, as Wotan
realizes. Unexpected, unfathomable and possessed of hidden knowledge, she
has the authentic air of divinity about her, and in the face of her prophetic
voice the tug-of-war over the Nibelung hoard suddenly looks embarrassingly
trivial. From this moment on, the local details of the plot are frequently interrupted by equivalent scenes of prophecy, all of which have the effect of lifting
the mere sequence of events to the mythic plane. (Operagoers unsympathetic
to the dimensions of Wagner's operas would say that they also have the effect
of retarding the *Ring* to glacial speeds.) Brünnhilde and Siegmund in Act II
of *Die Walküre*; the Wanderer and Mime in the first Act of *Siegfried*; Siegfried
and the dying Fafner in Act II, and Erda and Wotan in Act III; the Norns at
the beginning of *Götterdämmerung*; the Rhinedaughters and Siegfried in the
last act of the tetralogy; all these encounters serve little direct narrative
purpose, giving the stage over to ritualistic dialogue rather than forward-
moving action. The characters sound more like mouthpieces of some presid-
ing fate than individual beings – this is especially noticeable in Act III of
Götterdämmerung, where the Rhinedaughters shift very abruptly from playful
teasing to elemental gravity at the words 'Siegfried! Siegfried!'; and there is
also an impressive difference between Siegmund the ardent lover of Act I of
Die Walküre and the Siegmund who engages Brünnhilde in a series of cate-
chistically solemn questions in Act II. By shifting into this prophetic mode
so regularly, the *Ring* reminds itself of its concern with futurity. Instead of
just telling the story, as conventional operas tended to, it is preoccupied with
asking itself what is going to happen. In this respect too, Alberich's curse
weaves its thread through the whole fabric of the drama, because in every

case these rituals of prophecy founder on the loss of the future, the intractable sense of confronting an end.

This is literally staged for us as the tearing of the Norns' rope in the opening scene of *Götterdämmerung*. Through all its coilings and windings, the unbroken line of the rope stands for the continuity of history, connecting the past the Norns sing of to the future they peer into. It leads them even as far as the end of history, or at least the end of the gods, which the Third Norn prophesies (to the accompaniment of the descending 'twilight of the gods' motif produced by the inversion of Erda's music). The breaking of their rope, however, signifies a different kind of end: not the downfall of the existing order of things, which is how the scene functions in the original libretto of *Siegfrieds Tod* and which can be understood as a revolutionary prophecy in the political sense, but the rupture of the line leading from present to future, the disappearance of futurity that is so powerful a theme in Wagner's 'revolutionary' writings. On the brink of this rupture, the Norns lose the power of prophecy which is their purpose and their gift. They wind their rope tighter and tighter into a circle, forgetting that time is linear, imitating the destructive turnings and returnings of the ring. As the bassoons play the ring's own motif, the First Norn sings:

nichts mehr gewahr' ich:	I can observe nothing more:
des Seiles Fäden	I can no longer find
find' ich nicht mehr. . . .	the strands of the rope. . . .

Time itself appears to be darkening and fraying. The force that causes its decay is named by the Second Norn: 'ein rächender Flucht/ nagt mein Fäder Geflecht', 'an avenging curse gnaws at the mesh of my strands'. Alberich's deed is here correctly understood. The curse isn't so much a power to determine the future (a form of prophecy, that is) as the power that annihilates time. Accordingly, it is the motif of the curse which rings out at the very moment the rope breaks, not because the Norns are in any way implicated in the cycle of greed and destruction which Alberich specifically predicts, but because the baleful effect of the ring has here achieved its fullest manifestation, bringing a kind of death (a violent rupture) to the fabric of time itself.

As the curse motif fades, it is followed immediately by a gentle statement in the wind of the 'twilight of the gods' motif, recalling and fulfilling Erda's affirmation that everything ends. In the same way that Erda's prophecy in *Rheingold* effectively overarches the whole action of the tetralogy, telling us how it will end pretty much before it has had a chance to get under way, so the Norns' scene makes redundant the whole of the action of *Götter-dämmerung*, since the ultimate end happens at the opera's beginning. It casts a powerfully ironic pall over the radiant dawn music that introduces Siegfried and Brünnhilde, and particularly over the heroine's first words, which promise to send Siegfried off 'Zu neuen Thaten', 'to new deeds'. This embrace of things to come is rendered futile by what we have just witnessed. Appropriately, then, Siegfried's excursion into the world of adventures is instantly catastrophic (he is on stage for only a few minutes before he is caught in Hagen's trap). No heroic future is conceivable in the opera, nor in the cosmology of the *Ring* as a whole.

Perhaps the only stretch of unsullied optimism is the first act of *Die Walküre*. It ends with a gesture of magnificent confidence, Siegmund's cry 'so blühe denn Wälsungen-Blut!' ('then let the Wälsung race blossom'), matching the idealized dynamics of *Opera and Drama* in which enraptured sexual union conceives the future. The act leads us to this climax with extraordinarily patient steadiness. Its gradual ascent from the subdued lyrical melancholy and veiled menace of the first scene to the unmistakably sexualized exultant unsheathing of the sword is a wonderful example of Wagner's power to develop a single dramatic impetus over enormous spans. Though the conditions of Siegmund and Sieglinde's mutual discovery are unmistakably tragic – incestuous elopement is unlikely to be permitted a happy ending, and Siegmund tells us himself that he is one of life's perpetual victims – the act itself allows no thought of the future except that last ringing appeal to their unconceived child. The mythic dimension of the story only intrudes on Siegmund and Sieglinde in Act II, when Brünnhilde appears to call the former to his death. In her role as Valkyrie she speaks on behalf of an inexorable future: 'Nur Todgeweihten/ taugt mein Anblick', 'my gaze is meant only for those doomed to death'. Musically, the scene is organized as a series of stately repetitions, scored without the brightness of violins, the triplet figure in the timpani reverberating with dull insistence throughout the conversation as a quiet reminder of its fatality. In a pattern which by now we can begin to recognize as characteristic of the *Ring*, what is happening here is that the end is being announced before it is performed (as with Erda, the Norns and the *Götterdämmerung* Rhinedaughters). Death occurs proleptically, not simply a momentary event in the narrative but instead an idea overshadowing everything that precedes it. So Brünnhilde conducts Siegmund through the whole sequence of his death in advance, while the action seems frozen around them. With characteristic imaginative insight, Wagner's stage directions prescribe that the two lovers remain unmoving throughout the scene, Sieglinde asleep the whole time, so that Brünnhilde's appearance takes on the quality of a prophetic dream.

It is all the more poignantly ironic, then, that Brünnhilde imagines herself to have freedom of choice at this moment. Misunderstanding her role as the agent of destiny, she tells Siegmund 'Beschlossen ist's;/ das Schlachtloos wend' ich', 'it is decided; I will change the battle's destiny' – though 'Beschlossen ist's' literally means 'it is closed', 'an end has been put to it', implying that Brünnhilde believes that she can declare the future with finality. This is revolutionary talk. She speaks of turning – *wenden* – the course of history, as revolutions aspire to do. But the *Ring* doesn't put destiny in the hands of aspiring individuals (its greatest hero, Siegfried, is extraordinarily incompetent and thoughtless). The doom Brünnhilde announced to Siegmund is not reversible. All her brief rebellion achieves is to force the cyclical quality of fate in the *Ring* to be illustrated more explictly. Wotan ends up having in effect to kill his own son, an act which fulfils the nihilistic surrender of the future announced in his monologue earlier in Act II, and also powerfully reverses Siegmund's triumphant proclamation of the blossoming of the Wälsung tribe, since the father now destroys rather than creating his progeny. The inexorable logic continues in Act III, where Wotan completes the pattern by abandoning his daughter.

Brünnhilde's mistaken belief in the future as she talks to Siegmund comes from forgetting what she herself tells Wotan earlier in Act II:

Zu Wotan's Willen sprichst du,	You are speaking to Wotan's will,
sag'st du mir was du willst:	when you tell me what you wish:
wer bin ich,	who am I,
wär ich dein Wille nicht?	if not your will?

Until her divinity is taken away from her by Wotan's kiss, she exists only as the embodiment of an already determined power. (One might add that she hardly has her own will afterwards: her defiance of Waltraute could be understood as an effect of the curse on the ring, and she is later swiftly manipulated to do Hagen's will.) Another question is begged here, though: does Wotan himself have a will? That is, does the *Ring* follow the trajectory of his intentions, working out the future that he conceives? In the case of Act II of *Die Walküre*, it looks for a moment as if this is so. Brünnhilde's revolt is instantaneously and easily quashed by Wotan's superior power. Yet that power is actually the opposite of Wotan's will. It is in fact Fricka's will that is executed in the course of the act. Wotan's prophecy-instruction to his daughter, 'Siegmund falle!' ('Siegmund shall fall!'), is simply the echo of his wife's demand. However, it would also be too simple to cast Fricka as the one who determines the course of future events here. She doesn't just win a battle of wills with Wotan, as if this were a domestic tiff. Her argument works by exposing the contradiction in Wotan's own intentions. In other words, she explains to him what (as he despairingly admits to Brünnhilde) he of course already knows: that there is a fatal flaw in his own will. His final submission to Fricka's demand takes the form not only of a surrender of the will, but an abnegation of the possibility that he can have any relation to the future at all:

Was sie erkor,	What she has chosen,
das kiese auch ich:	I also choose:
was frommte mir eig'ner Wille?	what use is my own will to me?

This is a very far cry from the situation at the end of *Das Rheingold*, a triumphal procession which appears to stage the ascendancy not only of Wotan's present power but also of his plans for the future. Until the lament of the Rhinedaughters interrupts with its exquisitely timed reminder of what is being left behind, the scene is altogether a representation of progress, of movement forward. A bridge is created leading to a castle bathed 'in der Götter neuem Glanze', 'in the gods' new radiance', as Loge sardonically describes it: in every sense, the prospects appear bright. The central moment in this whole pageant of futurity comes when Wotan greets and names his new home, 'as though' (the stage directions tell us) 'seized by a grand idea'. The specific nature of his new conception is expressed in the orchestra, where the motif later associated with the sword Nothung here peals out its bright, confident sound for the first time in the tetralogy. As Fricka points out in *Die Walküre*, Nothung is a totemic expression of Wotan's will, his plan for the future. It is the agent which is supposed to ensure the continuity of the Wälsungs and enable the scion of the tribe to defeat Fafner and so recover Alberich's ring. When we hear its motif at the end of *Rheingold*, then, we are watching the whole plan form itself. Wotan is making the future we watch the gods striding towards. Majesty and pomp saturate the orchestral finale, a pompously brassy march which sounds supremely assured and triumphant, apparently celebrating the zenith of Wotan's power.

Yet there are three reasons for detecting an ironic quality in the exaggerated fanfare of the opera's last bars. First, there is Erda's prophecy, scored with chthonic eerieness and overriding Wotan's will (Erda makes him change his mind and leaves him uncertain about the future). Then there is Loge's aside to the audience, delivered with the flickering lightness that always characterizes his music; it too prophesies a future exactly the opposite of that envisaged by the gods: 'Ihrem Ende eilen sie zu,/ die so stark im Bestehen sich wähnen', 'they are hurrying towards their end, though dreaming themselves so strong'. Finally there are the Rhinedaughters, who manage to interrupt the triumphal march both musically and physically. Their plaintive appeal for their stolen gold stops Wotan 'on the point of setting foot on the bridge' (as the stage directions have it). With fine dramatic subtlety, it functions as a *reminder* – a turn to the past rather than the future, that is – which therefore suddenly makes the gods' procession look as if they are fleeing something left behind them rather than stepping into the glory lying ahead of them. All three alternative perspectives work in direct opposition to the progress of Wotan's will. The god's response, expressed in the overbearing and ponderous loudness of the finale, is simply to ignore them, hoping that the music of triumphalism will drown out both memory and prophecy.

It's a temporary victory, at best. The unfolding of the tetralogy shows increasingly clearly that Wotan's will is not a force capable of determining the future. Once again, we have to recognize that the law of the *Ring* is the law of Alberich's curse, bending and reversing every competing effort to chart a course through history even when the competition comes from the king of the gods. Wotan's will shows itself to be contained by the ring's motion of turning on itself; with a little eloquent prompting from Fricka, it becomes its own opposite in Act II of *Die Walküre*. The moment at the end of the act when he shatters Nothung on his own spear is the climax of this reversal. Insofar as the sword is the physical embodiment of his intent as conceived in the last scene of *Das Rheingold*, his destruction of it is an act of self-destruction. His will breaks itself. Brünnhilde is right when in Act III she tells Wotan that her disobedience was in fact obedience. Not because she rightly understood Wotan's 'true' intent (as she claims); she is right because Wotan's will has been shown to be its own opposite, and therefore to obey it is to disobey it and vice versa. His answer to her speaks with fierce insight of a circularity embedded in him, a revolutionary 'turn' (*Wandel*) that is once again not progressive but self-reversing: 'gegen mich selber/ ich sehrend sich wandte', 'in torment I turned against myself'. The only thing such a will is good for, he goes on, is self-destruction: 'in den Trümmern der eig'nen Welt/ meine ew'ge Trauer zu enden', 'to end my eternal grief in the ruins of my own world'. As he sings these words, the orchestra descends in a bitter cadence to near-silence – just a rolling timpani E flat – out of which the motif of the curse rises and falls. Wotan's power too is subject to the inertia of the ring (and of the *Ring*) which brings all ends to nothing.

Nevertheless, Nothung is forged again; the Wälsung tribe does blossom for at least one more generation; Alberich's plot is defeated, and the ring is returned whence it came – all apparently in accordance with Wotan's desire. When Siegfried manages to reconstruct his father's sword, it looks as if Wotan's will has been reinstituted. However, this action also is one of those events which is anticipated before it happens, in the ritualistic exchange between Mime and the Wanderer in the middle of Act I of *Siegfried*. Here once more the progress of the story comes to a halt, giving way to a mythic encounter. The game the two of them play is a portrait of space (Mime's questions) and time (the Wanderer's), articulating the dimensions of the *Ring*'s cosmos from bottom to top and from past to future. Out of the six questions exchanged, only one remains unanswered. Needless to say, it's the question about the future, which (according to the equation established at the end of *Rheingold*) is also a question about Wotan's will: who will make Nothung whole again? By the rules of the game, Mime's head is forfeit when he fails to know the future. The logic of the curse is being imposed again. Futurity is replaced by death. When, therefore, Siegfried reopens the future in the following scene by answering the Wanderer's last question, his deed is placed in a strange relation to prophecy. In one sense, it confidently fulfils the future the Wanderer predicted (Mime is told that Nothung can only be forged by one who does not know fear). More subtly, though, it seems to represent an unknown future, an unanswered question; it marks the point where the interchange of wisdom between the Wanderer and Mime breaks off. It bears repeating again that Siegfried does not know what he is doing (a characteristic that will be explored far more subtly in *Parsifal*). When Siegmund takes possession of Nothung, he does so as a sign of futurity ('so blühe denn Wälsungen-Blut!'). His son is driven instead by a restlessly energetic ignorance, a sense of everything he does not know. The counterpoint provided by Mime's gleeful plotting during the forging scene is more than just a comic effect; the dwarf's tyrannical plans highlight very precisely the extent to which Siegfried acts without understanding what lies ahead of him. Hence when the sword passes into Siegfried's hands it ceases to be a token of Wotan's effort to direct the course of events, and becomes instead a mere tool of the thoughtless present. Like the question game, it stops at the threshold of futurity.

Appropriately, it then redoubles the self-destructive logic enacted in Act II of *Die Walküre* and becomes the weapon which finally dismisses Wotan from the *Ring* altogether. The moment in *Siegfried* Act III when his spear is broken by Nothung obviously mirrors Siegmund's death, but it is not (as at first sight one might think) the inverse of *Walküre* Act II. It's a repetition of the earlier event: once again, a wheel has turned itself full circle. At both moments, Wotan's power shatters itself, because both spear and sword are his instruments. There isn't a real difference between the first occasion, when he destroys his own plan, and the second, when his plan destroys him. (In the same way, there is an equation between the end of *Die Walküre*, where he surrounds Brünnhilde with fire, and of *Götterdämmerung*, where she returns the favour; after *Die Walküre* he is no longer Wotan, appearing instead as the Wanderer, so both conflagrations are effectively funeral pyres for him.) The circularity of Siegfried's breaking of the spear is confirmed immediately afterwards by the orchestra. As Wotan gathers up the fragments and sings his last line in the tetralogy, we hear again the exquisitely poised ascent and descent of Erda's prophecy, the turn that produces the 'twilight of the gods' motif. What we are witnessing is not the passing of the old order in the face of the new (as the original, Young Hegelian, progressively revolutionary conception of the Nibelung story has it), but the completion of a 'revolution', a full turn, in which the sword goes from being the symbol of Wotan's intention to performing the final rounding of his will upon itself.

Yet again, the event has been at least obliquely foretold. In the first scene of *Siegfried* Act III, Wotan eventually announces to Erda, 'dem ewig Jungen/ weicht in Wonne der Gott' ('the god yields with delight to the eternally youthful one'), referring of course to Siegfried. This scene is the most complicatedly prophetic of all the tetralogy's many numinous interventions. Wotan's final speech, in which he willingly embraces his own end for the sake of (as he sees it) an end to Alberich's curse and a final 'erlösende Weltenthat', 'world-redeeming deed', very much belies what precedes it. His prior exchange with Erda is driven by an anxious effort to prevent the very end he finally welcomes. Over the relatively brief course of the scene, he takes over the prophetic voice from Erda, who has become incapable of speaking of the future, and answers his own question with his optimistic prediction of Siegfried and Brünnhilde's redemptive heroism. The form of that question, however, should make us pause. How, he begs Erda to instruct him, can one 'halt a rolling wheel' – 'wie zu hemmen ein rollendes Rad'? The turning of the ring governs what is happening, and, as always, Wotan's struggle is an effort to resist this revolution. In the score, the 'rolling wheel' is brilliantly figured as the scene begins by an adaptation of the rise and fall of the music of Erda's prophecy (the 'Erda' motif followed by its inversion, the 'twilight of the gods' motif). The ascent and descent has become a restless, rocking, urgent motion; Erda's serene assurance of the end of everything now sounds imminent, full of irresistible momentum. Nothing can stop this wheel. In the face of its movement, prophecy becomes superfluous, as Wotan understands when he dismisses Erda (and another cycle is turned here, since his words are accompanied by a smoothly lyrical version of the ascent and descent with which she initially predicted his doom in *Rheingold*). Talking about the future is a doomed enterprise under the ring's gravitational force. It's odd, then, that Wotan should go on to assume the prophetic role himself, and in fact his reading of the remaining course of events is wrong. Alberich's curse, he says, cannot affect Siegfried: is it then coincidence that Siegfried will be slain for the sake of Hagen's desire for the ring? Brünnhilde will, he says, redeem the world: but we have already seen that the end of *Götterdämmerung* resists the label 'redemption'. There is something impressive about Wotan's exultant faith in a future in which he has no place. Nevertheless, it's an illusory faith. He has himself just banished Erda – the mouthpiece of futurity – to eternal sleep, an act equivalent to the breaking of the Norns' rope. His 'prophecy' is really an attempt to give a certain interpretation to the scene we are about to witness, the breaking of the spear by Siegfried and Nothung. In Wotan's rather Hegelian view, this will be a revolutionary act, signalling the coming of the 'purely human' generation (a phrase much used in Wagner's revolutionary writings). But the overall logic of the *Ring*'s narrative dictates otherwise. The curse goes on functioning despite the god's belief in the untarnishable purity of Siegfried's motives, and, as always, its function is to distort and reverse optimistic pronouncements like Wotan's at the end of this scene.

It is something of a cliché in thinking about the *Ring* to say that its meaning shifted in the course of its composition from a progressive Feuerbachian one to a nihilistic Schopenhauerian one. Or, translating out of philosophical shorthand, the *Ring* can be understood to have surrendered its hopes for the future in favour of renunciation and negation. Something rather different suggests itself in the light of Wagnerian 'revolution'. The cyclical motion governing the *Ring* does indeed turn away from the promises of futurity which are so regularly raised in the course of the tetralogy. By reversing direction, though, something more is happening than a Schopenhauerian embrace of nothingness. It may be true that *Tristan und Isolde* goes nowhere – that is, desires only a release from desire, strives only to still its own action completely. The *Ring* is not quite that sort of story, though. It struggles with time, rather than always looking for ways to evade temporality, and its end looks more like a return to its beginning than the final release musically completed in the last bars of *Tristan*. Acts of foretelling, of prophecy, are bent around by the ring, but they are bent in a specific direction: backwards. The story becomes a series of recollections; progress into the future turns into continuous resumptions of the past. Famously, the *Ring* is packed with scenes of recollection, narrating things we have already seen happening, turning back to itself. This returning is the literal meaning of 'revolution' for Wagner. His writings bear witness to a revolutionary imagination that always finally turns its face away from prophecy and anticipation, looking back instead to the past.

CHAPTER SEVEN

Writing the Past

The critic Eduard Hanslick memorably referred to the central scene of *Die Walküre* Act II as 'an abyss of boredom'.[1] It's a shallow judgment, but nevertheless one can at least see what he was thinking. Wotan's long, sparse monologue has probably tested the patience of far more sympathetic listeners than Hanslick, presumably because measured by the basic conventions of nineteenth-century opera it seems like recitative protracted to numbing dimensions. The superficial eye also sees it as a scene with absolutely no action, though in many ways it is the tetralogy's crisis, the hinge of its plot. Wotan just talks. More specifically, he tells stories; he recollects things. It's one of the most characteristic features of Wagner's operas that for long stretches, often at critical moments, they give themselves up to the dramatic stasis of storytelling. As far back in his career as *Die Feen* he betrays a fascination with monologue, and in *Der fliegende Holländer*, *Tannhäuser* and *Lohengrin* his musical and dramatic imagination is often at its most innovative and distinctive at such moments: the Dutchman's introductory self-narration, Tannhäuser's chronicle of his pilgrimage, Lohengrin's answer to the forbidden questions. The tendency becomes increasingly marked, and the psychology more subtle, as Wagner's career goes on, reaching its zenith in Kundry's astonishing seduction-by-regression in the second act of *Parsifal* (the pinnacle of her erotic beguilement is to tell the naïve fool the history of his mother). One only has to think of Gurnemanz in Act I, or of virtually the whole third act of *Tristan* (in which a tiny, extraordinarily hurried burst of dynamic action is contained within huge and static monologues), to realize that Wotan's extended reflection on the story of the *Ring* so far is an absolutely habitual Wagnerian gesture. Siegmund and Sieglinde even fall in love by telling each other stories. In fact, in the prose drafts for Act I of *Die Walküre* Wotan appears onstage to plunge Nothung into the ash's trunk, but by the time of versification this crucial event has been turned into a recollected story, formally introduced by Sieglinde: 'O merke wohl, was ich dir melde!', 'mark well what I tell you'.

The change is symptomatic of Wagner's essential tendency to substitute narration for action. (In this case, no Hanslicks are likely to volunteer a complaint: Sieglinde's tale is a rhetorical masterpiece, assisted by music of fluent and seamless lyricism.)

The tendency becomes particularly conspicuous in Wagner's revolutionary years. Not surprisingly: something has to fill up the vacuum left by the always deferred, always imaginary deed of revolution. In the absence of the deeds which would overthrow the order of things and pave the way for the art-work of the future, Wagner's imagination often turns to the past, unreeling a series of fantastical, spurious, inventive narratives in his prose works. The same turn is everywhere manifest in the *Ring*, where the question of what is going to happen consistently transforms itself instead into the question of what has already happened. In other words, at the critical junctures of the drama people tell stories. There's a good reason for this. By initially beginning his dramatization of the Siegfried myth at the end, with *Siegfrieds Tod*, Wagner was required to insert scenes of narration in order to explain how we reached the point where his drama begins. The decision to stage some of these prior chapters in the story as *Der junge Siegfried* only extended his problem, for there was still a prehistory to be narrated during the course of the action. Only by finally reaching back to an absolute origin – the beginning of everything, as performed in the *Rheingold* prelude – can the serial generation of narratives be stopped, since that E flat is the first thing in the whole world, leaving nothing prior to be told. The structural requirements of the drama's reverse conception are however very far from being the only explanation for its compulsive storytelling habit. Narration means far more to Wagner than simply a way of getting necessary information across. It's the lifeblood of his art and the ground of his thought. What, after all, is more Wagnerian than Sieglinde's command, 'mark well what I tell you'? The nature of all his work is to sit its audience down and make them listen to the tale.

Not surprisingly, then, the burst of chaotic intellectual energy articulated in Wagner's revolutionary writings during the *Ring*'s gestation period ends in a retrospective rather than progressive mood, the exact reverse of the frenzied anticipation typified by his essay 'The Revolution'. The last and best of the prose manifestos of this period is 'A Communication to My Friends', written in July and August 1851 and printed, significantly, as a preface to the publication of the libretti of *Der fliegende Holländer*, *Tannhäuser* and *Lohengrin*. Here there is virtually no talk of either the life or the art of the future. Instead of looking forward to what will be coming, the essay occupies itself – as the *Ring* does – with retracing what has already happened. In fact, it's because the future seems so elusive that this turn to the past takes place. 'A Communication' exists in order to correct the misapprehension that Wagner's extant operas – the three 'romantic' ones – are in any way examples of the kind of 'drama' described in the prose works. Then as now, readers of *The Art-Work of the Future* and *Opera and Drama* tended to assume that they described in theory how Wagnerian opera was in practice supposed to function; an understandable misapprehension, but nevertheless a mistake, because the ideal drama described in the prose works is always a visionary entity. In the early 1850s, when Wagner's revolutionary writings began to attract attention as supposed manifestos of what one commentator famously called 'the music of the future', the confusion was more acute than it is today, since the musico-dramatic formulae of the prose works have even less to do with *Lohengrin* than they do with the *Ring* – and *Lohengrin* was all contemporaries knew of Wagner's most recent compositions. By publishing the three romantic opera libretti prefaced by 'A Communication', then, Wagner is drawing explicit attention to the *difference* between his visionary ideals and his actual practice as a composer. This is as much as to confess that the art-work of the future is by definition non-existent. Wagner's response to this admission in 'A Communication' is utterly characteristic:

> The contradictions to which I here allude [i.e. the contradiction of looking forward to a future which cannot be imagined actually existing], do not at all events exist for any one who has accustomed himself to regard a phenomenon with due allowance for its development *in time*. . . .
>
> . . . Thus I face towards *my Friends*, to render them a clear account of my path of evolution, in course of which those apparent contradictions . . . must be thoroughly unriddled.
>
> I will not however attempt to reach this end by the paths of abstract criticism; but will point out my evolutionary career, as faithfully as I can now survey it, by reviewing my works, and the moods of life which called them forth. . . . (I 283–6)

Theory and prophecy round on themselves and turn into autobiography's retrospective narration. As Lohengrin knows, the crucial question in the end is the question of origins: where do you come from, what is your nature? ('Woher die Fahrt? . . . Wie deine Art?')

By following this retrospective path, 'A Communication' becomes what none of the other prose works of this period manages to be: a powerful (if weird) interpretation of Wagnerian opera. As with Wotan's narration, it is the past, not the future, that unleashes meaning. Wotan discovers his own condition by recounting it; so Wagner also rewrites his existing work as a progressive unfolding of his true character as an artist. At the end of the progression lies the goal to which he now dedicates himself, the impossible vision of the future art-work now set out with straightforward pragmatic intent:

I propose to produce my myth *in three complete dramas*, preceded by a lengthy *Prelude*. . . .

At a specially-appointed Festival, I propose, some future time, to produce those three Dramas with their Prelude, *in the course of three days and a fore-evening.* (I 391)

Here, astonishingly, is the visionary prophecy that would make itself real a quarter of a century later at Bayreuth. It turns out that by rewriting the past, 'A Communication' is able to conceive the future.

There's plenty of evidence of the same tendency throughout the revolutionary writings, although never elsewhere capped by a similar flash of prophetic insight. Their most interesting passages, indeed, tend to be those where Wagner is giving his own versions of history rather than the speculative descriptions of the revolutionary drama. They read like historiographical versions of his enormously condensed and compressed libretti. In the same way that the texts of his operas are made by gathering up a mass of legendary or historical material and compacting it into a few essential incidents strung along a single plot, the prose works survey the history of melody or spoken drama or the Teutonic nations and organize those narratives into single lines of development, showing that the whole story of civilization can retrospectively be understood in terms of one essential tendency. This is of course only achieved by means of brazen oversimplifications and generalizations. Wagner drew heavily on the wealth of philological and antiquarian scholarship produced in Germany in the first half of the nineteenth century, without (as he is happy to admit) himself achieving thorough scholarly expertise in any single field. The fact that his histories are spurious doesn't diminish the power of the stories he tells, though. What matters to him is the effort to gather together disparate material into a single, cogent narrative, because once such narratives have been created the essential meaning of history (as Wagner sees it, of course) stands clear to the view. In *The Art-Work of the Future*, for example, he offers potted versions of the development of dance, music, poetry, architecture, sculpture and painting from classical antiquity through the Christian era into the present day, each in just a few pages. These reconstructions allow Wagner to interpret the history of European culture as a continuous decay from a state of natural, spontaneous expressiveness to the artificial and trivial entertainment-seeking of modernity, and to propose that each form of art has a 'world-historical task' (I 130) which can only be fulfilled when it has become part of the united art-work that expresses the 'free' and 'natural' state of the people, the *Volk* ('Folk'). (The invention of the study of aesthetics in eighteenth- and nineteenth-century Germany meant that Wagner had a number of possible models for this brand of historiography, most prominently Lessing, Schiller and Hegel.) This is a kind of symbolic history, closer to myth-making than scholarship. It interprets all the individual phenomena of culture as manifestations of some deep and universal tendency. The story of tragedy from Aeschylus through Shakespeare to Goethe becomes the story of the gradual alienation of the artist from his community, and the development of operatic melody since Gluck is read as a rape of nature ('so have we dug up the whole fair native forest of the Folk', II 58). His habit of storytelling allows Wagner to universalize his thinking. It's the same sort of process as Freudian psychoanalysis: whatever particular story one tells, its meaning turns out to refer to something essential and fundamental. Thus for Wagner the particular problems of opera, especially the relation between poetry and music, can be related to the whole course of European society's evolution.

At the heart of Wagner's mythic histories in the revolutionary writings lies a fantasy about a pure origin. Throughout the prose works we find him imagining a past state of perfection which has been corrupted and effaced by the progress of civilization (the main culprits – here Wagner follows Feuerbach and Proudhon – are usually Christianity, the State, and property). Humanity, he writes in the essay 'Kunst und Klima' ('Art and Climate') of early 1850, 'shall first reach Art when we completely turn our backs on such a civilization and once more cast ourselves . . . into the arms of Nature' (I 259). To this extent at least, utopia lies in the past, not the future. The idea in which this fantasy receives its fullest expression is the *Volk*, a romanticized idea of a 'people' or nation as the repository of pure and natural humanity untainted by artifice, civility, or indeed any of the trappings of social life; a reservoir of sheer instinct, untainted even by reflective thought. The *Volk*, says *The Art-Work of the Future*, is 'the plain and innate force of Life . . . unconscious and instinctive by its very nature' (I 79). It stands in the same relation to actual modern society as myth does to circumstantial history: the seminal, archetypal essence underpinning all reality.

Throughout his revolutionary writings, Wagner interprets cultural history as a continual falling-away from art's original and primal identity with the *Volk*. Operatic aria, for example, is a perversion of the healthy expressive spontaneity of folk-song; medieval Christian drama institutionalizes and dogmatizes the *Volk's* original representation of its own nature in its mythological plays; musical counterpoint is a self-consciously artificial, merely playful separation of the polyphonic unity of the *Volk's* voices into individual (and therefore self-serving) parts; and so on. Each new miniature history of society or art thus discovers its true aim in remote antiquity. The late 1840s and early 1850s was the period in Wagner's life when he was most intoxicated with the spirit of classical Athens. In *Art and Revolution*, the 'Grecian people' are the idealized embodiment of a *Volk* who find their communal identity expressed in their own drama. Witnessing his tragic art, the Greek 'found the noblest part of his own nature united with the noblest characteristics of the whole nation' (I 34). The subsequent history of the stage, Wagner writes, has divided individual from community and so destroyed the unity of the *Volk*; the golden age has been lost. (The story of the *Ring*, too, begins with a kind of fall, Alberich's original sin destroying the Rhinedaughters' state of natural exuberance and creating a world of masters and slaves.) The further back his stories go, the more they approach their ideal: a 'revolution' or turn in his revolutionary thinking, bending back to the past in its search for the art-work of the future. Narration is far more than just a technique for explaining things. A power is at work in the process of retracing the past, and this is the power sensed in the background as Mime and the Wanderer play their history-game in *Siegfried* Act I – Mime's failure to keep up drives him to an episode of hallucinatory terror – and wielded so devastatingly by Kundry in *Parsifal* Act II.

By definition, great powers can do a good deal of damage. The search for mythic, original purity is ambiguous even in *Lohengrin* – finding it means expelling it – while by the time of *Parsifal* the whole effort to reconsecrate the pure and atone for sin is presented with dizzying complexity. Wagner's prose writings, as usual, are not quite so subtle. His vision of the *Volk* is clearly a fantasy, as intellectually insubstantial as any addled New Age dream of returning society to nature. It is interesting because of the ideas about the relation between art and audiences which it allows Wagner to imagine. However, it also specifies a national, racial version of purity. Despite the fact that his prose works of this period (1848–51) usually rhapsodize about a universal humanity, undifferentiated by nation, class, gender or race, the very notion of an original purity which has been successively corrupted is a fundamental prop of nationalist and racist thinking. In 'Judaism and Music', Wagner claims that the Jews are in effect the opposite of the *Volk*. (At the end of *The Art-Work of the Future*, he metaphorically identifies the Exodus of the 'Israelites' with the *Volk*'s journey 'towards the Land of Promise', I 210, but this has little to do with his attitude to Judaism.) 'The Jew has never had an Art of his own' (III 90), whereas the *Volk* instinctively and intuitively turns its experience of Nature into art. Nineteenth-century anti-Semitism habitually cast the Jews as rootless cosmopolitans, divided by exile and diaspora from their own origins but also not belonging to the European nations and societies they inhabited. Thoroughly saturated with this stereotype, Wagner concludes that all Jewish expression is false because foreign, and artificial because irrevocably uprooted from its original soil:

> The Jew speaks the language of the nation in whose midst he dwells from generation to generation, but he speaks it always as an alien. . . . only he who has unconsciously grown up within the bond of [a] community, takes also any share in its creations. But the Jew has stood outside the pale

of any such community, stood solitarily with his Jehova in a splintered, soilless stock [*in einem zersplitterten, bodenlosen Volkstamme*], to which all self-sprung evolution [*Entwickelung aus sich*] must stay denied. . . . (III 84)

By definition, Jews are excluded from the natural, self-evolving community represented by Wagner's *Volk*. At once it becomes clear that the purity he fantasizes about everywhere in the revolutionary writings is exclusive, a closed circle of reciprocity between the people and their soil, like the brotherhood of the Grail in *Parsifal*.

This is not simply to point out Wagner's anti-Semitism, over which there is no doubt anyway, nor to argue for the intimate relation between his anti-Semitism and his utopian thinking, a point which has also been fully documented. What matters here is the way Wagner's storytelling tendency always involves more than just reciting or recounting events. It reaches back to visions of a fundamental origin, a numinous past which is a potent source of absolute ideals like 'nature', 'purity', 'humanity' – ideals which have a purely mythic status. Nationalism and anti-Semitism show that these fantasized origins are places of belonging, not just of beginning; places, that is, where (as in the case of Lohengrin) true identity is revealed, and where the proper order of nature is restored against the corruptions of history and civilization. The full importance of Wagner's nationalist and racist myths of belonging will be discussed later, at a point in Wagner's career where his writings meditate explicitly on the purity of blood and on the destiny of the new German *Reich*. These quasi-religious conceptions of sacred communities, with all their attendant political baggage, are, however, already present in the 1850s. Though classical Greece often appears in the revolutionary writings as the archetypal pure, original, ideal place, the version with the strongest hold on Wagner's imagination is the 'German fatherland' to which (at the end of his 1843 'Autobiographic Sketch') he swears 'eternal fidelity' (I 19). The *Volk*, despite its vague universalizing aura, is certainly a specifically German fantasy. Like many of the revolutionaries of the late 1840s, Wagner had imagined that the republican and democratic movements surging through Europe's cities would melt down the splintered kingdoms and grand duchies of the German-speaking people and forge a new, utopian pan-Germanic state. So the pure origin featuring so heavily in the revolutionary writings is a political touchstone, not just a story about how art or society used to be. It is laden with meaning; it is the image of a perfection which Wagner's imagination always circles around. The theme of purity is already dominant in *Tannhäuser* and *Lohengrin*: Elisabeth and Montsalvat both stand for a sacrosanct and inviolable perfection where truth, value and meaning ultimately reside. In the prose works, the notion of origins – the terminus of a journey back into the past – carries the same kind of mystical aura.

Recollecting the past allows history to pass over into myth. As the introduction to the autobiographical narrative of 'A Communication' says, the process of retracing an evolving series of events unlocks their fundamental meaning. For Wagner, this is never a matter of assembling and studying historical evidence in order to interpret the forces that it manifests (that is how historians work, not mythographers). He rewrites history in order to make it reveal its (always entirely Wagnerian) mysteries: the destiny of free humanity, the obliteration of property, the inevitable ascendancy of drama, the reuniting of the arts, or whatever grand secret his writing is in search of at the time. Nowhere is this tendency more obvious than in the craziest of all the writings of this period, *Die Wibelungen: Weltgeschichte aus der Saga* (*The Wibelungen: World-History as Told in Saga*), dating from early 1849. Attempting to synthesize medieval German history with the Nibelung legends, the essay situates itself at an imaginary point where the historical past intersects with myth ('the *Saga of the Nibelungen* is the birth-right of the Frankish stem', VII 262–3). Its flavour is nicely captured by Ellis's bemused summary: for Wagner, 'the [Nibelung] Hoard was also the Grail, and Friedrich [Barbarossa, the Holy Roman Emperor of the twelfth century] was Siegfried, and Siegfried was Baldur, and Baldur was Christ'.[2] Since 1846 Wagner had been meditating plans for an opera (or perhaps a spoken drama) on the life of Friedrich Barbarossa, an icon of German nationalism. In *The Wibelungen* this semi-legendary figure is merged with Wagner's more recent interest in the Siegfried legends, allowing for a translation of an already remote and romantic antiquity into mythic narrative. The Frankish royal family is identified with the Nibelungs, and the destiny of the Teutonic peoples is universalized as a perpetual inheritance of this myth, a heroic urge to 'keep or win the Hoard afresh' (VII 277). In the legendary stories of the sagas, Wagner claims, true history is written: 'Religion and Saga are the pregnant products of the people's insight into the nature of things and men' (VII 266). This faith licenses his attempt to compress a thousand years of history and a diverse range of literary material into a single, continuously unfolding revelation. The effect is exemplified by the comical series of equivalencies in Ellis's thumbnail summary: in myth, every story is analogous to every other, so that they can all be understood as different tellings of one story, held together by one fundamental meaning. Much the same thing happens in *The Art-Work of the Future* and *Opera and Drama*, where every history Wagner tells becomes a sign of the necessary and inevitable ascendancy of perfected drama.

For the revolutionary Wagner, it is ultimately myth rather than history which tells the truth about the past. Myth transcends the constraints and specificities of chronology, imposing its essential permanence on the phenomena of passing time. In other words, myth allows for misrepresentations and simplifications of history, which at their foulest extreme result in the kind of stereotyping and scapegoating demonstrated by habitual references in

'Judaism in Music' to 'our natural repugnance against the Jewish nature' (III 81). Wagner's imagination always searches for condensed representations of what it wants to explore. This might seem paradoxical, given the notoriously gigantic dimensions of his work – thick volumes, long operas, huge orchestras. The force of mythic material, though, lies in the disproportionate weight of its significance in relation to its content. Density is more important to Wagner, and more characteristic of him, than mass. His one exercise in 'historical' opera of the sort perfected by Spontini, Halévy and Meyerbeer is *Rienzi*, the longest of his scores (in its original version). Its size, though, comes (as in Meyerbeerian grand opera) from its wealth of incident; it's full of the crowdedness of history. The starker outlines of legend shape Wagner's more characteristic operas, where far less happens than in *Rienzi* but the density of conception and expression is infinitely greater. (*Die Meistersinger* is in this as in so many other respects an exception.) At its most powerful – for good or ill – his imagination cuts through the nuance and intertexture of history and establishes instead the monolithic bulk of myth. The 'whole strength of the portrayal', he writes in 'A Communication', 'could be concentrated on a few weighty and decisive moments of development' (I 367).

In the prose writings, this strategy works as a useful way of cementing his interpretations of history, finding the heart of the matter. *The Art-Work of the Future* reaches its climax by recasting its closing meditations on the role of the *Volk* as artist into the form of a legend (legendary tales being 'the ever fresh and ever truthful *poems of the Folk*', I 210). Wagner relates the story of Wieland the Smith, which he was at the time planning to turn into an opera. This brief narrative, he finally claims, contains the secret of the *Volk*'s nature and destiny: 'O sole and glorious Folk! . . . Thou art thyself this Wieland!' (I 213). At the beginning of the essay he had posed as the 'weightiest of questions' the problem: 'Who is then the Folk?' (I 74). By answering this question with the Wieland story, he performs the utterly characteristic manoeuvre of turning a problem about historical identity (who and where are the true people in whose name the revolution must be fought?) into a solution drawn entirely from legend. Which is as much as to say that it is an entirely fictional solution: Wagner would always rather tell stories than histories. The sacrifice of accuracy, though, brings with it a gain in power. This is the trade-off involved in myth, which our modern-day usage of the word preserves: take for example the phrase 'urban myth', which has come to refer to things which are not true but which everyone knows and takes for truth. Again, at its darkest this imbalance is the foundation of fascism, which imbues its lies with sheer atavistic force and so compels assent to them. Though there is of course a huge and important difference between Wagner's storytelling and mere propaganda, it's nevertheless true that he understands that narrative has far more elemental powers than simply the ability to recall what happened.

When he narrates his own career to date in the autobiographical section of 'A Communication', his own history as an artist is transformed into a quest for essential origins and powers. Each creative act, as he narrates it here, is an instance of the same compulsion: 'I must go back to the unadulterated Mythos' (I 360). The moment of discovering the Tannhäuser material is described as a revelation of the mythic *kernel* of history, its 'inner soul' as opposed to its 'endless trickery of outer [appearances]' (*unendlich bunter, äußerlicher Zerstreutheit*). It saves him from the seductions of mere history:

> . . . I was on the point of harking back, more or less, to the road of my *Rienzi*, and again writing a 'historical Grand Opera in five acts'; only the overpowering subject of Tannhäuser, grappling [*erfassende*] my individual nature with far more energetic hold, kept my footsteps firm upon the path which Necessity had bid me strike. (I 315)

The same victory is won when he comes across the medieval poem *Lohengrin*. Its first impression, he says, brought with it the trappings of historical costume drama, 'carved and painted saints and martyrs on the highways, or in the churches, of Catholic lands'. Gradually all these phenomena of medieval times and places fade away, leaving 'the myth of Lohengrin in its simpler traits . . . the genuine poem of the Folk'. He moves the story out of its chivalric Christian context and back into a primal, original space: it is 'one of man's earliest poetic ideals' (I 333). With the ability to identify different narratives as aspects of the same myth (Barbarossa equals Siegfried equals Baldur equals Christ) that drew the respect of Claude Lévi-Strauss, he goes on to narrate the Greek story of Zeus and Semele in order to show that *Lohengrin* is the same 'Mythos of the Folk' (I 335). A little further on in his career, 'A Communication' goes on to relate, he found himself faced with a choice between Friedrich Barbarossa and Siegfried as subjects for a new opera: 'Once again . . . did Myth and History stand before me with opposing claims'. The Barbarossa material represents a historical version of German national destiny, but, Wagner says, by reading the Nibelung sagas 'I sank myself into the primal element' of the idea of the German homeland (I 357). His immersion is a reverse journey through history:

> . . . I drove step by step into the deeper regions of antiquity, where at last to my delight, and truly in the *utmost* reaches of old time, I was to light upon the fair young form of *Man*. . . . My studies thus bore me, through the legends of the Middle Ages, right down to their foundation in the old-Germanic Mythos [*des alten urdeutschen Mythos*]; one [layer] after another, which the later legendary lore had bound around it, I was able to unloose, and thus at last to gaze upon it. . . . (I 357–8)

This sounds like an intellectual version of the quest for the Holy Grail. Wagner pierces through obstacle after shielding obstacle, persevering to the uttermost

limits of his search, where finally the radiant object of his desire is revealed
to him. It has been wrapped and hidden by the sedimentary deposits of
history (the '*later* legendary lore'), but the heroic archaeologist peels them
away in order to view the essence of 'Man' unclouded by all such obscuring
details. As the composition of the *Ring* poem shows, narration can find its
way to the origin of everything if it pursues its reverse course relentlessly
enough.

Not content with a retrospective autobiographical account of Wagner's
career as a search for myth, 'A Communication to My Friends' also mythol-
ogizes that career. That is, as well as narrating his quest for meaning it is itself
a revisionary quest, because it retrospectively revises the significance of the
three earlier operas in the light of its own effort to demonstrate the consistent evolution of Wagner the man and artist. As already mentioned, its aim
is to make the composer of *Der fliegende Holländer*, *Tannhäuser* and *Lohengrin*
look like the author of *Opera and Drama* and the progenitor of the Nibelung
tetralogy. The past has to be brought into line with the utopian future. Vision
thus requires revision. There cannot be any doubt that Wagner's three 'romantic' operas, however formally and imaginatively original, are saturated in the
aesthetics of that genre as it had developed in the early decades of the century.
This is precisely what 'A Communication' denies, though. It rewrites the
meaning of all three in accordance with its myth of the Wagnerian quest –
most astonishingly in the case of *Lohengrin*, where it actually comes up with
a brilliant and subversive interpretation, discarding the work's obvious fascination with the swan knight's mysterious holiness and siding instead with Elsa,
'this glorious woman, before whom Lohengrin must vanish, for reason that
his own specific nature could not understand her' (I 347). The heroine is rein-
terpreted to fit Wagner's current notions of fundamental meaning. 'She was
the Spirit of the Folk', he now says (I 347–8), and she leads him to the buried
primal myth, to Siegfried: 'It was "Elsa" who had taught me to unearth this
man' (I 375). Wagner even acknowledges here that he did not at the time of
composition in the 1840s fully understand the meaning of his own operas:
'this treasure trove of Knowledge lay hid, at first, within the silence of my
lonely heart: only slowly did it ripen into loud avowal' (I 348). He could
hardly be more explicit: true meaning is found only in retrospect, in autobiographical narration, in the archaeology of myth which uncovers what lies
'hid'.

At 'one blow', he writes, Elsa 'made me a Revolutionary' (I 347). But the
tale told in 'A Communication' is the very opposite of revolution. Given the
essay's stated aim of explaining the apparent disparity between Wagner's earlier
works and his post-1849 theorizing, what could have been easier and more
obvious than to portray 1849 as a revolutionary moment, when the past is
left behind and a new future appears? 'A Communication' could perfectly
easily have described the pattern of his career in such a way. From a

biographical point of view, in fact, this might well have looked like a more accurate account. Wagner's work before 1849 is visibly a product of existing operatic conventions, while after the revolution he strikes out in unprecedented directions and constantly breaks new ground. Yet the essay chooses to assert that no revolution took place. Instead, its myth is one of evolution. It seeks out the unchanging, essential, primal force of Wagner's creative life, developing continuously according to its own laws, its own Young Hegelian necessity. True, he refers to his embrace of the Nibelung material as 'an altogether novel path', the 'turning-point of my artistic course' (I 366, 367); but this apparent revolution is in fact (so the story goes in 'A Communication') really the next evolutionary stage in the line of development traced by the earlier operas. By revising the past in this manner, it claims that Elsa leads to Siegfried, *Lohengrin* to *Rheingold*, smoothly bridging the gap between 1848 and 1853.

Even in the altogether more worldly and historically-minded autobiographical narrative of *My Life*, written in the 1860s at the request of King Ludwig II, moments of origin are touched by myth. All the well-known stories of sudden inspiration – the *Rheingold* prelude appearing in a waking dream at La Spezia, the inspiration for *Meistersinger* arriving as Wagner stood in front of Titian's *Assumption* in the Frari church in Venice, *Parsifal* conceived on waking one fine Good Friday morning near Zurich – have an appropriately numinous air. Finding beginnings is a magical kind of storytelling. This is Kundry's secret: all but ageless herself, she conducts Parsifal back to his origin by giving him the name he didn't know he had. It is also the secret of the grief-struck *alte Weise*, 'old tune', of *Tristan* Act III, which both returns Tristan to consciousness (at the beginning of the act) and returns him to his fated birth. Like all the writings of the years between *Lohengrin* and *Rheingold*, 'A Communication' gestures towards the future: 'I now, as man and artist, press on to meet a newer world' (I 366). However, it knows more clearly than all the others that its most searching gaze is turned the other way. Narrative, not prophecy, is where meaning is found. It takes Wagner's revolutionary writings a long time to realize this, distracted as they are by their mistaken faith in a world to come. Nor should we underestimate Wagner's capacity for such faith (it accounts at least for his quite remarkable power to get himself in debt: indebtedness being a kind of act of faith in futurity). His ability to imagine the unimaginable shows itself everywhere, in his musical language, his political projects, even in his stage directions. Despite the vast originality of his conceptions, though, his is a peculiarly conservative art, or at least a nostalgic one. It dreams always of return. Tannhäuser goes home, Lohengrin goes home, Tristan goes home, Parsifal finds his way back. The pull of beginnings is more powerful than the promise of finales. So Wagner finds his material in myth, stories effectively consecrated by their antiquity; the bustling

sixteenth century of *Die Meistersinger* seems disconcertingly modern by comparison. At its most baleful, his appeal is purely regressive. The worst kind of
love of Wagner's art celebrates a retreat into romantic fantasy. King Ludwig
appears not to have been able to rid himself of those fantasies, while the Nazi
ideologues who exalted Wagner were playing on the obscure, atavistic power
of his immersion in Germanic myth.

With 'A Communication', Wagner's 'revolution' completes itself. It turns
around fully, closing the circle by explaining the future through a retelling of
the past, and interpreting that narration in turn as a path towards 'the final
fitting form [*die wahrhaft entsprechende vollende Form*]' of his creative essence,
the Nibelung project (I 391). Everything hinges on the narrative act, the
telling of the story. Without it, the past is just a series of mistakes that have
been left behind, while the future is (as we have seen) only a chimerical
dream. At the beginning of the (in)famous narration in *Walküre* Act II where
this chapter began, Wotan implies rather cryptically that what he is about to
say has been rescued from oblivion by his words:

Was keinem in Worten ich künde,	What I tell no one in words,
unausgesprochen	let it then remain
bleib' es denn ewig. . . .	unspoken for ever. . . .

This appears to be an oblique command to Brünnhilde not to repeat anything he will say; as Patrice Chéreau understood, Wotan is telling himself his
own tale. It also suggests, though, that his narration is not so much a recital
of the past as a conjuration of it. The mirror Chéreau placed in front of Wotan
in this scene is like Klingsor's mirror in Act II of *Parsifal*, imbued with the
power of summoning. Without his narrative, Wotan seems to say, nothing
happens. Accordingly, as the scene progresses the events he describes come to
life again. They do so orchestrally; the above words are sung to the bare
accompaniment of a deep E in the bass strings, and as Wotan proceeds the
musical texture mutates with him, a series of leitmotifs rising out of that bleak
foundation, recalling and representing each part of the story. This of course
is why Hanslick was so utterly wrong about the monologue. It lays out the
power of narration in Wagner's imagination more clearly than any other
example, because the interwoven sequence of musical motifs effectively
recreates the contents of the narrative. The orchestra allows us to feel what
happens as the 'unspoken' turns into speech. Instead of simply reproducing a
series of events in language, the monologue binds the past and future together
just as the autobiography of 'A Communication' does. Its music makes recollection visible, potent and dramatic: something is *happening* in the scene, the
score forces us to realize; it isn't just the repetition of things that have already
happened.

This is elusive territory, as always when one approaches the question of what music actually does. In chapters 5 and 6 of the third part of *Opera and Drama*, Wagner's thought (along with his prose) seems to become almost hopelessly tangled and obscure as he works to explain how it becomes possible for music, whose domain is 'the Unspeakable' (*das Unaussprechliche*), actually to speak, to narrate. The technique which achieves this, he argues, is the precise deployment of 'prophetic or reminiscent melodic-moments' ('ahnungs- oder erinnerungsvollen melodischen Momente', II 346): what have become known as leitmotifs. Either recollecting or anticipating '*the weightiest motives* of the drama' (II 347), these musical themes are meant to perform the role of storytelling as it is set out in Wagner's revolutionary writings. 'At their hand', he says, 'we become the constant fellow-knowers [*Mitwissern*] of the profoundest secret of the poet's Aim, the immediate partners in its realisement' (II 346). Like myth, motivic composition at once captures and fulfils the essential meaning of a story. The inexhaustibly subtle and fertile use of leitmotif is of course one of the most 'revolutionary' features of the *Ring*, and in this case, finally, 'revolutionary' is the right word. Leitmotif is (as Wagner struggles to say in these chapters of *Opera and Drama*) a mode of unifying time, making aural memories and anticipations bend the otherwise linear unfolding of a musical event into a perpetually circling structure. Motivic themes are

> Melodic Moments . . . in which we remember a Foreboding [*Ahnung*], whilst they turn our Remembrance into a prophecy [*Ahnung*]. . . . (II 347)

They twist time into a ring. Anticipation, memory and prophecy are bound together by leitmotif's power to predict and recollect dramatic action at an instinctive, non-verbal level. With the mastery of motivic composition, Wagner's understanding of the power unleashed by narration is at its most acute.

CHAPTER EIGHT

Staging the Past

One could summarize the revolutionary moment in Wagner's career as a composer by saying that between *Lohengrin* and *Das Rheingold*, music changes from an art of space into an art of time. Romantic opera (as discussed in Part I) is all about creating and exploring exotic space. *Der fliegende Holländer*, with its vividly pictorial orchestral effects and its juxtaposition of opposed worlds, is thoroughly imbued with this sense of musical geography, and in *Tannhäuser* and *Lohengrin* the dynamic tension between different locations – Venusberg, Wartburg, Montsalvat – energizes the scores' musical resources. *Lohengrin* in particular revels in that imaginative use of sonority in which, to use Adorno's expression (anticipated in *Parsifal* by Gurnemanz), 'time seems transfixed in space'.[1] Wagner's matchlessly vivid evocation of orchestral 'colour' is, as the word itself indicates, the musical equivalent of painting, an art which opens the visual dimension but more or less completely closes off the temporal. But the stress of revolution is exerted in the field of time. The vistas conjured up by a revolutionary imagination are prospects of futurity, not static landscapes of fantasy. Its watchword is change. Operatic romanticism draws attention to the difference between *here* and *there* (the stage brings to life all that which is unlike the world around it). Revolution, by contrast, speaks of the difference between *now* and *then* – which is why post-revolutionary regimes often create a new calendar, starting again at year one. *Tannhäuser* and *Lohengrin* are operas about here and there ('In fernem Land . . .', 'in a distant land'), but the *Ring* concerns itself with nows and thens: 'weißt du was daraus wird?', 'do you know what will become of that?' Its geographies are curiously vague and dreamlike. The spatial relationships have the fluidity and naïveté of myth, captured best when Siegfried asks whether Fafner's cave is 'nicht weit von der Welt', 'not far from the world'. Except perhaps in *Rheingold*, with its sharper vertical and perspectival organization – Nibelheim below, the river in between, the gods' world above, Valhalla in the background – we never know precisely where we are in the tetralogy. Yet, thanks to the constant recapitulation of events in narration, we are always intensely aware of *when* in the story we are. Time is no longer transfixed: the revolutions of Wotan's 'rolling wheel' have unfolded and freed it.

When one hears mention of Wagner's 'revolutionary' musical techniques and achievements, it's usually in the context of the future – of advancement, that is; Wagner makes the history of music progress. He frees opera from its dependence on closed, periodic forms and sequential 'numbers'; he begins to move the language of music out of the grammar of classical tonality; these and other familiar components of his originality are well known. Even in his own day, after the publication of his writings of the late 1840s and early 1850s, his art and his principles were popularly summarized under the label *Zukunftsmusik*, the music of the future, anticipating the vision of Wagner as a composer far ahead of his time. So he was: but he himself objected repeatedly and publicly to the popular label, and to the idea that he represented an avant-garde 'school' or tendency in music. It is a telling fact that the music of *Tristan*, which in many ways represents most obviously the aspect of his art that is 'revolutionary' in the progressive, forward-looking sense, was not supposed to blaze a trail into the future. Unlike the self-consciously experimental composers who at the end of the century would further stretch the boundaries of tonality and harmony, Wagner did not aim to be radical. *Tristan* was begun with the aim of producing a popular, easily performable work to bring in some royalties during work on the apparently unperformable *Ring*. As musically revolutionary as it is, then, it was not produced with an eye on the future. The same is true for many of Wagner's other drastic innovations. Like the harmonic language of *Tristan*, they are technical manifestations of his habitual urge towards expressive intensity, not attempts to revolutionize a genre per se.

As I have argued in this section, it is actually impossible for Wagner in this period to work towards the future. To this extent, then, the revolutionary quality of his music – in the *Ring* at least – has to be understood in the light of that other meaning of the word. The crucial musical achievement of these years is the discovery of a way of making music articulate the turnings of time, bending in on itself to create chronological structures – what *Opera and Drama* calls structures of reminiscence and foreboding. Music can thus tell stories, rather than simply functioning as a dazzlingly gorgeous palette for making pictures. In a more banal sense, music has always been an art of time: rhythm and sequence are its elements. But by saying that music in the *Ring* becomes an art of time, we're referring to something other than the architecture of musical form. What Wagner discovers is a way to make his score an agent of the power of narration. Music can participate in unfolding those essential relationships between *now* and *then*.

Chapters 5 and 6 of the last part of *Opera and Drama* go into quite explicit theoretical detail about how to achieve musical narrative. As always, though, the risk of attending to such details is that one begins to compare them with the existing scores, looking to see if the *Ring* matches the book's prescriptions. More important than the correspondence (or otherwise) between theory and practice is the fundamental principle involved in thinking of music in this way. That principle is captured in a casual remark in *My Life*. Wagner is recollecting (probably in 1869) his work on the orchestration of *Die Walküre* in 1855–6, the point at which he began to be distracted from progress with the tetralogy by thoughts of other projects. Sustained work on *Tristan* began in 1856, and the *Parsifal* material is occasionally mentioned in documents of the time. 1856 also saw the beginning of serious interest in a Buddhist drama of renunciation and enlightenment, *Die Sieger* (*The Victors*), which continued to occupy his imagination for another decade. The autobiography describes this subject's appeal in very striking terms:

> Apart from the beauty and profound significance of the simple tale, I was influenced to choose it as much by its peculiar aptness for the musical procedures that I have since developed. To the mind of the Buddha, the previous lives in former incarnations of every being appearing before him stand revealed as clearly as the present. The simple story owed its significance to the way that the past life of the suffering principal characters was entwined in the new phase of their lives as being still present time. I perceived at once how the musical remembrance of this dual life, keeping the past constantly present in the hearing, might be represented perfectly. . . . (*ML* 528–9)

Music is here granted an extraordinary double vision: its *now* is also a *then*, it bends the passage of time (as does the Buddhist idea of reincarnation, often symbolized by a wheel or ring) so that the present recuperates and includes the past. The future is notably absent. Wagner has at last rid himself of the distraction of futurity, a mirage which evaporates whenever he looks at it even in openly prophetic documents like *The Art-Work of the Future*. One could in fact make the same argument about the chapters of *Opera and Drama* dealing with music and time. Though they appear to give equal weight to reminiscence (the music of the past) and foreboding (the music of the future), the forebodings really turn out to be upside-down reminiscences; music always narrates, never prophesies. (Remember that Wagner always vehemently denied that he was inventing 'the music of the future'.) There's no need to wrestle with the theoretical prose, though. As always, the dramatically creative imagination is pithier and stronger. Thinking about *Die Sieger* enables Wagner to intuit the relation between music and reincarnation far more tellingly, and to focus on the 'revolutionary' (that is, time-turning) power of his scores – the art of 'keeping the past constantly present in the hearing'.

Alberich's curse is the event which pulls the *Ring* back towards itself even
as it recedes further into the past. When the circle at last closes around
Siegfried, amid the white heat of Act III of *Götterdämmerung*, the full force of
music's double vision reveals itself. Siegfried dies in the past. Up to this
moment of blindingly deluded recollection, he has not had a past: he rejects
the one Mime tries to concoct for him, refuses to listen to either Fafner or
Wotan when they tell him something of his prehistory, and is utterly bewil-
dered when the newly-wakened Brünnhilde also speaks of it. 'Nicht kann ich
das Ferne/ sinnig erfassen', he replies to her: 'my senses cannot lay hold of
distant things'. Hagen's potion is more or less redundant: it wipes away a
memory that had shown no signs of being able to retain anything anyway. As
his own words confess, what is out of his sight is out of his mind – until he
is stabbed with Hagen's spear. Then in an instant he is transported to *das
Ferne*, things far-away in both space and time:

Brünnhilde –	Brünnhilde –
heilige Braut –	holy bride –
wach' auf! öff'ne dein Auge! –	awake! Open your eyes! –
Wer verschloß dich	Who has closed you
wieder in Schlaf?	in sleep again?
Wer band dich in Schlummer so bang? –	Who has bound you so fearfully in slumber?
Der Wecker kam;	The awakener has come;
er küßt dich wach,	he kisses you awake
und aber der Braut	and again he breaks
bricht' er die Bande: –	the bride's bonds: –
da lacht' ihm Brünnhilde's Lust! . . .	Brünnhilde's joy laughs upon him!

The words indicate a *re*-awakening. Siegfried's fantasy is that he has returned
to perform his deed a second time. The music, though, belies him. It repeats,
as literally as possible given the different words, the sounds accompanying the
moment in Act III of *Siegfried* to which his memory has now turned: the
series of three tense chords with their increasingly ecstatic resolutions shimmering with the sounds of harps and high tremolo violins. Brünnhilde's awakening is pulled out of the narrative past and now happens again. In relation
to Siegfried's words, the repetition is poignantly ironic; Siegfried is (at last)
remembering what he should have known all along, but his dream of renew-
ing his love for Brünnhilde is only a deathbed fantasy.

Music works differently. It possesses the stage too fully to be understood
simply as the echo of Siegfried's deluded memory. It is not (ironically) *remembering* the past: it is *recreating* it. Brünnhilde actually now reawakens (in fact
the next words we hear after Siegfried breathes his last are Gutrune's nervous

account of how the Valkyrie has left her room in the night). The score refuses to see Siegfried's murder as the end of what began with his kiss in *Siegfried* Act III; it speaks with the same convulsive joy on both occasions, insisting that hero and heroine are united by death as fully as they were by love. After the grim fury of Act II, both of them are released from Hagen's enchantment as they were from Wotan's at the end of *Siegfried*, and the solemn celebration that ends the tetralogy can now get under way. More telling, though, is the way the score allows this to happen by reversing the onward flow of narrative. By accompanying Siegfried's death with the very music of Brünnhilde's birth (as a mortal being), it effectively undoes all the intervening disasters. Like the Buddha's gaze, it establishes the endurance of the past in the present. Tragedy is founded on the irreversibility of time: once things start going wrong they can't go right again. In Wagner's hands, however, music can not only remember what has passed but repeat it, keeping it (in the phrase from *My Life*) 'constantly present' rather than inevitably absent. There's no irony in the upward rush of the violins at Siegfried's 'wach' auf!' or the excited pulsing of the massed wind as he relives the kiss that wakes Brünnhilde, any more than there was in the identical passages in *Siegfried* Act III. Having fixed the ecstatic climax of Siegfried's career in these sounds in the earlier opera, the score can make it happen again, defying Hagen's apparently successful conspiracy. We thus find ourselves watching two moments at once, the *now* of Siegfried and Brünnhilde's oblivion and separation and the *then* of their mutual discovery and triumph. Music asserts a relationship between the two events which would otherwise be unimaginable. Contradicting the dramatic logic which tells us that one is the opposite of the other, as victory is to defeat, it makes them sound and feel the same, so that at the very moment of Siegfried's death he receives the full benediction of the past he had abandoned.

Two scenes of narration flank Siegfried's remarkable dying speech, both in their different ways demonstrating that telling stories in the *Ring* is far more than just a matter of communicating what has happened. The first is Siegfried's gradual recovery of his memory, during which he replays the events of *Siegfried* and so brings himself closer and closer to the doubled moment of Brünnhilde's awakening and his own death; the second is the funeral march, which conjures tremendous dramatic emphasis out of a surprisingly linear (and, by the standards of *Götterdämmerung*, relatively unsubtle) presentation of leitmotifs, recollecting the dead hero's history. Together, these scenes constitute a kind of saga. They see Siegfried, that is, through the eye of narrative, as someone about whom stories are told – not as the all-action hero idealized in *The Art-Work of the Future* and followed through the events of *Siegfried*. In the third part of the tetralogy, his nature is unreflecting, spontaneous, naïve immediacy. He says and does whatever comes to mind, and every occasion which presents him with an opportunity for thought or even choice is skimmed over with a kind of brutish dismissiveness. Wagner personally appears to have found these characteristics charming and indeed morally healthy. They chime with his view of the *Volk* ('With the Folk, all is reality and deed', I 135) as a pure force of nature unhindered by intellect, judgment or reason. Yet, by the merciful alchemy which transmutes the banality of his thinking every time it appears on stage, *Siegfried* the opera shows its hero as a figure diminished by the one-dimensionality of action. He *does* things, unstoppably – killing Fafner is child's play, no easier or harder than trying to cut a reed-pipe – but his actions are like the plots of those extravagant Meyerbeerian grand operas Wagner so deeply despised: superficial and empty, performed without understanding or meaning. The consequences of this foolishness are worked out in the first two acts of *Götterdämmerung* (and in *Parsifal*, one might add). Only in Act III does Siegfried's story change from action to narration. Prompted by Hagen (with malicious intent of course), he returns to Act I of *Siegfried* and runs through the plot of that opera again. Now, though, he is saying it, not living it, and as the scene proceeds it turns out that instead of him constructing the story, the story is actually reconstructing him, reassembling itself in such a way that he is finally able to know what it has been about.

Motivic composition is the agent of this change. In the most simplistic version of how leitmotif works in narration, we expect a straightforward correlation between the story narrated in a character's speech and the appearance of appropriate motivic material in the orchestra. Parts of Wotan's monologue in Act II of *Die Walküre* work more or less like this, although the steady interweaving of the motif particularly associated with him at this point (sometimes known as 'Wotan's frustration'), as well as the controlled gradual acceleration of the monologue overall, prevent it from ever having the effect of motifs merely strung together following the text. However, the section where he summarizes the events staged in *Das Rheingold* is accompanied by motifs associated with Alberich (and malice generally), the gold, the ring, Valhalla, and Erda, each appearing bare and self-contained around the vocal line, very much as if they were no more than illustrations. Siegfried's tale right before his death employs leitmotif with far more subtlety than this. Music does not merely provide the content of the story (Alberich → gold → ring → Valhalla → Erda). It is now the medium through which the individual elements *become a story*, in the sense described in the previous chapter: that is, a purposeful and meaningful narration of events. This is what makes it possible for Siegfried to change from someone who just enacts the plot – doing one thing after another, as directed by wiser instructors, and even the woodbird is wiser than him – into someone who tells the plot and so begins to understand it.

The scene clearly sets him up as a narrator. Prompted by Hagen to entertain the rest of the hunting party with a story, he announces 'so sing' ich dir Mären/ aus meinen jungen Tagen', 'I will sing you tales from my youthful days'. This is a formal performance in front of an audience: the men gather around him and punctuate his tale with eager questions. Music therefore has two roles. It supplies the straightforwardly illustrative motivic content, as in the passage from Wotan's narration; in this case, the sequence is (roughly) motifs associated with Nibelung smithing (representing Mime), Mime's 'starling song', Nothung, the tragic aspect of the Wälsung race (the mournful, stately motif prominent in *Walküre* Act I), the forest murmurs and the woodbird, Siegfried and Brünnhilde's mutual love, the magic fire and the magic sleep, and the lovers' destiny (the so-called 'world's inheritance' motif) – more or less a parallel version of the tale Siegfried recounts. However, music also and more importantly functions to convert this merely sequential content (Mime → Nothung → the forest → Brünnhilde) into a performance of storytelling, giving a simple series of events the cogency and the dramatic thrust of a tale. (Think of the difference between a list of chapter headings in a novel and the novel itself: one just outlines what is going to happen, like the purely illustrative use of leitmotif, but in the other we get to see it happening.) This is achieved by a brilliant use of markedly, urgently rhythmic motivic material. After a brief silence following Hagen's formal injunction to start ('So singe, Held!', 'So sing, hero!'), the story begins with a strong staccato statement of the Nibelung/smithing/Mime motif, which is essentially percussive, a rhythmic not melodic idea. The motif creates an emphatic and stable 6/8 metrical context, so that when Siegfried begins to sing he sounds as if he is reciting a ballad. Music is carrying him along, filling his words with a sense of movement. His story feels as though it is going somewhere, driven by the rhythmic impulse established at its start. As he reaches the point in the tale telling of his victory over the dragon, there is a brief slackening of the pace. Quickly, though, the strong metrical structure is re-established by rapid arpeggiated figures in the strings, a rippling, rocking movement which eventually shapes itself into the soft and steady pulsing of the forest murmur music. One gets a sense of how this rhythmic impulse shapes the music as a whole from the transformation it works on the Wälsung motif, here first played by a clarinet at Siegfried's words 'Wunder muß ich euch melden' ('I must tell you a marvel'). In Act I of *Die Walküre*, where it features so markedly, the motif always has an elegiac, solemn breadth, accompanying Siegmund's stories like a sigh. But in Siegfried's tale it is three times smoothly matched to the fast-flowing string figures, bringing out its own rocking quality, making it less a sigh than a song. Motivic references to the past are not just being quoted; they become incorporated into the new unfolding of Siegfried's life in his tale, part of the present moment. Under the steady pressure of the controlling rhythm, that life is – at last – gaining a direction.

There is a brief pause for Hagen to refresh Siegfried's memory, and the musical flow is slowed and unsettled by the eerie motif of magic transformation (initially related to the Tarnhelm). Briefly, an inertia comes over the score. The clarinets play a muted, slow, hesitant version of a motif whose heroic form in the first scene of *Götterdämmerung* Act I seems to represent Siegfried as 'Brünnhilde's arm'. Then the pace is resumed by another extraordinarily subtle piece of motivic integration. The Wälsung motif already heard in the tale appears again in the cor anglais. Its rhythmic shape has been strongly established in the scene, and now Wagner discovers that it bears a striking likeness to the sweetly leaping motif connected with Brünnhilde in *Götterdämmerung* (also marked by an ascending sixth). The latter melody springs up in the cellos as if it has evolved from the former. There is a clear sense of a thread having been picked up, the motif from the earlier part of the tale now generating its resumption. At the level of semiotic signification (what the leitmotifs 'refer to', as it were) this is a crucial moment, since (as Hagen knows) the hidden secret of Siegfried's tale is his forgotten love for Brünnhilde, and the score has at last discovered her music, setting him on the final path to exposing his own treachery by recollecting that love. Again, though, the storytelling function of the brief musical episode is more important. Where inertia threatened to halt the progress of the story and prevent Siegfried from fully reassembling his life, the smooth flow of one motif into another breathes rhythmic life back into his narration, leading him towards the final goal. The 'Brünnhilde' motif sets Siegfried singing again, and as it fades the divided strings resume the swift and steady rocking of the forest music. Now, though, as the motif suggests, the overall direction of this steady movement has become clear. The narrative is leading inexorably towards the recovery of Brünnhilde. Siegfried is now remembering, narrating and quoting the woodbird's words telling him of the sleeping maid surrounded by fire.

By this stage, music has taken over the function of memory. Siegfried hardly knows what he is remembering or saying. His usual spontaneous naïveté obviously prevents him from reflecting on the consequences of telling this part of his tale, but here his innocence (or ignorance) has gone a stage further: he's lost in his own narrative. The orchestra is slowly weaving the tapestry of his life back together again for him, its softly relentless metrical flow acting like a stream on which he is helplessly carried. Yet if Siegfried is lost in the past here, no longer aware of where he is and whom he's talking to, it is also true that he is finding himself in the present. His narration is giving him back his life as he tells it, rediscovering everything he forgot. Music's narrative impulse assembles the continuity and purpose of his story, linking its parts together as only narration can. He never understands the thread of his own existence until, in this scene, music turns it into a continuously moving story. So the rippling figures of the forest murmurs now merge smoothly into the rapid sextuplets and tremolo strings of the fire music, once again not just following the simple sequence of *then* (Siegfried went from the forest to the fiery mountain) but sustaining the rhythmic imperative of *now* (Siegfried is swiftly approaching the climax of his tale and the realization of his identity). Whereas at the beginning of the tale the metrical shape of the Nibelung motif served to define the song-like structure of Siegfried's recitation, the priorities have gradually been reversed; the orchestral texture is now rich and compelling, swamping the hero's sense of tale-telling. Effectively, the narration has turned into a re-enactment. The tale has reorganized and redirected Siegfried's past, and now his past has become 'present in the hearing' (the phrase from *My Life* again) and he is reliving it, its true purpose at last evident to him. The gradual process of recovery through narration is completed with the exquisite harmonic modulation over the word 'schlafend', as his story finally reaches Brünnhilde. Wind, horns and harp fill the score with ravishing, rapturous breadth and airiness. Siegfried, this music tells us, is no longer telling a story – or rather, storytelling has reached its zenith and made the past fully present. The orchestra isn't now incorporating motifs into narrative, but depicting the place narrative was trying to get to. So the driving rhythmic impulse disappears, because its goal has been reached. It has propelled Siegfried to his mountaintop: *back* to his mountaintop, one feels one should say, but in an important sense he is now there for the first time because (having forgotten his first stunned encounter with her) he now knows that Brünnhilde was the true goal of all his adventures. The story has reached its end. Consequently, Siegfried will in a few moments be dead; but 'end' also means purpose or aim, and his story has achieved that too, consummating itself in Brünnhilde's love. These two versions of his 'end' now coexist – hence his dying speech, when he is at once awakening his bride and expiring alone.

Left to itself after that speech, music decides to go back once more over Siegfried's past. The sequence of motifs in the funeral march adds up to something like an orchestral biography: two Wälsung-related melodic ideas familiar from Act I of *Walküre*, Sieglinde's music, Siegmund and Sieglinde's love, Nothung, two themes belonging to Siegfried (the one used prophetically in *Walküre* Act III and the horn-call), a lethargic version of *Götterdämmerung's* Brünnhilde motif, the curse. (As always with leitmotif, there could be other ways of describing details of the sequence, but the overall outline is unambiguous.) However, the march treats time and history in a manner utterly unlike Siegfried's tale. One can sense the difference intuitively. In the narration, the process of remembering the past is wound tight with dramatic tension, as the score gradually draws Siegfried towards the climax of his life, but the march summarizes that life with an audible sense of finality, heavy and monumental after the tale's atmosphere of fluid progression. This is partly to do with the way the march is punctuated by a series of tremendous repetitions of the simple four-note rhythm first given pianissimo on the timpani immediately after Siegfried's last words. These blaring climaxes dominate the march, and the intervening motivic 'biography' is interrupted and overwhelmed by their fatal reiteration. As the march proceeds, the motifs themselves tend to take on the same heavy, monumental quality as the four-note figure. They broaden out in tempo and are scored for ringing brass, and they loom hugely over the orchestral texture. Treated this way, the Nothung motif first and then the melody of Siegfried's horn-call appear less as elements of an unfolding story than as images graven on a tomb, grand but static. This, in fact, is the transformation the march as a whole works upon motivic tale-telling. If its musical sequence looks in outline like a biography, it is biographical only in the sense of an epitaph: a fixed and final inscription of a completed life. The march rears itself up as lapidary as a tombstone: this is what makes it such a reliable extract or 'highlight' from the *Ring*, because it freezes the play of motivic reminiscence into a single, monumental musical event. It's very rare nowadays to see the passage staged as an actual funerary procession, as Wagner's stage directions demand, and this reflects our feeling about the music, which seems to halt all motion in order to deliver its final testimony to the fallen hero. Leitmotif here works by gathering up the past and presenting it as a finished history rather than a dynamic sequence.

Put next to each other, the march and Siegfried's tale demonstrate the opposite extremes of Wagner's art of time. One unfurls the past in the present moment, allowing narration to reoccupy and relive *das Ferne*, far-off and forgotten things; the other is the music of death, recalling the past only as a series of events now terminated (just as the corpse of a hero embodies the completion and extinction of everything he has been and done). Between the two poles lies an astonishing range of resources. What the *Ring* does away with entirely is the conventional notion that musical drama proceeds from moment to moment, event to event, aria to duet to finale, the music at each point expressing or characterizing whatever stage the drama has reached. (Although there are admittedly stretches of *Das Rheingold* which have this effect: the moment when the gods grow old, for example, or Donner's thunderings in the final scene.) Instead it creates a kind of four-dimensional theatre, where each moment in the plot lives alongside other moments and overlaps with them, the orchestra opening pathways between nows and thens. Moving from creation to cataclysm, the tetralogy embraces the whole of time, and treats the element as if it were as fluid as water.

None of Wagner's other operas gives the same sense of infinitely flexible and permeable temporal structure. The earlier works generally operate in an expert version of the conventional fashion, following the course of their romantic plots and deploying music to characterize various moods and tendencies of the unfolding drama. *Meistersinger*, of course, is a consummately plotted artefact, and it's organized by the standard laws of comedy, which demand the resolution of complexities and the final drawing-up of threads – and also demand that the guy gets his girl, uniquely for Wagner (Senta's suicidal union with the Dutchman doesn't count). *Tristan* and *Parsifal* are by no means linear operas – both are deeply preoccupied with time and memory – but, for all the richness and intricacy of their musical language, they are directed by the working-out of large tonal structures which give them a strong shape: *Parsifal* sets up clear architectural contrasts between diatonic and chromatic musical characters, while the end of *Tristan* is a resolution of its opening harmonic ambiguities. In place of these coherent musico-dramatic structures, the *Ring* offers a web of repetitions, returns, reflections, narrations: the very epitome of Wagnerian 'revolution', bending back on itself to go over its own ground again.

The medium for these revolutions is leitmotif. Only in the *Ring* is motivic technique used in the kind of ways whose extremes are measured by the examples I've been exploring above. Another way of saying the same thing would be to point out that only in the *Ring* is it possible to treat motifs semantically – to give them names and associate them with specific objects, people and ideas, and to interpret the 'grammar' of their musical transformations as a way of expressing the dramatic evolution of those people or ideas. Earlier commentators' rather desperate efforts to label motifs in *Tristan* and *Parsifal* show by their very desperation that those motifs essentially function as raw material for musical and emotional development, not as means of referring to specific elements in the drama, while *Meistersinger* makes a masterful return to something like the technique of the three romantic operas, where motifs are used to make more distinctive and stable reference to a smaller number of fixed concepts. By contrast, the motifs of the *Ring* are points of reference around which the musical fabric weaves itself, enabling any moment in the tetralogy suddenly to find itself thinking or speaking of another moment. Used in this way, motivic technique is the exact equivalent in musical form of the *Ring* poem's compulsive preoccupation with narrative. Just as its characters are liable at any moment to indulge in storytelling, so its score is perpetually capable of the same act: turning around on itself and exploring the force of narration rather than action.

Part III of *Opera and Drama* sets out in theoretical terms the precise link between motivic composition and dramatic time, and these instructions are to a large extent carried out in the earlier parts of the tetralogy. In a crucial sense, though, the prescriptions of Wagner's book never translate themselves into the *Ring*. Once again, it's not a question of whether he follows his own detailed requirements for the initial appearance and subsequent use of motifs. There is a more fundamental difference between the theory and the score, since *Opera and Drama* (like the other revolutionary writings) is still tinged with the delusive fantasy of futurity which the *Ring* (or the ring) so comprehensively dismantles. Accordingly, in the book's account of 'root-motifs' ('Grundmotiven', II 347) Wagner lays as much stress on anticipation as on reminiscence, and justifies the whole system of motivic composition by describing it as a technique which unifies the drama – creating a 'Unity of Content' (II 344) – in order to show that the whole musico-dramatic structure is entirely determined by a single, authoritative, and fully understandable 'poetic Aim' ('dichterische Absicht'). In other words, he believes he has invented a method of binding time together, so that every moment of the drama exists either as a recollection or as a prophecy of the unfolding of a mastering intent ('Absicht'). Yet, as we've seen, this intent is purely visionary. The prose writings can (more or less) maintain their deluded faith in a unified relation between past, present and future, and in the power of the will to achieve its passage through time; but the *Ring* cannot. What this means in practice is that leitmotif turns out always to be a mode of narrative, not prophecy. In tune with the *Ring*'s most characteristic tendencies, its direction is backward.

This is hardly surprising. Contrary to what Wagner says in *Opera and Drama*, a musical idea can only take on the function of a leitmotif when it appears more than once – a banal point, but important in terms of the *Ring*'s understanding of time. Until the processes of repetition and transformation begin, any motivic fragment exists only as a way of characterizing the present moment in the drama. Hearing it for the first time, we hear it only as 'music'. Once it occurs again, it can gain the quality of reference or recollection. Wagner's theoretical claim is that in certain situations a musical idea can be filled with such a strong feeling of latent expression that the 'future course' (II 330) of the drama can actually be predicted (this is how motifs of anticipation are supposed to work). The sound, he says, creates the 'first thrill of [an] emotion' which 'predetermines' coming events 'by the force of its own need' (II 331). An example would be the distinctive melody to which Woglinde announces the condition of forging the ring, the so-called 'renunciation of love' motif. Its appearance is almost melodramatic: the score modulates out of the playful brightness of the Rhinedaughters' teasing into a solemn minor, and reverentially quietens itself, so that Woglinde's words are strongly isolated and highlighted, and the melody's foreboding character is clearly marked by contrast with the rest of the scene. Obviously, some new emotion is being summoned here, and the tragic implications of what

Alberich is about to do are in some sense being anticipated by the sudden temporary darkening of the mood. But these are all effects of the melody itself and its relation to its context: we are given a *feeling* of foreboding. *Opera and Drama's* claim that this feeling itself amounts to a prophecy is surely as fantastical as the position of the 1849 rhapsody 'The Revolution', which believes that saying the revolution is just over the horizon is somehow tantamount to making it actually happen.

It's the perpetual problem of futurity again: Wagner's writings always want to think that the 'force of need' actually brings about what it desires. Leitmotif can't achieve this, though, any more than pamphlets welcoming the revolution can bring about revolutions. Woglinde's melody gestures towards the future, but that gesture only becomes meaningful and substantial when the music reappears — strikingly, for example, as Siegmund prepares to draw Nothung from the ash — and so creates a relation between her words and everything that follows them. Simply put, a motif isn't a motif until we remember it from somewhere earlier in the drama. The more it seeps into the fabric of the score, the more motivic weight it accumulates as it reappears. Leitmotifs only function insofar as they have a history. Motivic composition is thus necessarily a process of continual recollection. There are no motifs of anticipation, any more than there are any self-fulfilling prophecies elsewhere in the revolutionary writings.

As a further example, take the apparently 'prophetic' citations of one of Siegfried's main motifs in the third act of *Die Walküre*. Towards the end of the increasingly fervent interchange between Wotan and his errant daughter, the lively character of this melody begins to work its way into the music, articulating the urgent hopefulness of Brünnhilde's cajoling. Its specific association with Siegfried could hardly seem clearer. It had first appeared when Brünnhilde consoled Sieglinde with a prophecy of his birth earlier in the act, and it now turns up again as she tells Wotan the same thing:

der weihlichste Held – ich
  weiß es –
entblüht dem Wälsungenstamm!

the most sacred hero – this I
  know –
will blossom from the Wälsung stock!

Every time she goes on to mention the hero by whom alone she deserves to be woken or the child Sieglinde is bearing, the theme dutifully appears (only its effortless integration into the accelerating tension of the scene prevents this from being obtrusively unsubtle). Then, at the close of Wotan's elegiac farewell, it is sung when the god predicts the one who will find his daughter, and when he forbids anyone who fears his spear-point to pass through the fire – two equally obviously 'prophetic' references to Siegfried. Is this not quintessentially a motif of anticipation? Well, no: its allusion to the unborn hero is precisely that, a recollection of the moment earlier in the act when Brünnhilde first sings the melody as she gives Sieglinde the name of her son-to-be. That is, it refers not to the future events of *Siegfried* (which both Brünnhilde and Wotan appear already to know, a typical instance of the permeability of time in the *Ring*) but to the instant where the hero is first mentioned and named. The mood of its appearances in Brünnhilde's arguments and Wotan's farewell is certainly prophetic, thanks of course to the words it accompanies, but the leitmotif itself does not look 'forward' to anything. It predicts Siegfried's eventual achievement of his bride, but only by referring *back* to the moment in the score when it receives its clear association with him. This is perhaps to belabour an obvious fact – we can't remember anything we haven't yet heard – but it is crucial to see that the musical nature of leitmotif depends entirely on its turn to the past. Its real function is not that described in *Opera and Drama*, which clings to the visionary fantasy that 'the eventual naked revelation' of an event or moment can be 'so conditioned by our preparatory feeling of [its] necessity, as to make us downright demand [it] in fulfilment of an expectation' (II 334) – which is as much as to say that wanting something to happen makes it happen (a kind of dilettantism of revolution, rightly sneered at by the anarchist agitator Mikhail Bakunin when he encountered Wagner in Dresden in 1849). Leitmotif is far better described by the suggestive phrase from *My Life*: 'the musical remembrance of . . . dual life, keeping the past constantly present in the hearing'. It's as if the music of the tetralogy obeys the law of Alberich's cursed ring: all forward movement ends up being a resumption and a reflection of what has happened before.

The reason for dwelling on Siegfried's tale-telling in Act III of *Götterdämmerung* is to show the extraordinary power and profundity the *Ring* discovers in its returns to the past. To say that leitmotif is always a structure of reminiscence is by no means to argue that the tetralogy's techniques of motivic composition are no different from the relatively simple use of reminiscence-motif which (as has long been recognized) had been widely exploited in opera before Wagner's career even began. Reminiscence-motif is, essentially, a process of quotation. A musical theme reappears in order to refer the listener back to the idea in connection with which it originally appeared. The technique allows for a certain amount of dramatic modification: alterations in the theme's dynamics, scoring or harmonic character can give its reappearance an ironic or poignant or triumphant quality. Basically, though, its function is that of an echo. It makes the sound of an idea or a person sound again, musically enacting the reappearance of that same idea or person. An echo isn't an exact repetition. It can be muted or distorted, appearing in a different place and with a different quality from its original. It is, however, always at bottom the same sound (one event creates both the first noise and its subsequent reverberations). In the same way, reminiscence-motif is a system of one-to-one equations. It only works if the echo can be heard as a direct reference to its prior source.

Wagner's breathtakingly imaginative and inventive expansion of this technique is best described as the discovery that motifs can be subjected to endless transformations and combinations, resulting in a continuously-evolving musical fabric which can shape the structure and progression of a whole score. (Even without technical analysis, it's somehow possible to *hear* the way that *Tristan* and *Parsifal* – gigantic works both – seem to evolve like a series of variations out of the initial thematic material of their preludes.) In the *Ring*, though, this description appears to contradict the fundamental truth that the direction of leitmotif – as of the work as a whole – is backwards, not forwards. In a formal sense, it is of course absolutely true that Wagner's genius expresses itself in exploring (and, in the concentrated density of *Götterdämmerung*, perhaps exhausting) the developmental potential of motivic composition. In the dramatic sense, however, the *Ring*'s leitmotifs – like Wagner's prose writings – are ultimately about narration, not progression. The real significance of the difference between them and the older, more naïve reminiscence-motifs is that returning to the past in the *Ring* is never simply a matter of repetition, quotation or echo. Narration is not a matter of merely reproducing what has happened, as Siegfried's death so eloquently reveals. Narrative *does* something. As in the prose writings, it makes meanings, rather than just recording events. Correspondingly, leitmotif is always a reminiscence of the past, but imbued with the *Ring*'s deep insight that memory and storytelling create new relationships between *then* and *now*. Motivic composition expertly wields the power that the prose writings aim for so clumsily (excepting 'A Communication', to be fair): the power to unlock the past.

Siegmund arrives at the beginning of *Die Walküre* as if he has come out of nowhere. The storm seems to have tossed him onstage as casually as if he were one of those shipwrecked Shakespearean characters, a Viola or a Ferdinand alone in their brave new worlds. Much of the tensely subdued dramatic power of the opera's opening scenes comes from the feeling that the characters are gradually and tacitly piecing together their relationships with each other, all of which seem entirely mysterious at first. Indeed, Siegmund's own problem is at heart that he doesn't himself know who he is (a problem he treats far more thoughtfully than his son will). His curiously evasive response to Sieglinde's question about his identity –

Friedmund darf ich nicht heißen;	I may not call myself 'Peaceful';
Frohwalt möcht' ich wohl sein:	I would wish to be 'Joyful':
doch Wehwalt muß ich mich nennen	but I must name myself 'Woeful'

– is a sign of this rootlessness. Like Parsifal, he appears to have mislaid his origin, but not in this case through sheer forgetfulness. The destruction of his family and the perpetual exile he has suffered since then leave him uncertain of his relation to his past. Nevertheless, like everyone else in the *Ring* he turns to narration in his efforts to grasp himself and his situation. In fact there are few better examples of this habit's compulsiveness than the beginning of the third scene of the act. As soon as Siegmund is left alone, he turns the immediately preceding events into a miniature story:

Ein Schwert verhieß mir der Vater,	My father promised me a sword:
ich fänd' es in höchster Noth. –	I would find it in direst need. –
Waffenlos find' ich	I find myself weaponless
in Feindes Haus;	in an enemy's house;
seine Rache Pfand	forfeit to his vengeance
raste ich hier: –	I rest here: –
ein Weib sah' ich,	I saw a woman,
wonnig und hehr. . . .	lovely and noble . . .

Remembering the one promise for the future that has been made to him, he shifts into narrative mode to try to define his passage through time. By recounting what has just happened he can understand the present moment as the 'direst need' which will bring about the event he has been waiting for. If *Die Walküre* were one of Wagner's prose works of 1848–52, this situation would be a perfect example of the self-fulfilling prophecies those writings put their deluded faith in. In good Young Hegelian fashion, Siegmund's 'need' (the Feuerbachian *Not*) would appear to generate its own fulfilment. So when he cries 'Wälse! Wälse!/ Wo ist dein Schwert?' ('where is your sword?') – Wagner can't resist a shamelessly melodramatic sustained tremolo at this moment – the question answers itself with glib immediacy: 'there it is', the ringing trumpet statement of the Nothung motif appears to say, before he's even finished asking.

As always in the *Ring*, however, the apparently prophetic intervention of the leitmotif here is really a memory instead. The motif doesn't wait for Siegmund to ask his question before making its appearance. It has already been quietly given (minus its leaping opening ascent, a change which substitutes a sense of distance for its usual vivid immediacy with extraordinary effectiveness) in the bass trumpet, at the beginning of the scene, before Siegmund begins the ruminations quoted above. In that place, it stands for the thought that prompts his words ('Ein Schwert verhieß mir der Vater . . .'). The score has to recall the promise first, before it can make its swift and decisive answer to his question. Yet even then, Siegmund lapses straight back into memory. Though light flashes on the hilt of the sword in reply to his desperate question, he doesn't go and find the answer that he has just been shown. He doesn't 'hear' the trumpet's response to his melodramatic plea: or at least, he doesn't hear it as an answer and a confirmation of his future. The motif becomes the main melodic idea of the musical fabric, but it weaves itself around his entranced memories of Sieglinde, which – needless to say – quickly take the form of yet more miniaturized storytelling:

Nächtiges Dunkel	Night's gloom
deckte mein Aug';	covered my eyes;
ihres Blickes Strahl	the beam of her gaze
streifte mich da . . .	touched me then . . .

Matching his mood, the orchestra discovers a gently lyrical version of the Nothung theme, which alternates with the motif's primary form to accompany his meditations. For all its momentary indication of the triumphant fulfilment of Feuerbachian need, then, the leitmotif is actually the sound of blissful recollection. Like Siegmund, the score prefers to dwell on the past rather than to take hold of Wälse/Wotan's promise.

It's no surprise that when Sieglinde enters – on the face of it, another immediate response to Siegmund's thoughts – she too insists on telling stories before any move towards mutual discovery and love can take place. She offers the story as a step towards the future:

Ein Waffe lass' mich dir weisen –:	Let me show you a weapon –:
O wenn du sie gewänn'st!	O, if you could win it!

But this momentary outburst of hope is in fact an invitation to narrative. As with the orchestral accompaniment to Siegmund's soliloquy, the sword works its way into the past. Sieglinde's tale explains its *history*. It does so, indeed, more thoroughly than she realizes, for the score's warm and gentle statements of the motif associated with Wotan (the 'Valhalla' theme) recall the final scene of *Rheingold* where the Nothung motif accompanies the god's salute to his new home. These two musical ideas provide the orchestral substance of her narration (the vocal line is justly famous for its fluid freedom, so all the motivic work is done by the instruments). As always, their function is not simply illustrative; they aren't there merely to point up her references to Wotan and the sword. They serve more importantly to locate the shared ground in the twins' pasts. They are the points of contact between Siegmund and Sieglinde: the sword Wälse promised the former is the sword witnessed by the latter, while Wälse/Wotan himself lies in both their memories, and of course is in the biological sense their 'origin' as well (we never hear any details about their mother: Wotan might as well have given birth to them by himself). Thus the motivic fabric of these fundamentally narrative passages is a pathway into the past, where the identities of Siegmund and Sieglinde lie waiting to be revealed. Only at the very end of the act is the sword (and its motif) made into a sign of future promise; and in the next act Fricka swiftly quashes that promise, precisely by reminding Wotan of its history ('Du schuf'st ihm die Noth,/ wie das neidliche Schwert', 'you provided [Siegmund's] need for him, as you provided the grim sword'). Siegmund and Sieglinde have to retrace and lay hold of their pasts before their (mistaken) hope can assert itself. That's why she says he has her own face and voice: go back far enough into their past and they turn out to be the same person, the same identity. The motivic 'discoveries' made by the orchestra – finding the sword, identifying their father – are, therefore, revelations achieved through memory, delving backwards so as to allow the characters to identify themselves. If they were no more than labels attached to the elements of the scene – which is in essence what reminiscence-motifs are – then narrative would be unnecessary. Siegmund could simply listen and look around him to find out what he needs to know. But leitmotifs are means of laying hold of the past, not just indications of prior events, and the score of the *Ring* can no more make itself progress without turning on itself in this manner than the story of the *Ring* can. The tetralogy confirms what the prose writings take a long time to admit: Wagner's art of time is an art of the past, and his 'revolution' takes the form of a backwards turn.

It has become something of a commonplace to approach the *Ring* via the two alternative philosophical enthusiasms that infected Wagner during its composition, Young Hegelian optimism and Schopenhauer's pessimism. Neither, I suggest, describes the way the tetralogy works. Its secret is neither revolutionary progressivism nor abnegation. It cannot embrace the future, but it also doesn't desire an escape from time and change. What it presents to us instead is a continuous reflection on the process of events, a story about telling stories. By the time it reaches *Götterdämmerung*, the score is so laden with motivic content that it seems as if everything that happens is spun out of what has happened before (almost any part of the opera could be mentioned, but take for example the orchestral transition between Hagen's watch-song and the Waltraute scene in Act I, an extraordinary compression of motivic fragments). The weight of the past hangs similarly heavily over the drama, as the Norns' prologue makes us feel. Alberich's curse converts that weight into a deadly force. It's the bleakest manifestation of a sense of the past: inescapable, inevitable, binding everything inside its unbreakable circle. And yet, the tetralogy also says, the curse's law isn't only punitive. Returning to the past, as Siegfried, his parents and (in Act II of *Die Walküre*) Wotan all find out, is a mode of understanding. Its revelations are ambiguous at best. There's still no pathway into the future, no ultimate 'redemption' which narrative can discover. Wagner is not and was never really a revolutionary (and the 'art-work of the future' always was and always will be a fantasy). Nevertheless, the dramatic and musical resources he pours into the art of narration themselves effected a kind of revolution: the *Ring* made opera into something that had never been imagined before. By going on telling and retelling its story, it invests Wagner's art with a force that even *Lohengrin* never really hints at.

This is not a book about what Wagner's work means, but about *how* it means. As the history of its production demonstrates wonderfully incontrovertibly, the *Ring* can mean many different things. That extraordinary fertility of interpretative potential, equalled in opera only I think by the richly ambiguous Mozart/Da Ponte collaborations, is a direct result of its discovery of the power of narration. Siegfried's death shows us that to remake action into a tale is to discover it again, to locate meaning in it, and in the process to come to a new understanding of that meaning. Stories are how forgotten things come back to life. By constructing itself as a gigantic series of recollections, the *Ring* makes it possible for us to go over it again, to retell it, as directors and performers have done and continue to do time after time. It is a wonderful irony that Wagner, so tyrannically (if inconsistently) assured of the meaning of his own work, should have created such a monumental testament to the power of reinterpretation.

PART III
Exile

CHAPTER NINE

The Art of Transition

The house near Zurich offered in 1857 by Otto Wesendonck for Wagner's use was christened the 'Asyl', 'refuge'. It seemed like the right name, redolent with the promise of coming to rest. As a political refugee, Wagner had not set foot in Germany since May 1849. In the intervening years he had been working on the *Ring* without hope of seeing it performed, or indeed of witnessing any of the increasingly numerous performances of his existing operas in his own country. With no formal employment, for solvency he depended on acts of patronage, supplemented by occasional concert engagements – the life of an itinerant musician, effectively, and his travels took him from his base in Switzerland around the edges of the forbidden homeland: France in 1850, Italy in 1853, England in 1855. Wesendonck's offer was meant to lay to rest as many of the disruptive forces in Wagner's existence as it could. He had already paid the composer's debts and subsidized his holidays; now, as the best available substitute for the impossible return to Germany, he was providing geographical stability. Wagner's letter accepting the offer is a hymn to the security of belonging somewhere:

> As though by magic, everything around me has suddenly been transformed!
> All sense of wavering must come to an end: I know *where* I now belong,
> *where* I can work and create, *where* I shall now find comfort and consola-
> tion, recovery and relief, and where I can now face, in total confidence, all
> the vicissitudes of my artistic career. . . . (*L* 363)

The 'refuge' was to represent the end of exile, a place for the displaced, where Wagner's life and art together would find their home (a similar sort of language attended the occupation of his house 'Wahnfried' at Bayreuth in 1874). The prospect collapsed only a matter of months after it had opened, and as Wagner faced up to the necessity of expelling himself from the Asyl, he wrote to Mathilde Wesendonck in terms of a permanent exile, as if the very idea of refuge is now unthinkable to him: 'Do you think that I, who fled from the world once before, could now return to it? . . . I can never, ever return to the world' (*L* 396).

As so often in his letters to Mathilde, this is the terminology of *Tristan und Isolde*. The words date from July 1858, during work on the composition of the opera's second act, which achieves one of its most enraptured climaxes as the lovers sing

heil'ger Dämm'rung	the sublime intimation
hehres Ahnen	of sacred twilight
löscht des Wähnens Graus	extinguishes illusion's misery,
Welt-erlösend aus.	releasing us from the world.

This, indeed, is the perpetual theme of the text of *Tristan*, a weird libretto by any standard. The lovers whose words overwhelmingly dominate the opera always seem to have their gaze fixed elsewhere, acutely aware that they do not belong in the world around them – the world which in their private mythology they label 'der Tag', the day, whose fading into 'twilight' is so thrillingly envisioned in the music accompanying the above lines. There is no *Asyl*, no refuge, in *Tristan*, except perhaps death; and even death is always described by the lovers as a longed-for release and transfiguration rather than any kind of fixed end. The whole opera is peculiarly pervaded by a feeling of displacement, or what the letter to Otto Wesendonck calls a 'sense of wavering'. In purely musical terms, this effect is intensified to the highest imaginable pitch by the score's harmonic language, which gives ears accustomed to the laws of classical tonality the impression of never coming home. The libretto has a rather similar effect. Since virtually nothing happens in *Tristan*, huge expanses of its text are given over to oblique recollections, elusive meditations, and pure rhapsodies like the four lines just quoted, all of which come to feel like poetic equivalents of the unfixed 'wandering tonality' (the phrase is Schoenberg's) of the score.[1] In terms of the plot, this mood of dislocation and displacement is conveyed by the fact that the opera's few crucial incidents are all errors. One potion is substituted for another in the first act; in the second, Melot the true friend turns out to be the betrayer; in Act III, Tristan and Kurwenal misinterpret King Marke's pursuit of Isolde. Everything seems out of place.

As always, Wagner's infallible theatrical instinct finds the most telling stage devices for articulating this mood. Each act of *Tristan* presents us with an offstage voice, a sound that has been literally dislocated – it has no location – so that for the duration of its song the opera is filled with an extraordinarily uncanny sense of happening somewhere else. In Act III the effect is produced by the wordless *alte Weise*, the 'old tune' played first by an invisible piper. Act II has Brangäne singing from her tower, one of the strangest moments in Wagner's whole oeuvre (of which more later). The opera proper begins with the unseen young sailor's *a cappella* song. The first words of *Tristan*, indeed, are a kind of miniature parable of the displacement that will afflict it throughout:

West-wärts	Westward
schweift der Blick:	the gaze wanders:
ost-wärts	eastward
streicht das Schiff.	the ship skims.

The invisible voice looks east as it is carried west. Opposite directions each exert their pull on the stage, so that (as with the sailor here) one always seems to be on the way to being somewhere else, and that destination is itself unfixed, maybe behind, maybe ahead. No wonder Tristan and Isolde themselves both seem to be unhinged, or cast adrift. Even before they fall under the spell of the potion, they both ask 'wo sind wir?', 'where are we?' (the question Wesendonck's Asyl was supposed permanently to answer). The offstage music that so memorably inserts itself into each act is a theatrical embodiment of the sense of exile underpinning this question.

Die Meistersinger von Nürnberg also begins with offstage voices. The curtain rises on the interior of a church, of which, say Wagner's stage directions, only the last few rows of pews are visible. We thus hear but don't see the massed congregation singing their chorale in praise of John the Baptist. The effect, of course, could not be more different from that achieved in *Tristan*. *Meistersinger's* disembodied voices are very securely located. They are enclosed together in a public building, engaged in a communal act of worship, and singing in good solid Lutheran harmony. There's no need to ask 'wo sind wir?'; we know exactly where we are and what is happening there. The only discordant note is sounded by the young lovers seen (again according to the stage directions) in the last row of the nave, exchanging fidgety glances rather than joining in with the rest of the town (musically, this is conveyed by the motifs from the prelude which wind distractedly between the lines of the chorale). This is our first glimpse of the tension between Walther and Eva on one hand and the civic and ritual life of Nuremberg on the other, a tension culminating in their attempt to elope and so exile themselves from family, town, Mastersingers, and the whole community. The question of whether Walther is willing to join the chorus – to sing along with Nuremberg, as it were, rather than going his own way – provides much of the opera's drama. We can tell from that very first scene, though, that the odds are stacked in favour of the community. Eva and Walther can do little more than share glances until the chorale is complete; the offstage chorus exerts an enormous gravitational pull. (A little later the point is made even more emphatically, when the outsider learns that the only legitimate way to win Eva is to join the community by becoming a Mastersinger.) The stately, massy sounds of the burghers celebrating their way of life together enclose the lovers as solidly and weightily as the walls of the church do. It's simply a question of how Walther's free spirit can be accommodated to this communal life. Sachs's job in the opera is to cobble the two together, to conduct the lovers to where they belong – ushering them into their proper *Asyl*.

Tristan (1857–9) and *Meistersinger* (1861–7) are the two theatrical products of Wagner's years of displacement. Admittedly, one could interpret the biographical facts differently. His exile technically began in May 1849 and ended with the full amnesty granted by Saxony in March 1862. Alternatively, the miraculously fortunate intervention of Ludwig II in March 1864 might be understood as the end of Wagner's years of increasingly troubled home-lessness after his expulsion from the Asyl; but he was effectively expelled from the King's company in December 1865. One could also claim with reason that Wagner never came to rest until he finally created his own house and his own theatre, at last the master of his Bayreuth domain in 1872. The completion of the *Ring* spans all these dates, but the tetralogy, as I've already argued, seems impervious to the effects of physical and chronological displacement; gifted with the power to turn in on itself and recollect itself, it preserves a quite remarkable stylistic and thematic coherence over the enormous expanse of its creation. *Tristan* and *Meistersinger*, however, manifest – in utterly different, indeed almost diametrically opposite ways – the issues of place, belonging, refuge, displacement and the 'sense of wavering' suited to a composer in exile. During the years of their composition, Wagner's bio-graphy is as marked by shifts and displacements as the 'wandering tonality' of his mature musical style. From the failed refuge of the Asyl he went to Venice; thence via Lucerne to Paris, where the *Tannhäuser* disaster of 1861 epitomized the sense of not belonging that clung to him and his works; after Paris, a number of brief temporary homes, ending in 1862 in Biebrich on the Rhine near Mainz; from there to Vienna, with a long excursion to Russia and back in 1863; and from Vienna anywhere he might escape his creditors, until Ludwig's private secretary found him in Stuttgart in 1864; so on to Munich, for a short-lived residence at the King's expense; and after his forcible expulsion from the Bavarian capital, settling eventually at the house 'Tribschen' near Lucerne in March 1866, where a secure household was at last completed by the arrival of Liszt's daughter (and Hans von Bülow's wife) Cosima.

From place to place to place: the art of transition. It's one of the most sug-gestive phrases Wagner used to describe his mature work, less dogmatic than the various familiar tags from his prose writings. This is perhaps because it was never meant as a public pronouncement. It comes from another letter to Mathilde Wesendonck, written from Paris in October 1859 (shortly after the completion of *Tristan*, to which work it refers):

1. Opera's two worlds. Framed by the elegant rococo decoration of the little theatre at Bad Lauchstädt, where Wagner made his first appearance as an opera conductor in August 1834, the wild territory of romance is conjured up in the stage's imaginary space.

2. Revolution: an end or a beginning? The final tableau of Patrice Chéreau's revolutionary production of the *Ring* at Bayreuth, first seen in 1976, and the most famous 'turn' in the stage history of Wagner's work. As smoke drifts over the ruins of a destroyed world, the assembled witnesses have turned round to face directly into the audience, as if to ask us: what now?

3. Chéreau's staging of the beginning of Wotan's narration in *Walküre*, Act II. Like the mirror, narration repeats things in order to allow them to be seen newly, or at least differently: reflection is both understanding and change.

4. Exile: Wagner as photographed by the Paris firm of Petit & Trinquart in 1860. Though the index finger is extended downwards as if to stress his location in *this* space, the hunted, antagonistic expression of the face betrays a sense of not belonging here, while the eyes stare intently towards an undefined elsewhere.

5. Desire as fulfilment: fantasies brought to life in Venus's grotto. In the first Bayreuth production of *Tannhäuser* (1896, under Cosima Wagner's direction), the hero lies dreaming in Venus's lap in the foreground, while his erotic dreams appear as mythological tableaux of seduction in a cloudy interior space. Here, the fantasy is Leda and the swan; their poses echo those of Tannhäuser and the goddess, smoothing the passage from the scene of desire to the visions it indulges in.

6. Desire as annihilation. In Hans-Jürgen Syberberg's 1982 film of *Parsifal*, the flowermaidens are sexual zombies, static, morbid and grotesque. Here they play in a 'garden' of toys and dolls, while the blind eye-sockets and rigid mouth of their creator's death-mask appear as the features of a leering voyeur.

7. Religion: the closing scene of *Parsifal* in the original version, preserved virtually unchanged from 1882 to 1933 (the photograph is of a 1930 performance). Holding the Grail, Parsifal is illuminated by a miraculous radiance which leaves everything outside the sacred space in shadow. All eyes and bodies are turned in worship towards him – except Kundry's.

8. *Bühnenweihfestspiel*: the convergence of opera's two worlds in one sacred space. A photo shows the auditorium of the Bayreuth Festspielhaus; on stage are the original (1883) sets for the Grail scenes of *Parsifal*. These two interchangeable temples of Wagner's art echo each other both architecturally (in the ranks of columns and the curved interior space) and conceptually. Both arrange spectators as witnesses of a central ritual displayed on the altar/stage.

Two stage models *(facing page)* from the 1896 production of the *Ring* under Cosima Wagner's direction, which adhered very closely to the original 1876 designs.

9. *(above)* The Valkyries' rock from *Die Walküre*, Act III.

10. Gibichung Hall from *Götterdämmerung*, Act I (with Siegfried's boat moored on the near bank of the Rhine).

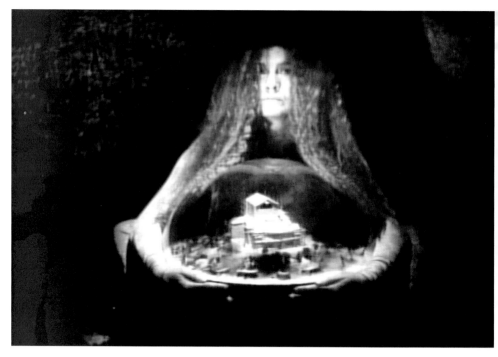

11. Kundry and the temple of art: an image from Syberberg's *Parsifal*. Moments before closing her eyes to bring the film to its end, Kundry (Edith Clever) cradles a model representing Wagner's theatre at Bayreuth, as if holding it in her womb. Which of them gives life to the other?

I recognize now that the characteristic fabric of my music . . . which my friends now regard as so new and so significant, owes its construction above all to the extreme sensitivity which guides me in the direction of mediating and providing an intimate bond between all the different moments of transition that separate the extremes of mood. I should now like to call my most delicate and profound art the art of transition, for the whole fabric of my art is made up of such transitions. . . . (L 474–5)

Although Wagner is thinking about 'mood' here – he goes on to cite as an example *Tristan* Act II's seamless progress from the height of ecstasy to the most sombre resignation – we recognize in these words a description of the essential character of his later musico-dramatic style. Entirely freed from the closed forms of all prior opera, where musical beginnings and climaxes and endings followed each other in sequence, Wagner's work from *Walküre* onwards achieves a continuity founded on continuous modulation. It is an art of perpetual change; not so much a structure as a dissolution of the geometries of structure into fluid, endlessly imaginative developments and adaptations.

In Wagner's writings on music from these years, especially 'Über Franz Liszt's symphonische Dichtungen' ('On Franz Liszt's Symphonic Poems', 1857) and *'Zukunftsmusik'* (*'The Music of the Future'*, 1860), it's clear that his theoretical preoccupations have become focussed on the problem of large-scale musical structure (rather than on the unity of verbal and musical genres, as in the revolutionary writings). As he suggests in the letter to Mathilde Wesendonck, the basic issue of his art now appears to be one of form: if his operas are not going to unfold in a series of self-contained units, how are they made instead? If he will not write melody in the traditional sense, because (as in a Mozart opera, say) one melody can only follow another as an entirely separate musical event, what will the substance of his music be? In 'The Music of the Future' – the quotation marks are part of the title, since the phrase is being used ironically – he claims to take his cue from Beethoven's symphonic procedure, which overcomes the 'fatal interspaces' between self-contained, discontinuous melodies by 'giving to the connecting-links between the chief melodies the full character of Melody themselves' (III 334–5). That is, the transitions between musical units become part of 'one vast, one solid piece of music, which in itself is nothing but one sole continuous melody' (III 335). Movement itself becomes substance – an appropriate creed for an exile.

In their different fashions, both *Tristan* and *Meistersinger* are about transition. From the very first bars of its prelude, *Tristan* is the quintessence of restlessness. Its two opening four-note phrases – the descending motif in the cellos, the ascending sequence in the oboes, overlapping in the anxious,

straining 'Tristan chord' – come from nowhere and go nowhere. One only
has to think of them and then call to mind the first bars of the *Meistersinger*
prelude to grasp at once the difference between located and dislocated music.
Tristan's opening takes us into a melodic and harmonic no-man's-land, and
from then on the opera keeps us out of place, restless in the sense that (as
the lovers perpetually tell themselves and each other) there is nowhere to
come to rest, no end to the 'sense of wavering' so acutely established in the
prelude. Tristan and Isolde's problem is how to get where they want to be,
or how to be somewhere other than where they are. Thus even amid the bliss
of apparent union during their 'Nacht der Liebe' ('night of love') in Act II,
there is no consummation. Instead, they share a joint desire for a yet more
perfect but unachieved state, 'holder Tod,/ sehnend verlangter/ Liebestod'
('sweet death, yearningly desired love-death'). Kurwenal naïvely believes that
he has brought Tristan 'home' by bringing him to Kareol, but his master dis-
abuses him in words which dissolve not only the notion of a 'home' but the
very idea of fixed space:

Wo ich erwacht,	Where I awoke,
weilt' ich nicht;	I did not stay;
doch wo ich weilte,	but where I stayed,
das kann ich dir nicht sagen.	that I cannot tell you.
Die Sonne sah ich nicht,	I did not see the sun,
nicht sah ich Land noch Leute:	nor did I see land or people;
doch was ich sah,	but what I saw,
das kann ich dir nicht sagen.	that I cannot tell you.
Ich war –	I was –
wo ich von je gewesen,	where I have been for ever,
wohin auf je ich gehe. . . .	and where for ever I will go. . . .

The words articulate the nowhere of the prelude, and also, in the last lines,
the endless, continuous movement that defines the opera as a whole. Tristan
has, he says, been somewhere and will be somewhere, so his actual experience is nothing but transition, going between.

There is none of this agonized restlessness in *Meistersinger* (notwithstanding
Sachs's interpretation of the riot as a manifestation of the world's *Wahn*
or illusion). It is by far the most homebound of Wagner's operas: *Land und
Leute*, land and people, are visibly and identifiably in place. Nevertheless, it
concerns itself with change. Meditating on Walther's unorthodox Trial Song,
Sachs says 'Es klang so alt, und war doch so neu', 'it sounded so old and yet
was so new'. His challenge is to reconcile novelty with tradition. The story
enacts a transition between generations, from the old-established models of
musico-poetic art catalogued by David and policed by Beckmesser to the
reinvigorated forms spontaneously achieved by Walther's songs. This, as is

embarrassingly obvious, is a parable of Wagner's own understanding of his operatic innovations. Like Walther, he disdains ossified musical conventions, believing that the artist's private inspiration justifies the creation of new forms appropriate to its individual expressive impetus (this is the argument of 'On Liszt's Symphonic Poems'). However, he also believes – like Sachs – that this spontaneous creative originality is not a break with existing forms but a way of giving fresh life and vigour to artistic traditions. As Sachs tells the other Masters in Act I:

Doch einmal in Jahre fänd' ich's weise,	But once a year I would think it wise
daß man die Regeln selbst probier',	that the rules themselves be
ob in der Gewohnheit trägem G'leise	tested, to see whether in the dull rut of habit
ihr' Kraft und Leben sich nicht verlier':	their strength and life had not been lost:
und ob ihr der Natur	and whether you are still
noch seid auf rechter Spur. . . .	on the right track with nature. . . .

Die Meistersinger is a work which performs these tests. It is peculiarly interested in trials and examinations – each act is centred around a scene of 'marking' and judging – but it is not only the individual performers who are tested. Via Sachs's ingenious stage-management, the institution of music itself is put on trial before the public (he refers to Walther as his 'Zeuge', a witness in the judicial sense), so that in the final scene the people of Nuremberg judge the Masters, rather than the Masters judging each other. The opera thus becomes a story of art in transition, moved back (to use Sachs's terms) into proper alignment with nature.

In *'The Music of the Future'*, Wagner metaphorically describes the effect of his own art on the listener in the same terms: 'it should exert on him somewhat the effect produced by a noble forest, of a summer evening, on the lonely visitant who has just left the city's din behind' (III 339). It's a passage into nature, in other words, just as the last scenes of the opera are, when the Masters and their art are moved out into the open and exposed to the fresh air of the prize song. Although Walther's audience experiences confusion and wonder at the unexpected originality of his art, they are made to parrot Wagner's conviction that it speaks directly to the hearers' feelings and so is 'swift and easy of understanding' (III 251). As the song unfolds they whisper to themselves, 'So hold und traut, wie fern es schwebt', 'So beautiful and familiar, though it soars far'. They know it is exotic and remote, and yet they understand and love it. (To be fair, Wagner had some justification for this view that the public understood his music instinctively, despite the critics' complaints that it was chaotic, formless and without melody; by the late 1850s he had become the most popular composer of operas in northern Europe, and even his more 'difficult' later works went on to draw enthusiastic audiences everywhere.) Beckmesser is the sacrificial victim of this rite of transition. He represents the aspect of the old order that is spat out as the communal tradition renews itself. The thing that makes him botch his performance of Walther's text is precisely his inability to change, trying to squeeze the words into his old melody because he can't come up with a new one. By contrast, Walther's song changes itself in mid-performance, altering tune and poem in the middle of the first stanza. His creation is the expression of a kind of continuous improvisation; where Beckmesser has to follow a script, inspiration comes to Walther in a dream. The contrast between them is therefore a (grotesquely uneven) battle between fixity and fluidity. Transition is itself the new law or 'rule' which is incorporated into tradition at the end of the opera.

Put side by side like this, *Tristan* and *Meistersinger* look like alternative interpretations of the notion of transition. The word can be understood in two ways with widely divergent implications. On the one hand – *Tristan's* hand, the side of 'night' in the lovers' terms – transition means the absence of a home or refuge, restless movement from place to place: being in transit ('wohin auf je ich gehe'). On the other hand – the 'day' side, the midsummer *Meistersinger* side – transition means continuity, inheritance, renewal, the smooth passing of a secure tradition from one place and generation to the next. In the first sense, the emphasis is on displacement and exile; in the second, on stability and belonging.

Wagner's 'art of transition' provokes the same two opposed interpretations. On the one hand, it appears to result in the dissolution of stable tonal relationships and regular musical periods. Hence what 'On Liszt's Symphonic Poems' calls 'this outcry about absence of Form' (III 243). Without the immediately apparent and graspable shapes of closed melodies and prepared harmonic resolutions, Wagner's new operatic style sounds like an endless series of displacements. On the other hand, as Wagner's own writing repeatedly claims, the art of transition results in an unprecedented wholeness. The 'new form', he says, is necessarily 'a form dictated by the subject of its portrayal and its logical development' (III 246). Instead of relying on a broken series of discontinuous melodies, 'everlastingly breaking and barring the musical flow' (III 342), the new art can portray all the shadings and modulations of a single dramatic subject, becoming 'a lucid exposition of its inner motives' (III 331). 'Stretch boldly out your melody', he imagines himself telling a composer in *'The Music of the Future'*, 'that like a ceaseless river it may pour throughout the work' (III 337). In this interpretation, continuous transitions are a way of maintaining coherence and continuity across the largest musical expanses, uninterrupted by the stops and starts of classical musical structures.

Wagner's self-styled 'most delicate and profound art', then, can be understood in terms both of formlessness and of coherence. A description in '*The Music of the Future*' of the Beethovenian symphony, which he takes as his forerunner in discovering the art of transition, gives a sense of both interpretations mingling and competing:

> . . . for here . . . the purely musical Expression enchains the hearer in an inconceivably varied mesh of nuances; rouses his inmost being, to a degree unreachable by any other art; and in all its changefulness reveals an ordering principle so free and bold, that we can but deem it more forcible than any logic, yet without the laws of logic entering into it in the slightest — nay rather, the reasoning march of Thought, with its track of causes and effects, here finds no sort of foothold. So that this Symphony must positively appear to us a revelation from another world; and in truth it opens out a scheme [*Zusammenhang*] of the world's phenomena quite different from the ordinary logical scheme. . . . (III 318)

Here Beethoven is credited with the continuous, fluid, 'inconceivably varied' musical fabric Wagner achieves in his own later work. The result is a sense of overall coherence and unity 'more forcible than any logic'; but at the same time it is also said to be free from logic and reason, a texture of wavering 'changefulness' which unlooses the sequences of 'causes and effects' and substitutes for them the sense of being removed to 'another world'. Transition is being treated simultaneously as an 'ordering principle' or a rule — its *Meistersinger* aspect, as it were — and also as an endlessly changeful 'mesh of nuances' which, like the eerie displacements of *Tristan*, move us into a world entirely unlike the here and now.

At bottom, these alternative meanings come down to the question of form in the broadest sense. With the full maturation of his characteristic style, Wagner absents himself completely from the existing forms of instrumental music (its sonata forms and scherzos and theme-and-variations and fugues and all the rest of its apparatus for organizing sound into perceptible structural units). What happens instead? Is it formlessness, or is it some huge new kind of form? Is it the world dimly envisioned and obscurely described by Tristan in Act III, the shadowy 'Weltennacht' ('world-night' or 'night-world'), where the only knowledge is 'Urvergessen', primal forgetting? Or is it the new, refreshed, natural artistic order heard by the people of Nuremberg in Walther's prize song, the new version of the rules that Sachs wants to take down from nature's dictation?

Both the Liszt essay and '*The Music of the Future*' mainly concern themselves with the idea of breaking the rules of form. With Liszt's tone-poems, Wagner is dealing with the transgression of classical symphonic structure, while the latter essay focusses specifically on the issue of melody as the basic unit of instrumental music. In each case, Wagner argues that traditional forms lack the full expressive potential required by the kind of conceptions that inspire the modern composer. He justifies Liszt's musical portraits of Orpheus or Prometheus, and his own 'endless melody' (III 338), by pointing out that their dramatic grasp of their chosen subjects can't be squeezed into formal structures which, he plausibly argues, derive their repetitive and foreclosed character from their origins in dance. But he is interestingly reticent when it comes to any actual description of the new art he and Liszt have arrived at instead. It 'involves a *secret*', he insists in the Liszt essay. We can't extract 'generally-applicable artistic rules' from Liszt's individual grasp of his subject; all we can talk about is the 'artwork and its impression on ourselves' (III 250). Likewise *'The Music of the Future'* explicitly refuses to 'clearly set forth all the single features of Melodic Form', also arguing that 'we now are drawing near the point . . . where the artwork alone can say the final word' (III 340). The lingering question of what replaces the old outworn forms is left open, to be answered only by referring to music itself, not to any formal theorizing. Fortunately, this invitation to refer the question of form to the 'artwork' itself is easily accepted, because both *Tristan* and *Meistersinger* are as preoccupied with this question as the essays are.

Form is what shapes, contains and gives definition to expression. An ancient analogy describes form as the body that clothes expression's soul, or as the outward shape of inward content. It hardly needs saying that *Die Meistersinger* is an opera about form. The guild of the Mastersingers exists in order to codify and preserve the specific shapes that the art of song can take. David's comic monologue and Kothner's solemn recitation of the *Tabulatur* in Act I both make it clear that the science of form is the essence of the Master's knowledge and skill. Beckmesser's behaviour as both 'Marker' and wooer betrays an exaggerated obedience to formal requirements. The whole competition in Act III is of course not just a battle between different forms but a contest over form itself: Walther and Sachs put the whole idea of the regulation and shaping of art on trial. One can hear the opera's fascination with this issue in the score. It is most obvious when the formal aspect of music is being treated parodically (parody works, after all, by drawing exaggerated attention to its own form). The extreme case is Beckmesser's tune, which cramps verbal expression into its metrically regular and fussily ornamental shape. The plucking and twanging of his lute give the melody an absurdly artificial and antiquated feel; even without hearing the way his competition song mangles its text, we'd be able to tell that it represents 'mere' form. The music of Kothner's recitation of the *Tabulatur* is more affectionately parodic, but still clearly mocks the flourishes and decorations which he adds to the words. His long coloratura-like excursion over the final syllable of the speech is obviously a joke at the expense of the idea of a formal ending.

As with Beckmesser's music, the score is here showing us what form itself sounds like. From this more or less satirical perspective, form manifests itself as redundant music (Kothner or Beckmesser's trills and warbles). Such musical moments stand out from the usual effortless Wagnerian flow of the orchestra, drawing explicit attention to themselves, advertising themselves as mere empty noise. There are also, however, many other parts of the score which highlight the presence of form without any parodic emphasis. *Die Meistersinger* is in fact virtually an encyclopaedia of musical forms. The opening chorale, the way that Act I ends with something very like a traditional operatic 'finale' sequence, Sachs's ballad in Act II, David's song on the Baptist, the processional marches and country dances of Act III, the hymn *Wach auf*, even the Watchman's little song: all these are occasions where the opera very deliberately clothes itself in specific generic shapes, taking on audible musical form. The same might be said of the brilliant part-writing with which Wagner indulges himself in this opera, so strikingly unlike his usual polyphonic 'mesh of nuances'. The muttered interchanges of the Masters when Walther is first presented to them effectively sound like an exercise in weaving together separate vocal lines. The riot scene takes this principle to a virtuosic extreme, since a huge number of separate parts are organized into energetic consonance, while the beautiful quintet is a jaw-dropping demonstration of the harmonious intertexture of solo voices which Wagner never allows himself elsewhere. Even the prelude – itself really an 'overture', a deliberate throwback to a traditional operatic form – concludes with a most uncharacteristic display of contrapuntal skill, fitting three of its major themes together as if to draw attention right from the start to this opera's fascination with the formal aspect of the craft of music. No wonder *Meistersinger*'s hero is an artist who is also an artisan.

Nor is form exclusively a musical matter in the opera. Far from it: music in fact becomes (as Sachs's horrific final speech makes bludgeoningly clear) a metaphor for the whole of society. The Masters are after all burghers as well as artists. Their concern with rules seeps from the field of music into the civic life of the town as a whole, of which they seem inexplicably to be the highest authorities. (It's Wagner's deepest fantasy played on stage, a city-state where the musicians are in charge.) From its opening tableau, the opera depicts a society governed (though perhaps only tenuously) by ritual. The embodied forms of communal life are vividly present: a church service, processions, roll calls, festivals and competitions, and of course the rite of marriage which governs the whole plot. Formal behaviour is everywhere, not just in its parodic manifestation as practised by Beckmesser, but in grave and dignified versions as well. The Masters are of course deeply conscious of bourgeois courtesy in their addresses and conversations, but even Walther and Eva, who stand as representatives of unconstrained spontaneity, recognize the requirements of

ceremony. Walther's initial questions to Eva in the church are painfully punc-
tilious, as befits a *Ritter* ('knight' – a landed aristocrat). More strikingly, Eva's
sweet echo of the crowd's comment at the end of the prize song interprets
all Walther's ardour not as the spontaneous expression of inspired love but
instead as the perfection of formal courtship: 'Keiner wie du so hold zu
werben weiß!', 'no one knows how to woo so graciously as you'. *Meistersinger*
never allows us to forget the presence of the shaping institutions of civic life.
The Act II riot seems like a sign of endemic social disorder, but note how
magically it dissolves at the mere approach of one rather feeble guardian
figure. The Watchman's regular, unchanging rounds, and his eloquently simple
call for a peaceful night, disenchant the temporarily frenzied streets as easily
as Parsifal's spear unmakes Klingsor's domain. When he is first heard after the
street battle, the orchestra is still echoing its riotous sounds, and his song
begins over dark whirling semitones in the bass clarinet. Quickly, though, it
pulls the bass figures into its own tonal orbit and calms them down; and with
the pious last line all the musical disturbance is pacified, the hushed strings
settling onto a serene cadence. However comical his effect, the Watchman is
as much an embodiment of the rules that order this community as the Masters
are. In his Act III monologue Sachs summarizes this aspect of his city by
referring to its 'treuer Sitten', 'faithful customs', its stock of ritual forms and
institutions on which its whole existence is securely grafted.

Sitten, customs, also shape and embody the world of King Marke's court.
The word is the centre of a brief but elaborate rhetorical fencing match
between Isolde and Tristan when they first come face to face in the opera.
His behaviour to her, he says, is constrained by what 'Sitte lehrt', what custom
teaches. She mocks him as 'du so sittsam,/ mein Herr Tristan', 'you so cour-
teous, Sir Tristan', and reminds him of another obligation dictated by custom:
atonement for unexpiated wrongs. Each is using the formalities of chivalric
courtesy to cover what at this stage has to remain silent between them. It's
not just a matter of using the language proper to a princess and a heroic
knight. Formal behaviour is the exact antithesis of the abandoned, exultant,
effusive passion which the two of them are jointly suppressing in this conversation. In the day–night dichotomy which they invent in Act II to explain
the relation between their love and the rest of the world, *Sitte* is the manifestation of the daylight world. Adultery, after all, is 'bad form', an offence
against the rules of courtesy (though not, as it happens, the rules of chivalry:
adulterous relationships are the essence of chivalric love – witness Lancelot
and Guinevere). As Marke complains when the lovers are exposed at the end
of Act II, their crime is not just a personal betrayal but an offence against the
whole social code:

Wohin nun Ehr'	Where now are honour
und ächte Art,	and true breeding,

| da aller Ehren Hort | now that the guardian of all honour, |
| da Tristan sie verlor? | Tristan, has abandoned them? |

The night-world imagined by Isolde and Tristan in their ecstasies defines itself in opposition to this kind of language. They never see what they are doing in the kind of terms Marke or Melot (or even Kurwenal or Brangäne) would use. They can't interpret themselves as adulterers or betrayers – which is one of the reasons why Brangäne's explicit warnings in Act II can't have the slightest effect on them. Hence at the end of Marke's long lament over lost honour, Tristan simply replies that he and the King no longer speak the same language. The whole issue of honour and custom is entirely irrelevant to him: 'was du fräg'st,/ das kannst du nie erfahren' ('what you ask, you can never be told').

The opening interchange between hero and heroine thus sets up an essential dichotomy in the opera. *Sitte* is the principle of the world they inhabit until they drink the potion, while their love – grimly unmentionable during those first tense exchanges – defines itself by its perpetual resistance to that world. There are few musical representations of the conflict, because it's so utterly one-sided: music is here absolutely on the side of that which cannot be expressed in or reconciled with the language of 'day' (in *'The Music of the Future'* Wagner wonderfully describes his new kind of evolving melody as 'a silence growing more and more alive', III 339). One very powerful instance, though, is the end of Act I, where the sounds of ceremony and form are clearly articulated in the massed chorus of the sailors and the trumpet and trombone fanfares heralding Marke's arrival. Simply by virtue of the way the drama is unfolding, Wagner here achieves the most acute tension between the world these sounds represent and the absolutely incompatible shared world of the lovers. The two are obviously about to come into extreme conflict, so the ringing fanfares ending the act are made to sound intensely ironic. Formal music has become a threateningly hollow sound, a sign of everything the opera will from now on try to evade.

In *Tristan*, then, transition expresses itself as a resistance to form. It's a movement away from that which shapes and embodies. The lovers seek a kind of disembodiment, and their words (like their music) strain the borders of intelligible definition in order to liberate them as fully as possible from any externally-given conditions, any 'ordinary logical scheme' as the passage on Beethoven from 'The Music of the Future' puts it. The more ecstatically (in Act II) or miserably (in Act III) Tristan and Isolde long for an escape from their surroundings, the more restlessly evasive and chromatic the score becomes. *Tristan* is in this sense a thoroughly antagonistic opera. Although held together by a motivic interplay more intricate and subtle even than that of *Götterdämmerung*, and by powerfully cogent deep harmonic relationships, its immediate aural effect is one of defeated expectations, unanticipated transitions, unresolved tensions – at every turn seeming to struggle against the imposition of structure.

In *Meistersinger*, by contrast, transition takes place under the aegis of form. It is a regulated process, implying a set of rules, and – more importantly – governed and sanctioned by ritual controls. Obviously enough, the main representative of newness in the opera is the prize song. It's absolutely characteristic of the general tendency of *Meistersinger*, then, that Sachs should encourage its creation via the metaphor of a marriage (when he advises Walther to match stanza to stanza as if making a 'rechtes Paar', a proper pair), and still more so that he celebrates its completion with a baptism. His christening speech before the quintet is intensely formal. As if the point wasn't clear enough, it begins with a resumption of the music of the opening chorale. This tells us two things. First, that this is an official moment: Walther's song is being formally adopted into the community according to that body's proper rites for solemnizing a new birth. Second, that the rite itself is thematically central, because the chorale is sung in honour of the original Baptist himself; Sachs is becoming John to Walther's Jesus, the forerunner and proclaimer of the holy authority of a new order. The scene, that is, is genuinely sacramental, not one of Sachs's comical exaggerations. The process of new birth is being inseparably tied to the sacrament of baptism. Transition is institutionalized and solemnized by the traditions according to which it is performed. Born in a dream the song may be, but it's quickly brought home. As Eva and Walther sing in the quintet, its melody will fulfil its purpose 'in der Meister vollem Kreis', 'in the full circle of the Masters'. The opera is about new things finding their proper place amid established forms.

These two works present, in very fully worked-out versions, the alternative interpretations of Wagner's 'art of transition'. They offer opposed meditations on the issues of movement and form; to adopt *Tristan*'s vocabulary again, they're as different as night and day. In fact one can hardly help noticing that where *Tristan* opens windows onto a mysterious, elusive, dislocated 'night-world', *Meistersinger* is set during the shortest night and longest day of the year. Sachs explicitly refers to the Tristan legend in order to reject it; this, he says, is going to be an altogether different story. The effect of Wagner's musical self-quotation at this moment is oddly disconcerting (quite apart from how blatantly it exposes the opera's concern with Wagner himself as artist-hero). When a few bars of the *Tristan* prelude suddenly bubble up in the *Meistersinger* score, they sound extraordinarily out of place. Of course, at a simple level it's a harmless joke; rather too much of Wagner's 'comic' opera, in fact, can be taken as a harmless joke – at a dangerously simple level. The music is meant to do no more than make reference to the story Sachs mentions, like a private reminiscence-motif. Yet it also cannot help emphasizing how utterly remote from Sachs's world the whole mood and action of *Tristan* are, an uncomfortable reminder of all the ways these two masterpieces seem to contradict each other. (Elsewhere in *Meistersinger*, discomfort is saved for Beckmesser, who gets enough of it to spare anyone else the need to feel any at all, as scapegoats do.) One evades form, the other embraces it. One elevates exile to a kind of artistic principle; the other is a hymn to an idealized *Asyl* where everyone can come home.

This in itself might seem like a symptom of artistic restlessness. After all, if transition rules Wagner's art between its early phase (ending in the Dresden non-revolution) and its final erection of its own temple with *Parsifal* and the Bayreuth Festspielhaus, what wider and more complete transition could there be than the distance between Isolde and Tristan's *Liebesnacht* and the Masters' Nuremberg? Both, it must be remembered, are fantasies. The lovers' frantic dreams of a permanent escape from the waking world are pure delusion, solvable only by death. *Tristan* makes it very clear that they are abandoned to a mutual fantasy. We see them often enough from the outside – from Kurwenal, Brangäne and Marke's point of view – to diagnose the madness of their passion; the wonder is how deeply the opera is able to take us inside it, making a hopeless private dream conceivable to the audience (we have the most astonishingly and unrelentingly effective of Wagner's scores to thank for this). But the Nuremberg of *Meistersinger* is a fantasy as well. It's a place where Wagner can imagine his own art, transparently figured in the persons of Walther and Sachs, performed and celebrated. This is the idea that realizes itself in the building of Bayreuth and the creation of an opera meant only for that stage; but in the 1860s, unlike the 1870s, it's still only an idea. At the time when he was working on *Meistersinger*, Wagner was in fact engaged in an attempt to bring it to life. Once the apparently unlimited and unstinted resources of the Kingdom of Bavaria had been offered to him by Ludwig, their first joint plan was the creation of a new theatre and a music school in Munich, to be devoted to model performances of Wagner's works, and, more generally, to house and disseminate an authentically German art much as (according to Sachs) the Mastersingers' guild had. But this dream dissolved under the laws of exile. Wagner was unable to hold on to his place of influence over the King. His plan for (as it were) a new Nuremberg in Munich proved itself to be as fictional as his version of the old Nuremberg. The idea that inspires *Meistersinger* turned out to be subject to the same displacements and restless transitions that characterize all Wagner's projects between Dresden and Bayreuth.

Tristan's fantasy is an apotheosis of exile. This is one of those achievements that one sometimes feels only Wagner could have come up with: embracing the state of transition so completely and enthusiastically that it convinces us that displacement and dislocation are forms of incomparable bliss. By rights, it should be a tragedy. Betrayal, doomed love and untimely death are the ingredients of an unhappy story, and the tension and disquiet of the opera's music might be thought of as the appropriate accompaniment to a tale of the sufferings of being out of place. Yet in Wagner's hands this is the least tragic of tragedies. Even the bleakest moments of Tristan's despair in Act III can metamorphose into ecstasy, as his delirium allows him to luxuriate in visions of Isolde's arrival long before the shepherd actually sights her ship. The lovers' monomaniacal surrender to their imaginary night-world becomes the opera's centre of gravity. Its focus, its sympathies, above all its music are so entirely on the side of Isolde and Tristan that their predicament becomes a kind of glory.

This is why it ends as it does, with the most drawn-out and full-blown of all Wagnerian climaxes. Isolde's *Verklärung* (transfiguration) or *Liebestod* (love-death) looks and sounds like an ascent to heaven, not a deathblow (her last words are 'höchste Lust!', 'highest bliss'). In these closing minutes, the restlessness of the opera's music becomes a way for the orchestra to fashion a kind of harmonic and melodic Jacob's ladder, rising higher and higher without (at first) any sense that the ascent need ever stop, and making each upward movement sound like an approach towards the most sublime and tremendous of destinations. In other words, the perpetual movement and constant transitions of exile are turned into steps on a stairway to heaven. Isolde's permanent sense of being out of place is allowed to become a condition of transfiguration. The comparison is not exact, but one might get a sense of what is happening by setting her situation at the end of *Tristan* next to that of Lohengrin in his final scene. Both are effectively banishing themselves from the world, turning their faces towards a higher and more perfect realm where they truly belong. In *Lohengrin*, though, this is a genuinely tragic catastrophe, because the hero's otherworldliness means he has been permanently exiled from the environment the opera inhabits. By contrast, the effect of Isolde's departure from the world is to make that world dissolve around her. Instead of being banished into her nightscape, she takes the opera there with her; the final chords of *Tristan* breathe only the most serene, magical contentment. Contemporary stage practice is interestingly revealing on this point. My experience may not be representative, but I personally have never yet seen Isolde die. Every staging I have witnessed has left her standing as the curtain goes down. This reflects the mood of the opera's end perfectly well. One doesn't feel that one is seeing the scene through Marke's eyes, looking at the dead bodies of two sadly deluded and star-crossed people. The more authentic interpretation seems to be that Isolde has at last discovered what she and Tristan have been searching for all along, the visionary rapture that is only available to those who expel themselves entirely from the daylight world. The *Liebestod* bathes the whole condition of exile in the rosiest imaginable glow, turning what ought to be a state of disquiet, pain and tragedy into *höchste Lust*, a happiness drifting beyond the limits of conception.

Turning back to *Meistersinger*, we can think of Sachs's Nuremberg as an alternative solution to the problems of exile and transition. As systematically unlike each other as the two operas are, they are at least linked by their earnest concern with these themes. But where *Tristan* decides to turn the problem on its head by exulting and glorying in the condition of being out of place, *Meistersinger* devotes itself to a solution: it fantasizes about *ending* exile, establishing an *Asyl*, a home. No other work of Wagner is as drenched and saturated by the spirit of place. Nuremberg itself has a weighty, felt presence in the opera. Its prime agent is the man the crowd calls 'Nürnbergs theurem Sachs', 'Nuremberg's beloved Sachs', the local hero who (it turns out) is also the hero of a locale, the (apparently) good genius of the town. His role in Act II is simple: to keep Walther and Eva in place, physically as well as in legal and moral terms. He functions like a closed gate in the town wall, frustrating their plans to escape everything that confines them. At the end of the act he pulls Walther into his house, effectively bringing him home. The prize song is thus born legitimately, under the proper parental roof. In Act III he tells Walther that the poetry is an art of locating things: 'Mancher durch sie das Verlor'ne fand', 'many have found what was lost thanks to it'. The *Wahn* (delusion or madness) he diagnoses in human affairs would be embraced by Tristan and Isolde, but he sets himself the task of fighting it off, carefully stage-managing the whole town in the final scenes so as to ensure that everything and everyone ends up in their proper place. For all his willingness to embrace the new and to bend the rules, Sachs is in fact a figure of implacable inertia and restraint, far more immovable object than irresistible force. He's the living embodiment of the nostalgic conservatism that suffuses the whole opera, the fond and warm fantasizing about a good old Germany which breaks into the open in the final speech.

The depth of this fantasy's appeal is revealed in Walther's prize song itself. So much attention, naturally, is focussed on the musical quality of the song – which is after all its significantly innovative aspect – that one tends not to pay much attention to what it actually says. It tells of the poet seeing two women in a dream, the first 'Eva im Paradies' ('Eve in Paradise'), the second the Muse of Parnassus. He awakens and finds both of them incarnated in his own beloved; he has won both Parnassus and Paradise 'durch Sanges Sieg', 'through victory in song'. This is intended as an elaborate and gracious compliment to Eva, and a celebration of the fact that she represents both womanhood (her namesake Eve) and, since she's the prize for which the Masters are competing, poetry (Parnassus, the Muses' sacred mountain). Walther knows that he's competing both for her personally and for Mastership according to the laws of the contest, so his song allegorically unites the two endeavours as the twin goals of the lover-poet. There's nothing particularly surprising about choosing the classical Muse to represent the poetic half of the pairing, but the reference to 'Eve in Paradise' makes us pause. Why choose the original sinner to represent 'das schönste Weib', 'the loveliest woman'? Because of the fact that she and Pogner's daughter have the same name, obviously enough. Yet the song adopts the Biblical myth with an extraordinary omission. Here is how the first stanza of the prize song describes the poet's dream:

. . . ein Garten lud mich ein, –	. . . a garden invited me in, –
dort unter einem Wunderbaum,	there, beneath a wonderful tree,
von Früchten reich behangen,	richly hung with fruit,
zu schau'n im sel'gen Liebestraum,	seen in love's blessed dream,
was höchstem Lustverlangen	boldly promising the fulfilment
Erfüllung kühn verhieß –	of joy's highest desires –
das schönste Weib,	the fairest woman,
Eva im Paradies.	Eve in Paradise.

The scene of seduction beneath a tree laden with fruit could not refer more explicitly to Adam's fall. In his dream, Walther is revisiting the primal, archetypal moment of disobedience, expulsion and exile. In the Lutheran world of Renaissance Nuremberg, Eve stands as the author of original sin; tasting the fruit of the 'Wunderbaum' and surrendering to the promise of 'höchstem Lustverlangen/ Erfüllung', she is the cause of mankind's irreversible exile from Paradise. Yet the prize song simply ignores the Bible's story of temptation and error. Walther finds his way back into the garden, a path for ever barred (according to the Book of Genesis) by the cherubim with the flaming sword. There he embraces his Eve and wakes (in the third stanza) to find that he has won Paradise again. His dream reverses the Fall. The original expulsion is undone, and the triumphant poet finds himself back in mankind's first God-given home, returned to Eden. There could be no more perfect illustration of the impulse of *Meistersinger* as a whole. In the quintet, Sachs, Eva and Walther all wonder about the real meaning of the dream and the song, anticipating that it will be revealed in the contest at the end of the act. The meaning turns out to be: you *can* go home again. The gates of Paradise are open, Walther's song proclaims, and the force of true love and truer music can carry us back inside our original refuge. *Meistersinger* works the same way, conjuring up a vision of artistic innovation and authenticity perfectly harmonized with social and civic life, a scene where the inspired musician-poet carries off all the prizes while the crowds salute and cheer.

Tristan commits itself wholeheartedly to an art of transition; *Meistersinger* dreams of bringing it to rest. One luxuriates in alienation, while the other is as much a paean to the idea of belonging as is the letter to Otto Wesendonck with which this chapter began. There's always an element of wish-fulfilment about Wagner's art; part of its power is the sheer excess of its romantic indulgence of its desires. In *Tristan*, though, those desires retain their unsettlingly extreme and hopeless quality. We can see that the lovers are lost and deluded even as the magic of the score compels us to share their delusion. *Meistersinger*'s fantasies are more nakedly, crudely self-satisfied; the opera banishes every hint of doubt about art's triumph and the artist's homecoming. Its closing music is uncannily like the pompous march of the gods at the end of *Rheingold*, except that this time there are no offstage voices to remind us of what the celebration is conveniently forgetting or leaving out. This is, or should be, genuinely troubling. The opera seems to be dealing with the problem of exile by taking possession of a fantasy *Asyl*, closing its doors (kicking out all undesirables on the way, in the person of Beckmesser), and then strategically forgetting that the whole business is just a dream. *Tristan* is often said to be the musical and dramatic *ne plus ultra* of desire; but in the Wagnerian canon that title really belongs to *Die Meistersinger von Nürnberg*, which gratifies its own desires so completely and wholeheartedly that it pretends they aren't mere desires at all, but presents them – like Walther's song – as a dream come true.

CHAPTER TEN

Desire

When Wagner had nowhere to go, he always seems to have ended up in Paris. The city figures in his biography as a kind of terminus of exile: always inimical, always somewhere he enters only to count the months until he can leave again, and always the scene of failure. It's appropriate, then, that Paris should have witnessed the first performances of music from *Tristan und Isolde* under Wagner's own baton. If *Parsifal* was created in a symbiotic relationship with Wagner's own theatre, intended only to be heard within its consecrated walls, *Tristan* – especially its opening prelude, which was the extract given at the 1860 Paris concerts – is the music of nowhere (the French capital being the closest approximation, in Wagner's cosmology). Here is how he describes the Tristan legend and its musical representation in a programme note for the concert performances of the prelude:

> Henceforth [i.e. after the drinking of the potion] no end to the yearning, longing, bliss and misery of love: world, power, fame, splendour, honour, knighthood, loyalty and friendship, all scattered like a baseless dream; one thing alone left living: desire [*Sehnsucht*], desire unquenchable, longing forever rebearing itself [*neu sich gebärendes*]. . . .
>
> . . . So in one long breath [the composer] let that unslaked longing swell from first avowal of the gentlest [tremor] of attraction, through half-heaved sighs, through hopes and fears, laments and wishes, joy and torment, to the mightiest onset, most resolute attempt to find the breach unbarring to the heart a path into the endless sea of love's delight. In vain! Its power spent, the heart sinks back to pine of its desire – desire without attainment [*Erreichen*]; for each fruition sows the seeds of fresh desire [*da jedes Erreichen nur wieder neues Sehnen ist*]. . . . (VIII 387)

Tristan also calls this particular kind of anguish *Sehnen*, yearning or longing, and recognizes it for a chronic and fatal condition. As the programme note explains, desire is condemned to feed itself, for even if it is momentarily satisfied, the moment merely begets further desire. The result is the most acute imaginable state of loss. Desire is by definition intensely focussed on what it does not have, a permanent consciousness of the absence of the thing desired. It's always nowhere. There is no cure: desire is 'unquenchable', 'forever rebearing itself', a self-generating torment. Tristan understands that nothing can mitigate it:

Für dieser Schmerzen	For the fearful pain
schreckliche Pein,	of these sufferings,
welcher Balsam sollte	what balm could
mir Lind'rung verleih'n?	grant me relief?

His mention of 'Balsam' briefly anticipates an echo in Act I of *Parsifal*, where Kundry brings Amfortas 'Balsam' from Arabia in the hope that it will ease the king's pain. A squire tells Gurnemanz that it has worked, at least for a little while, but the old knight comments gloomily, 'Die Wunde ist's, die nie sich schließen will!' ('it is the wound that will never close'). Permanent wounds run like a leitmotif through Wagner's imagination. Amfortas and Tristan's condition is not all that unlike the Dutchman's, suffering for all eternity, or even Kundry's own life of continuous damnation. Tristan, though, is the archetype for all of these incurable victims, because his suffering comes with no sin attached (never for a moment in the opera are we really convinced that adultery is a sin, not even during Marke's bitter speech at the end of Act II). His injury is not a punishment. It is simply the essence of suffering: longing for that which cannot be attained. The 'wound that will never close' is properly named desire.

I suggested in Part I that seduction (or abduction) is at the heart of the aesthetics of romantic opera. To an extent, that is, it permits desires to be gratified. It opens up magical or exotic scenes and allows its audience the vicarious thrill of feeling as if they have entered those enchanted spaces. The clearest Wagnerian representation of this effect is the Venusberg, a paradise of erotic satiety where every wish is immediately indulged. One can get a sense of how utterly different – and how immensely more sophisticated – the aesthetics of the mature operas are by comparing the Venusberg with Wagner's other staging of a sexual paradise, Klingsor's magic garden in Act II of *Parsifal*. Here there are no orgiastic scenes of indulgence, no instantly gratified desires. Venus's grotto works by parading enchanting visions before the beholder's eye, offering a surfeit of pleasure, promising to make flesh anything he can imagine. Klingsor's garden, by contrast, is a place of perverse innocence. His flowermaidens don't *know* that they are seducing Parsifal, nor does he in turn know that he is being seduced. Parsifal calls them 'schönen Kinder', lovely children, and indeed the whole atmosphere of the garden is one of pre-pubescent imitation sexuality, where erotic play is only a game. To this extent, they are the apt embodiments of Klingsor's peculiar power. Gurnemanz explains in Act I that the fallen Grail knight became endowed with magic after he castrated himself. Powerless to quell the urgency of desire (Gurnemanz calls it *Sünde*, sin) within himself, he decides instead to annul it; the result is that he learns how to conjure up the illusion of irresistible desire. He gains mastery over sexual longing by cancelling it (rather than by gratifying it to excess, as Venus does). Accordingly, the enchantresses that bloom in his castle appear childishly sexless even as they tease their victims. What his garden represents, then, is the strange emptiness of desire. In the Venusberg, you can have whatever you want: this is the law of romantic opera, satisfying its audience's longing for indulgence in illusions. In Klingsor's garden, you cannot have anything. You can only be teased by the shadow of satisfaction, and, as Kundry says, the flower maidens wither as soon as they are plucked, leaving you (like Amfortas) endlessly waiting for a relief that never comes: or, returning to the words of the programme note, 'the heart sinks back to pine of its desire'.

This strange quality of longing without attainment, desire cut off from its object, is essential to *Tristan*. It explains why the opera so often described as a fervid hymn to passionate love is in fact entirely chaste. Just as this is the least tragic of tragedies, it's also the most sexless of love affairs. For all their talk of rapture and bliss, the lovers treat their Act II tryst more as a chance to dream than an opportunity for consummation. Indeed they more or less ignore the fact that they are actually alone together, preferring to spend their time anticipating a more perfect moment of future union (in death). It's as if they voluntarily submit themselves to the law of desire, which denies any possibility of fulfilment. What do Tristan and Isolde actually want? Only at the most superficial level are they driven by the conventional lovers' longing for each other's presence. Far more deeply, they share a desire for oblivion. All their passion is really a death-wish. Their scene in Act II becomes more ecstatic the more it commits itself to a dreamily suicidal impulse. 'Lass' den Tag/ dem Tode weichen!' ('let the day give way to death!'), Tristan pleads, and though Isolde takes a little longer to be convinced, she eventually joins him in an entranced fantasy of complete extinction:

So starben wir,	So might we die,
um ungetrennt,	to be undivided,
ewig einig,	for ever one
ohne End',	without end,
ohn' Erwachen,	without awakening –
ohne Bangen,	without fearing –
namenlos	namelessly
in Lieb' umfangen. . . .	embraced in love. . . .

What they truly want, in other words, is nothingness: they desire nothing – which doesn't mean that they have no desire, but that (quite the opposite) they are utterly possessed by the compulsion described in the programme note, 'desire without attainment', a desire which by definition can go nowhere and achieve no object.

The broad musical progression of their long scene together in Act II eloquently confirms what their rather foggy conversation suggests. Isolde's excitement before Tristan's arrival is conveyed in breathless, bubbly, impatient music, rising to the sublime only when she takes hold of the torch and extinguishes it as if (she says) it were 'meines Lebens Licht', 'my own life's light'. When Tristan rushes onstage, the lovers gasp over each other in hysterical bursts of song, while the score – rushing strings and rapid fanfare-like brass – seems to be panting to keep up. This is impressively exhilarated music, but also almost melodramatic in its effort to express the maximum of hasty exuberance. It is, after all, the most conventional aspect of the tryst: the lovers' delight in finding themselves together at last. It quickly becomes clear, however, that the scene is not deeply interested in this delight. The eager pleasure conveyed early on dissolves quite rapidly, and what eventually replaces it makes it seem merely trivial by comparison. The scene finds its real centre of gravity when the orchestra arrives at the entranced murmur of the lovers' appeal to be drowned in darkness and nothingness:

O sink' hernieder,	O sink down,
Nacht der Liebe,	night of love,
gieb Vergessen,	grant me to forget
daß ich lebe. . . .	that I live. . . .

Unmistakably, this is a far deeper and more heartfelt desire than the giddy excitement of the scene's opening. We know anyway from the other two acts that both Isolde and Tristan are perpetually preoccupied by death. But when the same obsession appears in the midst of their mutual ecstasies, there can be no doubt that the kind of desire in which the opera is steeped is focussed exclusively on its own emptiness, its kinship with annihilation.

Another way of saying the same truth about *Tristan* would be to point out that the plot's crucial event, Brangäne's substitution of the love potion for the poison, is entirely irrelevant. At first sight, the device seems rather puzzling: are we to believe that the heights of impassioned dedication the lovers achieve in Act II are chemically induced? Does this mean that their love is not real? The questions are easily bypassed once we realize that the two potions are at the thematic level the same. There is no substitution. At best, the difference between love and death is a matter of postponement; what Isolde and Tristan intend to do in Act I is simply put off until the end of Act III. The whole intervening action consists of little more than the lovers slowly reversing

Brangäne's decision, committing themselves step by step to the shared death she tried to avert. The further their love progresses, the more thoroughly suicidal it becomes, climaxing in Isolde's solitary rapture as she extinguishes herself in 'höchste Lust', 'highest bliss'. When they choose to admit their love for each other, they choose in the same moment to die. Brangäne's switch merely protracts the process, allowing the opera to express the relation between love and death – *Liebestod* – as intensely and fully as possible. Death doesn't intervene tragically in their story, as it does in (say) *Romeo and Juliet*, where the lovers plan a future that is then denied them. Instead, it arrives as a kind of benediction, setting an apt and natural seal on Tristan and Isolde's passion. The love potion allows that passion to run in its proper channel, but doesn't change its destination; it's as deadly a poison as the vial Isolde initially chooses. Even before the business of the potions, Isolde knows the fatality hanging over Tristan and herself. 'Tod geweihtes Haupt!/ Tod geweihtes Herz!', she sings the first time in the opera her eyes fix on him: 'Head consecrated to death!/ Heart consecrated to death!' According to the story she tells Brangäne in Act I, she first fell in love with him as she stood over him with his own sword, ready to avenge her betrothed Morold. Death and love are always interchangeable in *Tristan*. Both mark the obliteration of 'day' by 'night', an extinguishing of light and a passage out of the world.

Desire, then, exists only under the shadow of death. Strangely, it never dreams of ending itself by achieving what it desires. Its only ambition is oblivion. Look at what Tristan says in his mournful delirium of Act III, as he envisions Isolde coming to him:

Die nicht erstirbt,	That which does not die,
sehnend nun ruft	now calls, yearning,
nach Sterbens Ruh'	to the distant healer
sie der fernen Ärztin zu.	for the peace of death.

'That which does not die' – the wound that never closes – is, as the programme note tells us, yearning or desire 'forever rebearing itself'. Specifically, it's a desire for Isolde's arrival. Here, though, it calls her not in order to satisfy itself with the joy of her healing presence, but because she will bring death – and indeed, as soon as she arrives Tristan is freed to breathe his last. This is the only healing desire can imagine, even from the beloved herself. (The last line of the passage quoted is punctuated with a bitterly discordant interjection from a stopped horn; promises of peace and healing quail before the Amfortas-like permanence of 'yearning'.) Unlike in the Venusberg, love conjures up no imaginary visions of satisfaction. Later in the act Tristan is allowed a passage of envisioned bliss. For a few moments he thinks Isolde is in his sight, the orchestra temporarily escaping its fever and melancholy to accompany his words with exquisitely sweet music:

Sieh'st du sie noch nicht?	Do you still not see her?
Wie sie selig,	How she, blessed,
hehr und milde	glorious and tender,
wandelt durch	travels over
des Meer's Gefilde?	the fields of the sea?

Yet the sweetness comes not from the delusion of Isolde's presence itself, but from the promise of extinction she brings with her: 'sie führt mir letzte/ Labung zu', 'she bears me a last relief'. The music of this vision is nothing like the excitement of Tristan's arrival in Act II. It is not depicting a lover's eagerness for his beloved, but something far more like Amfortas's pleading for death.

Suicidal raptures have a long and prominent history in Wagner's work. The Dutchman's longing for a devoted 'Engel' ('angel') is also a longing for the death that otherwise always eludes him. Senta, in turn, proves the completeness of her love by leaping off a cliff. Elisabeth and Tannhäuser both ultimately enact their mutual devotion by dying more or less spontaneously. Siegfried and Brünnhilde's paean to 'leuchtende Liebe' ('light-bringing love') also celebrates 'lachender Tod' ('laughing death'). There's nothing exclusively Wagnerian about this. A certain strain of melodramatic nineteenth-century romanticism always gloried in the conjunction of love and death, and Wagner inherited its luxuriously morbid mood from his theatrical family and his early cultural environment. Nevertheless, as with so many other conventions of late romanticism, he articulates it with such fervour and intensity that in his hands it somehow becomes original again, or at least gains a seriousness far beyond anything that could be achieved by clichéd melodrama. Tristan and Isolde's bizarrely contemplative discussion of their predicament in the middle of their Act II tryst (bizarre in that operatic adulterers usually have more of Don Giovanni's gusto) elevates the link between love and death into something like a mystical insight. To Senta, it seems perfectly conventional and straightforward: 'Hier sieh' mich, treu dir bis zum Tod!' ('See me here, faithful to you to the death'), she cries, in good operatic fashion, before hurling herself into the waves. Yet by the time of *Tristan*, this gesture, though still fundamentally unchanged – the gist of the lovers' conversation is the same as Senta's cry – has been transformed into a theme treated at massive length and with philosophical earnestness. As the contrast between the Venusberg and Klingsor's garden also suggests, it's as if Wagner's mature work has decided to explore something his earlier operas took more or less for granted. The romantic operas inherit the theme of desire's fatality as a convention of romantic aesthetics, but by the time of *Tristan* Wagner's work is trying to understand and express the essential significance of this theme.

At this stage, we've arrived at an interpretative crossroads. The remainder of this chapter will attempt to explain why, and by the end of the discussion it should be quite apparent which path this book is choosing to take. As we'll see in Part IV, the decision must necessarily be made before dealing in any detail with *Parsifal*, for decisions about how to understand Wagner's greatest and most troubling masterpiece are always at bottom decisions about how to approach Wagner's art in general. After all, more than any of its predecessors *Parsifal* revolves around the notion of *Erlösung*, redemption, and indeed stages the whole process of being 'redeemed' as explicitly and thoroughly as one can imagine, with its Christianized paraphernalia and its perpetual talk of sin and salvation. When we turn to face Wagner's habit of amalgamating love and death, we are at last confronting the question of redemption at its crucial moment. For Wagner's operas appear to insist that what I have called the suicidal tendency of desire is in fact a redemptive process. Love, they say, climaxes in deaths which are occasions of salvation and transfiguration.

This claim is seen at its clearest in *Der fliegende Holländer*. Both Senta and the Dutchman speak of his need for a faithful woman in terms of his being 'saved': her devotion to him is always presented in the context of redemption. The law of the Dutchman's curse dictates that it can only be broken by a woman wholeheartedly devoted enough to die for him, so love and death are brought together as the twin signs of 'Erlösung' or 'Heil' (both words, 'redemption' and 'salvation', are used frequently). The opera is very sure, therefore, that its hero and heroine's equally fervent longing to die is in fact their pathway to transfiguration. This is the basic claim of redemption in its simplest form: desire perfects itself in death, so the act of dying expresses and completes the saving power of love. With this model in mind, the rest of the operas can be understood the same way. Tannhäuser is 'saved' (from damnation at Venus's hands) by his love for Elisabeth, and, as the chorus proclaims at the end, his redemption is confirmed when he dies with her name on his lips. Brünnhilde describes her suicide as a longing 'des Helden heiligste/ Ehre zu theilen', 'to share the hero's holiest honour' – to be glorified in death like him, in other words. She immolates herself in the faith that their joint end will cleanse the world of Alberich's curse; once again, a loving death appears to be the avenue to redemption. Isolde dies in an ecstatic trance, as if discovering that extinction is indeed the portal into the blissful nightworld she and Tristan have all along dreamed of entering. Kundry too longs for a release which the opera finally grants her in the form of death; and though one can't say that she and Parsifal are lovers, Wagner's stage directions specify that she slowly sinks lifeless to the ground 'with her gaze uplifted' to him. Devotion, death and salvation are intermingled in her end as thoroughly as in Senta's or Tannhäuser's.

In every case, the operas are asking us to understand their ends, their conclusions, in a certain light. Interpreting death is always to do with interpreting ends, since (in tragic drama at least) death is the plot's way of signalling that its course is over: death is where stories reach their terminus. By representing death in terms of redemption, the operas deny that death merely annihilates or extinguishes the characters. They claim that their ends are in some sense happy ones. Again, *Holländer* is the most straightforward example, since (according to Wagner's instructions) Senta's suicide is immediately followed by the sight of her and the Dutchman in each other's arms, flying 'transfigured' towards heaven. *Tannhäuser* ends by reversing the Pope's excommunication of the hero and announcing 'Erlösung ward der Welt zu Theil', 'redemption has been granted to the world'. As already discussed at length, the case of the *Ring* is more complex, but there have always been people keen to interpret Brünnhilde's final actions as the deeds of pure love redeeming all the greed and guilt of the tetralogy. *Parsifal*, meanwhile, ends like *Tannhäuser* with a solemn and sacred chorus confirming 'Erlösung', although there has been almost nothing to mourn over here, since only Kundry (significantly) has suffered the usual Wagnerian fate of dying before being saved. In every case, redemption is offered as the final goal of the characters' striving and sufferings. Transferred to *Tristan*, this model provides an idealistic interpretation of the lovers' embrace of death. There's no reference to *Erlösung* in the opera, but if we understand all Wagnerian love-deaths as being gateways to transfiguration, then the oblivion Isolde and Tristan pursue so desperately might in the end be thought of as another version of redemption. Certainly the music of Isolde's last soliloquy could not be more ecstatically sublime, and the warm, serene, unruffled B major chords that bring the opera's opening motif to a kind of rest at the very end of the score breathe an atmosphere of benediction matching Wagner's closing stage directions, which call for Marke to make the sign of the cross (redemptively) over the lovers' bodies.

All this adds up to one fundamental claim: that death is a form of salvation. The end is interpreted as a climax, a consummation. Redemption sets a triumphant seal on the progress of the plot by converting its terminal event – the extinction of the main characters – into a mark of ultimate, sacred attainment. Brünnhilde, Isolde, Senta, the Dutchman, Tannhäuser, presumably Kundry, all expire surrounded by a nimbus of musical glory – those soaring, celestially orchestrated climaxes Wagner is so good at – as if their voluntary deaths are the capstones of their lives.

What, then, of the law of desire? How can this idea of redemptive consummations be squared with *Tristan*'s insight that the true nature of desire is emptiness, and that death is welcomed not because it transfigures and redeems, but because it stills and annihilates the otherwise infinite torment of longing? The 1860 programme note is very explicit: desire never reaches consummation, and that's what gives it its peculiarly intense force. In *Tristan*, love isn't the path to a redemptive death, but another version of Brangäne's poison, a form of oblivion. Once we realize this truth about *Tristan*, though, we have to begin questioning the whole concept of death-as-salvation throughout Wagner's work. To all appearances, redemption is the end that Wagner's operas desire. They want to persuade themselves and us that the deaths they stage can be interpreted as triumphs. But what if – as the 1860 programme note quite explicitly says – desire never achieves an end? What if the operas cannot have what they want? What if death is simply what it appears to be: annihilation, oblivion? The early operas resort to the most unambiguously explicit resolutions of such doubts, by providing material confirmation that death has been followed by redemption: the sight of Senta and the Dutchman taken up to heaven, the miracle of the Pope's staff. As Wagner's work matures, though, the questions become more pressing. The end of *Tristan* may look and sound like a blissful transfiguration, but everything that has preceded it indicates that this is the peace of oblivion, not of heaven. Similarly, who is to say that Kundry is saved as she expires, rather than simply achieving the nothingness she so desperately hungers for?

These questions have already been anticipated by the discussion of futurity in the *Ring* in Part II. Essentially, we're facing exactly the same interpretative choice: is there a redeemed, utopian future heralded at the end of a Wagner opera, or is there only destruction, an end that promises no new beginning, a death not followed by any ascent into a heavenly new world? 'Redemption' is a concept which encourages us to understand endings in the former of these ways. 'Desire' (as the programme note presents it) is its opposite. Redemption means that love and death are *for* something: they have a purpose, a goal, they end up getting where they have striven to go. Desire, as I've argued, is not a desire *for* anything; or it's a desire for nothing. It can never have what it longs for. It can always only be the state of longing. Redemption heals all sins and sufferings, but desire is the wound that will never close. These are two mutually contradictory ways of thinking about endings. One sets an idealistic seal on the struggles and sufferings of the plot, endowing them with a final saving transfiguration. The other denies that fulfilment and consummation have been achieved. There's no end to desire except annihilation (the word literally means 'bringing to nothing').

Why are these alternatives important? Why not just say that some of the operas end in redemption, like *Holländer*, and others (perhaps) do not, like *Tristan* or *Lohengrin*? The choice matters because it goes beyond questions about the individual operas. It speaks to one of the most distinctive and difficult aspects of Wagner's art. As an introduction to the character of that art, I once played two operatic overtures to a group of people unfamiliar with Wagner. The first, a conventional and unremarkable example of mid-nineteenth-century overture, was from Albert Lortzing's 1845 romantic opera *Undine*. The second was the prelude to Act I of *Lohengrin*, composed only three years later. When asked to compare the two extracts, most of the group mentioned the much more expressive character of the *Lohengrin* prelude, the consistency of its main musical idea – no switching from theme to contrasting theme, as in Lortzing's piece – and, more generally, the fact of its being simply more striking. One person found a very revealing way of putting these points: the *Lohengrin* prelude, she said, sounded as if it wanted something from her. What she was referring to was the quality in Wagner's art that overwhelms audiences with its massively assured and insistent self-expression. Probably not coincidentally, this was also a quality in Wagner's personality, remarked on by both friends and foes, and also (more reliably) by the very small number of people who managed to remain neutral after encountering him. By all accounts, his egotism was so titanic that it rose above mere selfishness into sincere fanaticism, a messianic insistence on the supreme importance of himself and his art. It would be both unfair and irrelevant to say that these personal traits were reflected in his art; but it's nevertheless true that his work is very deeply marked by a determination to achieve its effects as fully as possible: to get what it wants, in other words. Think of the volumes of his writings, full of a crusading spirit determined to justify its course, to convince everyone of its rightness and to condemn alternatives. As radiantly lovely as the *Lohengrin* prelude is, one has to recognize that it has something of the same quality: it focusses its imagination on a central idea – the descent, revelation and ascent of the Grail – and pursues that idea with merciless thoroughness, summoning up marvels of sonority in order to rivet our attention on the drama it wants to express. Or think of Wagner's insistence on creating a theatre exclusively for the performance of his own works under conditions entirely determined by himself and his appointed heirs. Then compare the astonishing originality of the *Tristan* and *Parsifal* scores, through which basically rather ordinary plots (doomed love, a heroic quest) are magnified and intensified so that every nuance of the drama is presented to the audience with the highest possible degree of earnestness, conviction and emotion. Like the Bayreuth theatre, the operas seem to say: in my hands all drama is unprecedently serious and worthy of attention, all themes are incomparably weighty, and the most essential meanings and revelations will be transmitted to the audience. At a fundamental level, then, Wagner's work has desires: it *wants* something. In Adorno's summary: '[w]hat specifically characterizes Wagnerian expression is its intentionality'.[1] His art wants to fill us with what it expresses; it wants to absorb its audience in itself. All art wants to achieve its aims, but there are few artists who make it comparably clear that they even have aims, let alone insisting that those aims are profoundly significant and intensely serious.

Nowhere in Wagner's work – not even in the most blatantly self-serving of the prose writings – is there a more complete satisfaction of an obvious desire than in *Die Meistersinger*. Hanslick found this quality even in the opera's music; in an interesting review of the 1868 premiere, he commented: 'Wagner knows what he wants; every note of the score speaks of intentions fully realized.'[2] At the level of the dramatic action, certainly, *Meistersinger* gets exactly what it wants. Walther (representing spontaneous, expressive, natural creativity) is publicly acclaimed; Sachs (the spokesman for the civic and cultural importance of art) is vindicated and glorified; Beckmesser the pseudo-artist is humiliated and expelled. Sachs is in fact the only successful plotter in all Wagner's operas. The plans he conceives (in stark contrast to Wotan, a figure to whom he's often compared) actually work out just as they were intended to. It's entirely appropriate that the opera's plot should centre on a competition and a prize. *Meistersinger* sets up the opposing camps, matches them against each other, and then makes sure the right side wins. This is precisely equivalent to the idea of *Erlösung*, redemption: everything turns out for the best, endings are interpreted as triumphs. Wagner's stage directions for the final tableau of *Meistersinger* suggest a scene uncannily similar in effect to the faintly comical picture of the Dutchman and Senta whooshing upwards in the light of the rising sun:

> Walther and Eva lean against Sachs's shoulders, one on each side; Pogner falls to his knees before Sachs as if in homage. The Mastersingers gesture towards Sachs with outstretched hands, as to their chief. As the cheering apprentices clap their hands and dance, the people enthusiastically wave hats and handkerchiefs.

Like the miracle of the Pope's staff, or the appearance of the fluttering dove signifying the Holy Spirit at the end of *Parsifal*, this is an unambiguous visual representation of satisfied, consummated desire. The goal has been reached, the proper end attained. Walther, Eva, Pogner, Sachs, the people of Nuremberg, and – most important – Wagner himself have all got what they want.

According to *Tristan*, though, desire doesn't flow so smoothly into attainment. As the programme note describes it, desire is actually a kind of resistance to consummations, to triumphant endings: 'one thing alone left living: desire, desire unquenchable, longing forever rebearing itself' (VIII 387). The sheer force of longing, shaped and driven only by the *absence* of the object of desire, disrupts the satisfaction of getting what was sought. At the end of *Tristan*, Marke explains that he was about to offer the lovers just what one would think they hoped for. He was ready, he says, to abandon his own claim and wed Isolde to Tristan. As soon as he sings the words, though, it's obvious that they do not touch on the lovers' real desires, which have entirely transcended mundane ambitions like getting married and living happily ever after. The opera resists any such simple resolution of its yearnings. It leaves the wound unclosed. The only end is death: not (I suggest) a redemptive death, which heals all wounds and sets a seal of benediction on desire's endless strivings, but simply the death that results from a terminal wound: fatality, oblivion. Next to this, Marke's offer seems as trivial as the business with the potions. Only in *Meistersinger* does Wagnerian love end up consecrated and consummated as marriage, because only in *Meistersinger* are Wagnerian desires allowed complete, unambiguous gratification. Everywhere else, desire's reward is death.

This is where our interpretative choice comes in. Either we understand these deaths the way the operas seem to encourage us to do, as moments of *Erlösung* or salvation, in which case we permit Wagner's works to have what they apparently want. Or we understand them the same way we have to understand the end of *Götterdämmerung*: not as triumph and redemption, but merely as a bringing-to-nothing (as Ellis might put it), an end beyond which nothing can be known. In this second interpretation, the quality of intense purposefulness that pervades Wagner's art suddenly seems less dictatorial (less charitable words for it would be 'tyrannical' or 'totalitarian'). This is because Wagner's desire – to make us feel what he wants us to feel and think what he wants us to think – might turn out to be like Tristan and Isolde's, a 'desire without attainment': *only* a desire, that is, and therefore something that cannot fulfil itself.

Tristan und Isolde is the work which most strongly communicates the real emptiness of desire, but in fact we can adopt this approach throughout Wagner's work – except, I think, in *Meistersinger*, which fulfils all its own wishes to a frankly alarming extent. Otherwise, it's always possible to doubt redemption. The suicidal love favoured by Wagner's characters (even Siegmund, more humane than most of Wagner's lovers, mentions death as he draws Nothung from the tree and claims Sieglinde) might actually signal desire's kinship with annihilation, suggesting that instead of getting you what you want, it gets you nowhere – like the all-powerful ring of the Nibelung, which maddens and destroys its possessors. In this interpretation, the art of exile reaffirms itself against the art of redemption. Instead of a Wagnerian art which always ends up securing what it is striving for (a prospect which, as the end of *Meistersinger* amply proves, ought to frighten anyone), we can envisage an art which contains a resistance to the process of consummating its own ambitions and achieving its desires.

I have already suggested that the *Ring* is the product of such an art. We can look further back than that, though. *Lohengrin* has come up very little in this discussion because its end is self-evidently complex and unresolved: there's no claim for redemption, except at the political level (with the disenchantment of Gottfried and the victory promised to the Germans). Elsa's love has very much the same annihilating tendency as Tristan and Isolde's, in that her desire for Lohengrin converts itself into an anxiety which ends up expelling its own object. Having (literally) got what she dreamed of in Act I, she makes herself lose it, and dies in a state of anguished yearning ('Mein Gatte! Mein Gatte!' – 'my husband, my husband!'). She has disenchanted the magic of romantic opera which – as in the Venusberg – fulfils all desires. She's the prophetess of Wagner's mature works, just as Wagner says she is in 'A Communication to My Friends' (although not for the reasons he gives there). Her unredeemed end is the result of a longing which banishes that which it longs for, and this resistance to gratifying desire is vital to the business of interpreting Wagner. Without it, all his operas are like *Meistersinger*: brilliant, beautiful, powerful, subtle artifices of wish-fulfilment, staging their own triumph, granting themselves a redemption they have invented on their own. But there is a force in the operas which does not heal all wounds and resolve all striving, a desire which is not conveniently confident of getting what it wants. Like Elsa, it exiles itself from redemptive endings, preferring instead the oblivion of Tristan and Isolde, the bare stage after the cataclysm at the end of *Götterdämmerung*, or Kundry's muteness. In Wagner's work there is a wound which never closes, and in the end that wound is worth more to us than the redemption which promises to seal it up.

'Redemption', of course, changes its meaning over the long course of Wagner's career. The argument I'm making here applies only generally. Each of the operas differently calibrates the opposition between redemption and emptiness, and the tension between the two becomes more subtle and intricate as Wagner's art develops. In *Der fliegende Holländer* there isn't really much choice. The conditions of the Dutchman's salvation are described early on in the opera, in Senta's ballad, and the rest of the plot therefore presents itself as the unfolding of the necessary actions. However fatalistic (and, for Erik, cruelly destructive) Senta's raptures are, it's always clear that they are in a good cause: redemption remains the clear goal of all the story's twists and turns. (That said, a brilliantly perverse 1978 production by Harry Kupfer at Bayreuth managed to deny it, presenting the whole story of the Dutchman as a hysterical delusion of Senta's, ending in her untransfigured and unredeemed suicide.) From this point on, the operas present increasingly ambiguous versions of *Erlösung*, until at the climax of *Parsifal* Wagner attempts again to stage a visible rite of salvation. One might describe this development in terms of a gathering resistance to the simplistic satisfactions of a redemptive climax. The last tableau of *Holländer* belongs to a thoroughly melodramatic theatrical tradition, one which always appealed to Wagner but which he was far too subtle an artist to leave unchallenged. Its rather clumsy directness fades very quickly from the operas, revived only at the close of *Meistersinger* (and even there apparently at Cosima's urging, against Wagner's better judgment).[3] Taking its place are endings where the passage from death to salvation is far less obviously marked, and where music replaces visible stagecraft as the main agent persuading us that redemption is at work – music, which (unlike that

tableau) never speaks directly and explicitly, and so allows alternative interpretations far more room to breathe.

One could also say, as have countless commentators on Wagner's career, that
his discovery of Schopenhauer's philosophical nihilism in the mid-1850s (after
Lohengrin but before *Tristan* and most of the *Ring*) fundamentally undermined
his earlier, more naïvely optimistic tendency towards triumphantly redemptive ends. The aspect of Schopenhauer's moral philosophy that appealed most
strongly to Wagner was precisely its effort to negate desire. The urge to get
what you want is, according to this philosophy, more or less the original sin;
for Schopenhauer, right action can only begin by denying one's own will.
His thinking systematically exposes the emptiness of desire, and calls for a
kind of self-annihilation, the ethical equivalent of Tristan and Isolde's voluntary deaths. It might be argued, then, that the claim I've put forward in this
chapter – that desire is, or can be, the opposite of redemption – is one Wagner
himself adopted wholesale from Schopenhauer. Not so, though. Under the
philosopher's influence, Wagner's concept of *Erlösung* changed more radically
in the late 1850s than at any other time in his career, but it remained nevertheless an idea of salvation. That is, Wagner was never a real pessimist.
His work never quite gives up the ambition of achieving redemptive climaxes,
of closing its wounds; correspondingly, it never denies its own will. He absorbs
Schopenhauer's pessimism into his own instinctive romantic idealism by
suggesting that the emptiness of desire is *itself* redemptive. In other words, he
believes Schopenhauer's insight can save us – whereas Schopenhauer himself
does not believe in any form of salvation, dismissing all such aspirations
as another manifestation of the deluded will. 'It is a question', Wagner writes
to Mathilde Wesendonck in December 1858, 'of pointing out the path to
salvation, which has not been recognized by any philosopher, and especially
not by Sch . . .' (*L* 432). The casual remark encapsulates the limit of
Schopenhauer's influence. Wagner embraces the philosopher's concept of
denying desire, only to turn that very denial into another form of *Erlösung*.
If this all seems remote and abstract, consider *Parsifal*. The opera's strenuous,
almost maniacal insistence on chastity stands for precisely the kind of
self-denial Schopenhauer theorizes – and yet *Parsifal* quite explicitly presents
it as a 'path to salvation', contradicting all the philosopher's thinking by
turning self-denial into a (Christian) virtue, a goal, something to be desired,
willed and chosen.

Wagner's usual names for this virtue are 'renunciation' or 'resignation'.
Wotan, Tristan, Sachs, Parsifal, all are supposed to be heroes of renunciation,
abandoning the delusory ambitions of the selfish will like good Schopen-
hauerians, in order to attain – like good Wagnerians – the rewards of
Erlösung. The equation would appear at first sight to be fairly straightforward:
recognizing the emptiness of desire equals renouncing the world equals

attaining a form of redemption. If this pattern held true, Wagner's operas would be having their cake and eating it too. They would have a way of converting annihilation itself into salvation. Renunciation would be an embrace of nothingness which nevertheless gains, in the end, everything it had given up, an abandoning of desire which in the end gets what it desired. Wotan rids himself of his lust for power and his hope for triumph over Alberich, yet in the end the *Ring* grants him at least an ambiguous kind of victory. Tristan embraces oblivion, yet (judging by the sounds of Isolde's death) oblivion does indeed turn out to be bliss. Sachs dismisses the world's 'Wahn' (illusion/delusion), yet ends up acclaimed by the world as its hero and lord. Parsifal discovers the meaning of suffering, yet ends all sufferings with a wave of his spear. It's exactly the same pattern as Wagner's reading of Schopenhauer, which embraces philosophical pessimism and abnegation as a 'path to salvation'. Here again is that fundamental urge to satisfy desire, to reach a longed-for goal.

However, converting renunciation into redemption is far less straightforward than the situation in *Holländer*, where Senta's plunge to annihilation is instantly succeeded by her ascent into transfigured glory. The mature operas are still powerfully shaped by that characteristic Wagnerian urge to get where they want to go and lay hold of the salvation they imagine for themselves. Yet they are also aware that desire is not so easily satisfied, nor wounds so easily healed. Renunciation is, after all, a way of acknowledging that all desires empty themselves into oblivion, not fulfilment. However much Wagner's operas attempt to turn that oblivion into a 'path to salvation', it remains a point of resistance. It's a sign of the law of exile reasserting itself − the law which dictates that the paths to salvation are barred and the goal is always out of reach. Can renunciation really be converted into *Erlösung*? If so, then the force of Wagner's desire would seem irresistibly complete. Annihilation itself would be transfigured into triumph, and *Meistersinger* would then have to be recognized not as an exception but rather as the model for all Wagner's operas: self-gratifying fantasies which expel all resistance to their wishes and insist that what they imagine for themselves is true, holy and achievable. We can see now how important that 1860 programme note actually is. Its vision of 'desire without attainment' matters deeply to the business of interpreting Wagner, for in the face of Wagner's masterfully powerful and coherent musical and dramatic imagination, we need to track down those forces in his work which do not work to achieve his goals, which keep his desires from being attained.

CHAPTER ELEVEN

Nirvana

In May 1856, about the time when his work on the *Ring* began to be distracted by thoughts of an opera on the Tristan legend, Wagner drafted the so-called 'Schopenhauer ending' of *Götterdämmerung*. In this version, Brünnhilde becomes a mouthpiece for the Buddhist notion of a final release from the world and all its endlessly perpetuated strivings and sufferings:

nach dem wunsch- und wahnlos	to the land without desire and delusion,
heiligstem Wahlland,	the holiest place of choice,
der Welt-Wanderung Ziel,	the goal of world-wandering,
von Wiedergeburt erlös't,	redeemed from reincarnation,
zieht nun die Wissende hin.	the enlightened one now goes.

The speech looks odd as a conclusion to the *Ring*. What does *Wiedergeburt*, reincarnation, have to do with the tetralogy's Nordic-heroic setting, in which death is brutally final and either Valhalla or the underworld awaits the slain? And why is Brünnhilde, impulsive and passionate even in her wisest moments, suddenly appearing as an 'enlightened' (*Wissende*) saint, serenely renouncing the futile torments of desire? The Schopenhauerian rhetoric makes little or no sense in the place for which it was originally planned. What it does illustrate, however, is a way of thinking about endings which had begun to nag at Wagner's imagination. It's a little nugget of *Tristan*-language that hasn't yet found its proper home, put in Brünnhilde's mouth for want of a better place. That same month, he made the first brief prose sketch for *Die Sieger* (*The Victors*), which was to dramatize an episode from the life of the Buddha. The 'Schopenhauer ending' would have been still more appropriately spoken by this drama's heroine, Prakriti, who enters the 'enlightened' community of the Buddhists by overcoming and renouncing her own 'desire'. (The plot turns on her love for one of the Buddha's followers, a union which can only be achieved if she accepts his vow of chastity.) One can equally well imagine the words incorporated into the nebulous trances of Act II of *Tristan*. It is not very far from the 'Schopenhauer ending' to the ecstasies of release invoked there, the 'nie-wieder-Erwachens/ wahnlos/ hold bewußter Wunsch' ('never-again-awakening, delusionless, sweetly-known desire') as one of *Tristan's* more memorably contorted phrases puts it.

Wagner had earlier summarized the essential insight he received from Schopenhauer in an excited letter to Liszt of December 1854. It is, he writes, 'the sincere and heartfelt yearning for death: total unconsciousness, complete annihilation, the end of all dreams – the only ultimate redemption!' (*L* 323). This is what Brünnhilde is made to embrace in 1856, and what provides the germ of the *Tristan* and *Die Sieger* projects which gradually displaced the *Ring*. Setting aside for the moment the question of how annihilation is also redemption – an equation I've already tried to cast some doubt on – the key notion here is an embrace of nothingness and absence, the idea that the direction of Wagnerian plots ('der . . . Wanderung Ziel', the goal of wandering, in Brünnhilde's words) is towards a serene nowhere. In this sense, Wagner's imagination is in the mid-1850s visibly becoming coloured by the conditions of exile. Not just political exile: for that kind of explusion always carries with it an enduring sense of relation to the now-forbidden home, a relation usually expressed (as it clearly is in *Die Meistersinger*) as nostalgia. The political refugee is always dreaming of returning to a very specific place. His exile orbits around it, controlled by the gravitational pull of the lost homeland. For Wagner, though, Schopenhauer and the Oriental philosophies which influenced him crystallized a more radical feeling of exile, one determined not by hopes of return to any central place but by an absolute, permanent, displacement. After his expulsion from the Asyl in 1858, and the series of meandering and largely abortive projects which followed, this feeling is prominent in many of his letters. The typical note of mournful resignation is struck as he writes to Mathilde Wesendonck in November 1859 after an enforced change of residence in Paris: 'I also know that I shall not establish another haunt for myself but, totally dispossessed, shall simply wait until someone closes my eyes for me' (*L* 479). Like the Brünnhilde of 1856, he imagines himself Buddhistically disburdened of the world, surrendering all desires except the hope for an escape from perpetual 'migrations' into the emptiness of death.

The Buddhist name for this condition of absolute dispossession and renunciation of desire is Nirvana. When Brünnhilde mentions the 'holiest place of choice', she means a place like this (although Nirvana is properly not a place but a state): separated entirely from all the troubled motions of the world, a haven of entire tranquillity. It's where you arrive once every other place has been given up, and it is therefore the goal of extreme exile, one which rejects dreams of returning home and embraces dispossession entirely. This, at least, is what Wagner implies in another letter written from Paris to Mathilde

Wesendonck. He is confessing his utter lack of fellow-feeling for France and everything French (and this is in March 1860, still a year before the *Tannhäuser* disaster confirmed how mutual the feeling was):

> I then feel quite wretched and homeless. And I ask myself: where do you belong? There is no country, no town, no village that I can call my own. Everything is alien to me, and I often gaze around me, yearning for a glimpse of the land of nirvana. (*L* 486)

In *Tristan und Isolde*, this is called 'das dunkel/ nächt'ge Land', 'das Land,/ das alle Welt umspannt': the dark land of night, the land which spans the whole world. It's a kind of negative space, which is why it is so often named as death, the opposite of existence. Schopenhauer defines it as the denial of the will to live (accounting for its other name in Wagner's imagination, chastity, the renunciation of the procreative urge). Surrendering all sense of involvement in or engagement with the world and its actions, one is left only with an unruffled awareness of nothingness, as if the exile has ceased even to think about the countries, towns and villages he has left behind and chosen instead to contemplate the empty ground of his own alienation.

More important than the details of Wagner's personal understanding of Schopenhauer and Oriental thought is the shift in dramatic conceptions to which the language of the oddly incongruous 1856 fragment testifies. The 'Schopenhauer ending' envisions a new and strange direction for drama to pursue. As the final gesture of heroism, it imagines an evanescence, a disappearance into empty space. Brünnhilde is made to announce her departure, as if the sum of all the *Ring*'s long and complex action is simply to wave the whole business away; enlightenment consists in dismissing all the bustle of the plot as mere 'desire and delusion'. 'Drama' is a Greek word meaning 'things that are done': actions, doings. A plot, correspondingly, consists of the unfolding of actions on stage. To yearn for a glimpse of Nirvana, though, is to imagine a space without events, a land of universal darkness and stillness. What sort of drama orients itself in this direction? One gets an idea of the answer from Wagner's sketch for *Die Sieger*, for the central plot of this drama as he outlines it in 1856 is in fact a neutralizing of action. Prakriti has to be brought to the point where she can choose not to do what she intially wishes to do. She denies her will, that is, and the sketch concludes at the point where the impulse which provides the material for the plot is joyfully stilled. Such tension as there is is provided by the antagonism of the Brahmins towards the Buddha, but the victory suggested by the title – *The Victors* – is not a triumph of one side of a contest over another (as it is at the ends of *Tannhäuser* and *Lohengrin*), but instead the victory over one's own will, the achievement of giving up the contest altogether.

If this doesn't sound like the most gripping drama, that might explain why the project was never realized, were it not for the fact that *Tristan und Isolde* is governed by exactly the same principle. Next to nothing happens in *Tristan*; the tension of the plot is supplied by the lovers' drift away from the sphere of existence altogether, unwinding and silencing all actions and finally departing like the Brünnhilde of 1856 into the Nirvana of complete stasis. *Parsifal*, too, has some of this glacially tranquil quality. Although its plot is organized around the more conventionally dramatic idea of finding something lost and healing something damaged, it eschews any sense of confrontation, slowing the action down to a dreamy crawl. Wagner's operas from *Die Feen* to the *Ring* have an undeniable tinge of melodrama. They exult in the exaggerated theatrical power of moments like Ortrud's sudden interruption of the bridal procession, Tannhäuser's erotic relapse in the Hall of Song, or Siegmund standing with his hands on the hilt of the buried sword. The tensions and climaxes of *Tristan*, *Parsifal* and even the busily plotted *Meistersinger* are far more subdued and oblique. When Melot betrays Tristan to the King in Act II, for example, all the ingredients of a crisis are prepared: the exposure of a crime, the surprise of the interruption, the lovers' guilt, the antagonism of the worlds of day and night. Kurwenal rushes in with a call to action: 'Rette dich, Tristan!', 'save yourself'. Agitated quavers in the strings seem to herald some decisive action, but instead Tristan and Isolde stand still, and the strings settle into a quiet tremolo, over which echoes of the love duet's most soaring theme are heard in the wind. When Tristan at last speaks, he addresses no one: 'Der öde Tag −/ zum letzten Mal!' ('bleak day, for the last time'). There is no conflict or crisis, only a brief glimpse of the land of Nirvana (death), a calmly melancholy sense of impending departure. Marke's long speech that follows is, notoriously, the very antithesis of drama, an extraordinarily static way for the plot to treat its pivotal moment. And if the end of Act II of *Tristan* is an extreme case, it nevertheless exemplifies a tendency noticeable even amid the swift action of *Meistersinger*, especially in the climactic third act, where Sachs orchestrates the plot more by his reticence than his actions. In succession he deals with David, Walther, Beckmesser and Eva, ensuring that each of them is ready for their role in the final unfolding of the drama, but doing so indirectly, almost passively, allowing them to proceed along their own paths with the gentlest possible nudges in the right direction; an unmoved mover like Gurnemanz, not a schemer like Wotan. Action leads only to chaos, as the sudden explosion of riot in Act II shows. Sachs seems instead to be operating from a position of quiet detachment; this is the note of sadness that Eva hears in his superficially boisterous cobbling-song ('Mich schmerzt das Lied, ich weiß nicht wie!', she tells Walther: 'the song grieves me, I don't know why'). Parsifal, too, is detached from the plot through which he moves, first by his entire ignorance and (after Kundry's kiss) by his determined aloofness. His first visible deed in the opera is a denial of action, breaking the bow whose use he has just boasted of. Later he tells Gurnemanz that during his long return to the domain of the Grail, his main effort has been not to use the spear: an anti-effort, as it were.

This is not to say that Wagner's three last dramas really breathe a spirit of Buddhist renunciation. Nirvana presents itself as the opposite of desire, a resigned freedom from worldly striving, but, as I've suggested in the previous chapter, Wagnerian versions of renunciation need to be treated with a lot of suspicion. Certainly the composer's own yearnings for a state of tranquil, unburdened peace had little to do with any austere withdrawal from worldly affairs. One might think (unfairly) of his predilection for luxury, hardly a Schopenhauerian or Buddhist habit of self-denial. More relevantly, his occasional yearnings for Nirvana went side by side with the most characteristic feature of his biography, a stupendously energetic and single-minded pursuit of artistic aims – a constant demand, more pronounced as the decades went by, that everyone else's desires and strivings be renounced for the sake of his own. In the operas too, Nirvana can be understood as a mask for desire. The exemplary figure here is Wotan. His enforced self-denial in Act II of *Die Walküre* leads him to what from one point of view is an orthodox Schopenhauerian outlook; abandoning his grandiose ambitions, he desires only *das Ende*, the end. (The *Ring* libretto was complete before Wagner read Schopenhauer, but we're not talking about influence here; what matters are the patterns and tendencies of Wagner's works as we now have them.) In his role as the Wanderer, Wotan appears to have achieved the appropriate detachment and resignation, bewildering Alberich in Act II of *Siegfried* with his carefree attitude to the fate of the ring. In fact, though, he clings to power, putting Mime in his place in Act I, forcing Erda to answer him in Act III, and later unable to restrain himself from violent confrontation with Siegfried. Only with the breaking of his spear does he achieve the full detachment of Nirvana, and the moment is marked by nothing like serene acceptance. He confesses his powerlessness ('Ich kann dich nicht halten', 'I cannot stop you') and quietly vanishes from the tetralogy. He never gives up power; Siegfried has to take it away from him by force.

In the three last dramas, renunciation is also a form of power (less clearly in *Tristan*). They are after all very far from being dramas of resignation. The triumphs won by their victors are climactic and decisive. Sachs and Parsifal both get their way, amid defeated enemies and communal celebrations, while Isolde's final vision – the *Liebestod* – converts the momentarily tragic outcome of the plot into an unmistakable victory, at least according to the most single-mindedly ecstatic music in the whole Wagnerian oeuvre. Whatever the operas' interest in moving towards a 'Schopenhauer ending', then, they are finally much more Wagnerian than Buddhist, manifesting the artist's dynamic will which always exaggeratedly glorifies its heroes and celebrates the success of its strivings. After Wotan, the real model of so-called renunciation or resignation is in fact Klingsor, a figure for whom self-denial (in the form of his castration) is quite explicitly a means to power (his magic arts). Though Parsifal is presented as Klingsor's enemy, the relationship is in this matter at least much more like that between Alberich and Wotan ('Licht-Alberich', 'light-Alberich', as he refers to himself): more of a doubling than an antagonism. Parsifal also has to be chaste before he can achieve power. Like Klingsor, his exposure to erotic experience (Kundry's kiss) results in erotic revulsion. He has to deny what Kundry reveals to him in order to become the saintly redeemer of Act III.

Hans Sachs represents a more difficult case. Not unusually for *Meistersinger*, false claims are being made here which the opera apparently does not recognize as such. In a letter to King Ludwig of November 1866, Wagner provided what is effectively a programme note for the beautifully meditative prelude to Act III (the passage was later adapted and reprinted in his collected writings). He describes it as a musical portrait of Sachs as 'man of resignation' (VIII 388), depicting a sorrow at the world's *Wahn* (delusion, madness) which has led to a calm sense of detachment. Later, in Sachs's monologue, the poet is made to express a kind of resigned despair at the constancy of *Wahn* in human affairs. Yet at the close of his meditation he sets himself the task of 'den Wahn fein lenken', 'subtly guiding the madness', in order to make it perform 'ein edler Werk', 'a nobler work'. This is hardly the language of detachment. Sachs is always in fact more cobbler than philosopher, always busy fashioning and assembling the plot rather than contemplating it from a distance. His 'resignation' does not prevent him orchestrating the whole town of Nuremberg in accordance with his wishes, nor is it much in evidence when the town reciprocally hails him as its father-figure in the final tableau. In this light, the Act III prelude sounds somewhat different from Wagner's own interpretation. The passage adapted from Wagner's letter focusses on the first theme heard, the heavy, drawn-out sigh of the strings whose final cadences are strongly reminiscent of the shepherd's bleak melody in *Tristan* Act III, and which (Wagner writes) expresses 'the bitter cry of the man of resignation who [shows] the world a cheerful, energetic countenance'. This theme is followed by a soft horn chorus intoning the music of Sachs's hymn *Wach auf*; the same music recurs a little later, 'with redoubled sonority' (VIII 388), and its warmer harmonies allow the 'resignation' theme to be led to the relatively cheerful conclusion Wagner describes. The hymn is at least as representative of Sachs as the first theme – it's his own composition, after all. So far from expressing resignation and detachment, it stands for Sachs's role as the symbolic and ideological keystone of the city, and thereby of the whole world of the opera. This becomes clear when it is sung in massed choir by everyone on stage in the last scene, a communal act of recognition and praise directed at the author of this hymn to the German, Protestant institutions governing Nuremberg. Immediately after the chorus has finished its enthusiastic welcome, the 'resignation' theme sounds again, before Sachs begins his reply. Again, so far from signifying detachment, it acts here as a bridge between Sachs and 'his' populace. However much it may stand for his inward melancholy, it nevertheless testifies at this moment to his public role, framing his formal address to the citizens of Nuremberg, and introducing the speech in which he establishes the rules of the competition that is to follow (a competition whose outcome he has already effectively determined). In the prelude, too, it is the hymn which determines the development of the 'resignation' theme, not the other way round. Sachs's resignation, such as it is, is always in the service of his public role, just as his gloomy recognition of the world's *Wahn* presses delusion into the service of noble works (rather than being the herald of a departure into Nirvana, as it is for the Brünnhilde of the 'Schopenhauer ending'). What does Sachs in fact resign or renounce? Only Eva's love: but although Eva tells him she is his if he wishes, this too is implausible, since the opera makes clear the bond between her and Walther right from its opening. Her love is not Sachs's to give up; his sexual self-discipline is as enforced as Klingsor's. In reality, Sachs's magisterial aloofness from his world is (again like Klingsor's self-mutilating chastity) a means of control. Where Pogner, Walther, Eva and (pre-eminently) Beckmesser flounder helplessly in their efforts to bring about what they wish for, Sachs's calm and disinterested demeanour actually allows him to manipulate everything around him extremely efficiently. If Sachs is a man of resignation, then resignation is not in fact the surrender of desires (and the threshold of Nirvana), but rather a more subtle means of achieving success.

Renunciation in *Tristan* is also at least potentially interpretable as a form of desire, rather than a Schopenhauerian abandoning of it. This opera comes far closer to the borders of Nirvana than either *Parsifal* or *Meistersinger*: there's no explicitly triumphal onstage climax, and the lovers end by passing into the otherworld of death (rather than being acclaimed as heroes, as Sachs, Walther, Parsifal and Amfortas are). Nevertheless, by renouncing the daylight world and embracing 'das . . . nächt'ge Land', the realm of night, they are consummating their long-deferred erotic desire. They aren't like Prakriti and Ananda, the lovers of *Die Sieger*, who genuinely have to rid themselves of their passion before they can be accepted into the Buddha's following. It's no secret that in *Tristan* death is a symbolic form of sexual consummation. With its series of gradually intensifying upward surges, prolonging the rise towards an always anticipated climax, Isolde's *Liebestod* is as close to being a musical representation of orgasm as one can imagine (correspondingly, her words are a dizzily confused blend of images of swelling, surging movement and sensory profusion). The abortive version of the same musical climax in Act II – interrupted by Brangäne's scream of warning – accompanies the lovers' shared fantasy of being 'hold Umnachten', 'sweetly enveloped in night', of entering 'ungemess'-nen Räumen', 'measureless spaces'. The music of sexual ecstasy is in the end indistinguishable from the fantasy of renunciation, of departing into a Nirvanic nowhere. And vice versa: the yearning for Nirvana is a form of sexual bliss. This is why Tristan and Isolde indulge in a mystico-philosophical tryst, rather than a straightforwardly carnal one. Their coitus performs the literal meaning of that word, 'going together', ascending into erotic rapture through the shared urge to depart (like the Schopenhauerian Brünnhilde) into another world. Though they abandon existence, they do so primarily under the impulse of desire, not renunciation, always dreaming of a more perfect satisfaction of their shared longings. The space their yearning reaches towards is a closer approximation to the land of Nirvana than any other in Wagner's work, and *Tristan* is correspondingly the slowest, least active of all the operas, the deepest exploration of a plotless drama. It's rather ironic – and significantly so – that this effect should be achieved through the *least* Schopenhauerian material: Tristan and Isolde's pathologically intense desires and passions come closer to Nirvana than Parsifal's chastity or Sachs's philosophic resignation. Significant, because the fact suggests how paper-thin Wagnerian gestures of renunciation really are. Desire has a far stronger hold on his imagination than denial. Ultimately, as suggested in the previous chapter, the will to redemption asserts itself over any form of resignation. However much *Tristan*, *Meistersinger* and *Parsifal* evidence a Schopenhauerian mood, they all end in ecstasy and victory, not monastic detachment.

It seems that we can't interpret any of Wagner's works as genuine dramas of serene self-denial. Perhaps this is another reason why *Die Sieger* never ripened into being, unlike all the other projects which absorbed his attention for an extended period: a story of Buddhist renunciation might in fact have been fundamentally alien to him. Yet the yearning for a glimpse of Nirvana persists. There certainly is some kind of change of direction in the later operas, prophesied in the 'Schopenhauer ending' with its themes of detachment, exile and unworldliness (or otherworldliness). The dramatic focus certainly also shifts, from melodramatically emphatic climaxes to expansive, meditative scenes which progress through the most refined and subtle adjustments. *Tristan* and *Parsifal* in particular feel almost like chamber operas, for all their vast dimensions and Herculean technical requirements. They have a concentrated contemplativeness which prefers to avoid grandly 'operatic' dramatic gestures. Another way of putting it would be to say that the tendencies visible in the composer of *Rienzi* finally vanish altogether in *Tristan*. Or, from a rather different point of view, one could say that the sheer slowness some people find unbearable in Wagner is most fully in evidence in *Tristan* and *Parsifal* – which, from the vantage-point of Nirvana, would of course be a compliment, since perfect renunciation would consist of no action at all (Act III of *Tristan* comes close). Where, then, can we locate the glimpses of stillness and silence in these operas? Where can we find the resistance to desire that Schopenhauer preaches? What signs are there of (to return to Wagner's paraphrase of this philosophy's ideal goal) 'total unconsciousness, complete annihilation, the end of all dreams'?

While rehearsing the prelude to Act I of *Tristan* for the Paris concerts of 1860 – the first time he heard it played – Wagner wrote to Mathilde Wesendonck: 'it was as though the scales had fallen from my eyes, allowing me to see how immeasurably far I have travelled from the world' (*L* 484). He meant, of course, that the musical language of *Tristan* seemed alien to anything a listener of 1860 could be familiar with. The phrasing is suggestive, though, with its image of distant space. It again brings to mind Brünnhilde announcing her departure, or the vision of radical exile in which existence itself is left behind. It's as if to say that music has become a force of detachment, alienation. This is a step – and a long one – beyond the aesthetics of romance, where music opens seductive paths into exotic and magical terrain. The *Tristan* prelude (Wagner's casual phrase suggests) removes the listener into unimaginable remoteness, so that the feeling is not of having arrived somewhere different, as in romance, but rather just a sensation of distance itself, of being far from home. It is also a step beyond the conceptions of music underlying *Opera and Drama* and articulated in the motivic compositional structures of the *Ring*. There, music acts as a quasi-language, in accordance with the theoretical writings' rather desperate faith that it can speak some determinate, specific, legible content. *Opera and Drama* describes it (sometimes, at least) as the language of feeling: a medium of psychological expression, and therefore also the language of desire, of the inner will. But in *Tristan*, it appears, music is the language of empty space: what it expresses is the vast gap between itself and 'the world'. Hence the phrase Wagner throws off the cuff in another letter to Mathilde Wesendonck from this period: the music of *Tristan*, he writes, is 'resonant silence' (*L* 427). Silent, because it makes no reference to the world, it has no linguistic content: a resonating absence, nothingness turned into sound. Like Nirvana, music represents a negative presence, a state of existence defined by its utter remoteness from existence.

Wagner's mature music has an enormous range of styles and expressive modes available to it, far too profusely inventive and diverse to be characterized by any single description. The rich diatonicism of *Meistersinger* is evidence enough that the *Tristan* prelude can't be taken as representative. Nevertheless, the prelude's hauntingly alienated quality stands for an essential aspect of music, one which becomes subtly and pervasively significant in the *Tristan* and *Parsifal* scores in particular: its inarticulacy, its lack of content. The opening of the *Tristan* prelude displays this aspect with something like visionary force. Silence emerges out of each of the ascending repetitions of the initial phrases like a continuation of the sound. The drastically unresolved melodic and harmonic character of those phrases gives them the quality of seeming to disappear into the subsequent silences, so that the bars of rest do not merely terminate the sound, but appear as extensions of the rising phrase in the wind; music *becomes* silent. At the same time, the lack of resolution makes those passages of silence sound pregnant with uncertain content. The ear waits for something to fill that space. Hence the emptiness has a kind of substance – we *hear* the silences, just as acutely as we hear the musical sounds. What we hear, though, is nothing: the ear experiences the absence of resolution just as it experiences the absence of sound. The sensation is precisely that of having travelled an enormous distance from the world – without arriving anywhere instead; a sensation of sheer removal, the ground pulled away from under us and only a forcible sense of nothing left in its place. Immediately before the first orchestral *tutti* finally gets the prelude moving uninterruptedly forward, that sensation is expressed in its simplest essence, with overwhelming directness. Twice we hear a bar consisting of no more than an isolated ascending semitone (first in the violins, then in the upper wind), played crescendo, followed by rest: a musical reach towards something not there, a motion into emptiness. Silence here seems the very condition of musical sound. Once this effect has been produced to such an extreme degree, it can't be effaced. The rest of the prelude, and indeed of the opera, seems infected by the positive lack of content felt in those first five silences. The prelude ends with sound being swallowed again by emptiness, and Act I proper begins with the eerily alienated sound of an invisible voice, as if music has indeed disappeared from the world and located itself nowhere instead. From here on, it always seems to be about to fall back into the groundless, placeless Nirvana of 'resonant silence'. Music is the language Isolde and Tristan strive towards, one which bears no relation to the daylight world but is instead entirely dark and mysterious (in Act I he calls her 'Des Schweigens Herrin', 'the mistress of silence'). The score's pervasive quality of elusiveness expresses their negative striving with extraordinary force. Music becomes the vehicle for saying nothing, speaking nothingness, making absence present and palpable.

As radical as the score of *Tristan* still seems (and it is hard to imagine how it must have sounded in 1860), in this aspect it communicates a perfectly simple truth about music. Music is dumb. Wagner himself always militated against that truth, finding a number of different ways of theorizing that music has an articulate communicative power. His insistence on the point is an aspect of the relentlessness of his desire. Convinced that his operas were meaningful, he demanded that their meanings be unambiguously represented to their audiences. Working in the medium of opera naturally lends music at least a veil of articulacy, in that it accompanies more specific modes of expression (words and visible actions). The *Ring* represents the fullest effort to absorb music into a linguistic system, aligning it via leitmotif with what the libretto says and the stage shows. Yet even in the *Ring*, music's essentially indeterminate character reasserts itself at crucial moments (notably the so-called 'redemption' motif at the end) to undermine its role in producing explicit, legible meanings. In *Tristan*, despite all Wagner's theorizing, it offers glimpses of a true Nirvana: not a state of apparent resignation which (like Wagner's melancholy self-pity in his letters, or like Sachs's detached air) merely cloaks the will and its desires, but a resonant emptiness which can't be pressed into the service of the will. We can't, that is, say what music *means*. It can't become part of a plot to lead interpretation towards conclusions as assertively triumphal as those of *Meistersinger* and *Parsifal*.

The more dramatic weight music carries, therefore, the more uncertainty there is in the meaning of drama. Hundreds of commentators have pointed out that one of the effects of Wagner's reading of Schopenhauer was that music gained precedence over plot and libretto in the hierarchy of operatic arts. Part of the weirdly static quality of *Tristan* and *Parsifal* as dramas derives very much from the way that the action of opera has largely moved from the stage (the events of the plot) into the orchestra. Wagner famously, though at least half sardonically, referred to his later works with the phrase 'deeds of Music brought to sight' ('ersichtlich gewordene Thaten der Musik', V 303). In other words, instead of music 'accompanying' the deeds visible on stage, as it essentially does in the system of motivic composition, the relationship is reversed: what we see on stage is just the 'accompaniment' in visual form to a drama that is taking place entirely in the score. The whole business of happening has moved into the terrain of music; that's where the action is.

How, then, can we talk about what happens in *Tristan*? In the motivic composition of the *Ring*, it is at least approximately possible to read musical events as if they were words or sentences. We are presented with relatively distinct and self-contained sounds which ask for some such translation. In Siegfried's death march, for example, the succession of distinct motifs approximates fairly closely to a verbal narrative (although the passage also has its own overall symphonic character – its monumental, gloomy grandeur – which has to be understood as greater than the sum of its motivic parts, and consequently not reducible to approximate verbal 'translations' as leitmotifs are). In the later operas, though, motifs do not isolate themselves so conveniently from the larger musical fabric. The musical structures of *Tristan* are deeply buried in the score: patterns of thematic development and variation over huge expanses of time, large-scale tonal relationships, extraordinarily subtle links between the most compressed and fragmentary musical 'motifs'. (These deep structures are of course present in the *Ring* as well, but the explicit play of leitmotifs appears visibly on their surface.) The only way to talk in detail about musical structures of this sort is through technical analysis, and *Tristan* is an inexhaustibly rich field for such detailed explorations. The job of analysis, however, is to identify and explain (and perhaps interpret) musical structures which the ear cannot immediately identify as such. The *Ring*'s leitmotifs are audible; familiarity with the music allows the listener to identify some of their basic associations with particular events or objects or people, and so to experience music as part of the language of the drama, part of the action of the plot. The deep structures of *Tristan* (and of the *Ring* as well) are not audible. Even after repeated listenings, very few hearers are able to say that one part of the opera is in the same key as another part hours distant from it, or that one motivic fragment is partially derived from another thematic element already heard in an extraordinary variety of different forms. It isn't possible to interpret the 'action' of the score of *Tristan* in anything like the same way one interprets the actions or words on stage.

It's like looking at a grand and complex building – a Gothic cathedral, say – from very far away. One can experience the overall outline of the architecture, receive a strong impression of its general style and character, and imagine intuitively that there must be powerfully harmonious relations among its details; but one can't actually see those details, the proportional relation between doors and façade or between tiers of arches and the cross-section of the whole building which would confirm the distant impression of organic harmony. Deep structures operate at a level below articulation. They're an aspect of resonant silence: we can't actually hear them, but their inaudible presence resonates through the experience of listening to each passage of the opera. In the same way, it's fairly easy to sense the unity and consistency of the score of *Parsifal*, the feeling that the whole massive opera breathes the same musical atmosphere throughout all its length. Technical analysis can account for this by picking apart the music's web of interrelations, but this again requires a level of explanatory detail which operates at a different level from what the ear hears. Interpretation is pushed down to the deep level of musical structure. Whatever meaningful relationships analysis can discover, they are not meanings that the score has spoken aloud.

In the mature operas, music's silences and secrecies replace the explicit staging of action. In scenes like the icily polite battle of wills between Isolde and Tristan in Act I or the dialogue of seduction and enlightenment between Parsifal and Kundry, it's obvious that the dramatically significant action is taking place at a level beneath the words the characters speak. One way of describing that level is to call it 'psychological' action, meaning that these are dramas of states of mind. Wagner had always been drawn to the dramatics of inner tensions, as is evident from the cases of Tannhäuser and Elsa, but in these earlier operas the character's inward crises are displayed visibly in their environments: we see Ortrud and Lohengrin battling for Elsa's trust, just as we see Venus and Elisabeth competing for Tannhäuser's soul. In the later operas, the psychological dimension of the plot is not so straightforwardly manifested on stage. It's not clear what the shared but tacit subtext of Tristan and Isolde's tense first exchanges is, nor is Parsifal's sudden access of enlightenment made explicit. (*Meistersinger* too has its reticences, especially with regard to the relations between Sachs and Eva and the nature of Walther's inspiration.) But if the later operas focus powerfully on shifts in the characters' consciousnesses, what more is that to say than that they dramatize things that aren't seen or said? Inward action is, more or less by definition, invisible.

Opera, of course, has a means of conveying things that aren't seen or said: its music, which acts separately from visible action and spoken libretto. To this extent, music 'represents' the invisible psychological action of the plots. Again, though, it does so without translating that action into something visible. Music keeps secrets. Asked to describe that which is unspoken, it doesn't turn it back into language. If it seems somehow to communicate the inward life of a character (as it accompanies their words or movements), it nevertheless at the same time preserves and communicates the inwardness of that life, its hiddenness and remoteness. Listening to the orchestra can't tell us what the characters are thinking and feeling. It can make us aware of the presence and the force of something that sounds like their thoughts and emotions, but it leaves them buried deep – especially in the later operas, which don't allow music to display feelings as nakedly as do (for example) Telramund's 'rage' aria in *Lohengrin*, or Alberich's boastful and threatening quasi-recitative in the third scene of *Das Rheingold*.

To the extent, then, that the later operas' centres of gravity shift towards the orchestra, they travel further and further from the world, pervaded by a sense of immanent silence and darkness. Isolde and Tristan hymn this 'heil'ger Dämm'rung', 'sacred twilight', during their tryst; and it is most fully achieved in Kundry's muteness during the last act of *Parsifal*. It also stands apart from the visible themes and events of the plots, though. The musical fabric of the scores achieves a quite extraordinary seamless and continuous texture, not so much the accompaniment to words and stage events as a symphonic drama of its own on which the visible action is carried. This relationship is architecturally literalized in the Bayreuth theatre, with its hidden orchestra pit: music becomes an invisible depth whose outer surface is the stage. Those depths are mysteriously remote, hidden. In *Tristan* and *Parsifal*, this is where music increasingly seems to belong – a transition announced by the unprecedented elusiveness of the former's prelude, and sacramentalized in the ritual scene at the end of the latter's first act, where sound ascends higher and higher (both in space and in pitch) into the invisibly resonant spaces at the top of the Grail temple. The nature of Wagner's later scores tends always towards remoteness. They celebrate music's wordlessness, its quality of being (to use a phrase of Tristan's) 'in keuscher Nacht/ dunkel verschlossen', 'darkly sealed up in chaste night'.

If music keeps itself far from the world of existence and experience, what is there to say about it? (We're still setting aside the kind of interpretations performed by close technical analysis.) Precisely that here, in the rich and subtle flow of the orchestra, the operas open glimpses of Nirvana. Music's essential silence, that is, counters the urgency of desire which drives the operas towards their victorious climaxes. In *Tristan's* language: if the plots tend towards a daylight world where final meanings are assertively staged (the epitome being the last speech and closing tableau of *Meistersinger*), then music surrounds them with a nightworld which exiles the operas from explicit and stable meanings, offering instead the impression of distance and emptiness.

This is not to say that it can't be brought back in line with the plots' desires. Much of *Meistersinger's* music presents itself as the depiction of the onstage world. The processional themes heard in the prelude, strongly associated with the Masters' guild, are recognizably public sounds; they have the quality of announcing and displaying something to an audience (as marches and fanfares always do). The various song melodies are also public, evidently enough since they are music meant to be played before specific hearers (as serenades and competition pieces always are). Still, though, the score can sometimes slip away into silence and remoteness, as it does in the opening phrase of the Act III prelude, before the *Wach auf* theme reminds it of its institutional obligations. Indeed, the orchestral preludes to the last acts of all three of the later operas seem to be sound on the edge of silence. The long slow ascent of the violins through three octaves, heard three times at the beginning of Act III of *Tristan*, unfurls into an extraordinarily barren stillness, each note a step further away from the world. Until it's rescued by the warm horns of Sachs's hymn, the 'resignation' theme similarly seems to be about to die away into nothing. The melancholy of the *Parsifal* Act III prelude is sharper, more pressing; but the opening notes still sound bare and aimless, the sound of Parsifal's penitential wanderings, monastically austere. Kundry's inarticulate shrieks and moans come as the climax to the prelude, and they are sounds which herald silence, the last struggles of her voice before it vanishes altogether. When Parsifal eventually appears, it's as a living icon of silence, masked and all but motionless, until Gurnemanz reconnects him to the opera's plots and purposes by identifying both him and the spear he carries. In passages like these, music is insisting on its power to remove the action into its own sphere of muteness. Each third act gathers itself from this opening position and regains its momentum, finding its voice again (though only barely in *Tristan*, where the long melancholy *alte Weise* on the cor anglais instils a dumb grief into the opera that is only overcome with Isolde's very last speech). Still, music has done enough to remind us that it contains an intimation of emptiness which the subsequent action can never entirely banish.

Nor do we need to go to the scores' most obviously melancholy passages to see this effect at work. Even in the lushest, most glittering love-music of *Tristan* there is a strange and striking reminder of the remoteness of sheer sound. Brangäne's watch-song at the heart of Act II sounds over orchestral music of incomparably rapt sweetness: soft, slow chordal sequences in the wind, rippling harps, lyrical melodies weaving among divided strings. Solo viola, violin and cello are particularly prominent (as well as violins in pairs and threes). Individuated from the body of the strings, they sound like voices, each singing a line of music distinct from the rest of the 'accompaniment'. Brangäne's own invisible voice – which seems to belong to an entirely different person from the fussing, twittering character we have seen on stage, if it belongs to a person at all – blends exquisitely smoothly into the orchestral flow. So smoothly, in fact, that actually to listen to her words involves a shock of startling incongruity. Impossibly, what the voice is saying is 'Habet Acht!/ Habet Acht!', 'be warned!' Nothing could possibly sound less like a warning, a call to pay attention, to be careful (literally 'have care!'). The music is utterly hypnotic and tranquillizing. Its own 'voices' – the individuated instruments – meander with blissful, dreamy abandon around the shimmering wind harmonies, locked in the lyrical trance the lovers' 'night of love' ('Nacht der Liebe') has called down on the scene. Brangäne's voice urges them (and us) to be aware of the world, but it is entirely subsumed by the wordless voices that inhabit and express an escapist erotic refuge. In effect, the music of the scene silences Brangäne's warning. It does so not by making her inaudible (as well as invisible), but rather by infusing the verbal content of the passage with an absolutely contradictory sonority. Under the hypnotic spell of the orchestra, words cease to communicate what they say, instead simply becoming music: Brangäne's voice ends up functioning only as a vocal line in the overall symphonic web. Music, in turn, ignores the world and defies language's call to pay heed to what it says. It exults in its self-absorbed dreaminess, in the soothing hush of beautiful sound. Its voices undo language: words melt into wordlessness, attention is lulled by entranced detachment. The watcher tries to call the scene out of Nirvana and back into the world, but – in a contrast that ought to be startlingly forceful, but is veiled by the gorgeous serenity of the scene – her own effort instead becomes part of music's blissful inarticulacy. When at the end of the watch-song Isolde gently asks Tristan to listen to the words of warning, he answers by (correctly) understanding what he's just heard merely as an expression of the Schopenhauerian denial of the will to live:

| ISOLDE: Lausch', Geliebter! | Listen, beloved! |
| TRISTAN: Lass' mich sterben! | Let me die! |

Music's hypnotic emptiness allows the possibility of refusing to listen. It's a crucial interpretative opportunity, because the operas become more and more insistent about saying what they want to say. The voice of Wagner's will sounds its warnings louder and louder: *Meistersinger* ends by turning Sachs into a speaking puppet mouthing his creator's words, warning of the imminent decay of Germany 'in falscher wälscher Majestät' ('under false foreign rule': read, the Jews), while *Parsifal* rants against impurity and sin. If music can silence and transfigure these speeches as thoroughly as it does Brangäne's, its power of detachment may well be 'redemptive' – but not at all in the way Wagner uses the word.

CHAPTER TWELVE

Politics and Fantasy

Wagner's years of rootless migration came to an end in May 1864 with a stroke so melodramatically sudden and so implausibly romantic that it seems to have come straight from the plot of an opera – *Fidelio*, perhaps, where an unexpected trumpet-call heralds the righting of all wrongs. Ludwig II's offer of unconditional protection and effectively unlimited resources was the kind of instantaneous reversal of fortune beloved of romance, and also usually confined to it. It was a gesture which blurred the boundaries between reality and fantasy, a biographical version of the architecture of Neuschwanstein in which Ludwig later tried to give weight and substance to his frothily romantic dreams. By his own account, the formative moment of his youth had been witnessing a performance of *Lohengrin* in 1861. His intervention in Wagner's career enacts the role of the quasi-divine emissary from a higher sphere, Lohengrin, to Wagner's victimized and suffering Elsa (their subsequent letters are full of protestations of sacred love, in the purplest prose). Wagner's reply to the King's first offer recognizes in the astonishing turn of events the signs of life imitating art:

> My dear and gracious King,
> I send you these tears of the most heavenly emotion in order to tell you that the marvels of poesy have entered my poor loveless life as a divine reality!

The brief letter closes with Elsa's language: 'In the utmost ecstasy, faithful and true, Your subject, Richard Wagner' (*L* 600).

Just as the King's first appearance looks like an operatic plot brought to life, the main theme of their subsequent relationship – at first at least – was their joint effort to realize Wagner's own 'marvels of poesy', his operas. Ludwig intended above all to supply the conditions in which the as yet unperformed *Tristan*, the incomplete *Ring*, the barely begun *Die Meistersinger*, and the projected *Die Sieger* and *Parsifal* would all become 'divine reality', performed on

stage under ideal conditions. Via the *fiat* of monarchy and its authority over
the Bavarian treasury, Ludwig would in effect be the medium through which
Wagnerian visions would be made flesh. Thus after the June 1865 premiere
of *Tristan*, Wagner writes to him: 'How beautiful, how beautiful indeed it is
for me to have been granted the miracle of truly witnessing and enjoying the
dream which my soul had long cherished!' (*L* 649). A dream come to life,
as it does (to rather kitschy effect) at Neuschwanstein, and also as in Act I
of *Lohengrin*, where Elsa conjures the knight out of her vision and onto the
stage:

Laß mich ihn seh'n wie ich ihn sah,	May I see him as I have seen him,
wie ich ihn sah sei er mir nah'!	As I have seen him let him come
	to me!

In a mood of equally dizzy rapture (at least partly affected, one suspects),
Wagner and Ludwig dedicated themselves to bringing about the same transition from private fantasy to theatrical actuality.

The command Lohengrin imposes on his bride tells her, in essence, not to
look too closely. Under the wrong kind of scrutiny, romantic dreams vanish.
In the case of the King and the composer, their mutual faith that 'reality'
could be like 'poesy' depended equally on a certain wilful blindness. Political
and economic realities dictated that it was not in fact possible for Ludwig to
act like Lohengrin, magically making all Wagner's wishes come true. Even
when it came to the more straightforward matter of putting the operas on
stage, the composer had to instruct his patron not to examine the procedure
too carefully. Ludwig urgently wanted to see *Lohengrin* performed for him
according to Wagner's directions, but when the production was planned in
1867 the only tenor Wagner thought capable of the role was Joseph
Tichatschek, who had been the first Rienzi and Tannhäuser back in Dresden
in the 1840s and was therefore far too old to incarnate Ludwig's fantasies of
radiant heroic purity. 'I ought', Wagner wrote to the King, 'to have begged
you to listen to the singer with your ears open, but not to observe him too
closely. . . . You ignored my warning: you stared at him with redoubled intensity; it was impossible for him to withstand this scrutiny: the vital illusion was
lost' (*L* 718). In this little parable the plot of the opera repeats itself. An
intensely questioning gaze destroys the fantasy which allows dreams to come
to life. Ludwig's naïvely romantic identification with Lohengrin must have
overlooked the fact that the swan knight's story ends in banishment, finally
confirming the incongruity between reality and dreams. Poignantly, the King's
idealized hero is undone in the opera by political machinations (in the form
of Ortrud and Telramund's plotting). As monarch of one of the largest German
states, Ludwig had a potentially important position in the conflicts of the later
1860s which eventually produced a unified German empire. However, the

intricacies of international diplomacy and the brutal realities of machine-age warfare, both of which were mastered by Bismarck's Prussia, had nothing to do with romantic fantasy. Realpolitik banished Ludwig's vital illusions. Political exigencies were also responsible for banishing Wagner from the King's company in December 1865, dooming their joint dream of creating a theatre in Munich where the composer's imaginings would be brought to life. The story of the period of their close association is, ironically, more like *Lohengrin* than either of them could have expected: it's the story of dreams undone by the 'redoubled intensity' of pragmatic realities.

It's tempting to go along with the tone set by their mutual correspondence, the romantic effusiveness which substitutes the language of opera for that of reality (or blurs the distinction between the two). Wagner's relationship with Ludwig, we might justifiably argue, was as politically meaningless as what one contemporary observer called the King's own 'tendency to become engrossed in his own fantastical world of dreams' (*WR* 176). For Wagner's art, the relationship was incomparably important, in that Ludwig's continuing support made possible the completion of the operas and of the Bayreuth theatre. Beyond this relation of simple patronage – a perfectly familiar phenomenon, though (as usual with Wagner) on an extraordinary scale – the rest of their shared language might be interpreted as pure fantasy. (From Ludwig's point of view it is of course a different story, since he suffered intensely from the contradictions between his fantasies and the realities of his position: but we're only concerned with Wagner here.) This sort of interpretation – where visionary dreams transcend pragmatic reality – echoes Hans Sachs's position in the oration that closes *Die Meistersinger*. He ends by declaring that art outlives politics:

zerging' in Dunst	should the Holy Roman Empire
das heil'ge röm'sche Reich,	dissolve into mist,
uns bliebe gleich	there would still remain for us
die heil'ge deutsche Kunst!	holy German art!

It's a curious inversion of the end of *Lohengrin*. There the romantic fantasy-figure disappears back into his invisible castle with its misty harmonies, leaving empire behind; here Sachs imagines that the political sphere fades away into irrelevance while music lives on. Ludwig would have ardently embraced this redistribution of the relationship between art and reality; he more than once suggested his willingness to abdicate his throne in order to devote himself entirely to Wagner.

Yet *Meistersinger* is quite explicitly a political opera. From the vantage-point of its Reformation-era setting it is willing to envisage the dissolution of the first *Reich*, the Holy Roman Empire, transcended by the endurance in art of what Sachs earlier calls the 'German and true' ('Was deutsch und ächt'). As a work of art completed and premiered in the late 1860s, though, it effectively hymns the advent of the second *Reich*, Bismarck's unified Germany proclaimed in 1871. Its earnest and enthusiastic nationalism is clearly not just a matter of 'German art' but of the idea of the German state as well. Moreover, that same nationalism, expressed in the form of romantic nostalgia, and secured by the scapegoating of Beckmesser and by Sachs's final warning against the corruption of authentic Germanness by insidious foreign influence, made the opera an apt vehicle for the propaganda of the third *Reich*, Hitler's fascist state in which the dissolution of the boundaries between fantasy and reality became the very opposite of harmless.

In *Meistersinger* nationalism is encoded in the sphere of art. The guild of Mastersingers stands for the authentic 'German spirit', to use a phrase recurrent in Wagner's writings of the 1860s. Proper guardianship of this spirit is therefore represented through a proper appreciation of music and song. This corresponds exactly to the principle underpinning Wagner and the King's relationship: art and reality are interchangeable, or at least liable to overlap. As we've seen, though (and it's obvious enough anyway), this is an idea which shies away from close scrutiny. Indeed, there is still an enduring reluctance to look too closely at this aspect of *Meistersinger*. When the scholar Barry Millington published an article drawing attention to the fact that Beckmesser stands in Wagner's imagination for the Jews, vehement protests and denials followed.[1] This was not, surely, because of any possibility of doubt over Millington's basic argument. Wagner's writings unambiguously and repeatedly cast the Jews as the opposite of true music and of healthy natural identity, as Beckmesser is Walther's opposite. The real cause of resistance must surely have been a reluctance to associate the opera with anti-Semitism, and therefore (by inevitable extension, given Wagner's posthumous adoption as the Nazi state composer) with Hitler's attempted genocide. When thinking about *Meistersinger*, it is easy to appreciate the appeal of letting ideas of empire and German history dissolve, leaving behind only music.

In the same way, Wagner's political writings of the later 1860s – primarily 'Über Staat und Religion' ('On State and Religion') and 'Was ist deutsch?' ('What is German?'), both unpublished until the 1870s, and *Deutsche Kunst und deutsche Politik* (*German Art and German Policy [Politics]*) – claim that their only real concern is with art. Political problems are glibly interpreted in terms of cultural issues, just as they were in the prose writings of the post-revolutionary 1840s and 50s. The crisis Wagner thinks is facing German identity as a whole is described in terms of the degenerate state of German theatre and of the popular press. As Sachs's speech insists, questions of nationhood and empire blur into questions of aesthetics and culture. 'On State and Religion' was originally written privately for Ludwig's benefit, in answer to a request to explain the changes in Wagner's political thinking since the time of those earlier prose writings (which the King had studied intently). Wagner quickly denies that he is responding in any political capacity at all:

> My youthful friend will surely not expect me to give a categorical account of my later views on Politics and State: under any circumstances they could have no practical importance, and in truth would simply amount to an expression of my horror of concerning myself professionally with matters of the sort. (IV 9)

Fair enough, one is tempted to say. The political speculations that follow in this and the other documents are indeed airily fantastical and utterly remote from the 'practical' circumstances of Bavaria in the years leading up to German unification. The artist, Wagner goes on to say, is necessarily remote from such concerns: he 'may say of himself: "My kingdom is not of this world;" and, perhaps more than any artist now living, I may say this of myself . . .' (IV 9; cf. John 18: 36). We've already had cause to scrutinize these gestures of unworldliness, however. Here again, as with the matter of Wagner's (mis)use of Schopenhauer, Wagnerian renunciation may well be a mask for Wagnerian desire. In this case, the artist's claim to be apolitical and unworldly, to dissolve the sphere of politics into the sphere of art, masks the essential political meaning of his art in this period. It's at this point that closer scrutiny becomes necessary. Under the intoxicating influence of his apparent power over the monarch of a German state, Wagner did indeed indulge in fantastical theorizing about the role of a king in relation to his people, and the destiny of Germany as a whole. Yet these fantasies should not be treated as merely operatic excursions into the realm of politics. Looked at more closely, they function in the reverse direction as well: they reveal the thoroughly political significance of the operas.

Once again, the hazily overlapping relationship between art and reality is central to understanding how this reversal works. Ludwig's appearance in Wagner's career casts the relationship in a distinctive light. As the latter's initial letter puts it, reality has been transfigured by the 'marvels of poesy'. Apparently guaranteeing the fulfilment of Wagner's work, bringing his operatic and theatrical visions to life, Ludwig represents the *Lohengrin*-like entry of dreams into the actual world (with no prying Elsa whose scrutiny might bring about a tragic outcome). This transfiguration is achieved by ignoring or suppressing pragmatic details: as Lohengrin suppresses any questions about his exact nature, as Wagner and Ludwig tried to ignore the economic and political costs of their dreams. Hence the transfiguring touch of art imagines itself as an ascent above merely pragmatic and utilitarian concerns. (This attitude persists with audiences who object to 'political' productions of Wagner's operas, presumably because they believe that all such concerns belong only outside the theatre.) Once reality has been brought into line with the marvels of poesy, there is no need to be concerned with strictly political or functional questions. All that matters, as Wagner (of course) and the King (less rationally) agreed, is opera. Empire can dissolve into mist as long as art endures. So Sachs says, and so the Wagner-Ludwig fantasy concurs. Art and fantasy transcend politics.

Yet the most striking thing about Wagner's political writing of the period is how it turns this very mode of thinking into the fundamental basis of a militant nationalism. Transcendence itself turns out to be an aggressively politicized idea. The nationalistic tone of the end of *Meistersinger*, that is, is not an anomaly; nor is Sachs's claim that art stands apart from empire an honest one. Like many other commentators in Germany at the time, Wagner was preoccupied with the idea of Germanness, the question of what might make the disparate German-speaking states into a unified *Volk*. It's hardly the mode of thought appropriate to an exile, or to a disciple of Schopenhauerian dispossession and resignation, but the miraculous intervention of May 1864 at one stroke moved Wagner from an unfixed nowhere to an apparently permanent place in the inner sanctum of Bavaria. Correspondingly, his writing becomes saturated with the rhetoric of national identity, of a secure and fixed place.

In the absence of a unified German empire, this place is conceptual or ideological rather than geographical. There is no single 'Germany', politically speaking; but everywhere in his writing there are references to a 'German spirit', a notion of Germanic identity which transcends the fractured political condition of the Teutonic peoples in order to gather them together at the spiritual level. This naturally begs the question: what is the specifically German spirit? How does it reveal itself? Or, in the title of the brief meditation written in 1865, 'What is German?' The essay begins with an etymological answer (and here it is clear how far we are from the language of exile, the art of transition):

> [Jacob] Grimm . . . has proved that 'diutisk' or 'deutsch' means nothing more than what is homelike [*heimisch*] to ourselves . . . 'deutsch' is what is plain (*deutlich*) to us, the familiar, the wonted [*uns Gewohnte*], inherited from our fathers, racy of our soil [*unserem Boden Entsprossene*]. (IV 152)

'German', that is, means that which belongs to itself, possesses itself, is in its proper place. Germanness is a quality or a power of incorporating everything into a fixed identity, an irresistibly centripetal force. Everything that comes within its orbit is sucked into its own nature (the explicit contrast in 'What is German?' is with 'the Jews', who have no homeland and insinuate themselves into other cultures: Wagner refers to them as 'an utterly alien element', IV 158). It is thus effectively self-defining: 'German' means that which is German and not anything else, which refuses to be anything other than German, which inhabits its own being securely and inviolably.

Evidently, the logic of nationalism is at work here. We exist, the argument

goes, by virtue of being utterly unlike everyone else. The seeds of a later, far
more strident Aryanism are also obvious enough in this kind of thinking, and
they begin to sprout in Wagner's last essays, which translate Grimm's etymol-
ogy into a spurious biology by raising the notion of blood purity. In the
writing of the 1860s, though, this idea of a self-defining, self-sufficient
Germanness takes a more surprising turn. Extrapolating from Grimm's original etymological answer to the titular question, 'What is German?' goes on
to give the idea of inviolable self-possession a Schopenhauerian twist. To be
defined purely by the permanence of one's own identity (Grimm's definition)
is also, Wagner argues, to be indifferent to everything external. That is to say,
because the 'German spirit' is self-defining, it's also exclusively self-interested,
concerned only with its own nature, aloof from other matters. This leads the
essay from its etymological foundations to a purely ideological nationalist
rhetoric, fervently triumphalist in tone. The German spirit

> was the first to publish to the world – that the Beautiful and Noble came
> not into the world for [the] sake of profit, nay, not for [the] sake of even
> fame and recognition. And everything done in the sense of this teaching
> is 'deutsch'; and therefore is the German great; and only what is done in
> that sense, can lead Germany to greatness. (IV 163)

Germanness is now defined as disinterestedness. It stands for a separation of
'the Beautiful and Noble' from 'profit'. As it appears in this passage, it is given
a negative definition; Wagner here tells us what the German does *not* think
and feel, what he stands apart from. His idealism has no ulterior purpose. It
is not *for* profit or fame. A version of Schopenhauer's doctrine of the denial
of the will is clearly at work here, for Wagner's 'German spirit' characterizes
itself by its absence of purpose.

In the course of the much more extensive essay *German Art and German
Policy*, though, the negative definition is recast in positive form. Discussing
the remarkable flowering of German culture in the age of Goethe and
Schiller, Wagner puts the matter in extremely revealing terms:

> Here came to consciousness and received its plain expression, what *German*
> is: to wit, the thing one does for its own sake, for the very joy of doing
> it; whereas Utilitarianism, namely the principle whereby a thing is done
> for [the] sake of some personal end, ulterior to the thing itself, was [shown]
> to be un-German. (IV 107)

This is more or less identical with the definition given in 'What is German?'
Immediately, though, Wagner makes a crucial step forward in his argument:

> The German virtue herein expressed thus coincided with the highest prin-
> ciple of aesthetics . . . according to which the 'objectless' [or 'purposeless';
> *das Zwecklose*] alone is beautiful, because, being an end [*Zweck*] in itself, in

revealing its nature as lifted high above all vulgar ends it reveals at like time that to reach whose sight and knowledge alone makes [the] ends of life worth following; whereas everything that serves an end is hideous, because neither its fashioner nor its [audience] can have aught before him save a disquieting conglomerate of fragmentary material, which is first to gain its meaning and elucidation from its employment for some vulgar need. (IV 107–8)

To paraphrase: both Germanness and art are defined by their anti-utilitarianism, by the fact of being ends in themselves rather than means to some ulterior purpose; consequently, Germanness and art transcend 'vulgar' (*gemein*) desires and functions (such as profit, fame or recognition, or any other pragmatic or utilitarian measure of value). The 'German spirit' is the spirit of the aesthetic, of art. (The theory of art's purposelessness is itself a legacy of the age of Goethe and Schiller, deriving from the hugely influential theories of Kant.) Needless to say, this provides the theoretical ground for Wagner's consistent assertions that the political revival of the German spirit can only happen in the form of a regeneration of German art. Equally obviously, Wagner has his own art in mind (as in *The Art-Work of the Future* and the other revolutionary writings). His plans to build a music school in Munich (at Ludwig's expense) loom large in *German Art and German Policy*. In the institution of the theatre, he claims over and over again, 'there lies the spiritual seed and kernel of all national-poetic and national-ethical culture' (IV 69); hence 'the supremely salutary effect of a genuine German Art-revival' (IV 110–11) – a revival clearly to be begun with the model performances of his works, conveniently freed by Ludwig's patronage from any concern with profit, fame or recognition.

Wagner's definitions cement the relationship between Germanness and art at a fundamental conceptual level. One idea lies at the very heart of these answers to the question 'What is German?': the dialectical opposition between aesthetic/German anti-utilitarianism (purposelessness, 'the thing one does for its own sake') and worldly, vulgar pragmatism, whose actions are impelled by degraded desires (such as the profit motive) and performed to serve ulterior ends. The German is otherworldly, spiritual, detached; its opposite (variously associated with France, the Jews, bourgeois life, commerce, and bad music) is enmeshed in the order of modern life, the world of everyday reality. This polarity crops up everywhere in the political essays. *German Art and German Policy* begins by quoting the political theorist Constantin Frantz, who contrasts 'the tyranny of . . . materialistic civilization' with the 'forces of mind and spirit' needed 'to bring about a nobler culture' (IV 37). In terms of artistic achievement, tyrannical materialism is represented by what Wagner calls 'the French spirit': 'the loftiest spheres of its imagination were everywhere delimited by tangibly and visibly realistic life-forms' (IV 84). Reality, that is, exerts its pragmatic weight to drag the creative imagination down from embracing the ideal. Both art and politics, then, are fields in which two tendencies are at war. On one side is 'the realistic force of Need [*die reale Kraft des Bedürfnisses*]', the pragmatic demands of real existence; on the other side, 'the ideal power of supplying that which is unreachable by the highest demands of Need' (IV 128), a transcendent spiritual domain entirely separate from mere everyday desires and purposes, a law unto itself, a thing done purely for its own sake. According to this systematic opposition, therefore, the 'German spirit' is essentially apolitical. As Sachs's final speech envisages, it lets the material domain of empire fade away, preserving itself in the purely aesthetic realm of 'holy German art'. Wagner reads the history of the Thirty Years War as a demonstration of this inverse relation between art and politics. 'The nation', he writes, 'was annihilated, but the German spirit had passed through'. Political defeat and spiritual victory are understood to be interchangeable effects of the same cause. Other nations survived because they kept a pragmatic eye on worldly profit, submitting to 'the laws of political advantage'; but precisely because Germany 'could never bend before the laws of this advantage', its uncompromised spirit meant that 'a German Folk could rise again' (IV 161).

How, then, do Wagner's writings actually envisage the operation of the political sphere? If they insist on such a thoroughly romantic transcendence of pragmatic politics, what do they have to say about the operation of society? The questions shouldn't just be ignored, because at the same time as Wagner declares that art and the German spirit transcend mundane reality, he is also writing about the national destiny of Germany and the regeneration of society. (It's the same paradox as Ludwig's: however intense his dedication to romantic fantasy, he was still the King of Bavaria, and thus inevitably a political being.) Most of the time in the writings of this period, Wagner's predictable bias bends his arguments towards the sphere of art, so that the discussion of material and historical questions quickly turns into arguments specifically concerned with the theatre. The end of *German Art and German Policy*, for example, is naked propaganda for Wagner's proposed new theatre in Munich. Creating a place 'exempt from all the needs . . . of a daily traffic', dedicated to idealistic goals 'beyond all ends of utility', would (he writes) give the German spirit 'a fitting habitation in the system of the German State' (IV 133, 135). This is as much as to say that a theatre dedicated to Wagner's works would itself be a representation of regenerated German identity (a view that would persist through the creation of the Bayreuth Festspielhaus). Politics is placed squarely inside the theatre; the 'German State' discovers and reveals itself on stage. Yet the political writings are not exclusively vehicles of artistic propaganda. In 'On State and Religion' – the brief, strange and

fascinating meditation originally written at Ludwig's request and meant only
for him – Wagner does deal directly with the idea of the political nation and
its institutions. It's by far the most interesting of this group of writings, because
it pursues the fundamental opposition between pragmatic realism and anti-
utilitarian idealism in directions which touch directly on the confusions of
reality and fantasy that resonate throughout the period of Wagner's relationship with Ludwig.

Following Schopenhauer, 'On State and Religion' begins by describing
human nature as at bottom mere blind egoism, made up (like animal nature)
of actions and desires that respond to the stimulus of immediate needs. The
state, it goes on to explain, arose simply as a means of mitigating the anarchy
that would otherwise result in a community of egoists. Its purpose is to
provide for as many of its people's immediate needs as can be reconciled with
mutual security. Its function is pragmatic: the 'necessity of establishing some
workable agreement among the myriad blindly-grasping individuals into
which it is divided' (IV 11). However, in accordance with the dialectical opposition governing all these essays, the state also contains, at its head, a representation of the aspect of human nature that potentially strives for something
higher than purely selfish gratification. This is the monarch, an individual set
above the strife and desires of individuals in order to administer in his own
person the ideals of justice and 'purely-human interests' (IV 12). (The fantastical nature of this argument, and its almost hilariously obvious appeal to
Ludwig's mystical tendencies, are not at issue here: all that concerns us is the
structure of Wagner's ideas.) In the person of the King, the state and its
citizens therefore achieve an image of a political ideal which transcends
the mundane egoism of human nature. Here, Wagner argues,

> at this summit of the State where we see its ideal reached, we therefore
> meet that side of human apperception [*Anschauungsweise*] which, in dis-
> tinction from the faculty of recognising the nearest need [i.e. mere egoism],
> we will call the power of *Wahn*. (IV 13)

For once Ellis does a small service by refusing to translate *Wahn*, since the
word immediately recalls Sachs in Act III of *Meistersinger*, a resonance we'll
shortly look at. The most accurate translation of the concept as Wagner
muddily presents it here would be 'ideology' (that is, the imaginary aspect of
social and political relations). However, the most convenient way of thinking
about it is to recall the basic opposition between pragmatism and aesthetic
anti-utilitarianism which Wagner makes so much of in this period. On the
one hand, the state caters to its citizens' immediate, pragmatic, functional
needs. On the other hand, in the institution of monarchy, it caters to their
Wahn: a 'form of apperception entirely opposed to ordinary cognisance' (IV
13), a purely aesthetic, entirely non-utilitarian mode of thinking – fantasy, in

other words. *Wahn*, usually translated as 'delusion', is here being understood as a purely imaginary dimension of political life. The example Wagner goes on to give is patriotism (a perfect example of what would now be called ideology). In entire contradistinction to the citizen's egoism, which places self-interest above any other interest, patriotism is his willingness to sacrifice his own life for the sake of the state. A phenomenon like this, Wagner claims, can only be accounted for by the existence of an entirely fantastical aspect to the state. *Wahn* raises the citizen 'beyond and above his common notions of the nature of things' (IV 16). It makes him transcend pragmatic egoism and rise into the sphere of the imaginary, the aesthetic, the German, everything which in Wagner's scheme is lifted above the material, the vulgar, the sphere of everyday reality. 'On State and Religion' thus unfolds the dimension of the aesthetic, the anti-real, in the course of a specifically political argument. *Wahn* is a power of making fictions, or a tendency to believe them. It describes perfectly the language exchanged by Wagner and the King, with its allegiance to dreams and fantasy, its insistence on transfiguring reality with the 'marvels of poesy'. Yet whereas the transfiguration usually claims to dissolve the pragmatic sphere (as Ludwig tried – unsuccessfully – to ignore the political dimension of being Wagner's patron), in 'On State and Religion' it reveals how it is embedded in a nationalist, monarchist, conservative idea of the state.

Distinguishing *Wahn* ('this wonder-working intuition') from 'the ordinary practical mode of ideation [*Vorstellungsweise*]' (IV 25), Wagner is imagining two different kinds of civic and political consciousness. The latter addresses itself to the ordinary business of everyday experience, the immediate needs of the citizen. Substituting fantasies and fictions for those mere realities, the former lifts the mind 'above all notions bound by Time and Space' (IV 25). What it finds there is not a depoliticized Nirvana, though, but the domain of transcendent monarchy and institutionalized religion, the ideal aspect of the state. As the essay confesses, 'the highest associate tendence [*die höchste gemeinsame Tendenz*] of the State could only be kept in active vigour through a form of Wahn' (IV 17). Delusion props up the political order. That's why it is exemplified by patriotism, a feeling which, however visionary or imaginary, serves a clear utilitarian end by inspiring militant allegiance to the state. In 'On State and Religion', then, the purely imaginary, anti-pragmatic, ego-transcending force of *Wahn* is very far from being 'objectless', 'an end in itself'. This makes explicit something clearly implied by the equation between aesthetics and Germanness made in *German Art and German Politics*. *Wahn*, the sphere of the aesthetic and the fantastic, does in fact have an ulterior purpose, and that purpose is nationalism itself. By identifying the German spirit with that which transcends utilitarian politics and (like art) serves only itself, Wagner's political thought is actually defining the whole sphere of the aesthetic, the spiritual, the unworldly, the sphere of *Wahn*, as the proper medium of Germanness. In the context of the late 1860s this is quite blatantly a utilitarian political purpose. Art heralds the coming of a unified, authentic German nation. Wagner may imagine that nationalism of this sort only occurs within the walls of a theatre, but the mere idea of the German nation at the time inevitably involved an awareness that it would actually create itself in the most pragmatic way imaginable, by imposing military defeat on competing European powers. His long essay on Beethoven, written during Prussia's successful campaign against France in 1870, includes at its end a pointed analogy between artistic and military manifestations of the 'German spirit':

> [Those who wish to may] Scoff at us . . . for attributing to German music this unbounded significance; we shall as little let ourselves be led astray thereby, as the German nation allowed itself to be misled when its enemies presumed to insult it on the ground of a too well reasoned doubt of its unanimity and staunchness. (V 125–6)

This is the voice of Wagner as patriot. Praising Beethoven's greatness in the field of art slips easily into the patriotic *Wahn* of nationalism, where the German spirit manifests itself in its armies as well as its symphonies.

The falseness of the essays' self-declared ideal of aesthetic transcendence is played out in Sachs's treatment of *Wahn*. His monologue endorses *Wahn* in explicitly utilitarian terms, as we've seen. He diagnoses the riot that ended Act II as a demonstration of the emptiness of human experience, but this Schopenhauerian pessimism doesn't stop him trying to use *Wahn* in order to re-engineer his community. By mastering fantasy 'ein edler Werk zu thun' ('in order to perform a nobler deed'), he is giving it exactly the kind of pragmatic ulterior purpose that (according to the essays) art is supposed to be untainted by. Indeed, the whole plot of *Die Meistersinger* could not more forcefully give the lie to this Kantian notion that art serves only its own purposes. 'What is German?' tells us that the German spirit, the artistic spirit, is by its nature detached from 'profit', 'fame' or 'recognition'. Yet in the opera Walther's song is quite deliberately directed to a specific ulterior goal, winning the competition and thereby gaining Eva. Nor does he only profit from the economy of Pogner's rules. He gains fame and recognition as well by performing his song in public, using it to win over the audience. The song may begin in the realm of anti-utilitarian fantasy, as a dream, but it ends absolutely in the political sphere. It fulfils its public purpose in the closing scenes, where it gains a still more fundamentally political meaning. As well as winning the contest and converting the crowd, it becomes the defining moment in the regeneration of the community – a regeneration swiftly translated by Sachs from Nuremberg to Germany as a whole. Art, Sachs says, is a national enterprise, and therefore a nationalist enterprise. Walther's triumph unites the citizens of Nuremberg – precisely exemplifying the political essays' argument that the German spirit can only be revived through German art. However much both the essays and the opera try to claim that this revival is a purely spiritual one, there can be no doubt that they direct art towards the goal of a nationalism which corresponds exactly to the ruthless militarism of Bismarck's forcible creation of the second *Reich*.

This is why Beckmesser has to be expelled. It's not just that he is a bad artist, although this is how *Meistersinger* tries to present the matter. The closing scenes are all about the construction of a properly, exclusively *deutsch* (that is, belonging-to-itself) community, inspired by and organized around art. This community, this newly unified state, can only be authentically *deutsch* – 'inherited from our fathers, racy of our soil', as 'What is German?' has it – if it gets rid of all alien elements. Beckmesser lacks the 'German spirit'. He is a utilitarian pragmatist, not a transcendental fantasist; he makes art by rules (as Wagner says the French do in *German Art and German Politics*), he insists on worldly forms and routines, he has no appreciation of Walther's natural, spontaneous, dreamy inspiration. His humiliating failure as an artist in the song competition is therefore not just a signal of his musical incompetence, but the demonstration of his un-Germanness, his foreignness to what is *deutsch*: and so he has to go, as comprehensively exposed and defeated as possible. His story shows us that art's claim to occupy a detached, self-contained aesthetic sphere actually involves a deliberate (and in this case aggressive) exclusion of everything outside it. This exclusion may present itself as transcendent unworldliness, but it is more properly named as nationalism, whose rejection of everything outside itself is not mystically aloof but straightforwardly prag- matic. The new German nation built itself on the military defeat of Austria and France. The third *Reich*'s vision of a regenerated Germany, of course, founded itself on an exclusive nationalist myth of the 'German spirit' that expressed itself with horrific and unimaginably brutal pragmatism. Which is not to suppose that the ideology of the 1930s can be equated directly with Wagner's imagination in the 1860s (although Wagner did choose to republish 'Judaism in Music' in 1869); but the Nazis' adoption of Wagner's art as an icon of their version of the 'German spirit' shows all too clearly what is involved in Wagner's own identification of politics with aesthetics. Fascism begins with the politics of fantasy, erecting a transcendent ideology of the state which it then claims is pure, self-defining, answerable only to itself, and unquestionable from any merely worldly position. It raises the state into the sphere of *Wahn*, 'madness', far removed from all 'common notions of the nature of things' (IV 16). When Wagner uses this kind of language to describe his own art, we need to realize once again that the pose of detachment and transcendence masks an urgently pragmatic and political desire: the desire for Germanness, for an authentic nation, 'transcending' everything opposed to (or beneath) it by force if necessary.

The latter sections of 'On State and Religion' deal yet again with the opposition between idealism (transcendence, purposelessness, Germanness, renunciation, *Wahn*) and pragmatism (materialism, worldliness, foreignness, desire, reality). This time, the context is a discussion of religion.

> *Religion*, of its very essence, is radically divergent from the State. The religions that have come into the world have been high and pure in direct ratio as they seceded from the State. . . . Its basis is a feeling of the unblessedness of human being, of the State's profound inadequacy to still the purely-human need [i.e. the longing for something higher than merely material, egoistic needs]. Its inmost kernel is denial of the world. . . . (IV 23)

This sort of language should by now be very familiar. Religion, the essay is saying, is like art, fundamentally distinct from and opposed to the sphere of the everyday. Wagner continues in openly Schopenhauerian terms. The religious consciousness, he writes, recognizes 'this present world', the world of reality, as only 'suffering and illusion' (IV 24); it leads us to 'voluntary suffering and renunciation' (IV 25). As always, though, Wagner won't stop at Schopenhauer's pessimism. Beyond suffering and renunciation lies (inevitably) redemption, 'the measureless lofty joy of [overcoming the world]' (IV 26). Schopenhauer himself dismissed Christianity as just another form of blind desire, another manifestation of the egotistic will. In 'On State and Religion', though, the Christian religion is identified as a specifically positive form of transcendence, not sheer pessimistic denial but redemption. Heaven replaces Nirvana. The absolute detachment Schopenhauer recommends becomes itself a 'measureless lofty joy', just as the detached self-sufficiency of *deutsch* is the grounds for an assertive nationalism, a proclamation of *Deutschland*.

Wagner's account of how religion enacts this transcendence again demonstrates his desire to go beyond Schopenhauer's negative philosophy, to proceed from renunciation to redemption.

> The wondrous, quite incomparable attribute of religious Dogma is this: it presents in positive form that which on the path of reflection [*des Nachgedenks*], and through the strictest philosophic methods, can be seized in none but negative form. That is to say, whereas the philosopher arrives at demonstrating the erroneousness and incompetence of that natural mode of ideation [according to which] we take the world, as it commonly presents itself, for an undoubtable reality: religious Dogma [shows] the other [i.e. transcendent] world itself, as yet unrecognized; and with such unfail-

ing sureness and distinctness, that the Religious, on whom that world has dawned, is straightway possessed with the most unshatterable, most deeply-blessing peace. (IV 26–7)

To paraphrase again: philosophy (Schopenhauer's, of course) can discover that the real, pragmatic, utilitarian world is empty and meaningless, but all it can do then is recommend denial and renunciation of the real. Religion actually reveals a transcendent, spiritual, anti-utilitarian world, and therefore offers a redemption after renunciation. Ordinary modes of thought, rooted in the world of everyday experience, cannot comprehend religion. Yet its virtue is to show anyway what lies beyond that mundane world. Thus Wagner argues that religion has been corrupted and degraded by its efforts to explain its transcendental intuitions in the language of reality, 'dragged before the tribune of common . . . apprehension' (IV 28). Its truths should instead have the force of pure revelation, which the everyday world 'has to take on authority' (IV 27). They can be seized only by 'Faith', 'sincere, undoubting and unconditional' (IV 28). Religion represents the aesthetic, anti-pragmatic sphere. Notably, though, Wagner's argument at bottom claims that it enforces this sphere as a pragmatic necessity. Like extreme nationalism, it demands assent. Its utter separation from worldly modes of thought and experience means that it can only appear in the world in the form of 'Dogma', an unquestionable, inexplicable truth. In the same way that the unworldliness of the 'German spirit' translates into a desire to overcome the exterior world politically and militarily, the transcendence of religion translates itself into a total ideological assertion.

Here in miniature are the politics of *Parsifal*. In Wagner's last opera, the forces of fantasy and of nationalism are represented as religion. The community longing for purity and unity is no longer named Germany, but appears instead as the brotherhood of the Grail. The transcendent purposelessness of art is translated into an opera which enacts a religious rite, so that art celebrates and deifies itself. At first sight, everything about *Parsifal* claims to be anti-utilitarian, spiritual, mystical. Such claims need to be treated with the utmost scepticism (and, vitally, they're denied by the opera itself, as we'll see in Part IV). The idea of art's holiness, like the idea of art's Germanness, exploits transcendence for nakedly ideological purposes. These apparent renunciations of the everyday world are at the same time props of a militant nationalism and a dogmatic religiosity – tendencies which become all too explicit in Wagner's latest prose works. Insisting on preserving art's sacred immunity from the world involves doing what Lohengrin does, what Ludwig tried to do, sustaining fantasy only at the cost of silencing pragmatic questions.

Yet opera is a pragmatic business, as no one knew better than Wagner. It is the most cumbersomely material of artistic genres. Wagner's conceptions may be visionary, fantastical, transcendent, but their existence nevertheless presupposes the bricks and mortar of the theatre, the sweat of musicians, the obstructive three-dimensionality of costumes and props and sets. Likewise, art may pretend to be sealed up in an inviolable holy of holies, and Germanness may pretend to be a matter purely of the spirit, but aesthetics and politics are equally vulnerable to Elsa's questions: what is your real nature? Where do you come from? These are the questions of a sceptical, probing reality, and dogma's purpose is to silence them by declaring itself aloof from them − again, just as Wagner and Ludwig hoped to screen their theatre of dreams from the mundane inquiries of politicians and the public. As *Lohengrin* demonstrates, though, and as Wagner's rapid fall from the immunity of royal grace in 1865 equally testifies, repressing pragmatic questions only makes them likely to be asked more pointedly. The more the essays of the late 1860s speak of transcendence, the more they expose their thoroughly political character. The same contradiction stands visibly before the eye in Ludwig's later project, Neuschwanstein. For all its airy lightness and delicacy, it irresistibly impels us to ask (like Elsa) how it got there. It is meant to be the purest flight of fancy, the image of an unearthly Montsalvat, but it also bears witness to the most worldly power: only a monarch could have done such a thing. Fantasies of art are built on pragmatic foundations, just as fantasies of nationhood are propped up by artillery and the jackboot.

It is worth remembering, then, that the last phase of Wagner's career is not only that of *Parsifal* but also that of Bayreuth. The elevation of art to the otherworldly sphere of religion coexists with the practicalities of financing and building its visible, material home. Adopting Jesus's words for his own, Wagner in 'On State and Religion' says 'My kingdom is not of this world' (IV 9). This is wrong: not only that, but any such claim needs to be positively denied, as we need to deny *Parsifal*'s claim to be a sacred opera. Yet despite the evidence of Wagner's nationalist rhapsodies of the 1860s, his art knows that it belongs to the body as well as the spirit, the sphere of reality as well as that of fantasy. The Festspielhaus at Bayreuth is material evidence of that. Faced with the kind of fantasies that occupy Wagner's imagination in the last decade of his career, there's a real need to bring art back to earth. *Parsifal* might look like the worst possible guide to any such effort, but the genius of this most extraordinary creation of Wagner's astonishing imagination is that it brings back everything those transcendental fantasies falsely claim to have overcome.

PART IV

Religion

CHAPTER THIRTEEN

Purity

In the closing exchanges of Act II of *Parsifal*, Kundry – herself accursed – calls down on the hero what he will later call 'ein wilder Fluch', 'a savage curse'. Her imprecation is the fearfully agitated climax of the descent into fury, pleading and self-hatred she has undergone since her kiss changed Parsifal's pure innocence into conscious purity. This is what she sings:

[*into the background*]	
Hilfe! Hilfe! Herbei!	Help! Help! Here!
Haltet den Frechen! Herbei!	Stop the miscreant! Here!
Wehr't ihm die Wege!	Bar the roads to him!
Wehr't ihm die Pfade! –	Bar the paths to him! –
[*to Parsifal*]	And should you escape from
Und flöh'st du von hier, und fändest	here, and find
alle Wege der Welt,	all the roads in the world,
den Weg, den du such'st,	the road which you seek,
dess' Pfade sollst du nicht finden!	that path you shall not find!
Denn Pfad und Wege,	For the path and the roads
die mir dich entführen,	which lead you away from me
so verwünsch' ich sie dir:	I thus curse for you:
Irre! Irre, –	*Irre! Irre* – [wandering/error]
mir so vertraut –	so faithful to me –
dich weih' ich ihm zum Geleit'!	I consecrate you to its guidance!

With the last lines, sung to music that for a few bars is oddly tender, she gives him into the hands of her own guiding force. Summoned by her call, Klingsor immediately appears to try to stop Parsifal. But although he thinks he is the power that controls her, it is not in fact to him that she has given Parsifal, and the hero dismisses his magic with effortless swiftness. The force that has directed Kundry, and to which she now consigns Parsifal, is named by the word 'Irre!' With this malediction, Kundry is pronouncing two interchangeable decrees. Its paired meanings are conveyed by the cognate English imperative: err! Latin *errare* means 'to wander' (as in 'knights-errant', the adventuring heroes of chivalry). To wander is also to go wrong: hence 'error', straying from the right path, making a mistake. Parsifal is doomed not to find the right road (the repetitions of *Weg* and *Pfad* in her curse imbue this fate with demonic insistence), and at the same time to be in a state of error.

This fierce curse, whose consequences stretch through the invisible chasm of time between Acts II and III of *Parsifal*, is the last gasp of exile in Wagner's work. Almost literally so: the final syllable of the speech is virtually the last articulate sound Kundry will make before falling into self-imposed muteness. In rehearsals for the 1882 premiere, Wagner authorized it to be sung an octave higher than it's written in the score, which translates it into a shrieking high B. With that explosion of energy, exile exhausts itself. The act that follows is an extended double homecoming, bringing Parsifal back to the domain of the Grail and then allowing him to return the brotherhood of the Grail to its original state of purity by healing Amfortas and reinstituting the eucharistic rite. As Gurnemanz assures him,

War es ein Fluch,	If it was a curse
der dich vom rechten Pfad vertrieb,	that drove you from the right path,
so glaub', er ist gewichen.	be sure that it is broken.

In Act III, error (*Irren*) has supposedly been repudiated. Parsifal's wanderings are over, and his ignorance has been replaced by calm confidence in his redeeming duty; Amfortas's sin is expiated; Kundry's ancient crime is absolved; everyone is back on the right track. The transitions and migrations of exile are laid to rest. Intensely ritualistic, the act stands as the terminus of a trajectory in Wagner's work that leads towards complete occupation of its own territory. As we've seen, this tendency is powerfully present in *Die Meistersinger*, with its nostalgic conservatism and its fantasies of *deutsch* belonging. The end of *Parsifal* fulfils what is only a prophecy in Sachs's closing speech, as he issues a warning against imminent invasion and degeneration, and envisions 'holy German art' as the only impervious force of resistance. That vision comes true (or at least presents itself as having come true) in the closing act of Wagner's last opera, where art – Wagner's art, of course – has clothed itself in the rituals and iconography of Christianity, and celebrates the restoration of a sacred brotherhood. The impure element (Kundry, who is at once female, Semitic, and unchaste) is baptized on stage, as if opera has taken on itself the role of administering the rites of purification. This too had been anticipated in *Meistersinger*, whose third act also contains a baptism in the domain of art: but whereas Sachs half-jokingly christens a song, in *Parsifal* it's music – the opera itself – that claims to be the actual site of the Christian sacrament. Once

Kundry's baptism – the first ritual of admission into a holy community – has been taken care of, the act proceeds to sanctify itself by restaging its peculiar version of the sacrament of communion. Act I had also ended with a staging of the eucharistic rite, but there it was *watched* by Gurnemanz and Parsifal, both of them to some degree misunderstanding what was happening there. At the close of the act, Parsifal remains unenlightened, a failure marking the limits of the Grail's revelation; he can't be made to participate in the process undergone by the brotherhood. Gurnemanz, meanwhile, fails to grasp who Parsifal is, as the invisible voice that repeats the prophecy of the 'pure fool' after the rite effectively points out. In the last act, though, the sacramental scene cancels the vagaries and doubts and displacements of exile, breaking Kundry's curse by achieving a religious certainty – a faith – that it is on what Parsifal calls 'der Rettung . . . Pfad', the path of salvation. So Gurnemanz welcomes his return to Montsalvat as a baptismal end of 'Irrfahrt', 'error-journeying':

. . . und langer Irrfahrt Staub	. . . and let the dust of long wandering
soll jetzt von ihm gewaschen sein.	now be washed away from him.

All this striving to escape the curse of error, this language of right and wrong paths, indicates more clearly than anything else the real significance of *Parsifal*'s religious trappings. It should be needless to point out that the opera is not in fact a sacramental event, only a representation of one, however force-fully it asserts the contrary. Its symbolism and its scenery are no more thoroughly Christian than those of *Tannhäuser* or *Meistersinger*, or for that matter *Tosca* or *Don Carlos*. The fact that it enacts Christian rites and dis-courses on the theology of atonement (in the Good Friday scene) does not mean that it is a kind of liturgy, any more than the fact that a painting represents the crucifixion means that painting is a religious object. What turns such a painting into a specifically Christian artefact is its being made into an icon (usually by being placed in a church, above an altar). Likewise, Beethoven's *Missa solemnis* (or any other musical setting of the liturgy) would only be a Christian event if its Kyrie, Gloria, Credo and so on were actually sung in the course of a mass. Performed in the concert hall, it's just a musical work clothed in the language of Christianity and informed with a religious sensibility – exactly as *Parsifal* is.

The significant matter is the nature, the character, of that religious sensibility. In Wagner's opera, it takes the form of an overriding concern with purity and sin. Overriding, because the polar opposition between the two governs the whole thematic universe of *Parsifal*, as is evident if we contrast the later work with earlier Wagnerian versions of the same theme. *Tannhäuser* is organized around the same opposition, as to an extent is *Lohengrin*. In the two early operas, though, sin and purity are only aspects of a broader, more fundamental ethical opposition between good and evil (in *Lohengrin*) and right and wrong (in *Tannhäuser*, which concerns itself mainly with the hero's choices, his vacillation between antithetical ideals). There the religious concepts are essentially aspects of morality, but in *Parsifal* they gain a tremendous independent force. Reversing the situation of the earlier works, the moral sphere is now only a subset of the religious. It's not at all clear what is 'evil' about Klingsor, or what is 'good' about the Grail knights, in any ethical sense. What is absolutely unambiguous is that Klingsor is impure and that the brotherhood aspires to purity: these are the terms of *Parsifal*'s 'religion'.

Kundry's curse cuts to its heart, because purity means a disciplined adherence *den Rettung Pfad*, to the one right road, while sinning is defined as straying, losing the way. The knights strive to remain loyal and constant to the rules and rituals of their community; Klingsor devotes himself to disturbing them, distracting them, seducing them from the right path into his mazy garden of error. The opposition between staying right and going wrong constitutes the whole system of the opera's religion, as comparison with the earlier works again shows. Klingsor and the Grail Knights' war is entirely against each other, unlike in *Lohengrin* where Ortrud's evil encompasses general characteristics of falsehood and malice, and represents a threat to the whole social and political order. *Tannhäuser*'s situation is closer to *Parsifal*'s, in that there is nothing obviously wrong with Venus except for the fact that she stands as the impure antithesis to the Landgrave's chivalric code. Nevertheless, the plot of *Tannhäuser* takes place within a whole social structure, the Pope and Hermann its respective sacred and secular heads, which determines that one kind of behaviour is correct and orderly, and the other kind (Venus's kind) is not. However implausible this structure may be, it is taken for granted by everyone in the opera's world, Tannhäuser himself included. As in *Lohengrin*, religion is part of the ethical and cultural order of society, so its demands and its values have a kind of unquestionable and universal validity – which is why the crime of even mentioning Venus's name calls forth the whole apparatus of guilt, penance and pilgrimage. In *Parsifal* nothing seems to exist outside the weirdly mirrored worlds of Klingsor on one hand and Montsalvat on the other: no society, no ethical norms, no larger moral universe. The geography and chronology of the opera are equally dreamy and vague. All that matters is the attempt of the Grail brotherhood to maintain its integrity: specifically, to heal the breach in its perfection made by Amfortas's error, a breach materially represented by the permanent wound in his body. The community needs to return to its right path: and its 'rightness' in this sense is not a matter of morality or choice (it has nothing to do with how they behave in the world), but simply a question of staying true to the pure faith, avoiding error. Gurnemanz explains this logic to the Squires in Act I as he describes what it means to be a servant of the Grail:

Die seinem Dienst ihr zugesindet	You who were called to its service,
auf Pfaden, die kein Sünder findet,	on paths no sinner can find,
ihr wißt, daß nur dem Reinen	you know that only to the pure
vergönnt ist sich zu einen	is it permitted to be one of
den Brüdern, die zu höchsten Rettungswerken	the brotherhood, which the wondrous power of the Grail
des Grales heil'ge Wunderkräfte	strengthens for the highest deeds
stärken . . .	of salvation . . .

The Grail knights are the elect, chosen for the sake of their purity to be members of a sacred community. What matters about them most is not what they do but what they are.

Accordingly, the religion of *Parsifal* is extraordinarily introverted, self-regarding, like a sacramentalized version of the absolute self-absorption of Tristan and Isolde. As in *Tristan*, the characters' actions – indeed, their very power to act – seem incidental, if not entirely irrelevant. Far more important are their *natures*. This is why the opera is so relentlessly concerned with chastity. With unsettling effect, the moral antagonism one might expect to find in a plot like this is translated entirely into the field of sexuality, so that instead of being a battle of good against evil, the contest of the Grail and Klingsor is between chastity (purity) and eroticism (sin). Sexual discipline is not so much an ethical choice (something one does) as a bodily state, an entirely introverted kind of holiness, dedicated to keeping watch on one's own body. Indeed, to be chaste is to resist action, to maintain one's purity by renouncing temptation – a static, negative virtue. This is entirely in keeping with the nature of the Grail knights. Their essential mission is to keep to the one right way (it's interesting that where Act I speaks of 'Rettungswerken', '*deeds* of salvation', and hints vaguely about crusading knights fighting in distant lands, Act III refers more acutely to 'der Rettung . . . Pfad', salvation's path). Thus Amfortas fears for the adventuring Gawain, 'wenn er in Klingsor's Schlingen fällt', 'if he should fall into Klingsor's snares'. Leaving the domain of the Grail is itself a risk, because it means wandering (erring) from the safe paths. The risk is materialized by the seductions of Klingsor's garden, which tempt the straying knights to forget the way of salvation and dally instead in an enchanted erotic realm. In Kundry's double nature, the opera's central dichotomy is made even more starkly visible and material. Within the realm of the Grail she appears as an unsexed 'wilde Weib', 'wild woman', whom the young knights compare to an animal. Under Klingsor's power, she changes into an erotic temptress. The actual crime for which she has been eternally cursed – laughing in the face of Christ – fades strangely into the background compared with the more vivid and threatening sinfulness signified by her sexual power. She tells Parsifal in Act II that her curse can only be ended when she looks again into the saviour's face, undoing her ancient sin. Yet Parsifal ignores it entirely in his reply, insisting that her salvation depends only on turning away from her desires:

Auch dir bin ich zum Heil gesandt,	I am sent for your salvation also,
bleib'st du dem Sehnen abgewandt.	if you renounce desire.

At first glance – and this impression needs to be quickly corrected – *Parsifal*'s profound interest in sexuality looks like another instance of the transcendentalism always latent in Wagner's thought, the elevation of spirit over body (or matter) which is such a prominent theme of *German Art and German Policy*. Chastity appears to stand for transcendence, because it rejects the body, striving to keep the spirit untainted by sensual 'desires'. From its first note, that strikingly bare and austere sound, *Parsifal* superficially gives every impression of being a thoroughly idealizing work, one which refuses the sensory indulgence usually offered by Wagner's rich aural and dramatic imagination in favour of a disciplined spirituality. It celebrates the rites and faiths of a community centred around a sublime object, the Grail, which reveals itself through waves of immaterial radiance and sound. Its villain is a magician who attempts to drag the spirit down into what Amfortas calls 'die Welt der Sünden', 'the world of sins'. Its obsession with purity in itself looks like a straightforward rejection of everything worldly and corporeal. Its characteristic sound is a blended, distanced, shimmering orchestration, colluding with the Bayreuth theatre's fantasy that music is not produced by real people playing physical instruments but emerges instead from some immaterial space (like the invisible voices singing from the obscure heights of the dome in the temple scene of Act I).

All this is true: and yet *Parsifal* is, quite emphatically, the most bodily of Wagner's works (the *Ring*'s ecstasies and torments are more psychological). By comparison with *Tristan*, which systematically dematerializes everything it touches, *Parsifal* is absolutely mired in flesh and blood. *Tristan* – superficially Wagner's most pagan, erotic work – casts a spell of abstraction over its world: its concerns are relentlessly metaphysical rather than physical. Strangely, *Parsifal*, which ought to be his most spiritual drama, presses in exactly the opposite direction. Its religious concerns are located in the body: its metaphysics are expressed through dramas of the flesh, from Klingsor's self-mutilation and Amfortas's wound to the fresh blood that flows on the tip of the spear when Parsifal returns it to the Grail temple at the close. Klingsor's mistake, in fact, is to think along the very lines that Wagner thinks in his essays of the late 1860s. Striving for spirituality (so Gurnemanz tells the story in Act I), he castrates himself in the hope that such an extreme annihilation of the body will enable him to transcend it. This is not what *Parsifal* means by chastity. Kundry bitterly mocks Klingsor for his mistake: 'Bist du keusch?' ('Are you chaste?'), she taunts him, the violins screaming her chromatic laugh.

Around the time he was working on *Parsifal*, Wagner was busy in print again, this time with a series of writings sometimes collectively referred to as the 'regeneration essays': 'Modern', 'Publikum und Popularität' ('Public and Popularity'), 'Das Publikum in Zeit und Raum' ('The Public in Time and Space'), all of 1878; 'Wollen wir hoffen?' ('Shall We Hope?'), 1879; 'Religion und Kunst' ('Religion and Art'), 1880, and its three continuations, 'Was nützt diese Erkenntniß?' ('What Boots This Knowledge?', 1880), 'Erkenne dich selbst' ('Know Thyself', 1881), and 'Heldenthum und Christenthum' ('Hero-dom and Christendom [Heroism and Christianity]', 1881). These essays inherit a set of familiar themes from the work of the 1860s: the decay of German civilization under the influence of bourgeois and Jewish materialism, the mission of the German spirit to redeem European culture, the faith in 'that spirit's highest manifestation in an Artwork' (VI 122, 'Shall We Hope?'), art's destined role in taking over the proper functions of religion in place of a degenerate church and state. Yet there is a striking difference between the writing emanating from Munich and Tribschen during the *Meistersinger* period (1861–7) and the Bayreuth essays of 1878–81. Instead of being founded on a reiterated opposition between transcendent spirit and degraded matter, as the earlier writings are, the familiar aesthetic and political themes are now based on an obsessively corporeal rhetoric. Like *Parsifal*, the 'regeneration essays' are fundamentally concerned with flesh and blood. That elusive abstraction 'the German spirit', which defined itself by its removal from the distractions of matter, now mutates into a question of the German body.

All the essays ring changes on one central faith:

> ... the religious conviction that the degeneration of the human race has been brought about by its departure from its natural food, the only basis of a possible regeneration. (VI 242, 'Religion and Art')

Words like 'degeneration' and 'regeneration' in Wagner's writing irresistibly invite thoughts of his constant and ambiguous concern with redemption. They imply the passage from error to salvation which, in one way or another, is traversed so frequently in his work. All those broken curses scattered through the operas – the Dutchman's, Tannhäuser's, the ring's, Kundry's – are at the simplest level signs that salvation is in process, and the Bayreuth essays are no less concerned with redeeming the tragic conditions of existence. But whereas redemption had always before been presented as a kind of spiritual transfiguration, what the Wagner of the late essays means by 'regeneration' is something astonishingly, bizarrely literal: a change in the physical constitution of the human being. The prescription for a regenerate humanity thus depends on a purification of its material nature: its food (Wagner argues the necessity of a vegetarian diet) and its blood. When in 'Hero-dom and Christendom' Wagner writes of the 'noblest cleansing of Man's blood from every stain' (VI 283), it sounds at first reading like metaphorical language, as if what the phrase really refers to is the kind of spiritual and moral 'cleansing' performed by Parsifal at the end of the opera, in his declaration 'Sei heil, entsündigt und gesühnt', 'be healed, purified and atoned'. In fact, though, the essay means a literal purification of the bloodstream, just as Parsifal's act of healing involves the literal closing of a bodily wound. The ideal of regeneration can only be achieved through a transformation which is dietary and racial, not transcendentally spiritual:

> It certainly may be right to charge this . . . dulness of our public spirit to a vitiation of our blood – not only by departure from the natural food of man, but above all by the tainting of hero-blood of noblest races with that of former cannibals now trained to be the business-agents of Society. . . . (VI 284)

Accordingly, Wagner's hope for a religious regeneration is grounded on an equally literal faith that the blood of Christ provides the necessary cleansing agent. The essays veer wildly between symbolic interpretation of the eucharistic blood – where it stands for a Schopenhauerian embrace of suffering and self-denial – and a peculiarly literal interpretation, according to which its purifying force works in the sacrament of communion by a process of *physical* transfusion, so that 'the partaking of the blood of Jesus . . . might raise the very lowest races to the purity of Gods' (VI 283). In the end, though, religion is never merely symbolic. The eucharist is a rite of food and blood. Wagner's insistence on its redemptive force merges into his entirely material concern with diet and race; and there is nothing symbolic about either his horror at vivisection and his recommendation of vegetarianism or his revulsion at the idea of Jewish blood mingling with Aryan. The 'regeneration' essays have an almost hypochondriac obsession with thoughts of contaminated bodies and physical violence. Their dietary mania and their racism – the two most prominent themes – both indicate a return of Wagner's imagination to matter, to earth, to literal body and blood.

This is exactly where Klingsor fails. His self-mutilation is impelled by a belief that sin resides in the body and virtue in the spirit – which is very much the faith of *German Art and German Policy*, with its visions of aesthetic detachment and anti-utilitarian transcendentalism. It is also a faith handed down in the Christian tradition: the spirit is willing, but the flesh is weak. Yet however much *Parsifal's* insistence on chastity and renunciation makes the opera look as if it assents to this belief, Klingsor's extreme effort to mortify the flesh is in fact its original sin, the primal error from which everything wrong in the drama proceeds. He is right that impurity is located in the body; Amfortas's wound visibly confirms it, and the erotic female bodies inhabiting Act II are equally sinful. Klingsor's mistake is not realizing that purity is located in the body too (as the substitution of physical 'regeneration' for spiritual 'redemption' in the Bayreuth essays shows). Amfortas's cure has to be performed by a kind of totemic repetition of his wound: Parsifal touches the spear to his side again, and its point is then bathed in visionary blood. The place where sin happens is also the place of salvation. There is no escape from the body in *Parsifal*. The usual Wagnerian remedy for torment like Amfortas's is death, signifying the spirit's redemptive release from the afflicted body (think of the Dutchman, Tannhäuser or even Tristan). It's very striking that *Parsifal* ends instead with regeneration. Only Kundry suffers the familiar transcendental release, and she is a special case which we'll look at more carefully later (for now it's enough to point out that she is healed and 'redeemed' *before* she expires in the final Grail scene: the real moment of her salvation is when she screams herself awake at the beginning of Act III and discovers that she is at last free, in possession of her own body). In Klingsor's dialogue with Kundry at the start of Act II – a scene in which power relations are brilliantly inverted, since she torments him as much as he torments her – he confesses that his self-mutilation has not stilled his 'Schrecklichster Triebe Höllendrang', 'most fearful hell-bent urge'. In *Parsifal*, the sin of lust, of bodily craving, even survives castration.

However much the opera feels as though it breathes a rarefied spiritual air, its ties to corporeal matter are reiterated throughout the plot. The first events we witness are the introduction of two figures marked by errant bodies, the dishevelled and distressed Kundry and the sickened Amfortas. The plot proper begins when a dead swan thumps onto the stage, a moment so prosaically earthy that it almost always raises a few giggles in live performance. Parsifal's assault on Kundry when she tells him of his mother's death begins a series of strange intimacies between the two of them that together act as a kind of gestural, physical mime or dumb-show of the unfolding drama, a representation of its progress in bodily form: his violent but ignorant grief here in Act I, their kiss in Act II, her penitential washing of his feet in Act III. The relation between Amfortas and Parsifal is also communicated corporeally. Asked at the end of Act I whether he understands the rite he has just witnessed, Parsifal only answers (according to the stage directions) with a clutch at his heart and a shake of his head. Gurnemanz misinterprets the silent gestures as empty ignorance, but silence is always laden in *Parsifal*, and what the two movements really indicate is the stirring of the opera's central redemptive principle, *Mitleid*. The word means 'compassion', and its superficial reference is to an idea of sympathetic identification with another's sufferings. A moral idea, in other words: Wagner's late essays refer to what he calls 'Schopenhauer's Ethics' (VI 260, 'What Boots This Knowledge?'), meaning that the only possible basis of religion and morality is a denial of individual self-interest, achieved through compassion for all the inhabitants of a blindly destructive universe. In *Parsifal*, though, *Mitleid* is made literal, physical, a bodily event rather than an ethical intuition. Like the English words 'compassion' and 'sympathy', *Mitleid* etymologically means 'suffering with'. So Parsifal's enlightening stroke of compassion takes the form of a corporeal repetition of Amfortas's pain:

| Die Wunde sah ich bluten: – | The wound I saw bleeding: – |
| nun blutet sie mir selbst. . . . | now it bleeds in me. . . . |

At the moment when his body encounters sin exactly as Amfortas's did – the moment of Kundry's kiss, which also seduced the king – Parsifal literally 'suffers with' him. His body becomes Amfortas's body. *Mitleid* is brought down to its most brutally physical form. This is what was prefigured by Parsifal's convulsive response to the ritual of communion; his body feels its first pang of pain.

Though Gurnemanz doesn't realize it, the brief convulsion is also a direct answer to the question he has just asked: 'Weißt du was du sah'st?' ('Do you know what you saw?'). For the archetypal instance of *Mitlied* in the literal, corporeal sense – *Parsifal*'s sense – is the sacrament of communion, where the body and blood of Christ are ingested by the worshippers. (I'm referring to what is staged in the opera, of course, not trying to intervene in any theological arguments about transubstantiation.) As they sit for their eucharistic meal, the knights sing to each other about how the bread and wine are being ritually incorporated into their own bodies:

Nehmet vom Brod,	Partake of the bread,
wandelt es kühn	change it boldly
zu Leibes Kraft und Stärke . . .	into bodily power and strength . . .
. . . Nehmet vom Wein,	. . . Partake of the wine,
wandelt ihn neu	change it anew
zu Lebens feurigem Blute. . . .	into life's fiery blood. . . .

The whole liturgy of the rite in Wagner's opera is obsessively concerned with the two elements of blood and body. So are the two interruptions in the rite made by Amfortas, once in each act: both times he delivers an anguished rhapsody on his own physical torment and the blood flowing from his wound. These scenes are the climactic demonstrations of *Parsifal*'s corporeality. They strip the Christian sacrament down to its material essence, the display and consumption of a redemptive body. As Wagner's 'regeneration essays' theorize, they reduce the ideas of atonement and salvation to the literal process of sharing in the body of Christ. This is a rite of *Mitleid* in the same physical sense as Parsifal's moment of corporeal identity with Amfortas. When he clutches silently at his heart after first witnessing it performed, he is understanding it better than Gurnemanz appreciates, because he is feeling the bodily suffering the rite commemorates.

In the scenes when *Parsifal* enacts the mysteries of its religion, then, it is most fully preoccupied with flesh and blood. The 'holy German art' prophesied at the end of *Meistersinger* and brought to life in Wagner's temple-theatre with the creation of *Parsifal* is a profoundly corporeal, material religion. Its holiness doesn't involve a flight from the earth into transcendence, despite the opera's shimmeringly spiritualized mood. Its sacred object is the body, the same body that is wounded and eroticized as marks of its sinfulness. In the noxious Bayreuth essays this equation underpins a maniacal insistence on the need for a cure, a physical regeneration of the diseased and impure body into an untainted one. To some extent, the opera shares this kind of thinking. The imagery of washing and curing that pervades Act III seems to echo the essays' revulsion at uncleanliness, and Parsifal's central mission is to close Amfortas's wound and make his body whole again. This suggests a straightforward path of purification, like the project imagined at the end of 'Public and Popularity' – the 'cure of ills inevitable in the evolution of the human race' (VI 81). In *Parsifal*, though, there is never a simple path from sickness to health. This is the meaning of Kundry's curse, against which even an entirely enlightened and pure hero is apparently defenceless. To say that the opera is a dramatic enactment of the 'regeneration' theories is to ignore its extraordinary symmetries of sin and sanctity, its *Mitleid* that conjoins pure and impure bodies, its constant commingling of sacred and profane blood. There have always been people who prefer to think of it as a sublime artefact, the closest thing to a sacramental experience that the secular world of opera could provide. There have also always been people for whom it is the product of a diseased imagination, exuding a perverse, decadent pseudo-holiness which dresses up sensual ecstasies as religion, and which is unhealthily fascinated by the sex and violence around which its ideas of 'purity' revolve. *Parsifal* probably polarizes opinion more powerfully than anything else about Wagner. Indeed, its own story sets holiness against decadence, as if to dramatize the two extremes of thinking about his art: the devoted Wagnerism that treats him with religious reverence, and the critique that discovers in his work the nadir of self-indugent and over-stimulated aestheticism. But both interpretations of *Parsifal* – as the purest or the most tainted of Wagner's works, if not of all operas – are blind to its mixed, fluid nature, its astonishing power to traverse and interweave the very oppositions it seems to set so starkly against each other. We've observed this vital tendency in Wagner's operas before: in the oscillations between enchantment and disenchantment which complicate the black-and-white worlds of *Holländer*, *Tannhäuser* and *Lohengrin*, in the *Ring*'s power to reverse its own directions, in *Tristan*'s acute understanding that the fullness of desire merges into the emptiness of renunciation, even perhaps in *Meistersinger*'s effort to ally renewal (Walther) with nostalgic conservatism (Sachs). In *Parsifal*, however, the stakes are at their highest, since the polarity it offers is between sin and salvation. What makes it the summit of Wagner's work is its power utterly to undo the banal simplicity of that polarity, generating instead an inexhaustibly subtle interplay between light and dark, soul and body, heaven and earth.

That power is incarnated in Kundry. She stands apart from everyone else in *Parsifal* because of her explicitly double nature, the fact that she inhabits both extremes of the opera's world. Her agonized transitions between the two, accompanied by unmusical and inarticulate groaning and/or laughter, reveal the cost of traversing the range of Wagner's imagination; there's no glib, comfortable synthesis here, no naïve idea that opposites can be 'united' in some stable happy medium. Wagner is not that sort of artist. His imagination is demonic and disruptive. It leaves its contradictions open, gapingly so (as the irreconcilable Young Hegelian and Schopenhauerian *Ring*s coexist with each other). Much of its volcanic energy comes from its failure – or refusal – to achieve a middle ground. Kundry is tormented by those unreconciled energies throughout Acts I and II, contradicting and resisting everything that is said to her, always acting out opposed roles at once. Yet although she's the most extreme case, she's far from the only character in the operas with schizophrenic tendencies. Tannhäuser always seems to want to be other than where he is, and his thoughts and feelings are perpetually reversing or contradicting themselves. Elsa's pure love and faith slide swiftly into self-destructive doubt. Brünnhilde goes from love to vengeful fury to love again in the course of *Götterdämmerung*, each transition taking place with unsettling abruptness. Kundry is the climax of this restless instability in Wagner's art.

What she embodies above all is the inseparability of sin and salvation. Any analogy between the opera and the 'regeneration' essays' fantasies of purity founders on her: she's both the demonic temptress – Klingsor conjures her with the names 'Ur-Teufelin', 'Höllen-Rose', 'primal she-devil', 'rose of hell' – and the one whose temptation enlightens Parsifal and makes possible the work of redemption. She appears in Act III as the Magdalene, the saint who is also a sinner, whose penitential awareness of sin actually constitutes her saintliness. There's no peaceful resolution to the contradictions of her nature in this act. Although the trajectory of healing and curing is clearly at work to some extent, in that she is presumed finally to be free of her devilish and unchaste aspect once she reawakens in Act III, the opera never straightforwardly grants her a newfound purity. Her silence – the richest, most resonant silence in all Wagner's work – disables the kind of facile redemption

announced by the chorus at the end of *Tannhäuser*, or even the more shadowy
ecstasies of Isolde's 'höchste Lust!' ('highest bliss'). She keeps herself apart from
the prophecies and theologies exchanged between Parsifal and Gurnemanz,
though her silence perhaps acts as a reminder during the latter's exposition
of the meaning of Good Friday that she herself witnessed the drama of
Calvary. She likewise stands apart from the work of miraculous healing performed in the temple, though again, her silence perhaps draws tacit attention
to the fact that the agent of Amfortas's fall is present in this scene alongside
the agent of his restoration to health. As I've argued earlier (in chapter 11),
silence doesn't choke off interpretation, but opens space for it. Kundry may
be healed and purified, as the opera certainly implies, but there is nothing
actually to tell us so. Instead, all we have in Act III is her almost continuous
presence on stage, an embodied remnant of the erotic damnation that plagued
the prior acts, a mysterious incarnation of error.

Kundry's effect is always to remind any scene of its antithesis, to shadow
anything that happens in her presence with a sense of its equal and opposite
reaction. This makes her the enemy of everything that is dogmatic about
Wagner's art and thought, and the tutelary goddess of all the ambiguities and
reverses his operas are so rich in. In *Parsifal*, she epitomizes the strange doub-
lings that work their way so prominently through the drama. They pervade
the score as well: the similarities of shape between the music of Klingsor's
domain and that of its supposed opposite, Montsalvat, have often been pointed
out. The flower maidens' chorus, for example, strikes a faint echo of the
Dresden Amen in its second phrase (at 'laß mich dir blühen', 'let me bloom
for you', an offer oddly analogous in itself to the unfolding of the Grail
shrine), a relation perhaps enforced by the shared key of A flat. In more
sinister vein, the leaping, falling and twisting melody which opens Act II,
associated with Klingsor and his world, is a feverish and angular transformation of the opera's first theme, to which the invisible voices in the Act I ritual
scene will sing Christ's own words, 'Nehmet hin mein Blut . . . Nehmet hin
meinen Leib', 'take this my blood . . . take this my body'. Klingsor is, after all,
a fallen Knight of the Grail.

Relations like these suggest the kind of opposition in which the antithetical poles are inextricably linked. Sin and purity may be opposed extremes,
but they're the extremes of the same scale. One can't be thought of apart
from its relation to the other (the Kundry effect again). For the sake of illustrative contrast, compare *Lohengrin*, where purity equals transcendence. In the
earlier opera, the Grail and its emissary cannot touch the earth. They retreat
from the contagion of contact with a sinful world, which makes it all too
easy for Ortrud to drive Lohengrin back into the sanctuary he came from.
Though *Parsifal* denounces sin and error far more vehemently than does
Lohengrin, the fact is that its representations of holiness have none of the aura

of inviolable detachment which in the latter work is the very condition of the Grail's existence. Indeed, there's an almost paranoid quality about Amfortas's and Gurnemanz's Montsalvat, a feeling that damnation is always pressing against its borders. Yet Parsifal's awakening into redemptive knowledge takes place at the very heart of the domain of sin. Lohengrin's purity is inevitably destroyed by his intimacy with Elsa; there's an impossible contradiction in his attempt to be her lover and also to remain a mystery to her. But Kundry's seduction creates Parsifal. He does not even know his own name until she sings it to him; then she tells him his own history and genealogy; and finally her kiss, the climax of his gradual loss of innocence, is the very touch that makes him 'pure'.

The opera's sacred rite is itself poised tensely between holiness and sin – or rather, more accurately, it conflates them with extraordinary density and subtlety. Its central object, the holy of holies, is the Grail: not a talisman of untouchable purity as in *Lohengrin*, but a vessel full of blood. The ritual performed at the end of Act I celebrates the presence of the Grail, and, by analogy, the blood and body of Christ at the Last Supper. Yet in both Acts I and III there is a far more prominent icon of blood and flesh on which the rite indispensably turns: Amfortas himself, whose body, wounded by the same spear that pierced Christ on the cross, and continuously leaking blood, is an obvious totemic substitute for Christ's. Amfortas's suffering is thus a permanent re-enactment of the crucifixion. As the rite begins, therefore, he experiences a disturbingly masochistic ecstasy, in which – by the process of literal *Mitleid* – his flesh and blood become Christ's:

. . . des Weihgefäßes göttlicher
   Gehalt
	. . . the divine content of the
	   sacred chalice

erglüht mit leuchtender Gewalt; –	glows with radiant power; –
durchzückt von seligsten Genusses Schmerz,	transfixed by blessed joy's pain,
des heiligsten Blutes Quell	I feel the fount of holiest blood
fühl' ich sich gießen in mein Herz . . .	gush in my heart . . .

. . . von Neuem sprengt er das
   Thor
	. . . again now it bursts open
	   the door

daraus es nun strömt hervor,	through which it streams forth,

hier durch die Wunde, der Seinen
   gleich. . . .
	here through the wound, a
	   wound like His. . . .

We learn that the ritual can't take place without Amfortas. It's not just that he is the appointed guardian of the Grail, though. He's also the sacramental icon itself, the suffering body to which the brotherhood is dedicated. Act III takes place not on Easter day, as one might expect from its themes of restoration and renewal, but on Good Friday, the day of the wounded and broken body and the flowing blood.

Amfortas's agony is thus central to the rites of the Grail community. And yet, of course, his wound and his pain are also quite explicit marks of sin. Seduced by Kundry and stabbed by Klingsor, he is acutely conscious that he brings the contagion of sin into the centre of the holy ritual. So far from making him an unworthy celebrant of the Grail's rites, though, his damaged body is symbolically interchangeable with the flesh and blood consumed in the eucharistic *Liebesmahle* ('love-feast'). He is the sacramental body and the sinful body at the same time. His gush of 'heiße Sündenblut' ('hot sin-blood') in Act I prefigures the crimson light later exuded by the Grail. By Act III, the gory carnality at the heart of the rite can no longer be veiled in symbolism. Violently pressed by the assembled knights to renew the long-abandoned ritual, Amfortas tears open his robe, letting the wound flow again; and this suicidal impulse is instantly followed by Parsifal's arrival and the second revelation of the Grail, confirming the equation that identifies Amfortas's poisoned blood with the purifying contents of the chalice.

There is no better example of how Wagner's operas unchain themselves from the tendentiousness of his prose writings. In the second section of 'Religion and Art' there is a brief excursion into the early history of civilization, specious even by the standards of Wagner's habitual shallow historicizing, in which he describes how at the dawn of human history a violent and brutal culture separated itself from the primal purity of 'Brahmin' India. The result (he says) is that 'blood and massacre . . . still rage throughout the human race', 'a malady which necessarily kept [humanity] in progressive deterioration' (VI 230, 231). Hence the advocacy of a bloodless vegetarian diet. It seems a little surprising that this revulsion at 'blood-guiltiness' ('Blutschuld', VI 231) should go hand in hand in the essays with a determined faith in the purifying power of Christ's blood as celebrated in the sacrament of communion. Wagner appears to resolve the apparent contradiction by insisting that what is consumed in the eucharist is not flesh and blood but bread and wine, although trying to make sense of the essays' regeneration theory at this point is perhaps treating it with more respect than it deserves. In *Parsifal*, all such vegetarian compromises are abandoned. 'Blood-guiltiness' (in the figure of Amfortas), along with a corresponding 'body-guiltiness' (as it were) in the figure of the unchaste Kundry, are unmistakably central to the work of purification. Accordingly, the sacred ritual is a thoroughly carnivorous one. Its liturgy, sung by the boys and youths, insists that transubstantiation has taken place. First the boys equate the meal of the last supper with the flesh and blood of Good Friday:

Wein und Brod des letzten Mahles	The Grail's Lord once changed
wandelt' einst der Herr des Grales,	the wine and bread of the Last Supper,
durch des Mitleid's Liebesmacht,	through compassion's loving power,
in das Blut, das er vergoß,	into the blood which he shed,
in den Leib, den dar er bracht'.	into the body, which he broke.

The youths respond by affirming that Christ's body and blood have in turn been changed 'in den Wein, der euch nun floß,/ in das Brod, das heut' euch speis't', 'into the wine, now poured for you, into the bread, which today feeds you'. As the principle of *Mitleid* dictates, there is a literal transfer from body to body. Beneath the symbolism of pure, wholesome bread and wine there lies a deeply corporeal worship of the brutality of Good Friday, the same violence which is marked on Amfortas's body, and which repeats itself at the moment of Parsifal's enlightenment: 'Amfortas! Die Wunde!' ('the wound!'). It is impossible to extricate the opera's rituals and dramas of purification from the gory, suffering, sinful body which they are supposed to cleanse and regenerate. *Parsifal's* religion celebrates not transcendence but incarnation.

So the stage action at least implies: but this is to say nothing of *Parsifal's* music, which has such a striking consistency of texture and atmosphere that it demands to be understood as the defining element of the opera's singular mood. It's the least dramatic of Wagner's scores, in the sense that it relies far less on the play of contrasts and tensions than any of the other operas. Even *Tristan und Isolde*, which comes closest to *Parsifal* in the overall coherence of its idiom, relies far more noticeably on climactic surges and accelerations, on resolutions forcibly withheld, on suppressed energies and abrupt explosions. Compare the strained, yearning silences of the *Tristan* prelude with the pauses of the prelude to *Parsifal*: where the former have the quality of reaching into palpable nothingness, the latter come as pauses for breath, returns to an equipoise from which music can begin again. The separate motivic themes of the prelude are kept very distinct from each other, spaced apart by silences, so that in each case one seems simply to be moving on to the next melodic idea: a much calmer, more stately progression than can be found anywhere else in Wagner's overtures. What unifies the sound of *Parsifal* is not the seamless progress of small-scale motivic development, the sense of continual variation that structures the intricacies of *Tristan*, although such development is certainly at work (there's a remarkably close relation between the main motivic elements of the score, and an endless inventiveness in the use of them which is well beyond the capacity of a book such as this to explore). It's the mood or *quality* of *Parsifal's* music that maintains itself so distinctively, the 'feel' of its sound, never better described than in Debussy's brilliant remark that the opera sounded as if lit from behind.

Transparency, luminosity, an ethereal refinement so intense as to make the music sound almost abstract or intellectual: *Parsifal* breathes this kind of air from the bare yet expansive unison of its opening melodic line to the unearthly light of its last chorus. Even the flower maidens' music, so naïve that it verges on a kind of delicate banality, lends erotic seduction an airy lightness and thinness that allows us to hear how close they are to fading ('wir welken und sterben', 'we wither and die'). Kundry's enchantment is also strangely quiet, almost dry. Her role as temptress never disturbs the mood; indeed, the opening exchanges between her and Parsifal in their long Act II scene take place above one of the stillest, most distant passages of the score. 'Fern – fern ist meine Heimath', she tells him – 'far, far away is my home-land' – and that feeling of a secret still being kept goes on to pervade every-thing she says up to the fateful kiss. Likewise, the opera's most agitated sections still take place under some degree of musical restraint. Energy is never released as openly and forcefully as in *Tristan* or the *Ring*. The knights' furious assault on Amfortas in Act III is part of a marching chorus, controlled by the heavy and steady rhythm and underpinned by the tolling bells which, however dissonant they are made to sound here, give the passage something of the solemn gravity evoked so powerfully throughout the ritual scenes. The after-math of the kiss in Act II calls up the score's most frantic sounds, especially as Kundry's rage and desperation increase, but even here what we hear tends to be a progressive fragmentation of the musical flow, a disintegration into sharply discontinuous units of sound, rather than a more exaggeratedly tormented atmosphere. The music retains its characteristic lightness and undemonstrativeness, that is: its abstraction just seems to be harsher than usual. (The section where Kundry explains her curse, narrating her offence against the suffering Christ, is a good example of this effect.) Thanks to this impres-sion of intense, sustained coherence, music seems to exert a more definitive pressure on *Parsifal* than any other work of Wagner's except *Tristan* (where the effect is reinforced by the extreme slowness and emptiness of the stage action – or inaction).

What is the meaning of the opera's distinctive musical character? Its first impression is easily named: purity. There's an unearthliness to this score which is best felt by comparison with other achievements of Wagner's mature mastery, especially *Götterdämmerung*. There, the orchestral content is almost suffocatingly dense and weighty, incomparably vivid in its drama, forceful in its emotional expressiveness. Set it beside *Parsifal* and one begins to feel that Wagner's last opera is strangely empty: it's too serenely preoccupied with the beauty of form and the subtlety of musical thought to bother itself with expression. (Can there be any music that is so overwhelmingly stirring while at the same time conveying no emotional or dramatic content as the 'transformation music' of Acts I and III?) Unearthly without rapture, radiant without brightness, *Parsifal*'s score might well be understood to correspond to the drama's apparent ideal of chastity. Its relatively rectilinear polyphony – again best sensed by contrast, in this case with the sinuous interwovenness of *Tristan* – likewise seems to bespeak a faith in the single path of purity, as opposed to the multiplicity and deviousness of error. In 'Religion and Art' Wagner encourages this sort of view of the score:

> ... we must recognize that Music reveals the inmost essence of the Christian religion with [matchless] definition ... for, as pure Form of a divine Content freed from all abstractions [*als reine Form eines gänzlich vom Begriffe losgelösten göttlichen Gehaltes*], we may regard it as a world-redeeming incarnation of the divine dogma of the nullity of the phenomenal world itself. (VI 223)

Music's own emptiness, that is, is the sign of its sacred purity: it's untouched by the sinful world. This is an idea we have encountered before, but here it is given a significantly religious twist: the Schopenhauerian otherworldliness to which music tends is now described as a 'dogma' and associated with a particular form of spirituality (that of Christianity). One can hear this conception of music in *Parsifal*. It's easy enough to interpret the score's distinctive radiance as the mystic glow emanating from the Grail, washing away the impurities of the 'phenomenal world'.

As usual, though, the essays are propounding as 'dogma' something which the opera is not so certain of. The view of music in 'Religion and Art' does in fact ascribe it some kind of specific content (*Gehalt*), 'divine Content', even as it claims that music dissolves the world. Yet *Parsifal*'s music is surprisingly averse to explicitly sublime gestures. Compare the exquisite prelude to *Lohengrin*, which thematically at least concerns itself with the same terrain as *Parsifal*. Everything about it expresses a celestial 'content': its marvellous use of the high strings, its solemn and serene melody, the way it slowly gathers that melody to an impressive climax, turning its sublime radiance into 'dogma'. If one now calls to mind the long opening melody of *Parsifal*, the musical essence of the whole score and the source from which the rest of the opera flows, it's immediately clear that we have the same serene otherworldliness without any of the rapture, any of the shimmering brightness, any intimation of the divine. Even the more obviously sacred sounds heard subsequently in the prelude, and of course throughout the opera as well – the Dresden Amen and the so-called 'Faith' motif that first sounds gently in the wind, both of which are strongly redolent of church music – are reticent, almost barren, by contrast with the visionary ecstasies of the Grail music in *Lohengrin* or of any number of other instances of Wagnerian exaltation.

Indeed, the opening melody has an unmistakable downwards pull. Its slow ascent though a whole octave ought to sound more like a complete journey than it does; instead the turn back down at the centre of the arching melody weighs heavily on its character. In the Good Friday scene of Act III, the same tense rise and fall sets Parsifal's cry of grief over the sorrow 'des höchsten Schmerzentag's' ('of the day of highest sorrow', or perhaps 'most sublime day of sorrow'). (It makes sense that at triumphant moments, such as the end of the opera, we hear a version of the opening phrase which ascends to a brighter and more assured end, straightening out the grieving turn.) If this is a 'world-redeeming' sound, it shows the same kind of redemption at work that we shall later see in Kundry's silence: a mimed, bodily salvation, laden with the memory of suffering, performed through the inertia of incarnation rather than the sublimity of transcendence. Both Kundry and Parsifal himself achieve a state of 'purity' only after having travelled along the paths of error: they bring the memory of going wrong with them when they finally arrive at their goals. The opera's musical character isn't bathed in an unambiguous holiness either. Indeed, that opening melody will later shape the music of body and blood in the ritual scene of Act I; it sounds very apt for the scene's recollection and representation of suffering. Much of the distinctive sound of *Parsifal* lies in its shadowiness: that's part of the brilliance of Debussy's remark, noting that the luminosity of the score has the effect of silhouetting its content. In the Act I ritual scene, the temple plunges into almost complete darkness (according to the stage directions) before the Grail's bloody light illuminates it again. That is a better image of the 'purity' of this score than any suggestion of its transcendent holiness. If it reveals the essence of religion at all – which we should surely doubt – it does so only on this drama's terms, where salvation is shadowed by suffering and taint. Much of the music of *Parsifal* is redolent of suffering, and even when it isn't – as for example in the blissful pastoral of the Good Friday meadows in Act III – the drama forces it into conjunction with suffering (which is what Good Friday memorializes). If this is purity, it's a purity that remembers its cost: not washed clean of error, as the essays imagine, but silently remembering and recording what it has left behind.

CHAPTER FOURTEEN

Bühnenweihfestspiel

By his own reckoning, Wagner never wrote an 'opera' after *Lohengrin*. The published title pages of the post-revolutionary works cast about for other words to describe themselves. 'Music-drama' is probably today's most popular choice for those who still believe that it is beneath Wagner's dignity to be lumped in with the rest of the 'operatic' repertory (as if *Così fan tutte* or *Otello* or *Peter Grimes* has less serious dramatic credentials). Yet only one of his works is officially – according to the title page – a 'Musikdrama': *Die Meistersinger von Nürnberg*, whose very theme is the categorical distinction between old and new ways of setting words to music – between mere outmoded 'opera', which throughout four decades of Wagner's writings is consistently condemned as a senseless Beckmesser-style garble of empty sounds, and the new practice exemplified by Walther, where music serves the purposes of dramatic intelligibility, and drama in turn expresses the spirit of music. The label given to *Meistersinger* is therefore part of that work's specific propaganda on behalf of Wagner's own art. Elsewhere he prefers other terms. *Tristan* calls itself a 'Handlung', 'drama', or perhaps (since the term has an unconventional flavour in German) 'action'. The *Ring*, completed in 1874 amid strenuous work towards the Bayreuth project, is labelled 'Bühnenfestspiel', 'stage festival play', and its component parts become a 'preliminary evening' followed by three 'days', as if they are events in time and space – the same implication as the 'happenings' of twentieth-century performance art – rather than scores printed on paper. Created in symbiosis with the Bayreuth theatre, *Parsifal* echoes the *Ring*'s title but adds a sacramental twist. It describes itself as a 'Bühnenweihfestspiel', one of those compound German coinages consisting of enough elements that the grammatical relation between them begins to hover freely: 'stage-consecration festival play', perhaps, or 'sacred stage festival play'.

These efforts to colonize new realms of vocabulary in the name of Wagner's art were originally motivated by a desire for generic distinction. According to the theory advanced in *Opera and Drama* – written in the interval between

Lohengrin ('romantic opera in three acts') and the mature works – the whole genre of 'opera' is founded on a mistake. From its beginnings it has misunderstood the relation between music and drama, Wagner explains. Accordingly, the corrected genre he intends to found with his Nibelung tetralogy needs a new name, one appropriate to the seminal role played in its creation by a purely poetic intent: hence 'music-drama' (although in Wagner's 1852 book it's simply called 'drama', 'the genuine drama'). The new term is thus meant to represent an altogether new *kind* of artistic event (or at least a return to the lost perfection of classical Athenian tragedy). It testifies to Wagner's formal and structural originality. By changing opera's appearance to such a radical extent, at every level from the kind of language used in the libretto to the dimensions occupied by the work as a whole, he seems to have made it unrecognizable by the standards of what went before. So 'music-drama' ends up referring to a whole subsequent genre, not just to Wagner's achievement, although he is by heavy implication credited as the only begetter of the new genre: subsequent 'operas' which emphasize dramatic impact rather than musical richness – *Wozzeck* rather than *La Bohème*, say – might also be thought of as 'music-dramas'.

Those who still prefer to use the term for Wagner's later works are in effect declaring their partisan allegiance to the revolutionary aspect of Wagner's art and theory, the feeling that after *Lohengrin* he began to work on something altogether new. (It's one of the possible ways one labels oneself as a 'Wagnerian'.) The same was true in his own day, as in the course of the 1850s, 60s and 70s he gained an enormously prominent reputation as the foremost composer of a new kind of music, and consequently also gained a set of devotees, as perceived reformers do. From the retrospective vantage-point of his brief 1872 essay 'Über die Benennung "Musikdrama"' ('On the Name "Musikdrama"'), Wagner himself interprets the label in exactly this way:

> I certainly have reason to suppose that this term was invented for the sake of honouring my later dramatic works with a distinctive classification; but the less I have felt disposed to accept it, the more I have perceived an inclination in other quarters to adopt the name for a presumably new art-genre [*Kunstgenre*]. . . . (V 299)

As he points out, 'music-drama' is a word that has evolved in response to his revolutionary theories and practices, but it's also a term that he feels unwilling to use as a 'classification' for his own works. (He's interestingly silent about *Meistersinger*, a self-declared 'Musikdrama' which explicitly colludes in 'Wagnerism' by staging the public acclamation of 'a presumably new art-genre'.) The odd series of experimental labels actually attached to those works clearly demonstrates a dissatisfaction with 'music-drama', which the essay goes on to dismiss as a 'wholly senseless word' (V 300). Wagner denies the

implication of his own programmatic theories as advanced in the revolutionary writings: that he is responsible for creating a genre. In documents like *The
Art-Work of the Future* and *Opera and Drama*, theory is an effort to prescribe
how a work of art should look. It gives the formulae for generating individual works, explaining the formal principles and technical details that should
shape the ideal 'drama'. It maps out a genre, in other words, and 'Musikdrama'
seems like an apt word to contradistinguish that kind of creation from the
genre of mere 'opera' against which it defines itself. To use the term is to
point to something distinctive about the formal and technical character of
Wagner's later works, to recognize a mature Wagnerian style. It's certainly true
that such a style exists; it's also true that this style represents an achievement
of gigantic originality and inventiveness; it's largely true as well that there is
a perceptible connection between Wagner's mature musico-dramatic idiom
and the kind of ideas argued in *Opera and Drama*, and that the revolutionary
writings are correct in sharply differentiating that style from the existing forms
of the genre of opera. By refusing the word, however, Wagner's later
works (except *Meistersinger*) are rejecting the idea that they advocate or
belong to a genre at all. Rather than submitting to any sort of classification,
each one finds something new to call itself. They don't think of themselves
as being like each other. Naming opera, it turns out, is not a matter of
grouping works together according to their formal characteristics or their
demonstration of partisan theoretical positions. Since they aren't markers of
revolutionary originality, what does the use of these increasingly eccentric
names – *Handlung, Bühnenfestspiel* with its *Vorabend* and *Tage, Bühnenweihfestspiel* – mean instead?

Whereas the word 'opera' was originally rejected because it denoted a genre
founded on a formal error, by the 1870s Wagner objects to it on more pragmatic grounds. His long and difficult preparations for the first Bayreuth festival began in 1871, with performances at that point announced for 1873 (in
the event they did not take place until 1876; the second festival, devoted to
Parsifal, was in 1882). There were three basic tasks: fundraising, building the
theatre, and assembling a company of musicians and technicians. The last of
these involved him in a series of visits to opera houses all over Germany, in
search of singers who might be able to take roles in the *Ring*. In effect, he
was taking a snapshot of the state of German opera. His conclusions are
recounted in the 1873 essay 'Ein Einblick in das heutige deutsche Opern-
wesen' ('A Glance at the German Operatic Stage of To-Day'), a document
which ends up washing its hands of the whole business of 'opera'. Wagner's
judgments here have nothing to do with the formal composition of musico-
dramatic works themselves: it made no difference which parts of the repertory Wagner saw performed, since his interest was exclusively in the theatrical
and musical *execution* of whatever opera happened to be staged in the local

theatres as he passed through each town. As he passes comment on the various performances he attended on his tour, distinctions which would have been absolutely fundamental in the theoretical writings of 1848–52 are notably ignored. For example, the earlier generic differentiation between mere 'opera' and his own proposed 'genuine drama' can be directly translated into a distinction between Meyerbeer and Wagner. The antagonism between their respective approaches to drama is effectively a microcosm of the whole theoretical argument. Yet in the 1873 essay *Der fliegende Holländer* and Meyerbeer's *Le prophète* appear on the same page, treated as part of the same repertory and subject to exactly the same kind of discussion: performances of both works illustrate the absurd operatic practice of making senseless cuts in the scores. The state of German opera transcends all categories of genre: 'I found the same inability to hit the right method displayed in every class of operatic music, Mozart's as much as Meyerbeer's' (V 263). With the pragmatic requirements of the Bayreuth project in mind, 'opera' ceases to be a formal or theoretical concept and becomes instead a matter of performance, an institutional event rather than a set of artistic works. The word 'opera' describes a situation in which the philistinism of directors, the incompetence of performers and the degraded tastes of audiences collude in a theatrical practice that consists only of 'all the senseless tricks a tortured fancy can conceive' (V 269). In an imaginary paraphrase of what audiences understand by the word, the essay brilliantly captures the sheer emptiness of genre:

> It is 'Opera; which has nothing to do with either mirth or earnestness, but – simply *Opera*. Why doesn't the prima donna sing us something pretty?' (V 277)

That is, opera has no content, aesthetic or theoretical or otherwise. It's just a word denoting what goes on in an opera house, the absolutely trivial and meaningless brand of entertainment to which all musical drama (whether *Don Giovanni* or *Le prophète* or *Lohengrin*) is reduced once it finds itself in the grip of German theatres.

In the essay 'On the Name "Musikdrama"', Wagner decides that 'opera' is consequently the only appropriate name, in the end, for any and all kinds of contemporary works, as well as any and all genres of the existing repertory.

> Now I advise my professional competitors to retain the designation 'opera,' on second thought, for their musical works intended for the present theatre: it leaves them where they are, gives them no false colour. . . . (V 302)

Wagner is saying that terminology is a matter of *place*, not of genre. Any other name for new works would create the (false) impression that they stood somehow apart from the system of equally senseless performance and reception which 'opera' designates. This system is 'where they are'. The institutional and cultural arrangements of the 'present theatre' set the conditions for the nature of opera. It's not a matter of the proper relations between music and drama, or of any other theoretical or aesthetic question. All such refinements are irrelevant under the existing conditions of performance; where opera happens, in the theatre as Wagner finds it, every artistic conception turns into the same kind of event. Art is boiled down to the lowest common denominator shared by opera's inept performers and inert audiences:

> One thus can find no line to part the putative artistic action from those before whom it is set. The two dissolve into one brew of the most repulsive mixture. . . . (V 277)

Throughout his writings from the early Paris articles on, Wagner is always sensitive to the reciprocal relation between art and its audiences, but with the vision of Bayreuth coming closer and closer to reality, this issue becomes absolutely central. As this image from 'A Glance at the German Operatic Stage of To-Day' indicates, he ascribes to the theatre a kind of poisonous alchemy, transforming everything inside it into the revolting ferment which is 'simply *Opera*'. Hence in the extremely interesting essay 'Über Schauspieler und Sänger' ('Actors and Singers'), begun soon after the foundation stone of the Bayreuth Festspielhaus was laid in May 1872, he claims sweepingly that 'Our theatres are opera-houses' (V 195): any kind of drama – musical or not – performed in them effectively becomes 'opera', because the word tells such works 'where they are'. We can see from this blanket assertion how completely genre has dropped out of the equation. Once it's on the contemporary German stage, anything, even a spoken play, might as well be opera. In turn, 'On the Name "Musikdrama"' points out that the word itself is etymologically no more than the plural of Latin *opus*: it means 'works', created things, without any reference to their generic or artistic nature. Wagner sardonically comments that this apparently casual and vague designation is in fact entirely apt: 'a deep-set [*tiefer*] instinct here expressed a thing of nameless nonsense' (V 302). The genre is a non-genre. All its name tells us about is 'the modern stage and the relation into which the spectator is brought thereto' (V 194).

Refusing to name themselves by this word, Wagner's works are making a statement not about their artistic nature but about where they are and what they do. Likewise, the new terms they devise for themselves do not primarily refer to the kind of works they are (their genre, or the theoretical principles they articulate). They speak instead of the works' *situation*. 'Opera' names the situation of musical drama on the existing German stage; Wagner's invented terminologies prophesy not just the *idea* of Bayreuth, which had been anticipated back in 1851 (in 'A Communication to My Friends') as a necessary consequence of the generic nature of the Nibelung tetralogy, but the actual building, the place in which the works they name will discover 'where they are'. The Festspielhaus itself embodies a different set of conditions under which musical drama can come to be. At his speech during the rain-soaked festivities over the laying of the foundation stone, Wagner connected the actual physical nature of the building with the idea of drama's relation to its audience (the relation whose degraded version is 'opera'):

> In the proportions and arrangement of the room and its seats . . . you will find expressed a thought which, once you have grasped it, will place you in a new relation to the play you are about to witness, a relation quite distinct from that in which you had always been involved when visiting our theatres. (V 324–5)

With his doggedly literal translation of 'Gedanke' as 'thought' (rather than 'idea', which would read much more naturally in English here), Ellis actually highlights the strange significance of Wagner's language. The Festspielhaus is being described not just as the result of an architectural concept, but – more strikingly – as a thought made stone (or wood and brick, in this case): 'The cloud has found a resting-place, whereon to take material form' (V 328).

We could describe that thought thus: opera is not an artefact but an event. Opera *happens*: in a particular place, at a particular time, before particular people, embodied by particular performers amid particular scenery, bound up in a web of material relations which together define what the given work is – or, more accurately and more significantly, what it does. In relation to the time and place and circumstances of the first Bayreuth festival of 1876, the central notion in Wagner's thinking in the early 1870s, the name of what the work does, and of where it is, is *Bühnenfestspiel*, 'stage festival play' – the name of the *Ring*. With this word, the tetralogy imagines itself as the same kind of creation as the Festspielhaus itself. Drama and building equally are attempts to erase existing conventions and contexts of performance, replacing them with a reinvigorated 'festival' that celebrates both the work (*Spiel*) and the physical stage (*Bühne*). The *Ring* may be an altogether new kind of work, as partisans of inimitable Wagnerian originality declare, but more importantly, it happens (so it dreams) in a new kind of way. All its meanings, everything about its nature, are concentrated in the fact of performance. Even after more than a century in which the building, the audiences, and (by inevitable extension) the works themselves have gone through mutations unimaginable to Wagner in the 1870s, the ghost of this fundamental inspiration still haunts the Festspielhaus. A large marble tablet is embedded in its otherwise almost featureless foyer, on which is inscribed the dates and cast list of the 1876 *Ring*. The building can't ever be separated from the performances that gave it its first life.

The *Ring*'s beginnings are overshadowed by incapacity, impossibility, the revolution that didn't happen and the theatre that didn't exist. As argued in Part II above, these pressures govern *Opera and Drama*'s metaphors of insemination and birth; the actual moment of delivery, when a poetic idea clothes itself in the flesh of drama, is always deferred. Wagner's misty generic speculations about the relations between music and drama thus define an originality, a new conception of how opera should be, which is precisely that – a conception. After one of the longest (and most painful) gestations in the history of drama, the building at Bayreuth brings what was conceived in the late 1840s to birth. In the 1870s, no more faith is pinned in the theoretical ideal of *Musikdrama*. Originality of conception doesn't matter. Opera has become not a new idea, a new genre, but a *deed*. 'Handlung', 'action', is how *Tristan* names itself, despite being as abstract and uneventful as opera can be. The name doesn't refer to any quality of the contents of the work, which would be better described as a 'meditation' (or perhaps, punning on the opposite of action, a 'passion'), but rather to the idea that in performance *Tristan* makes a certain spirit manifest: something occurs in it. The essay 'On the Name "Musikdrama" ' comes up with a famous phrase to describe this process (in a much more satirical vein than many subsequent citations of the passage allow for): 'I would gladly have called my dramas *deeds of Music brought to sight* [*ersichtlich gewordene Thaten der Musik*]' (V 303). Music's invisible, immaterial, undefined expression is made incarnate in a *Handlung*.

The label *Tristan* tags itself with thus prefigures the basic shift away from the position of the abortive revolutionary period, a movement completed on 13 August 1876 when the opening note of *Rheingold* first made its way out of the hidden orchestra pit of the Festspielhaus. Instead of a theoretical concern with music's relation to drama, a relationship which can get no farther than conception, the key question about opera becomes the relation of music to the stage. This is how Wagner dissects the word *Musikdrama* in his essay on the term:

> . . . certainly the greatest difficulty is to place 'music' in a proper position towards 'drama', since it can be brought into no equality therewith. . . . The reason surely lies in the fact that the word 'music' denotes an *art*, . . . whilst 'drama' strictly denotes a *deed* of art. . . . The primary meaning of 'drama' is a *deed* or *action* . . . By its name one now denoted for all ages an action [shown] upon the stage, and, to lay stress on this being a performance to look at, the place of assembly was [in ancient Greece] called the 'theatron', the looking-room. . . . But Music is placed in an utterly false relation to this 'show-play' [the literal translation of *Schauspiel*, play], if she is now to form but a part of that whole . . . she must neither stand before nor behind the Drama: she is no rival, but its mother. She sounds, and what

she sounds ye see upon the stage; for that [purpose] she gathered you together. . . . (V 301–2)

The last phrases are quite definitive. What is intended by the impossible word 'music-drama', Wagner says, is something whose purpose is to make itself manifest in a theatre, before an audience ('she gathered you together'). Music is still a mother and a womb, as in *Opera and Drama*, but now there is an emphatically instantaneous birth: the stage brings music to life. Wagner leaves the world of opera behind with *Lohengrin* ('romantic opera in three acts'). It's an appropriate bequest, because the production of *Lohengrin* on one of those everyday German stages where the overview of 1873 says opera belongs – Liszt's production at Weimar in 1850 – marked the beginning of the early works' entry into the ordinary repertory. *Lohengrin* (and even more so *Tannhäuser*, 'grand romantic opera in three acts') proved popular with that very 'brew' of theatre administrators and audiences Wagner came to see as the essence of 'opera'. After 1848, his career moves towards the goal of *Handlung*, where works exist not as scores to be taken up (and mangled) by any theatre willing to pay for them, but instead as events which make something manifest: not musical drama, nor *Musikdrama*, but music 'made visible' in the 'deed' of performance. This tendency is completed in 1876, where *Rheingold*, *Walküre*, *Siegfried* and *Götterdämmerung* are no longer operas or even artefacts of any sort, but a 'preliminary evening' and three 'days'. Bayreuth removes them from the sphere of created art and makes them into events in time and space.

Both the idea and the actuality of Bayreuth are deeply founded on the notion of incarnation, bringing something to material life, making it visible. Wagner creates his own theatre as a place where opera happens, and in the process reveals itself to be something other than 'opera' as every other stage in the world would represent it. Hence the Festspielhaus imagines itself as far more than just a convenient home for Wagner's works. It's a festival space devoted to the power of theatrical representation. Within its walls, something that would just be an opera anywhere else becomes a *Handlung* or a *Bühnenfestspiel* or a *Bühnenweihfestspiel* in the act of performance. At the start of this book I cited Nietzsche's bitter attack on the mere theatricality of Wagner's genius. His only mistake was to have expected something else. At Bayreuth, Wagner's imagination consummates the fundamental tendency of his works, their innate and urgent desire to reveal themselves, to make their spirit visible, to be not just words and music but deeds. To adopt a phrase from his 1878 'Ein Rückblick auf die Bühnenfestspiele des Jahres 1876' ('A Retrospect of the Stage-Festivals of 1876'), this is 'the idea which found shape in the Bayreuth [festivals]' (VI 97). Theatre is the proper home of Wagner's art (something too easily forgotten in the age of recorded sound) – a transfigured theatre, necessarily, since the conditions of performance need to be entirely unlike those Wagner observed in mere 'opera houses'; but nevertheless an actual stage, an actual auditorium, a place where the printed marks of score and libretto and stage directions are changed into the dynamic event of theatrical representation.

With *Parsifal*, we reach the logical conclusion of the idea that work and theatre are different dimensions of a single creative act. In 1876, the *Ring* became a *Bühnenfestspiel*, a celebration of the stage on which it was performed. In 1882 there is a crucial addition: *Parsifal* is the *Bühnenweihfestspiel*. The root *weih-* signifies consecration, the actual event or process which makes a space sacred. In this case, the space in question is of course the Bayreuth theatre. Celebration becomes sacramental; the festival of 1876 is now a religion. Hence the process of making *Parsifal* visible, putting it on the stage, is imagined as a kind of revelation, but – significantly – one that only occurs within the sacred domain. Recalling the rehearsals and performances later in 1882, Wagner writes that 'all that passed within the walls of that house during those two months' was 'governed by a consecration that shed itself on everything without the smallest prompting' (VI 303). His reference to the walls, the boundaries of the building, is not accidental. Exactly as (in the opera) the Grail can only be uncovered within the temple at Montsalvat, *Parsifal*'s *Weihe* (consecration) only works within its own temple. So Wagner attempted to prevent its performance on any other stage; and in the decades after his death *Parsifal* was performed more regularly at Bayreuth than any of his other works, always adhering to the precise sets and details of interpretation established in 1882. It did not receive a new production in the theatre until 1934, by which time every other one of the operas except the then rarely performed *Holländer* had already gone through two new stagings. Even Wieland Wagner's version, given at the first postwar festival of 1951, was not replaced until 1975, and was religiously given every year during those two and a half decades except 1974.

By turning representation (the principle of drama in performance) into revelation (the principle of religion), the notion of *Bühnenweihfestspiel* again alters and refines the kind of event *Parsifal* imagines itself to be. It is no longer enough just to celebrate the act of making a work visible, as *Bühnenfestspiel* does. Religion demands assent to the spirit it reveals: it requires faith. The audience is in turn transformed into a congregation, not only witnessing what is made visible on stage but somehow actually participating in the rite, and so (like any other congregation) declaring their membership of a community united by their common faith. *Parsifal* doesn't just stage redemption but thinks of itself as actually performing it, just as (according to Christian doctrine) a sacramental event changes the nature of those who participate in it. 'We are one body', the congregation says in the liturgy of the eucharist, and *Parsifal* imagines itself incorporating everyone in the theatre into the healed and purified community of the Grail. We're here at the opposite extreme from what Wagner in the 1870s comes to mean by 'opera'. With that word he denoted the way the operatic repertory, its performers, administrators, and its audiences all dragged each other down to their lowest level. *Bühnenweihfestspiel* is the antithesis: the work and all who perform and watch it are lifted together into a higher state.

It needs to be said that these are analogies with religion, not an actual substitution of the forms and rites of Christianity for the procedures of operatic performance. *Parsifal* may think of itself as an act of faith, but it is still musical drama rather than sacramental rite. This is very clear even from Wagner's own 1882 retrospective essay, for all its language of consecration and revelation. What he talks about in detail is the exceptional perfection achieved in matters of staging, vocal technique, dramatic gesture, and so forth, all the technical details of theatrical performance to which Bayreuth is really dedicated. The language of religion signifies the spirit in which *Parsifal* is supposed to be given and received; the opera is not a sacred rite, nor does it ever really mistake itself for one. *Bühnenweihfestspiel* works instead to redefine the *context* of performance, just as the 1876 festival did. Thus instead of claiming that *Parsifal* actually is a holy opera and its performance a sacramental event, its real aim is to define the way the work should be performed and understood. It's not meant to convert us to the Christian faith; its religion is no more than the religion of this opera and its theatre.

The key meaning of *Bühnenweihfestspiel* is its effort to foreclose interpretation. By imagining performance to be analogous to ritual, it insists that the audience submit entirely to its 'faith'. The sacred space is not just constituted by the stage. It's the whole of the Festspielhaus, including of course the auditorium, where the spectators are. They are included in the walls within whose bounds consecration happens. Hence in the same way that Wagner insisted on a symbiotic relationship between this opera and its theatre, there is a communion of understanding between the work and those who gather to watch it. *Bühnenweihfestspiel* is the extreme refinement of Wagner's lifelong fantasy that his operas reveal meanings in some absolute, unambiguous, instantaneously efficacious way. Merely to watch *Parsifal* (in its appointed place) is, the name suggests, enough to receive its benediction. This had not been the case with the festival *Ring* of 1876. The *Bühnenfestspiel* celebrated the performance of Wagner's art, but its further meanings were left uncertain (as we've seen, this is a characteristic effect of the tetralogy, which is unable to determine its overall direction). By the 1870s Wagner's own idea of what the *Ring* performances were about was concentrated around his visions of a revitalized German nation. An account of preparations for the staging of the *Ring* published in 1872 speaks of the 'secret' of both Bayreuth and the Nibelung drama being 'the *genuine Essence of the German Spirit*' (V 316), and

Bühnenfestspiel is supposed to make this spirit visible as a theatrical deed, and so inspire a reawakened national culture. Yet the 1878 'Retrospect' comments rather mournfully on the failure of any of Germany's leading lights to pay attention to what happened in 1876, let alone to give it support in the form of covering the debts the festival incurred. Wagner writes with delight and pride about the spirit of performance itself, the dedication and achievements of singers, designers and musicians. Events on stage are a cause for celebration (Wagner tactfully represses the disappointment he felt with much of the inscenation of the 1876 *Ring*), but they have not (he confesses) revealed the larger meanings intended by the festival. With *Parsifal*, this last imperfection of theatre – the fact that it can't guarantee how it will be seen, no matter how perfect the performances and how ideal their context – is supposedly removed. By analogy with a religious rite, the work in performance enacts its own meanings. One doesn't ask what the sacrament of baptism (for example) is 'about': anyone who participates in the rite doesn't think of it as signifying or referring to purification, but actually as making pure. Interpretation is not at issue. Everyone present is involved in the sacramental process; anyone who dissents from the meaning of the rite just doesn't attend. That is the logic of *Bühnenweihfestspiel*, and the reason why it withdraws entirely from the operatic repertory. You have to go to Bayreuth to experience *Parsifal*, it claims, and if you do then you have by that very act participated in the redemption the work is 'about' (more accurately, the redemption it *performs*). The alternative is simply to stay away. There is no way of sitting in the audience at a performance of *Parsifal* and misinterpreting what is happening, in the same way that Christians who have not undergone the rite of baptism cannot participate in the sacrament of communion. It's the climax of Wagner's lifelong insistence that everyone was either for him or against him, and of the quality in his work (a quality I've elsewhere named desire) which demands our assent to what it wants to express. *Bühnenweihfestspiel* claims to leave no room for error.

As Wagner's tyrannies go, this one is very easily resisted. In a perfectly clear and straightforward sense, *Parsifal is* part of the operatic repertory, an opera like any other. Vastly more people have seen it at a theatre other than the Festspielhaus than at Bayreuth, and, as in any other theatrical situation, their ideas about what they saw will have been as various and unpredictable as they would have been if they had been watching any other opera: probably more so, in fact, since *Parsifal* is by the standards of the operatic repertory a work of unusual complexity, reticence and resonance. The surprising thing is not that the implications of *Bühnenweihfestspiel* are purely fantastical, but that they exerted their influence for so long. The first opera house to dare to break Wagner's posthumous ban on staging *Parsifal* in profane theatres was New York's Metropolitan Opera, separated by an ocean from the anger of

Bayreuthian disciples (and not subject to European copyright agreements), and even the Met waited until 1903. The tradition of withholding applause when the curtain comes down on Act I is still maintained at Bayreuth, an eerie (and by now utterly *pro forma*) submission to the attitude of reverence *Bühnenweihfestspiel* calls for. It is still not entirely unusual to find members of a *Parsifal* audience trying to persuade themselves that they are more worshippers, or at least sacramental celebrants, than operagoers – even outside the walls of the Festspielhaus, where *Bühnenweihfestspiel*'s own principles dictate that the quasi-religious function of performance no longer applies. Yet for all this, *Parsifal* cannot disguise the fact that it is a theatrical event, not a ritual.

Nor, in fact, does it truly attempt to. For the key to any dramatic performance is incarnation, the process of making something visible in time and space, the principle to which Bayreuth is dedicated; and incarnation is *Parsifal*'s deepest idea. The manifestation of spirit as body (or blood) might be a sacred event, but, as we've seen, it might also be a reminder of sin and suffering, as it is on Good Friday, and as it is in the persons of Amfortas and Kundry. Once alternative possibilities are opened – and *Parsifal* is inexhaustibly rich in double versions of the same idea – then the fantasies of *Bühnenweihfestspiel* are immediately halted. Error, the substance of Kundry's curse, creeps in the walls of the sacred space, as Kundry herself silently enters the temple of the Grail. Bayreuth can be a place of incarnation, a stage where art comes alive, but what it can't do is sanctify that process. Wagner's effort to make his theatre function in this way in the last years of his life is, quite obviously, a doomed project, just as his widow and his son's successive (and perhaps increasingly half-hearted) attempts to preserve the staging of *Parsifal* exactly as it was in 1882 were also doomed.

The composer's own profound sense of the nature of theatre could have told them why. Incarnation means the entry of something transcendent into time and space. That's what the stage does; the very meaning of Bayreuth is that it makes works into events, turns an art into a deed. To try to define this deed as a ritual is to insist that it perpetually retain the same form. But time and space are subject to change, as a glance at photographs of the 1882 performances forcibly recalls: those costumes and sets and attitudes seem so infinitely far from our own sensibilities that it is almost impossible to imagine *Parsifal* conceiving of itself as a sacred rite while clothed in such forms. (I suspect many contemporary operagoers' instinctive ideas of what transcendence and ritual look like would be closer to the style of Wieland Wagner's productions, sublimely austere and immaterial.) In an 1878 essay, 'Das Publikum in Zeit und Raum' ('The Public in Time and Space'), Wagner himself recognizes that the original meaning of a work is lost as the place and date of its original performance recede or disappear. He is describing the futility of attempts to revive Mozart's operas on the late nineteenth-century German stage:

> If we would rightly judge and perfectly enjoy the 'Zauberflöte', we must get one of the spiritualistic wizards of to-day to transport us to the Theater an der Wien [where the *Magic Flute* was premiered] in the year of its first production. Or do you think that a modern performance at the Berlin Court-theatre would have the same effect? (VI 91)

Incarnation invites error. When the spirit becomes flesh, it is subject to the vagaries and laws of the time and place it appears in. Thus (as Wagner had always known) any theatrical performance exists in some kind of dialogue with the audience before which it is staged and the world to which they belong. This dialogue invites interpretation, even in the case of the *Bühnen-weihfestspiel* and its effort to foreclose the possibility of error or uncertainty. Gloomily, Wagner argues in 'The Public in Time and Space' that changed audiences and performance contexts inevitably fall into error. Noting the impossibility of his own contemporary world understanding *Don Giovanni*, he tries to claim that 'every intelligent person should reflect that not this work must be altered to fit our times, but ourselves to the time of "Don Juan"', if we are to arrive at harmony with Mozart's creation' (VI 90). So the essay ends with the image of the genius swimming against the current of time, always resisting the notion that art is subject to historical change. This is certainly how he wants to think of *Parsifal* as he recalls the 1882 festival. The performances, he writes, 'bore our souls away from the [familiar] world'; the significance of the event was 'the blessed sense of world-escape [*die Weihe der Weltentrückung*]' (VI 312). Again by analogy with religious ritual, *Parsifal* is imagined as something that can preserve its own spirit apart from, and untouched by, the mundane material world of change and decay. Yet his comments on Mozart's operas themselves demonstrate a keen and disillusioned understanding of the fact that drama is a live art which moves through time: one incarnation is different from another, like the two manifestations of Kundry, or the relation between Christ's wounded body and Amfortas's, or between Amfortas's sickening wound and Parsifal's redemptive repetition of the same pain in his moment of *Mitleid*. As the essay itself admits, there's no going back to the time and place of *Don Giovanni* or *Die Zauberflöte*.

This is why Bayreuth is Wagner's most characteristic creation, and also his greatest. In relation to *Parsifal* in particular, it dreams of doing away with the errors of time and space. It is supposed to be a temple in which the opera will always remain the same, separate from the world (and so never performed elsewhere), always continuing to manifest its original meanings as Wagner understood them; an operatic Oberammergau, where sacred drama is continuously preserved. And indeed, remarkably, the Festspielhaus has succeeded in being a place exclusively devoted to Wagner's work, and still kept under the administrative control of his descendants. Far more importantly, though, it has proved itself to be something very different from a sacred enclosure where *Bühnenweihfestspiel* preserves its unchanged rites. It turned out to be a place devoted to incarnation: year after year, it clothes Wagner's scores in flesh, makes them visible, brings them to life. Its double-sidedness is a perfect image of Wagner's Janus-faced genius. On the one hand it was imagined as a temple where change could be prevented, a theatre entirely under Wagner's control, unsullied by the incompetence and indifference of other opera houses, a place where his works could be preserved and immortalized, their meanings transmitted without interference to audiences with every performance: the very epitome of Wagnerian desire. In this aspect, the Festspielhaus represents everything that is dogmatic and overbearing about Wagner's art, its effort to insist that its meanings are single and unchangeable and incontrovertible. Yet on the other hand Bayreuth creates the conditions where Wagner's works turn into performed events, actions in time and space, continuously renewed through history in front of different audiences and in ever-changing contexts; a place where the operas clothe themselves in the messy, impure flesh and blood of performance; a place where Wagner's genius continually comes to life again. In this antithetical aspect, his theatre represents everything about that genius that is committed to the art of drama, that understands the operas not as monumental abstractions (such as they become when we listen to a recording) but as dynamic events displayed before an audience. It's easy to see in this case how the latter – and greater – aspect of his work overrides the former. The evidence of history is there: Wagner's works *have* changed, renewed themselves, received different interpretations, from a very young Wieland Wagner's ultra-conservative nationalist staging of *Meistersinger* (the only festival production seen during the war, in 1943 and 1944) to Götz Friedrich's leftist view of *Tannhäuser* in 1972, from the first *Holländer* in 1901 to Harry Kupfer's 1978 production which told more or less the opposite story about the same work. Simply put, Wagner's desires have not been followed at Bayreuth. There's no irony in this, though. The Festspielhaus was created on the understanding that opera is not a static art but a dynamic one, that performance is its true home. Wagner himself laid the foundations for the living energy of interpretation, and his works have borne him out, displaying in his own theatre their apparently endless capacity for fresh incarnations and renewed meanings.

The process is imaged for us in *Parsifal*. After the hero has watched the ritual of the Grail for the first time, in Act I, Gurnemanz asks him – like a good Wagnerian – 'Weißt du was du sah'st?': 'do you know what you have seen?' He thinks of the rite as a *Bühnenweihfestspiel*, a sacred event which is self-interpreting, revealing its significance as it happens, leaving no room for error. Parsifal is expected to receive the meaning of the performance as an immediate revelation. He shakes his head dumbly, though. *Bühnenweihfestspiel* doesn't work: Parsifal needs to *understand* something, not just to see it. (It's one of the masterstrokes of the opera that this understanding can only come to him through the agency of Kundry's sin.) Only when he returns to the temple in Act III, with fresh eyes and an entirely different consciousness, can he renew the rite. It takes change to make the performance go on happening. Not just change: it takes error too. Kundry's spell at the end of Act II tells him that all his ways and paths will be cursed except for those that lead him back to her; hence it's only by returning to her that he can re-enter the domain of the Grail (he arrives there in Act III only minutes after she does). The path of error is inseparable from the path of renewal. In the face of the sacramental delusions of *Bühnenweihfestspiel*, the Bayreuth festival stands as a physical monument to that deepest of *Parsifal's* insights.

CHAPTER FIFTEEN

Transformation Music

If *Parsifal* were a more straightforwardly melodramatic opera – more like *Tannhäuser*, say – then the climax of its second act would by rights be its end. The plot's main strand is wound up as soon as the hero repossesses the spear and, making the sign of the cross in the air, uses it to destroy Klingsor and all his works. There is even the requisite miracle to mark the moment when good triumphs over evil. To the accompaniment of a rippling harp glissando – an oddly conventional musical gesture – the spear Klingsor hurls at Parsifal hangs motionless over his head. As in the third act of *Götterdämmerung* when Siegfried's dead arm raises itself to pull the ring away from Hagen's covetous lunge, a higher power briefly reveals itself, its otherwise inexplicable presence acting like a seal on the plot's defeat of malevolence. Miracles can't be argued with. More or less by definition, they are the last word in all conflicts or uncertainties, the final court of appeal, as it were. In *Götterdämmerung*, the necromantic gesture of Siegfried's arm immediately precedes Brünnhilde's last entry, effectively raising the curtain on the drama's final scene, a sign that the coda has begun (the glissando harp in *Parsifal* even sounds like a curtain going up). Parsifal's triumph is swift and absolute. As well as dealing finally with Klingsor, he announces in the same moment the conclusion of the other main thread of the plot, Amfortas's wound and its hoped-for cure. In fact, his grammar rather strangely indicates that the two resolutions are one and the same. This is what he sings to Klingsor as he takes hold of the miraculously suspended spear:

Mit diesem Zeichen bann' ich deinen Zauber:	With this sign I banish your enchantment:
wie die Wunde er schließe, die mit ihm du schlugest, –	as it [the spear] closes the wound which you struck with it, –
in Trauer und Trümmer stürze die trügende Pracht!	may your false splendour plunge into misery and ruin!

'As' it heals Amfortas, let it destroy Klingsor: how are the two events analogous or simultaneous, except by a logic that says this is the instant of complete triumph, the resolution of all the plot's tensions at once? In a sense, *Parsifal* is finished at this point. There is no conflict in Act III (the struggle between Amfortas and the rest of the brotherhood only happens because they don't yet know that the work of healing is already complete). The battle is over. All that remains is the working-out of Parsifal's prophesied role.

Yet as soon as Parsifal's words are finished, everything about the scene speaks of a mood utterly foreign to triumph. The music over which he announces Klingsor's defeat and Amfortas's cure is as close to a direct echo of *Lohengrin* as *Parsifal* gets, all high tremolo strings and soft wind chords. As he finishes, a tremendous fortissimo mimes the destruction of the magic castle, and a downward rush in the violins (one of Kundry's themes, heard at her first entry in Act I) represents its fall. Yet from this moment on, both musically and dramatically, the act empties itself into barren stillness. A motif of falling semitones (the musical interval at the centre of *Parsifal's* infinitely subtle orchestral web) recurs in strident repetitions, but fades steadily as it proceeds, coming to rest in one of those peculiarly strained and obscure near-silences which the opera uses so effectively. Out of this hush the horns repeat the falling semitone motif, laid over a linked motif of four rising semitones which is identical in shape with the seminal 'yearning' theme of *Tristan und Isolde*; the sound has all the bleak poignancy of *Tristan's* third act, without a hint of *Lohengrin*-like transcendence. It is an orchestral version of what the stage directions call for in the scenic action: at the instant of Parsifal's victory, he finds himself in an empty desert, scattered with faded flowers. Radiant harps and miraculous interventions are utterly forgotten. We may have arrived at the resolution of the plot, but it looks and sounds like a wasteland.

At this point Parsifal turns back to Kundry – who has mysteriously survived the annihilation of everything else in Klingsor's domain – and sings the most intriguingly cryptic line in all Wagner's operas: 'Du weißt,/ wo du mich wieder finden kannst!': 'You know where you can find me again!' (In the text as collected in the *Sämtliche Schriften und Dichtungen*, the lines are: 'Du weißt –/ wo einzig du mich wiedersieh'st!', 'you know where once again you will see me'; since the line is central to my thinking about the performance of the opera as well as its internal significances, I have on this one occasion preferred to cite the revised version, which is the one always heard on stage.) The first syllable of 'wieder' is sustained at length while an oboe and a bassoon repeat the melancholy, disquieting combination of rising and falling semitone motifs. We hear them once again after he finishes, the descending fragment in horns and massed wind, the ascending one answering in trumpets and lower strings, sounding against each other like two lines converging towards some mysteriously absent point of resolution; then, with a last moan in the wind and the fading diminuendo of the timpani, Parsifal walks offstage and the act ends. The only figure left in the waste is Kundry. She acts as a reminder of why the opera has not ended in triumph here; she's unfinished business. Though an incontestably powerful supernatural miracle has come sponta- neously to Parsifal's aid and enabled him to recover the spear and dissolve Klingsor's spells, it hasn't – inexplicably – protected him from Kundry's curse. The end of Act II is heavy with the weight of that curse, the bleak threat of endless wandering (*Irren*, error), conjured up by the semitonal motivic frag- ments (we'll hear them again at the end of the Act III prelude, right before Kundry's moan). Instead of triumphal resolution, what we see and hear at this climax of the plot is a quiet collapse into desolation. It is the beginning of a long journey through error, not the end of a quest. Hence Kundry's mute presence: she's a disquieting remnant, the embodiment of a sinfulness and a suffering which have been 'left over' (as it were) from the sum of Parsifal's holy victory over evil. Indeed, all the musical and dramatic signs suggest that the force of her 'error' has won out over Parsifal's heroism; the stage shows a place of barren ruin, not a scene of restoration. Her own position at the end of the act is unsettled, and also unsettling: both defeated and saved together, it seems, restored to herself but abandoned in the desert, as much the victim of her own curse as Parsifal is.

This, presumably, is what his last words to her refer to. They seem to turn the tables on her curse. She had laid her malediction on every path leading him away from her, every step he might take in search of his own redemp- tive goal: 'den Weg, den du such'st,/ dess' Pfade sollst du nicht finden' ('the way which you seek, that path you shall never find'). His answer, if that is what it is, implies that it is she who will now be in search of him – not the other way around, as in the terms of her curse. He is holding out some kind of offer of salvation for her. At the same time, the words show that salvation lies in her own hands: '*you know* where you can find me again'. Which of them is it that will lead the other back to the right path? Kundry appears to hold the key to the final resolution which has so strangely failed to happen here at the end of Act II; yet she is the one who remains fixed in place amid the waste as the curtain comes down, while Parsifal begins the journey that can't be ended until it brings him back to her. There is nowhere for either of them to go. The plot is lost in a dizzying limbo.

One event untangles the maze of error and allows the true resolution of the story to begin, and it's the first dramatic (rather than musical) event of Act III: Kundry's awakening. This takes the form first of an invisible moan, then the appearance of her body 'ganz erstarrt und leblos' ('entirely stiff and lifeless'), as the stage directions have it, and then a terrible scream into life. Her passage back to the domain of the Grail is entirely mysterious. Neither Gurnemanz nor Parsifal says anything about how it might have happened,

while she herself of course insists on saying nothing at all. As it's staged at
the beginning of Act III, it is a passage through death; that scream is a kind
of birth-pang. Later, Parsifal tells Gurnemanz the story of his own long
journey from the end of Act II to the Good Friday meadows of Act III, and
it turns out to be a story from chivalric romance, a passage through 'zahllose
Nöthen,/ Kämpfe und Streite' ('countless distresses, struggles and battles').
Kundry's parallel journey seems to happen instantaneously, its narrative contained in that one inarticulate shriek. She simply appears again, and in doing
so summons Parsifal back to her, just as her curse dictated. It's almost as if
she is a magnet whose polarity has reversed itself. At the end of Act II she
expels Parsifal out to his wanderings, remaining in place herself at the centre
of the waste; in Act III she draws him back to the domain of the Grail, herself
now become its static and silent heart.

It might seem an overstatement to claim that she is so central to
Montsalvat and its community. Her presence in Act III is more usually interpreted as a piece of antifeminist propaganda not entirely unlike the scapegoating of Beckmesser in *Meistersinger*. Her dutiful and penitent silence, the
argument goes, is *Parsifal's* misogynist fantasy of the role of woman in redemption. Purification for Kundry means becoming a servant, prostrating and
muting herself before the brotherhood, kneeling in front of Parsifal and
washing the dust from his feet with her hair, and finally dying with her eyes
raised to him in sacrificial submission as he is anointed king. In this (not at
all implausible) interpretation, she's redemption's sacrificial victim, the female
sinner silenced and enslaved as payment for the restoration of the exclusively
male holy community. Yet in the bleak suspension and emptiness of the end
of Act II, the one certainty remaining to both her and Parsifal is that the
completion of their aborted journey lies in her power. You know where you
can find me again, he says to her. In the desert of error they are mired in
together, the implication is that he does not know how to find himself, that
his place depends on hers. Likewise, there is only one thing we know about
her passage back to Montsalvat. Berating her for her silence after waking,
Gurnemanz reminds us of something he said in Act I:

Hast du kein Wort für mich?	Have you no word for me?
Ist dieß der Dank,	Is this my thanks
daß dem Todeschlafe	for having once again
noch einmal ich dich entweckt?	roused you from the sleep of death?

She has not just mysteriously come to life in the Grail's domain: she has done
so *again* ('noch einmal'). In the course of his narrations in Act I, Gurnemanz
refers to the other time he awoke her in the same place ('Sie – wieder da',
he exclaims in Act III: 'She there again'): when Amfortas lost the spear and
gained his wound. More tellingly, he also recounts how she was found 'hier

in Waldgestrüpp',/ erstarrt, leblos, wie todt' – 'here in the forest undergrowth, numb, lifeless, as if dead' – when Titurel first built the castle to house the Grail. What we see at the start of Act III is something that has in fact happened twice before. Kundry's forest resurrections together mark the history of the Grail community: its founding, its fall into sin, its restoration to purity. Whereas the rest of the plot moves through a trajectory of dramatic change, setting up problems (Parsifal's ignorance, Amfortas's 'sin', the lost spear, and so forth) and then resolving them, Kundry lives through a series of repetitions, each one bringing her back to life in the same place. Her story, like that of the opera itself, is one of returning. She is also effectively the foundation of all the other stories; she's the point the opera keeps coming back to, just as her corpse is pulled out of the forest and brought back to life at every crux of the brotherhood's history (and indeed in Gurnemanz's narration it sounds almost as if Titurel built Montsalvat on the spot where her 'lifeless' body was discovered). Parsifal's last words to her in Act II are surely an enlightened intuition of this truth. He seems to know where she belongs, and to know that she will end up there again, even while he himself is condemned to wander in error until she reawakens.

Indeed, one could describe the enlightenment he receives with her kiss as an initiation into the mystery of recurrence. The first thing that he realizes as he sheds his naïve innocence is that what is happening to him is something that has happened before, when Amfortas fell. The kiss is itself a repetition. *Mitleid* (as *Parsifal* understands it) hinges on this idea: it's the experience of re-experiencing something. The same logic determines Amfortas's cure at the end of Act III. Parsifal touches the point of the spear to his side, saying 'die Wunde schließt/ der Speer nur, der sie schlug' ('the spear which struck the wound now closes it'). It's part of the opera's deep interweaving of opposites: wound and cure are mirror images of each other (and this is another reminder of Kundry's central significance, since by this logic she who caused Amfortas to fall into sin must also be present at his restoration and atonement). In the same way, Parsifal seems to realize at the end of Act II that Kundry's curse is also a blessing, because although it dooms him to the wrong paths, it also promises his eventual return to her, and her eventual return to Montsalvat. That is perhaps why the word 'wieder', 'again', receives such emphasis as he sings his last line to her. What needs to happen in the last act of the opera, he knows, is the repetition of events. The first thing he says in Act III is a blessed realization that something is happening again. 'Heil mir, daß ich dich wieder finde': 'Praise be [literally 'salvation to me'], that I have again found you' – a line the stage directions say is addressed to Gurnemanz, but which would more powerfully correspond to the last line of Act II, and more accurately reflect the path of his return, if spoken to Kundry. He then asks to be led back through the events he witnessed in Act I, first at the level of ideas (as Gurnemanz explains the relation of suffering to salvation in his Good Friday homily) and then literally: the 'transformation music' works its magic again and he is brought back into the presence of Amfortas and the Grail.

Throughout *Parsifal*, things aren't so much just happening as happening again (*wieder*). The prelude begins with a highly formal extended reiteration, a double doubling of the original theme. It first appears in bare unison, and is then immediately repeated with the addition of richly decorative, exquisitely blended orchestral colouring. This two-part structure is itself then repeated, with chromatic intensification but preserving the exact contours of the first statement. Nowhere else in Wagner do we begin with so strong a sense of echo. The theme appears to answer and mirror itself, and this process takes place in a self-contained musical 'paragraph', coming to a complete and lengthy stop before new thematic material is introduced. At the beginning of Act I proper, the first phrase of the original theme is again heard in completely self-contained form, played by offstage trombones with no orchestral accompaniment: the most deliberate and emphatic possible repetition, as if the melody is demanding to be heard not just as an abstract musical idea but as the very sound of the opera's rite. Indeed, as Gurnemanz calls the squires to their morning prayer, all the main thematic ideas of the prelude are reiterated in order, with equal deliberation and emphasis. The music there presented as a motivic introduction to the drama is now revealed to be the actual form of liturgy and worship in the domain of the Grail (later in Act I the opening fourfold structure will be exactly repeated as the eucharistic rite begins).

Repetition is of course the very essence of ritual events. Forms, ceremonies, words and gestures are prescribed elements of a rite. What marks them off from everyday events is precisely the fact that they are supposed to be repeated with every performance, their fixed nature inseparable from their sacramental character. The way *Parsifal* begins – with strongly-marked repetitions of distinct musical material – gives a very strong sense of entering into this sort of chronology, unveiling a world structured by ritual's potent regulation. The overall architecture of the work is highly symmetrical, the first and third acts with their parallel structure (Gurnemanz–Kundry–Parsifal scenes in the forest leading to Amfortas scenes in the temple) flanking the antithetical second act. *Parsifal* has even been mapped out as a kind of geometric diagram, most interestingly in Wieland Wagner's version, the 'Parsifal cross', where the events of the opera are arranged along two axes that mirror themselves around the central point of their intersection (the kiss). However plausible or otherwise such diagrams are, they testify to the intensely formal character of the opera: formal not in the sense of *Meistersinger*, which argues over and weighs up the structures that shape experience, but in the sense of architecture itself, the feeling that *Parsifal* is less an unfolding story than an arrangement of dramatic space. This is the impression given by the prelude, with its stately presentation of distinct musical material, entirely unlike the symphonic and contrapuntal *Meistersinger* prelude or the sustained dramatic development of those to *Lohengrin* and *Tristan*. What we subsequently see on stage exudes the same quality. Everything seems foreordained, governed by an insistent order that makes individual events into parts of a larger architecture.

The life of Montsalvat in particular is sustained by ritual and repetition, literally so in the case of its master Titurel. He is a corpse prolonged by the rite of the Grail (another unsettling confusion of living and dying bodies, like Christ and Amfortas and Kundry). His brotherhood feeds off the same ritual, withering away when Amfortas refuses to repeat it. Outside the specifically ceremonial community of the knights, though, the same quality pervades the action. Kundry's curse (the one she suffers under, not the one she pronounces at the end of Act II) is represented by her compulsive hysterical laughter, a form of repetition which reminds her of her primal sin (laughing in the face of Christ) and results over and over again in her victims' fall into erotic impurity:

kehrt mir das verfluchte Lachen wieder –	then my accursed laughter again possesses me:
ein Sünder sinkt mir in die Arme!	a sinner sinks into my arms!

This tells us that the whole action of Act II up to the kiss is the re-enactment of a scene performed many times before, Klingsor's conjuration included ('Meinem Banne wieder/ verfiel'st du heut'', he tells Kundry: 'you are enslaved *again* today to my spell'). A cycle is broken with the kiss, but only through the process of *Mitleid*, which as we've already observed is itself a mode of repetition. At this point the Act I rite recurs in Parsifal's entranced inward vision: 'Es starrt der Blick dumpf auf das Heilsgefäß: –/ das heilige Blut erglüh't . . .' ('my gaze fixes dully on the sacred chalice: the sacred blood glows . . .'). Immediately he is convinced of his need to go back, to do something again (but differently). That strange final command or appeal to Kundry – 'you know where you can find me again' – could be a motto for the whole work, though, not just the particular path of salvation laid out in front of Parsifal once he has recovered the spear. In so many words, it is what Titurel says to Amfortas, and what Amfortas says to the brotherhood, and what they in return say to him; it's the call of the Grail itself, preserved in its shrine to be perpetually unveiled in the rite; it sums up Kundry's appearances at Montsalvat, since she was there before the temple itself was; it's the form of Klingsor's power over both Kundry and the Grail knights, both of whom are irresistibly drawn into his orbit.

The words could just as appropriately be carved on the Bayreuth Festspielhaus. No other major theatre is so entirely devoted to the law of repetition. Except in the aftermath of World War II, when it was used for various different purposes including some local opera performances, only Wagner's work has appeared on its stage. His operas go on being found there again. Like Kundry's body, they are repeatedly taken and brought to life. Right from his early days, Wagner's imagination was preoccupied by this idea of inifinite repetitions. The melodramatic pathos of *Der fliegende Holländer* is based on the way a pattern repeats itself throughout eternity; everything that happens in that opera too has happened before, until Senta finally proves herself 'treu . . . bis zum Tod', 'faithful unto death'. We've considered the force of repetition in the *Ring* at length already; here it only needs to be added that the tetralogy's power to bend time back on itself is institutionalized in the idea of Bayreuth, where the *Ring* is guaranteed to run its course from creation to apocalypse again and again. In both the *Ring* and *Holländer*, recurrence is strongly tinged with destructiveness. Satan inflicts the same kind of curse on the Dutchman (as the story goes in Senta's ballad) as Alberich lays on the ring, each trapping their victims in inescapable plots. The same fatalism finds its way into *Parsifal* as well, in the forms of Amfortas's permanent wound and Kundry's permanent affliction of laughter. At Bayreuth, these curses initially manifested themselves through a form of dramatic ossification. As if Wagner was Satan or Alberich, his heirs felt themselves bound by the law of his theatrical will. When the administration of the theatre passed to Cosima, her explicit goal was the most faithful possible adherence to the ideas of dramaturgy and musical execution established at the 1876 and 1882 festivals. Wagner was to live in his grave like Titurel, preserved for ever by the continuous unveiling of his works.

Titurel doesn't come back to life in *Parsifal*, though. When we first hear him in Act I, there's an incongruously necromantic quality about the appearance of his voice; we can't forget that we are hearing a corpse singing. Letting Wagner's invisible and disembodied voice continue to resonate around the Festspielhaus after his death must have had the same effect: inspiring for members of the community placed under his leadership (the Grail knights all but worship Titurel as their founder and head), but disturbing for other witnesses. One of the small surprises of the opera is that Titurel's death is forgotten after the swift and total reversal of mood when Parsifal re-enters the temple bearing the spear. Amfortas has longed to die while his father demanded to be kept alive. Neither gets his wish in the end, yet in both cases the result seems better as it is. The singing corpse is replaced by the silent but whole body. Titurel is left in his grave, while his newly-healed son says nothing more once he is cured.

This reminds us that while the old king is left to die, there is a character in *Parsifal* who is subject to a kind of resurrection. Three times found 'leblos', 'lifeless', and restored to life, Kundry images an entirely different kind of repetition from the model presented in the Grail rite and implicitly adopted by Cosima (and by other, later Wagnerians who maintain the idea that the purpose of Bayreuth, not to mention any other place where the operas are performed, is to preserve and give voice again to the dead body of the composer by attempting to exhume his supposed 'intentions'). Her third and final awakening, the one we witness in Act III, leaves her fully healed and (almost) perfectly silent, like Amfortas in the closing moments. Whereas Titurel's ossified brand of immortality kept him shut out of sight, invisibly issuing commands, Kundry is strikingly *present* during the last act of *Parsifal*. Although she does little and says less, she is there throughout. It's a very different kind of presence from Titurel's, and a very different kind of recurrence from the daily-repeated ritual that keeps him alive. Gurnemanz captures its essence as he watches her: 'Wie anders schreitet sie als sonst!', 'how differently she moves from before!' She has come back to life, again, but the repetition marks a change: she is different. That difference is in fact what communicates itself most strongly throughout the act. Because she tells no story and contributes virtually nothing to the action, more or less the only thing her presence conveys is how altered it is from any of the ways she has appeared before.

Her silence opens out breathing room for a mysterious sense of change. By the time of Titurel's funeral rites, the Grail brotherhood has entirely lost whatever faint grasp it may have had on the idea of change. They're horrified by the mere fact of his death – though Gurnemanz, more humanely, comments that it just means he was 'ein Mensch wie Alle!', 'a man like everyone else'. They are still more horrified by Amfortas's refusal to reiterate the ceremonies of the Grail. In chaotic and furious chorus they repeat Titurel's command from Act I, 'Enthüllet den Gral!', uncover (or 'disclose') the Grail. They have been reduced to desperate ventriloquism; now that the living corpse can't speak for itself, they try to speak for it. So the circle of devoted Bayreuthians gathered around Cosima set themselves the impossibly necromantic task of making the Festspielhaus speak as if its lord and founder were still alive. With Kundry's mute reincarnation, though, an utterly different set of possibilities emerges. As Parsifal says at the end of Act II, she knows where to return to; she knows how to make things happen again. Importantly, though, this return also marks a break with the past. Unlike the rite of the Grail, which refreshes body and blood by constantly offering the same source of nourishment for consumption, Kundry's journey back to life is a form of change. She takes on a new form, a new way of moving. Just as importantly, these differences are allowed to speak for themselves. There is no voice to interpret the nature of repetition for us. She's simply *there*, a new version of something we saw before, and a version whose meaning lies only in its newness. There's nothing else to say about her except that she has returned, but returned 'anders', differently. The first of these mysterious reincarnations came before the building of the temple; Titurel raised his shrine on the site where Kundry awoke. In doing so, he petrified the idea of renewal into a ritual and a community based on rigid, deathly repetition. Wagner's temple risked doing the same to his own body of work; and yet Bayreuth, like Montsalvat, can't forget that it is a site of repetitions which are subject to silent change, founded on a body always being brought back to new life — not a corpse clinging ghoulishly to its old existence.

Why does Kundry awaken in Act III with a scream? Like everything else about her in the act, the question is partly unanswerable. Curiously, though, that scream turns up earlier in Wagner's work. It is a repetition, albeit a most oblique one, of a passage in his 1870 essay *Beethoven* (which is at once a eulogizing description of Beethoven's genius, an attempt at a philosophy of music and a celebration of a distinctively German tradition in art). In a characteristically imprecise but ingenious appropriation of ideas supplied by Schopenhauer, he connects the philosopher's theory of dreams (which interestingly prefigures Freud's) with his own conceptions of music's articulate power. Dreaming is understood to be the activity of an 'inward-facing consciousness' (V 68) entirely distinct from the ordinary mode of everyday perception enslaved to the outward appearance of things. It signifies another mode of knowledge and experience, one that can't be accounted for by egotistical reason and deluded observation. (One way to understand the distinction would be to recall the dualism of 'day' and 'night' in *Tristan*; dreaming here stands for the lovers' night, the waking world for the oppressions and falsifications they ascribe to day.) Wagner suggests an analogous distinction between 'the *light-world*', 'the visible world' whose corollary in the individual consciousness is 'the operation consequent on *sight*', and 'a *sound-world*', the domain of music, which enters consciousness at a level as distinct from light and reason as dreaming is from waking (V 68). Like dreams, music bypasses the world of appearances, speaking instead to some purely inward aspect of being. Through 'this inner life', the essay goes on, 'we are directly allied with the whole of Nature, and thus are brought into a relation with the Essence of things that eludes the forms of outer knowledge, Time and Space' (V 69). The sound-world is somehow a vehicle for immediate knowledge of the world's nature, a mode of insight into the essence of things (*das Wesen der Dinge*). Citing Schopenhauer's interest in prophetic or clairvoyant dreams, Wagner finds the same kind of immediate insight expressed in a primal act of sound: 'From the most terrifying of such dreams we wake with a *scream*'

(V 69). The scream is revelation in the form of sound, an expression of the act of dreaming, of an intuitive knowledge transcending everyday reason and grasping the deep nature of reality. Prior to any word or any thought, it's the momentary articulation of existence itself – not the mundane existence of 'Time and Space', but the essence (*Wesen*) of being. So, Wagner claims, we can understand 'the Scream in all the diminutions of its vehemence, down to the gentler cry of longing, as the root-element of every human message to the ear' (V 69). With the waking scream, the sound-world (Tristan and Isolde's 'night') reveals itself as the inward and essential basis on which the light-world ('day') rests and which its delusions obscure.

The scream is thus the archetype of music itself. Its eruption out of dream is the 'root-element' of everything addressed to hearing; the '*art* arising from this element' is the art of pure sound (V 69). Music, the essay goes on to say (following Schopenhauer closely), is 'itself a world's-Idea [*eine Idee der Welt*], an idea in which the world immediately displays its essence [*Wesen*]' (V 72). It is a language directly and incontestably felt rather than rationally understood:

> If the scream, the moan, the murmured happiness in our own mouth is the most direct utterance of the will's emotion, so when brought us by our ear we understand it past denial as utterance of the same emotion; no illusion is possible here . . .
>
> . . . [music is] an art aris[ing] from this immediate consciousness of the oneness of our inner essence with that of the outer world. . . . (V 71)

Parsifal doesn't allow us to interpret Kundry's scream quite so securely as a form of revelation. She doesn't become the mouthpiece of Schopenhauerian thought, as Tristan and Isolde do (superficially at least) and as the *Beethoven* essay does. It is true that after she wakes illusion is broken: she has been literally disenchanted, freed from the compulsion of Klingsor's wizardry. Yet whatever insight she may drag with her into the waking world, she nevertheless keeps her secrets. As usual in Wagner's writing, *Beethoven* wants to find a way of arguing that sound communicates essential truths with unambiguous, irresistible directness. Kundry's scream clearly doesn't reveal any explicit meanings, though. Gurnemanz has no idea what has happened to her; he's frustrated by her silence. If it articulates the inward and essential revelation of dream, it's correspondingly true that (as *Beethoven* admits) '[w]hat it here has seen, no tongue can impart' (V 73). Whatever Kundry knows lies outside the domain of language. Hence her silence: the cry is a step beyond speech.

The accidental resonance between Act III of *Parsifal* and the argument of *Beethoven* suggests a way of thinking about the changed nature into which Kundry is reborn. If the scream is the primal articulation of the 'sound-world', and therefore an archetypal instance of music, Kundry's silence is also music's

mute presence. She loses her voice in order to enter a different mode of articulation. Up to this point, her voice has always been at war with itself. The
struggle is acutely dramatized at the beginning of Act II, where her broken
sentences and violent alternations between despair and anger represent her
effort to speak against Klingsor even as her will is being invaded by his possession. Her self-lacerating laughter is the sound of a mouth turned bitterly
against itself; even her kiss at the opera's moment of transformation offers sin
and salvation together, the work's polar extremes contained at the same instant
between her lips. Perhaps, then, there is nothing remotely punitive about the
muteness she imposes on herself in Act III. The first time we hear her scream,
when Klingsor forces her to waken in his castle, the cry is prelude to the torments of language. He flings mocking questions at her, and she appears unable
to resist replying: her voice is dragged out of her. This is the same tyranny of
voice by which Titurel rules. As with the ancient king, Klingsor's commands
are a means of forcing repetition; the one insists on Amfortas continuing to
perform his office, the other likewise sends Kundry 'wieder zum Dienst',
to serve again. Kundry's last croaked words are 'Dienen . . . dienen': 'to serve,
to serve'. Even as it expires, language is still caught in the nexus of power
and submission. Silence, though, breaks the spell at last (just as it represents
Kundry's relief from her grotesque laughter). The shriek of Act II is clearly
the sound of suffering; Kundry goes on to articulate her misery in language
barely beyond the level of a scream ('Ach! – Ach!/ Tiefe Nacht . . . /
Wahnsinn . . . Oh! – Wuth . . .', deep night, madness, rage). When it's repeated,
though, it marks a change, a transition out of language into a different state.
Beethoven likes to call this new state an understanding of 'the inner nature
[*innere Wesen*] of things' (V 69), and to argue that music is the direct expression of such a revelation. *Parsifal* suggests a different – and, I think, a much
more telling – interpretation. Kundry's last scream is here an escape from
the deadening repetitions and compulsions of commanding language into a
changed silence; and music, correspondingly, is not a ritual voice, but a form
of muteness also full of the possibilities of difference.

This isn't always how music works in the opera. *Parsifal* is not like *Tristan
und Isolde*, sustained by an art of transition, formed by sounds that are always
in flux. It is closer to *Die Meistersinger* in its ambivalence about musical change.
Yet where *Meistersinger* works hard to reconcile continuity with difference,
hoping to contain the transition to Walther's new art within an undisturbed
repetition of the guild's German spirit, *Parsifal* augments the tension between
change and continuity almost to breaking-point. At one extreme, its music
shifts and dissolves like a tonal kaleidoscope, as restlessly fluid as *Tristan*'s
without the surcharge of expressive desire that gives the latter score its sense
of straining endlessly *towards* something. At the polar extreme, *Parsifal* distils
the diatonic stability of much of *Meistersinger* into monumentally firm

expanses of sound, music as heavy and fixed as stone. The epitome of this aspect of the score is the Montsalvat bells. Sound here becomes a massive vibration of architecture, the music of gigantic objects heavily and repeatedly struck. The bells emerge out of the orchestral welter at the end of the first transformation scene, and the score surrenders completely to their inexorable pounding repetitions; Wagner writes a fermata over the bar in which they sound alone, and adds a note explaining that their repetitions can go on as long as needed. This bar is the gravitational centre of repetition in the opera. Music has become entirely absorbed into ritual. Over and over again the bells toll their simple sequence, marking the ceremonial life of the Grail community, summoning it to its daily iteration.

Their rhythm is projected backwards and forwards from this central moment, giving the latter part of Act I its distinctive sound. We hear it first, not coincidentally, immediately after Kundry disappears from the stage (though it's interesting that she doesn't actually exit: the stage direction says that she sinks into the undergrowth 'und bleibt von jetzt an unbemerkt', 'and from now on remains unseen' – a curiously suggestive piece of phrasing, as if she is still somehow invisibly present throughout the rest of the act). Her dim, shifting, chromatic music dies away; there is a brief pause; then the stately, steady march of ceremony begins. Its characteristic motif is more of a rhythmic pulse than a melodic or harmonic idea. Certainly the feeling of rhythmic stability overtakes the vocal lines: the exchanges between Gurnemanz and Parsifal right before the transformation scene sound almost un-Wagnerian in the way they submit natural speech rhythms to the insistent pulse of the orchestra. At the end of the transformation music, this main motif reveals itself as an orchestral version of the tolling bells. The derivation is absolutely unmistakable; the motif strikes up again in the strings as the bells fade away, carrying the echo of the ritual tolling through the subsequent choral march, and it resumes after the sacramental hush of the Grail's unveiling to accompany the knights' militaristic procession through the rest of the ceremony. The whole rite is thus framed by the essential character of the bells' music, changeless, insistent, repetitive, the expression in sound of the first words of the ceremony:

Zum letzten Liebesmahle   At the last love-feast [the Last Supper],
gerüstet Tag für Tag. . . .   prepared day by day. . . .

The knights proclaim that their rite is the infinite and regular reiteration of the event it commemorates. To an overwhelming degree, that's also the meaning of the rhythmically and harmonically stable aspect of *Parsifal*. What has happened before will go on happening afterwards, preserved and sanctified in the form of ritual. You know where you can find this music again.

Yet the revelation of the sound of Montsalvat's bells, the unveiling of the ritual scene on stage, arrives after a passage – a journey – through musical chaos. Three times during the 'transformation music' the dominant rhythmic pulse of the surrounding music dissolves into an aural avalanche. The bells and their attendant motivic figure separate sound into perceptibly distinct units, organizing music as geometrically as the following ritual organizes the community into a series of choreographed choruses and processions; but the triple eruption in the transformation scene momentarily throws rhythm, melody and harmony into a wrenchingly dense mass, no longer architecture but a stupendous ruin of assembled fragments. What we're listening to here is the difference between repetition and transformation. The potent drama-turgical idea that inspires this passage of music is another of those utterly Wagnerian masterstrokes. Instead of simply replacing one scene with another, altering the place of the stage action by the usual method of taking one set away and installing the next, *Parsifal* requires us to believe that its stage space dissolves and reassembles before our eyes. That's how we arrive at Montsalvat. Correspondingly, the scene of musical and dramatic iteration has to build itself out of a few brief minutes of complete decomposition. Change has to happen; and *Parsifal* not only visibly and aurally stages and orchestrates that change, but places it in the most direct possible juxtaposition with the insistent changelessness of Montsalvat. Transformation music unveils the rite. There has to be a passage through change and difference before repetition can be established again.

The opera's central moment of dramatic change, the kiss and its aftermath, is scored to the same musical chaos. Parsifal has to undergo the violent passage through change before he can become the repetition of Amfortas and the instrument for re-establishing the Grail rite. (In Hans-Jürgen Syberberg's brilliantly weird film version of the opera, the change is visibly incarnated: Parsifal not only becomes a different person, but a person of different gender.) His visionary monologue following the kiss falls repeatedly into the sonic maelstrom established in the Act I transformation music. The logic of *Mitleid* presents the moment as a strict repetition, binding Parsifal's mind and body to Amfortas's with the inexorable necessity imaged in sound by Montsalvat's tolling bells; but the score vehemently insists on change and dissolution. Revelation strikes Parsifal with a chaotic rather than an enlightening force. He here discovers his own nature and mission, instantaneously understanding the world of salvation and sin within which he had until now been help-lessly ignorant (he was as naïve in the face of Kundry's eroticism as when asking Gurnemanz 'Wer ist der Gral?', 'who is the Grail?'). Yet the new know-ledge unsettles and dissolves his world: wisdom is confusion. What he realizes about sin and sanctity is that they are chaotically interwoven:

Oh, Weltenwahns Umnachten:	Oh, benighted madness of the world:
in höchsten Heiles heißer	in the ardent craving for highest
Sucht	salvation
nach der Verdammniß	to thirst for the source of
Quell zu schmachten!	damnation!

The Grail knights, with their pathological conviction that all error is sin and only purity is perfection, never understand Parsifal's tormented insight. That is why they cannot understand Kundry (even the sympathetic Gurnemanz knows nothing about her real nature). She is the very embodiment of transformation, always turning into her own opposite, and so she stands outside Montsalvat's conceptual field. All the squires want to know about her is whether she is on the right side of their black-and-white world:

. . . doch ob heilig du,	. . . whether you are holy,
das wissen wir grad' noch nicht.	that we are still not at all sure of.

The failure of this mode of thinking becomes increasingly clear in Act III. Transformation has here worked its strange magic; as Parsifal says to Gurnemanz (another line that resonates most strongly with respect to his awareness of Kundry), 'Verwandelt dünkt mich Alles', 'everything seems changed to me'. Yet the bells of Montsalvat toll the same implacable iteration as they always have done. The transformation scene of Act III, like that of the first act, centres on the repeated C–G–A–E peal; nothing has changed, because ritual does not permit change. In truth, however, everything is different. The four notes are now harmonized in such a way that they sound utterly funereal (they are also scored in unison with contrabass tuba and timpani, making for a darker and duller resonance). The distinctively steady rhythmic pulse associated with Montsalvat is here transferred to the bass strings and given a dragging quality, made to sound forced, obsessive, claustrophobic, everything that the subsequent funeral march of the knights will show the brotherhood to have become. Repetition reveals itself to be deathly. We don't hear the fractured, chaotic music that erupted in the first transformation scene, because transformation is precisely what is missing. Horrifically, nothing at Montsalvat is different from how it was in Act I (Titurel was really no more alive then than he is at his own funeral). Music, though, can express this sameness in a different light: the bells play the same notes, the processional quality is unchanged, and yet an utterly dissimilar atmosphere governs the repetition. As at the instant of Parsifal's enlightenment, repetition and alteration are experienced at once, in disturbing conflict. Like Kundry herself, music contains as its essence this power to be the same and yet different. If the Grail rite in Act I is dedicated to ignoring or suppressing that truth, then it's a lesson that needs to be learned. After Parsifal's saving intervention, the last chorus of the opera is thus a hymn to difference-within-sameness: 'Erlösung dem Erlöser!', the redeemer redeemed. The phrase in itself is a transformation within a repetition, the same word reflected back on itself and made its own object (which is perhaps why it has struck so many commentators as a cryptic pronouncement). The 'Erlöser' is both redeemer and subject to redemption, renewed, differently incarnated. Wagner sets the words in ten separate choral parts and, in absolute contrast to the stern unisons of the ritual scenes, allows them to flow over each other with melting sweetness, dissolving 'Erlösung' and 'Erlöser' into each other. Warm and stable harmonies reign – Montsalvat is not about to become a home for the agonized chaos of transition – but the blended sound has lost all the stern resonance of the bells, and the march-like dotted rhythms pervading both ritual scenes have been smoothed out into an ethereally serene texture. *Parsifal* ends with music that is quite clearly still the sound of the Grail, but equally certainly a new version of it.

In this sense, Parsifal's promise to Kundry – 'you know where you can find me again' – is an invitation to change. Ritual reiterates its unchanging demands, but music works mute transformations. Travelling back over old ground, both Parsifal and Kundry find that everything is different. So with everything in *Parsifal*: things happen again, but the real principle governing its symmetries is transformation rather than dull repetition. So too with Bayreuth itself. Like Montsalvat, its founding principle is a dedication to preserving and repeating that which it holds holy. Yet Montsalvat was built on Kundry's resurrected body, and remains haunted by the doubleness and contradictoriness of her nature; and the Festspielhaus too is a place whose repetitions are always really transformations.

CHAPTER SIXTEEN

The Grail

With the founding of the Bayreuth festival, Wagner's career makes a kind of return to its beginnings in the world of theatrical romance. *My Life* recollects the impression anything connected with the stage made on the young Wagner, in a passage I quoted in the first chapter:

> . . . a set, or even a flat . . . or a costume or even only a characteristic piece of one, appeared to me to emanate from another world, and be in a certain sense interesting as apparitions, and contact with all this would serve as a lever to lift me out of a monotonous everyday reality into that fascinating demoniacal realm. Everything connected with the theatre had for me the charm of mystery, an attraction amounting to intoxication. . . . (*ML* 13)

It might seem perverse to assert a link across fifty years between this childish enchantment and the Festspielhaus project. What to the ten-year-old Wagner looked like fairyland must have felt in the 1870s like the most deadeningly pragmatic of places. 'Everyday reality' rarely made itself so strongly felt in his life as when he set himself to rounding up the money needed for the building, and the sets and costumes and singers needed for the performances. The child's fantasy depends of course on never looking too closely at the machine which houses the ghost; make-believe works best when you can't see it being made. At Bayreuth, Wagner was forced to operate every cog in the machine, pulling every string that made the stage pictures move and sing. Like an operatic Wizard of Oz, he found himself hidden behind a curtain manipulating everything that would have appeared to the child as 'demoniacal' magic. There is a great deal of evidence to indicate just how disillusioning he found the experience of the 1876 festival in particular, when the swimming nixies and grim dragons of his imagination had to be mechanized and stitched together. 'I feel only a dull pain in my soul', he wrote to the soprano Lilli Lehmann about a week after the last performance, adding '[t]here is so much that we shall have to put right next year' (*L* 859). Doing things differently might not have helped, though, when the root of the disenchantment lay in doing them at all. An anecdote tells of him jokingly remarking that having invented the invisible orchestra, he now wished he could come up with an invisible stage.

Nevertheless, the Festspielhaus tries its very best to express the magic of stage illusion. Its fundamental architectural principle is the abolition of the audience's 'everyday reality' and a corresponding fullness of illusionistic representation on the other side of the proscenium. The vast stage, surrounded by expansive areas for storing and manoeuvring scenery, permitted a full range of scenic effects even with the bulky demands of late nineteenth-century technology. Hiding the orchestra and doubling the proscenium simultaneously distanced the audience from the action and presented it to them as a self-contained stage picture, effectively anticipating the entirely imaginary yet powerfully immediate 'space' conjured up on a film screen. Darkening and simplifying the auditorium changed it from the social space of conventional theatregoing into 'an actual "theatron", i.e. a room made ready for no other purpose than . . . looking' (V 335). In this respect, it is once again a standing monument to the particular character of Wagner's genius. Nothing could be more characteristic of him than the devotion of enormous care and energy to the production of illusion. If childhood fantasy inevitably collapses in the face of 'everyday reality', Bayreuth is conceived as a systematic effort to reverse that fall. All its technological ingenuity and architectural innovativeness together adds up to the 'lever' referred to in the passage from *My Life*, a tool for shifting experience across into the territory of romance.

With the perfection of this machinery, Wagner's art turns itself finally and completely into 'apparitions'; an art of the visible clothed in the aura of invisibility, of manifestations from another world. This is the character of romantic opera, with its heightened sense of fiction and the supernatural. One doesn't usually think of the Wagner of the 1870s and 80s having anything to do with romantic opera, although considering how deeply Wagner's early sensibilities were saturated in the magical illusionism of the genre – the same section of *My Life* mentions that Weber's *Der Freischütz* in particular 'affected my imagination with characteristic intensity' (*ML* 13) – it is extraordinary that he should have left the conventions of romance so far behind. There is really very little about *Tannhäuser* to indicate that its composer could also produce *Siegfried* or *Tristan*. At Bayreuth, nevertheless, Wagner not only resurrects the idea of a magical theatre, but works out that idea with an earnestness and a concentration that would have been inconceivable to him in the 1840s. *Lohengrin* was his farewell to romantic opera, and it shows us exactly why the genre is being left behind. In its story, the gap between this world – 'everyday reality' – and the magical otherworld of romance becomes tragically unbridgeable.

Elsa cannot simply live out her dream; she falls victim to her nagging sense of the difference between vision and reality, her inability to pretend that Lohengrin is real and no questions asked. Again, though, the Festspielhaus is a kind of return to the perfectly romantic condition of *Lohengrin's* first act, where a dream comes to life and works its magic in the everyday world, before the troubling need to ask questions arises. Its design suppresses everything that might remind the audience that they are in a theatre, to the point that watching an opera there is supposed to be an experience that transcends illusion. Art's dreams are made to look as if they have come true; so Wagner both inherits and intensifies the aesthetics of romance. Devoting the building to perfect illusionism, he at the same time tries to banish that sense of a *deliberate* illusion, of make-believe, which romantic opera's overblown and exotic fantasies necessarily carry with them. It's as if he takes the child's intoxicating submission to fantasy and insists that it is real experience, no pleasurable temporary indulgence in theatre's imaginary space but an actual exposure to the magical otherworld. Elsa's problem is that she knows she is being asked to suspend her disbelief. One hesitates to imply an exact analogy between Lohengrin and Tinkerbell, but that's how romance works; if you choose not to believe it, it goes away. With the completion of the Bayreuth project, Wagner makes the final necessary adjustment: there is now (the theatre seems to say) no choice but to believe.

In *Lohengrin*, romance dwells out of sight, in a far-off land, inaccessible by everyday paths ('In fernem Land, unnahbar euren Schritten . . .'). There, the swan knight tells his enraptured audience, a sacred chalice resides, given by angels into the keeping of the purest of men, invincibly holy, withdrawing from any profane touch. The opera's prelude charts this combination of revelation and concealment; a shimmering haze of sound swells, fills itself out, descends, reveals itself in glory, then swiftly retreats into the almost inaudibly lofty registers from whence it came. Nothing could be more magically sublime than the Grail and its attendant sounds in *Lohengrin*, but equally, nothing could be more remote and distant. In the 1840s, that is the story of romance. Illusion preserves its enchantment by keeping its distance from the everyday world. With the building of the Festspielhaus, though, comes the creation of an opera which returns to the world of *Lohengrin* while abandoning its conditions. *Parsifal* takes place within the very same 'distant land' Lohengrin tells his listeners they can never approach. We are there as soon as the curtain goes up, and by the end of the first act the opera has led us into the heart of Montsalvat, allowed us to watch the sacred rite, and exposed the chalice itself. Indeed, whereas the whole plot of *Lohengrin* turns on concealment, on the hiddenness of the Grail, the action of *Parsifal* revolves around unveiling it. Lohengrin explains in the course of his narration:

| So hehrer Art doch ist des Grales Segen, | The Grail's blessing is of so high a nature, |
| enthüllt – muß er des Laien Auge fliehn. . . . | that if unveiled, it must flee the eyes of the uninitiated. . . . |

'Enthüllt' refers to the process of revealing something by removing a covering: being literally discovered, or disclosed (un-closed). It is the commanding word at the centre of the ritual in *Parsifal*, the word which makes the rite happen. 'Enthüllet den Gral!' Titurel intones, ordering Amfortas to open the concealing shrine in which the vessel is kept; and after his son's agonized protests have exhausted themselves, he repeats 'Enthüllet den Gral!' and the ceremony begins. As Parsifal assumes the leadership of the brotherhood, he re-initiates the rite with the same formula (the opera's last words but for the ethereal final chorus):

| Nicht soll der mehr verschlossen sein: | No longer shall it be locked away: |
| Enthüllet den Gral, öffnet den Schrein! | Reveal the Grail, open the shrine! |

Parsifal displays what *Lohengrin* keeps hidden. This isn't a breaking of the earlier opera's taboo. After all, Gurnemanz sounds a lot like Lohengrin when he tells the naïve boy that no earthly path leads to the Grail ('kein Weg führt zu ihm durch das Land'), and that no one can approach it unless called. Magic still has to hide itself away from the profane touch of everyday reality. The difference between *Lohengrin* and *Parsifal* is simply the existence of the festival theatre. On the stage of Wagner's own temple (where *Parsifal*, of course, was exclusively meant to be performed), mystery need not hide itself to preserve its integrity. Illusion and reality, the two worlds between which romantic opera crosses and which it loves to set in opposition to each other, are melded. In any theatre other than the Festspielhaus, Elsa might confront magic with her disenchanted questions – what are you? where do you come from? – and receive the answer that it is all smoke and mirrors, greasepaint and stage fire. At Bayreuth, where the contradiction between stage illusion and visible reality seems to be banished, the answers instead are: I am sacred and I come from a higher realm. The Grail sheds its radiance over the stage and into the auditorium, crossing the invisible space occupied by the orchestra and entering the audience's world. In doing so, it signifies the fulfilment of the child's excited fantasies. In *Lohengrin*, the 'other world' that arouses the ten-year-old's intoxicated imagination has to be kept strictly 'other'. Romance's aesthetics work by insisting on the distance travelled between magic and the everyday, so that art becomes a brief window opening out onto vistas of enchanted terrain – scenes which (like Lohengrin's audience at the end of Act III) we can hear about and wonder at, but never enter. *Parsifal*, however, lets us occupy enchanted space, just as the Festspielhaus (by comparison with other nineteenth-century theatres) lets us mistake stage illusion for real presence.

All Wagner's work – dramatic and literary – is about itself. Other composers of opera have been interested in things like human passions or moral challenges or social relations or political issues; what interests Wagner's imagination more than anything else is art. That half-comical confession of childish excitability in *My Life* reveals an early fascination with a kind of power, the 'rough magic' (Prospero's phrase) of theatre. As Wagner's career goes on, the fascination becomes conscious of itself, and his work begins to ask itself over and over again about the nature of the imaginary, the illusory, about the peculiar power of stage representation. The romantic operas deal with captivating supernatural powers; the *Ring* presents itself as a new kind of drama, a manifestation of the art-work of the future, and at the same time profoundly concerns itself with the telling of stories; *Tristan* seeks a mode of existence separate from the laws of the everyday; *Meistersinger* argues over the nature of inspiration and the civic function of art; *Parsifal* hopes to turn opera into sacramental *Bühnenweihfestspiel*. Nor is it only a matter of the operas' explicit themes and structures. More fundamentally, Wagner's work goes on working deeper and deeper into the question of how it appears, and what kind of power it exerts. One feels this most clearly in its extraordinary expressive range, its endlessly inventive recourse to the most exaggerated and intensified musical and dramatic modes, its sense of always being at full throttle even in its moments of serenity or restraint. Out of this quality comes the realization that what it most habitually aims for is not artistic perfection but artistic *effect*. It's as if Wagner dedicated himself to learning the thaumaturgy which impressed itself on him in his childhood. (I mean that by way of illustration only; this book intends no claims of any sort about his biography.) From this perspective, there is no further to go than Bayreuth. The building (and the connected notion of exemplary festival performances) stands as a self-contained solution to Wagner's most fundamental concern: how to endow his art with its proper nature, and to place it in the proper relation to its audience.

We have to think of it not simply as a pragmatic project, impelled by professional dissatisfaction at the way opera was performed, but rather as an extension of the operas themselves, a creation in parallel with musico-dramatic composition. The scores themselves contain the dream of music as an invisible atmosphere and of drama as a separate and self-contained ideal world (in architectural terms, a hidden orchestra pit and an auditorium focussed entirely on the stage). Less so *Holländer*, perhaps, since it proceeds in a series of relatively conventional dialogues and monologues, and tends to use the orchestra as a way of accompanying or 'illustrating' the stage action; but with the first scene of *Tannhäuser*, a visionary pageant displayed in a magical recess and dramatized by orchestral sound, Wagner's operas begin to imagine a Festspielhaus for themselves, where music will appear as an emanation of the spirit of the drama, and the action will appear like a vision unfurled before the audience. It is meant as the space in which art achieves its effects, where the intense desire pervading the operas – their effort to present themselves to us as directly and irresistibly as possible – can be fully unleashed. In Wagner's thought at least, this is more than just a matter of better performances enabled by better conditions. Bayreuth exists to turn art itself into a process of revelation. It is the place where the Grail can at last be seen.

The relationship between *Parsifal* and Bayreuth hinges at its deepest level on the image of the Grail and the act of its unveiling. For the Grail is an archetypal terminus, an object whose true meaning is no more than the end of the quest to find it. The medieval romances on which Wagner drew as sources for *Lohengrin* and *Parsifal* are vague and contradictory about what it is, what it does, who is in search of it, and where it might be found, yet all the stories agree that it is the goal of the highest of quests. Like Bayreuth, it represents conclusion and fulfilment. At the moment when the Grail is found, desire is answered by revelation. Displayed on stage by *Parsifal*, it represents the terminus of Wagner's imagination in every sense, the visible sign that his work's continuous quest to reveal its power and its meanings has arrived at a consummation. When it appears, all there is to do is celebrate and worship. This is the icon around which the Festspielhaus is built, in the same way that great cathedrals have been built to house sacred relics and assemble their devotees. After Wagner's death, Cosima's strict legal and artistic control over Bayreuth led commentators to call her 'the guardian of the Grail', and when the Metropolitan Opera staged the first unauthorized performance of *Parsifal* in 1903 one German writer spoke of a *Gralsraub*, a 'theft' or 'rape' of the Grail.

In *Lohengrin*, the chalice has to remain the object of a quest rather than the end of it. Because that opera is firmly set in a human, historical world, the Grail beckons as an impossibly distant ideal. It stands as a promise or an aim, something Wagner's art can point towards. This position recurs in the *Ring*, *Tristan* and *Meistersinger*, all of which end with gestures in the direction of a redemption whose nature they have laid out in their course. Thus Sachs and Walther together define a 'holy German art' whose fruition is prophesied in the final oration; Isolde and Tristan speak obsessively of the nightworld where they belong, and in the *Liebestod* she passes out of sight into that other space; Brünnhilde promises the end of the accursed world at the end of *Götterdämmerung*, leaving a bare stage for utopia to build itself on. The end of *Lohengrin* is thoroughly ambivalent, though. The opera may herald the presence of the Grail, but it leaves the quest incomplete. Indeed it admits that by its very nature the quest is unachievable: no earthly pathways lead to the Grail. Like the prose writings that follow the completion of *Lohengrin*, it opens up an infinitely wide chasm between desire and fulfilment. Wagner's art can imagine its own perfection, but only by admitting at the same time that its goal remains remote. Hence the restless intensity of longing in *Tristan* and the *Ring*, which make the idea of perpetually elusive ends their basic dramatic and musical principle (an art of transition and deferral in the former, of reversal and retrospection in the latter). It is true that *Meistersinger* grants its own wishes, but in the form of propaganda, a solution which to my eyes at least is unworthy of Wagner's genius. Only in *Parsifal*, which resumes and satisfies the desire haunting the close of *Lohengrin*, is there a symbolic completion of art's trajectory. At Bayreuth, Wagner's work no longer needs to think of itself as wanting to be elsewhere or aiming at something out of reach. *Parsifal* secures its own fantasies of revelation and redemption (its hero doesn't need to die to be redeemed, unlike in all the other operas bar *Meistersinger*). Properly housed in the theatre it consecrates, it presents itself as the fulfilment of everything Wagnerian opera desires for itself: a work of art revealing its own transcendental nature, transforming the audience gathered to watch it, communicating its secrets without ambiguity or deferral. The Grail – more specifically, its visible presence on stage – is the symbol of this completion.

You cannot ask questions of the Grail, as Elsa learns the hard way. In this sense too it represents a terminus: the end of meaning and of interpretation. That's why it doesn't matter what sort of object it is. The only important thing is to reach it, and once that quest is complete any further questions are superfluous. Its mere presence replaces all doubts with the instantaneous and unshakable certainty of revelation. For Wagner, the theatre always hinted at this kind of knowledge. On the stage, imagination is free to operate according to its own laws, while the audience ideally consents to submit to those same laws, temporarily accepting things it knows to be impossible, surrendering to the demands of an illusory world. With *Parsifal* and Bayreuth, that romance finally turns into religion. The make-believe domain of the stage is bathed in the light of the Grail, and the imaginary laws by which its illusions are sustained are presented instead as articles of faith. If the essential character of operatic romance is its fantastical otherworldliness – the feeling that the stage conjures up an alternative space to reality – then *Parsifal* claims to make that other world fully and immediately present, no longer a temporary illusion subject to sceptical questions, but what 'On State and Religion' calls a dogma. With the icon of the Grail, art presents itself at last as an incontrovertible reality of its own. It is no longer 'about' anything; it doesn't have to make that sort of sideways reference to the world outside the theatre. It isn't a mirror held up to nature, enabling its audience to reflect on what they see. The Festspielhaus turns out the light by which nature is visible, and replaces it with a radiance emitted from the stage. Art illuminates only itself. The domain of romance has sealed itself off from the everyday world, as thoroughly as the Grail bars all profane paths to Montsalvat. In this hermetically sealed theatrical space, no questions are supposed to be asked about how art relates to the reality it excludes.

Why, then, is the unveiling of the Grail in *Parsifal* attended with so much tension and conflict? The battle between Parsifal and Klingsor is positively inert by comparison with the internal strife within the walls of the temple. Each revelation of the chalice takes place only after a furious struggle between the communal demand to display it and Amfortas's desperation to keep it hidden. One might equally well ask the same question about the Festspielhaus. Why is its history also so persistently marked by struggles over the revelation of Wagner's art? Instead of silencing questions, Bayreuth has made a habit of raising them. Even before the advent of openly controversial – not to say confrontational – production styles in the 1950s, the festival was a magnet for various kinds of scepticism and discontent, not to mention the site of bitter struggles over control of Wagner's legacy. Like the act of disclosing the Grail, performances at Bayreuth seem to be unable to banish echoes of Elsa's disillusioning doubt. As *Lohengrin* demonstrates, revelation is a dangerous business. The only immaculate purity is perfect concealment, avoiding all contact with the mundane world. This is the thought that torments Amfortas; he can't bear to reveal the Grail because doing so brings its sublime perfection into direct contact with his own tainted mortality. Wagner's half-joking aspiration towards an invisible theatre involves the same recognition that disclosing his operas in performance necessarily exposes them to profane hands and eyes. Although the Grail is in itself the image of consummate perfection and of the resolution of all doubts and uncertainties, the actual moment of its contact with an imperfect world is highly charged with tension.

This, after all, is the other basic meaning of operatic romance. If the laws of romance free the imagination from its obligations to reality, allowing the artist to assert his visions as otherworldly truths, it's nevertheless also true that its stories repeatedly express the dangerous incompatibility of enchanted terrain and ordinary experience, the tragic conjunctions between its magical Lohengrins and its human Elsas. This was pre-eminently true of the genre of German romantic opera which so entranced the young Wagner. In that reminiscence of childhood enchantment recalled in *My Life*, the excited sense of danger is palpable: the theatre is a 'demoniacal realm', and merely touching anything associated with it offers the thrilling sense of crossing into forbidden territory. Wagner's own brand of romance keeps returning to that moment of transition, investing it with conflicted energy: Senta poised on the brink of dedicating herself to the supernatural world, Tannhäuser constantly pulled back and forth across the border between Venus's and the Landgrave's domains, Lohengrin's forbidden question irresistibly drawing attention to the precariousness of his magical presence. Acts of revelation turn out to be unstable; that is why both *Parsifal* and Bayreuth attempt to perfect the process. Achievements of equally consummate mastery, they endow romance's illusions with unprecedented power, seeking to submerge the tensions of the earlier operas in the Grail's pure radiance. Yet even within *Parsifal*, revelation is a struggle.

The best way to get a sense of what this means is to visit the basement of the museum that now occupies Wagner's house Wahnfried in the town of Bayreuth. On display here, in a darkened room, are a number of original stage models from early productions, most dating from the period of Cosima's direction of the festival (1883–1906), a few from the following two decades. The little boxes of light and colour preserve exact details of how those early stagings must have appeared. We have other records of those productions, in the form of two-dimensional paintings or photographs, but although they convey visual schemes and scenic arrangements, they give too strong a sense of pictorial rather than theatrical space. They position us perfectly in relation to the perspectival illusion of the stage scenery, making the set look like a painterly representation of whatever location it is supposed to represent. They also blur the details just enough to hide our sense of stage machinery, particularly so of course in the case of paintings such as Joseph Hoffmann's designs for the 1876 sets, which are still the most widely-known representations of the visual aspect of the first *Ring* cycle. A painted or engraved reproduction of a stage picture is necessarily going to translate the visual language of theatre into something closer to a direct representation of nature: it will take a prop that is supposed to represent a tree (say) and make it look even more tree-like. Early photographs have something of the same quality: they're fuzzy enough to hide the artifice of assembled props and painted flats. In the models preserved at Wahnfried, though, we get a sudden, very startling glimpse of the mechanics of illusion. Each scene reveals itself as the product of an arrangement of painted flats and three-dimensional props (often concealing a series of stairs and platforms), all reproduced in miniature. Looking around the models from different angles, what we see is not a scenic illusion, or even a representation of imaginary space, but a wonderfully intricate contrivance in *real* space. We observe how each separate flat produces a specific part of the stage picture, placed in careful relation to the others. We notice how the props allow certain kinds of movement around the stage and into the wings. Everything looks like artifice, rather than (as in a photograph) an approximate representation of some natural location (forest hut or hall of song or ship's deck).

At the same time, it's impossible not to be struck by the thought of how strange – from our later point of view – Wagner's operas must have looked in these settings. Though the Bayreuth theatre was quite advanced for its day, and has remained technically innovative throughout its history, the nineteenth-century stage apparatus now looks unimaginably creaky and crude, and the dominant visual style – a lush naturalism – strikes the contemporary eye as something out of a comic-strip. (Even in 1876 and 1882, many in the audience found the scenic representations weak and unimaginative.) It is all but impossible to imagine Wagner's dramas clothed in the forms preserved for us in these models. The winged helmets and bearskins of the 1876 *Ring* have in fact become a kind of cultural joke about Wagner in general, turning up in cartoons and parodies as visual signs for a specifically Wagnerian kind of silliness. They are elements in a scenic vocabulary which seems utterly remote from us: the dead language of nineteenth-century romantic natur- alism and heroism. Equally, the stage properties used to convey such visual effects – the flats and constructions and props – strike us as only drawing more attention to their artificiality the more they try to pass themselves off as nature. Amid all the artistic and historical significance of the early festivals, amid all the dense theoretical and symbolic weight attached to them, the models in the Wahnfried basement intrude with a disorientingly strange reminder of how the first *Ring* cycle and the first *Parsifal* (and the subsequent Bayreuth premieres between 1886 and 1901) must actually have revealed them- selves. As the visitor stares at them, the whole domain of romance, the whole apparatus of transcendence constructed so surely by Wagner's work, collapses like Klingsor's castle. Because the stage technology and scenic language which they record look so foreign, our sense of what Wagner's operas were origi- nally like changes instantly. One stops thinking about emotional impressions, acoustic marvels, dramatic impact, or indeed about any artistic questions at all. The imagination fixes instead on the physical form of the works in per- formance. (An exercise which partly reproduces the effect of looking at the Wahnfried models is to remind oneself that Brünnhilde's horse Grane is required by the stage directions to appear at various points in the drama – and appear he did in all early Bayreuth productions. Now picture to yourself the closing moments of *Götterdämmerung* with a live horse being led around the scene.)

This is an unfair reaction, of course, a reflex of prejudice. The models are fascinating and exquisitely beautiful artefacts; and in fact nothing else in Wahnfried has quite such a tangible historical aura about it, such a power to open a window onto the past. The point is that our scenic expectations – indeed, our fundamental visual instincts – have changed beyond recognition since the early decades of the twentieth century. What actually confronts us in those models is something otherwise taken for granted: our sense of the possible visual forms of Wagner's operas, our basic and instinctive sense of their *appearance*. It's only when presented with a completely alien form of visual representation that we realize how deeply our overall idea of the operas is bound up with our assumptions about what (roughly) they look like. Even those who have never seen the operas in performance will still have some internal visual vocabulary, however vague, which is instinctively applied to them. In my own case it derived from the cover pictures of the boxed LP recordings of the *Ring* in my parents' record collection. Those four images were enough to crystallize a dim sense of intense, misty light, a visual sense which, however faint, became part of my idea of what the *Ring* was as I listened my way through the recordings. For the most part, our overall idea of the operas is to do with their sound and their story. Thinking of what the *Ring* is, one is largely imagining to oneself a musical and dramatic artefact. With due allowance for the intervention of different conductors, these aspects are essentially derived from Wagner himself: he is the author of the musico-dramatic substance which forms most of our idea of his works. Our sense of what they *look* like, however, has very little to do with Wagner. As we've seen, even Wagner himself was alienated by the visual forms that appeared in front of him in 1876 (though not those of 1882: and, correspondingly, the basic scenic vocabulary of *Parsifal* has proved to be surprisingly coherent over much of the work's performance history). When we encounter a scenic style utterly unlike our basic expectations, we're made to realize how different this aspect of our idea of the operas is from the musical and dramatic dimensions. Story and score can't really change that much, but a work's appearance is subject to extraordinary alterations, depending on stage technology, the visual conventions predominant at any particular cultural moment, the habits of directors, and so on. Looking at the models of early Bayreuth performances, one is forcibly reminded that there is no such thing as a 'correct' or authoritative scenic form of the works: partly because these productions, despite being authorized by Wagner himself or his immediate heirs, look so peculiar to our eyes; more importantly, because they so clearly show how much the operas' visual appearance depends on the conventions and mechanics of theatrical illusion, which have changed dramatically since 1876, and will of course go on changing.

What happens when we encounter unfamiliar production styles is that our idea of what the work 'is' – the idea we take for granted – is suddenly confronted by a feeling that the work could be something different. No one has to go to Wahnfried to appreciate the point. The confrontation is played out over and over again, all over the opera-performing world, every time a 'controversial' new production of one of Wagner's works makes an appearance. It's almost always the visual sphere – what the operas look like – that turns out to be the point of controversy. After we had watched Act I of *Tristan und Isolde* in Heine Müller's highly abstract 1993 Bayreuth production (designed by Erich Wonder), a friend said 'there's supposed to be a boat': by which he meant that he expected – and that Wagner's stage directions demand – some kind of literal representation of a boat, some boat-like appearance. When such visual expectations are contravened, the effect is often a sense that we are watching something other than the opera we thought we were going to see (this at any rate is the tenor of many of the angry comments that inevitably follow controversial new stagings). In fact, the controversy itself largely depends on this sense of missed expectations. Few productions in the history of Wagner on stage have been as contentious as Patrice Chéreau's 1976 Bayreuth *Ring* (designed by Richard Peduzzi), but the root cause of contention did not in fact lie in the staging itself. Because the production was widely distributed on television and video, there were many people – myself included – for whom it was the first *Ring* they had ever seen. Without a prior and strongly different sense of what the tetralogy 'ought' to look like, there was no controversy: Chéreau's version, utterly convincing on its own terms, simply became my idea of the *Ring* – thus ensuring that I would be suitably surprised and unsettled by subsequent stagings. Indeed, once the 1976 *Ring* had become part of operagoers' expectations, the controversy faded just as easily. By the end of its run at Bayreuth it was being hailed as a classic version, and its own brand of naturalism has become a benchmark by which more avant-garde stagings can now be criticized. The same thing happened with Wieland Wagner's postwar 'New Bayreuth' style. On its first appearances, audiences with traditional expectations were predictably stunned, if not outraged. Within a few years, the timeless and mythic quality of Wieland's productions, and especially their smooth visual abstraction, had become conventional, and so formed the expectations of a new generation – just in time for those assumptions to be shattered by the politically and historically specific style of Chéreau or Götz Friedrich, whose 1972 *Tannhäuser* marked the moment when 'New Bayreuth' became 'old Bayreuth'.

All debates about new productions of Wagner testify to the fact that the appearance of his operas is both part of, yet at the same time slightly different from, their *nature*, their existence. We cannot help thinking of them as necessarily having visual form (and of course, despite the distractions of audio recording, visual form is properly an aspect of their being: they are theatrical artefacts). At the same time, we are forced to realize that their visual form is not like their aural and linguistic form. There is a disjunction: difference and change creep in. Between what the operas *are* (printed score, libretto and stage directions) and the way they *appear* (revealed in performance), there is a transition. A hidden distance is crossed, as between Acts II and III of *Parsifal*, and the gap is full of tension and difficulty ('Kämpfe und Streite', as

Parsifal puts it: 'struggles and battles'). Making the transition, the operas are shifting from the domain of art into that of artifice. Their purely aesthetic nature is muddied by that other aspect of their being, compromised by the errant, erratic world of appearances.

The feeling that a drama we thought we knew has appeared in an altered guise, still itself and yet changed (like Kundry in Act III), reminds us how deeply art's magic illusions are bound up with the materials of the stage. This, I suggest, is the real secret of the childish excitement remembered in *My Life*. The language of the brief autobiographical passage is entirely that of romance: a spell is cast, a supernatural realm seems to be opened, the mundane world dims before it, and the entranced hero falls into helpless 'intoxication'. All of these perfectly conventional ideas recur with the utmost majesty and intensity throughout Wagner's work, symbolizing in every case the power of art itself, the irresistible seductions of the operas' own 'fascinating demoniacal realm'. Yet the vehicle of this magic, as Wagner remembers it, is the mechanical apparatus of theatrical make-believe: 'a set, or even a flat . . . or a costume or even only a characteristic piece of one' – the very objects which, as recorded in the Wahnfried models or the early cast photographs, seem now to speak of everything about Wagner's art that is *not* imbued with otherworldly potency. Though that art is indeed intoxicated with romantic yearnings towards transcendence, there is something compelling about the thought of those desires being stimulated by fragments of theatrical detritus. Wagner conjures up visions of Montsalvat while holding in his hands a piece of a fake temple of the Grail.

The joint fantasy of *Parsifal* and the Festspielhaus is to present Wagner's work as if it were just 'there': immediate, present, fully possessing our experience, communicating itself as directly as possible. It's the consummation of an idea central to the aesthetics of romanticism, the dream of art as an autonomous imaginative world. This idea is made literal in the Bayreuth theatre, with its unprecedented emphasis on the illusionistic stage space, and symbolized by the holy Grail, an icon of pure and immediate revelation. By hiding the orchestra, making the audience invisible to itself, and cancelling the usual social activities attendant on opera, the Festspielhaus tries to forget that it is just a theatre; it wants the dramas it displays to appear in the guise of real presence, not artifice. By staging a sacramental celebration of its own content, *Parsifal* tries to forget that it is just a work of art; it also wants to appear as an actual rite of sanctification, not merely the representation of one. Opera and theatre each strive to make transcendence manifest, to bring us into the presence of romance. Like the notion of 'deeds of Music brought to sight' (V 303 – the more usual translation is 'deeds of music made visible'), or the definition of 'Dogma' (IV 26) in 'On State and Religion', they imagine something immaterial and otherworldly becoming incarnate without losing any of its aura of sublimity. This is Wagner's art's most exalted idea of itself: an earthly revelation of a higher world, redemption glimpsed for real.

Once again, the Grail is the central symbol. As the *Lohengrin* prelude tells (according to Wagner's 1853 programme note), the sacred chalice is a heavenly object which was miraculously carried down to earth and placed among men. The prelude goes on to depict it being withdrawn again, but that is the tragedy of romance; in the 1870s and 80s Wagner simply stops the motion halfway, leaving the Grail visible on stage, and romance becomes religion. Incomparably more than any other object, the Grail itself is simply 'there', as Wagner's art imagines itself to be. It symbolizes presence itself: whatever it is, whatever it does, all that matters about it is that it be in our keeping and before our eyes. Representing its own nature in the icon of the Grail, Wagner's work wants presence to negate interpretation. The question of what the Grail actually is – a critical, interpretative question, a question about meaning – is supposed to be cancelled out by the mere act of the chalice being found and revealed. At least part of the reason *Parsifal* unveils its light is that it wishes to blind us with radiance.

Yet it's this very question which is inescapably raised in the theatre. Each time one of the operas takes on a new theatrical form, we are prompted to ask again: what is the work? Our sense of difference, of change, undercuts the idea that the operas are simply 'there'. Their visual aspect, their appearance, interferes with the romantic perfection of their presence. Instead, the moment of revelation, the point of contact between art and the world, comes with a question mark attached. It's a moment of uncertainty; and uncertainty invites interpretation. That sense of estrangement felt so strongly in the basement of Wahnfried is the fundamental condition of interpretative efforts. We can't start looking for answers until we feel that a question has been put to us. Nothing operates more powerfully to open up space for such questions than the mechanics of theatrical artifice, the endlessly variable visual dimension of Wagner's works, because the effect of those works' appearance on stage is to make us wonder *how* his art reveals itself – rather than just sitting back and surrendering to its revelations.

When particularly controversial productions make their appearance, one of the most predictable responses is the outcry that the director and designer have set themselves against Wagner and the work, resisting or contradicting the very opera (and its author) they were supposed to be performing. To an extent, this is perfectly true. There is indeed an essential and powerful tendency in Wagner's art to deny interpretation, to banish all questions, to refuse all possibility of difference, a tendency that attains its *ne plus ultra* in the image of the Grail. My claim throughout this book has been that to a greater and more significant extent, the charge is absolutely false. At heart, Wagner's work is riven with tension and preoccupied with change, raising unresolved questions that are far too energetic to be suppressed by its fantasy that it knows all the answers. Elsa's interrogations can't be silenced; and even in Montsalvat itself, in the holy of Wagnerian holies, these tensions break out in tormented strife at the moment when the Grail is supposed to be revealed. Asked to show itself, Wagner's art erupts with uncertainty about its own nature. There could be no more apt manifestation of this quality than the shock of estrangement generated by an opera's unexpected new appearance. Over the past hundred years, innovative stagings have expressed a truth Wagner grasped at the age of ten, one his work never forgot: art's transcendental romance is founded on the strange artifice of appearance.

Interpreting Wagner means asking his work to show us its questions, its uncertainties and ambivalences, its errant restlessness, its unhealed wounds. Hard as it often strains to hide these pressures, they go on shaping it right through his career, all the way to the very end of *Parsifal* in the Festspielhaus in 1882. Even at the climactic instant when the sacred light of revelation and redemption is conjured again out of the darkness, the opera sounds out an appeal for exposure, a demand to be brought to sight and so into the view of our questioning gaze. Uncover the Grail; open the shrine.

Notes and Further Reading

CHAPTER ONE   *The romance of opera*

The relationship between Nietzsche and Wagner has been intensively studied: for a philosophical standpoint, see Roger Hollinrake, *Nietzsche, Wagner, and the Philosophy of Pessimism* (London: Allen & Unwin, 1982); a more broadly musical and aesthetic account is Dietrich Fischer-Dieskau, *Wagner and Nietzsche* (New York: Seabury, 1976). The history of German romantic opera is best traced through the relevant chapters of a recent authoritative survey, John Warrack, *German Opera: From the Beginnings to Wagner* (Cambridge: Cambridge University Press, 2001). See also Winton Dean's section on 'German Opera' in *The New Oxford History of Music, Vol. 8: The Age of Beethoven, 1790–1830* (London: Oxford University Press, 1982), and, for a broader overview which includes some excellent illustrative material, Barry Millington, 'The Nineteenth Century: Germany', in Roger Parker, ed., *The Oxford Illustrated History of Opera* (Oxford: Oxford University Press, 1994). For a full selection of writings on musical aesthetics in general from the period 1719–1848, see Peter le Huray and James Day, eds, *Music and Aesthetics in the Eighteenth and Early-Nineteenth Centuries* (Cambridge: Cambridge University Press, 1981).

1   Friedrich Nietzsche, *The Birth of Tragedy and The Case of Wagner*, trans. Walter Kaufmann (New York: Vintage, 1967), pp. 172–3.
2   Edward Lippman, *A History of Western Musical Aesthetics* (Lincoln: University of Nebraska Press, 1992), p. 190.
3   See Lippman, p. 193.
4   Oliver Strunk, ed., *Source Readings in Music History from Classical Antiquity to the Romantic Era* (New York: Norton, 1950), p. 803.
5   From Hoffmann's 'Der Dichter und der Komponist' ('The Poet and the Composer', 1819–21); Strunk, p. 788.
6   Strunk, p. 804.
7   Quoted in Lippman, p. 187.
8   Strunk, pp. 780–1.
9   Strunk, p. 788.
10 Barry Millington, 'The Nineteenth Century: Germany', in Roger Parker, ed., *The Oxford Illustrated History of Opera* (Oxford: Oxford University Press, 1994), p. 215.
11 Strunk, p. 760.
12 Eduard Hanslick, *Music Criticisms, 1846–99*, ed. and trans. Henry Pleasants (Harmondsworth: Penguin, 1950), pp. 35–6.

13 Nietzsche, p. 171.
14 ibid.

CHAPTER TWO *Myths of the artist*

Paul Bekker, *Richard Wagner: His Life in His Work* (1931; repr., Westport, CT: Greenwood, 1971), points out the autobiographical significance of the heroes of *Holländer*, *Tannhäuser* and *Lohengrin*. The aesthetic implications of Wagner's writings from Paris are very interestingly discussed in Thomas S. Grey, *Wagner's Musical Prose* (Cambridge: Cambridge University Press, 1995). The essays collected in David C. Large and William Weber, eds, *Wagnerism in European Culture and Politics* (Ithaca: Cornell University Press, 1984), illustrate the depth and breadth of Wagner's influence, far beyond his exclusively artistic legacy; for one aspect of the latter, see Raymond Furness, *Wagner and Literature* (Manchester: Manchester University Press, 1982). On early nineteenth-century anti-Semitism, see Léon Poliakov, *The History of Anti-Semitism, Vol. 3: From Voltaire to Wagner* (London: Routledge & Kegan Paul, 1975); Jacob Katz, *From Prejudice to Destruction: Anti-Semitism, 1700–1933* (Cambridge: Harvard University Press, 1980); and, in relation to romantic thought and culture, Paul Lawrence Rose, *Revolutionary Antisemitism in Germany from Kant to Wagner* (Princeton: Princeton University Press, 1990). Some flavour of opera as a social event in the mid-nineteenth century is conveyed by John Rosselli's brief but evocative section 'Opera as a Social Occasion', in *The Oxford Illustrated History of Opera* (see notes to chapter 1). For a detailed study of Wagner's actual relation to Betthoven's legacy – as opposed to the fiction of 'A Pilgrimage to Beethoven' – see Klaus Kropfinger, *Wagner and Beethoven* (1974; English ed., Cambridge: Cambridge University Press, 1991).

CHAPTER THREE *Enchantment*

For the English reader, relatively little substantial critical attention has been paid to the romantic operas. Thomas S. Grey, ed., *Richard Wagner: Der fliegende Holländer* (Cambridge: Cambridge University Press, 2000), in the Cambridge Opera Handbooks series, gathers seven excellent studies of the first of them. Otherwise, the brief essays collected in the English National Opera/Royal Opera series of Opera Guides (originally under the general editorship of Nicholas John) offer the best selection. The volume on *Tannhäuser* (1988) is no. 12 in the series, that on *Lohengrin* (1993) no. 47. Particularly notable are Carolyn Abbate on the music of *Tannhäuser* and Thomas S. Grey on *Lohengrin's* musico-dramatic style. Among surveys of Wagner's work which discuss the early operas' progression towards the composer's mature achievement, see in particular the relevant sections of Carl Dahlhaus, *Richard Wagner's Music Dramas* (Cambridge: Cambridge University Press, 1979), and Barry Millington, *Wagner* (1984; rev. ed., London: J.M. Dent, 1992; Princeton: Princeton University Press, 1992). Examples of 'bewitched' criticism of Wagner are too numerous to cite. Michael Tanner, *Wagner* (London: HarperCollins, 1996; Princeton: Princeton University Press, 1996), is an interesting recent case of a generally thoughtful study which at crucial moments decides that its subject is in fact beyond analysis and interpretation.

1   Ulrich Müller and Peter Wapnewski, eds, *Wagner Handbook*, trans. John Deathridge (Cambridge: Harvard University Press, 1992), p. 107.

CHAPTER FOUR   *Disenchantment*

The political and cultural meanings of Parisian 'grand opera' are explored in Jane Fulcher, *The Nation's Image: French Grand Opera as Politics and Politicized Art* (Cambridge: Cambridge University Press, 1987). Wagner's turn to a revolutionary historical consciousness under the influence of Feuerbach in particular is lucidly explained in Bryan Magee, *Wagner and Philosophy* (London: Penguin, 2000). All general critical studies of Wagner pay at least some attention to the transition from more traditional operatic forms to his mature style; those by Dahlhaus and Millington (cited in the notes to chapter 3) give particularly succinct accounts. Contexts for Wagner's originality are explored in Robert T. Laudon, *Sources of the Wagnerian Synthesis* (Salzburg: Musikverlag Katzbider, 1979). More specifically, Grey's *Wagner's Musical Prose* (see notes to chapter 2) offers a subtle and powerful argument about the developing possibilities of a 'speaking' or semiotic music in Wagner's work.

1   *The Works of Heinrich Heine*, trans. C.G. Leland, 12 vols (London: Heinemann, 1891–1905), vol. 4, p. 244.
2   See Carolyn Abbate, 'Orpheus and the Underworld', in Opera Guide 39: *Tannhäuser* (London: John Calder, 1988).

CHAPTER FIVE   *Writing the future*

On the prelude to *Das Rheingold*, see Warren Darcy, *Wagner's 'Das Rheingold'* (Oxford: Clarendon, 1993). Helpful paraphrases of Wagner's theories can be found in Alan David Aberbach, *The Ideas of Richard Wagner* (Lanham, MD: University Press of America, 1984), and in John Deathridge and Carl Dahlhaus, *The New Grove Wagner* (New York: Norton, 1984). See also L.J. Rather, *Reading Wagner* (Baton Rouge: Louisiana State University Press, 1990). An introduction to the Young Hegelian philosopher most influential on Wagner in his revolutionary period is Eugene Kamenka, *The Philosophy of Ludwig Feuerbach* (London: Routledge & Kegan Paul, 1970). Analysis of the role of anti-Semitism in Wagner's theoretical thinking and his artistic practice presents hugely difficult problems; though some will feel that the book is too polemical to be critically effective, Paul Lawrence Rose's *Wagner: Race and Revolution* (New Haven and London: Yale University Press, 1992) marshals detailed historical evidence in support of a compelling basic thesis. See also Marc Weiner's book cited in the notes to chapter 13. The governing sexual metaphor of *Opera and Drama* is highlighted in Frank W. Glass, *The Fertilizing Seed: Wagner's Concept of the Poetic Intent* (Ann Arbor: UMI Research Press, 1983), a study which makes the idea central to Wagner's whole creative practice. Grey's *Wagner's Musical Prose* (see notes to chapter 2) also explores the gendered language of *Opera and Drama*. The subject has been richly complicated and extended in Jean-Jacques Nattiez, *Wagner Androgyne* (1990; English ed., Princeton: Princeton University Press, 1993), a brilliantly adventurous essay in Wagner's peculiar (and, in Nattiez's reading, peculiarly consistent) hermeneutics.

CHAPTER SIX   *Staging the future*

Two articles by Warren Darcy reflect on Wagner's alterations to the conclusion of the *Götterdämmerung* libretto: 'The Pessimism of the *Ring*', Opera Quarterly 4 (1986), 24–48; 'Redeemed from Rebirth', in Leroy R. Shaw, Nancy R. Cirillo and Marion S. Miller, eds, *Wagner in Retrospect* (Amsterdam: Rodopi, 1987). Very many books have been devoted in English alone to the meanings of the *Ring* tetralogy. A sense of the changing possibilities of socio-political interpretation could be gained from George Bernard Shaw, *The Perfect*

Wagnerite (1898), reprinted in Dan H. Laurence, ed., *Shaw's Music*, 3 vols (New York: Dodd, Mead, 1981); Deryck Cooke, *I Saw the World End* (Oxford: Oxford University Press, 1979); and Sandra Corse, *Wagner and the New Consciousness* (London: Associated University Presses, 1990). Varieties of psychological (or psychoanalytical) interpretation can be assessed in Robert Donington, *Wagner's 'Ring' and its Symbols* (London: Faber and Faber, 1963); the last chapter of Catherine Clément, *Opera, or the Undoing of Women* (Minneapolis: University of Minnesota Press, 1988); and Nattiez's *Wagner Androgyne* (see notes to chapter 5), which also offers an ingenious reading of the *Ring* as an act of musicological criticism.

CHAPTER SEVEN *Writing the past*

Rose's *Wagner: Race and Revolution* (see notes to chapter 5) and his *Revolutionary Anti-semitism* (see notes to chapter 2) deal with the cultural stereotyping of the Jews in the mid-nineteenth century. Elizabeth Magee, *Richard Wagner and the Nibelungs* (Oxford: Clarendon, 1990), is a detailed scholarly study of Wagner's historiography and mythography in the revolutionary and post-revolutionary years. Among the mass of scholarship on Wagner's understanding and use of antiquity and legend, a quirkily interesting work which evokes the mythic dimension of his recourse to antiquarian material is Jessie L. Weston, *The Legends of the Wagner Drama* (London: D. Nutt, 1896).

1   Hanslick, *Music Criticisms*, p. 146.
2   Quoted in Ernest Newman, *The Life of Richard Wagner*, 4 vols (London: Cassell, 1933–47), vol. 2, p. 81.

CHAPTER EIGHT *Staging the past*

Deathridge and Dahlhaus's *New Grove Wagner* (see notes to chapter 5) is perhaps the most useful standard account of Wagner's revolutionary position in music history. The question of how *Opera and Drama* relates to Wagner's compositional practice is fully discussed in Jack Stein, *Richard Wagner and the Synthesis of the Arts* (Detroit: Wayne University Press, 1960), with particular reference to the use of leitmotif. The scene of Siegfried's death is the focus of David J. Levin, *Richard Wagner, Fritz Lang, and the Nibelungen* (Princeton: Princeton University Press, 1998), a penetrating study of the importance of narration (and one which reaches rather different conclusions from those implied here). Levin is responding in particular to two accounts of the *Ring's* narrative tendencies: the chapters on Wagner in Carolyn Abbate, *Unsung Voices* (Princeton: Princeton University Press, 1991), and James Treadwell, 'The *Ring* and the Conditions of Interpretation', *Cambridge Opera Journal* 7 (1995), 207–31. A sophisticated discussion of the possibilities of leitmotif can be found in Grey's *Wagner's Musical Prose* (see notes to chapter 2).

1   Theodor Adorno, *In Search of Wagner* (1952; English trans., London: Verso, 1991), p. 63.

CHAPTER NINE *The art of transition*

A full study of Wagner's comic opera in English is John Warrack, *Richard Wagner: Die Meistersinger von Nürnberg* (Cambridge: Cambridge University Press, 1994), in the Cambridge Opera Guides series. (Not surprisingly, Warrack presents a much more optimistic view of the work than the one I offer here.) The relevant volume in the Opera Guide series (no. 19) of the English National Opera/Royal Opera is also useful; that on *Tristan und Isolde* (no. 6) is disappointing. For a general account of *Tristan*'s significance in music history, the best source is again the *New Grove Wagner* (see notes to chapter 5). See also Carl Dahlhaus, *Nineteenth-Century Music* (Berkeley: University of California Press, 1989).

1   See Barry Millington, ed., *The Wagner Compendium* (London: Thames and Hudson, 1992), p. 236.

CHAPTER TEN   *Desire*

Peter Conrad, *A Song of Love and Death* (London: Chatto & Windus, 1987), is an approach to the genre of opera centred around its stagings of desire (especially forbidden or subversive desire); the sections on Wagner are rich in interesting readings. Throughout his later writings on Wagner, Nietzsche rails intermittently against the hypnotic quality of the operas. The sharpest articulation of his efforts to resist the Wagnerian spell is *Der Fall Wagner* (*The Case of Wagner*, 1888); for a compact English edition see Friedrich Nietzsche, *The Birth of Tragedy and The Case of Wagner* (New York: Vintage, 1967). By far the subtlest analysis of this hypnotic dimension of Wagner's aesthetic character – the essential dimension, in my view – is Theodor Adorno, *In Search of Wagner* (1952; English trans., London: Verso, 1991). Alas, though short, Adorno's critique is so subtle as to be almost impossibly dense. A lucid, eloquent, rather mournful description of Wagner, roughly comparable to Adorno's in its perceptive ideological critique and its appreciation of the composer's contradictoriness (though in no other ways), is Thomas Mann's essay 'The Sorrows and the Grandeur of Richard Wagner', available in Thomas Mann, *Pro and Contra Wagner* (London: Faber and Faber, 1985). Rather surprisingly, Mann's essay is still the best single general account of the kind of artist Wagner is. Wagner's use (or abuse) of Schopenhauer has been much discussed: Magee's *Wagner and Philosophy* (see notes to chapter 4) is a very recent and very clear summary, one which sees a much more direct and unambiguous influence than I am suggesting. Adorno (pp. 143–4) casts a much more sceptical eye on Wagner's adaptation of a philosophy of pessimism.

1   Adorno, *In Search of Wagner*, pp. 44–5.
2   Hanslick, *Music Criticisms*, p. 119.
3   See Ernest Newman, *Wagner Nights* (1949; repr., London: Pan, 1977), p. 414.

CHAPTER ELEVEN   *Nirvana*

Schopenhauer's thought can be pursued at second hand in Bryan Magee, *The Philosophy of Schopenhauer* (Oxford: Clarendon, 1983), and Patrick Gardiner, *Schopenhauer* (London: Penguin, 1963). With reference to various different elements of Wagner's art, Adorno's *In Search of Wagner* (see notes to chapter 10) asserts that it tends to the very opposite of resignation; and he points out that in the *Ring* as well as *Tristan* 'the ascetic ideal is itself confused with sexual desire' (p. 145).

CHAPTER TWELVE   *Politics and fantasy*

Ludwig has been a perennially fascinating subject for later biographers; the most recent of a number of English accounts is Greg King, *The Mad King* (London: Aurum, 1997). A biography which includes some specific attention to Ludwig as a patron (and victim) of the arts is Wilfrid Blunt, *The Dream King* (London: Hamish Hamilton, 1970). For the historical context of Wagner's nationalism, see Michael Hughes, *Nationalism and Society: Germany 1800–1945* (London: Edward Arnold, 1988), and Edmond Vermeil, *Germany's Three Reichs* (London: A. Dakers, 1944). The interrelations of nationalism, musicology and fascism are explored in Pamela Maxine Potter, *Most German of the Arts* (New Haven and London: Yale University Press, 1998); the story of musical culture in Nazi Germany is told in Erik Levi, *Music in the Third Reich* (New York: St Martin's Press, 1994). See also Jeremy Tambling, *Opera and the Culture of Fascism* (Oxford: Oxford University Press, 1996).

1 Barry Millington, 'Nuremberg Trial', *Cambridge Opera Journal* 3 (1991), 247–60.

CHAPTER THIRTEEN *Purity*

The chapter on *Parsifal* in Linda Hutcheon and Michael Hutcheon, *Opera: Desire, Disease, Death* (Lincoln: University of Nebraska Press, 1996), offers a powerful reading of the materiality of the opera's bodies; see also the relevant sections of the same two authors' *Bodily Charm: Living Opera* (Lincoln: University of Nebraska Press, 2000). In the Cambridge Opera Handbooks series, Lucy Beckett, *Richard Wagner: Parsifal* (Cambridge: Cambridge University Press, 1981), is a useful introduction, though committed to a reading of the opera which many will find implausible. A new full-length study has appeared very recently: Peter Bassett, *Wagner's Parsifal* (Kent Town, Australia: Wakefield, 2001). Its subtitle – 'the Journey of a Soul' – accurately reflects its fairly conventionally spiritual focus. The Opera Guide on *Parsifal* in the English National Opera/Royal Opera series (no. 34, 1986) is particularly valuable for two essays on the music, one by Robin Holloway describing its essential unity, the other by Carolyn Abbate focussing on its narrative properties. The material basis of Wagner's anti-Semitism is exhaustively explained in Marc A. Weiner, *Richard Wagner and the Anti-Semitic Imagination* (Lincoln: University of Nebraska Press, 1995), with reference not just to the 'regeneration' essays but the whole of the composer's oeuvre.

CHAPTER FOURTEEN Bühnenweihfestspiel

For a valuable glimpse of the actual atmosphere of the 1876 and 1882 festivals, as well as those conducted in the following decades under Cosima's supervision, see the collection of reminiscences in Robert Hartford, ed., *Bayreuth: The Early Years* (Cambridge: Cambridge University Press, 1980). Wagner's thinking about the institution of the theatre is discussed in detail in Dieter Borchmeyer, *Richard Wagner: Theory and Theatre* (Oxford: Clarendon, 1991). Frederic Spotts's *Bayreuth* (New Haven and London: Yale University Press, 1994) is a lively, detailed and searching history of the festival, especially strong on the theatre's prehistory and the early productions. Adorno (see notes to chapter 10) identifies the fiction of *Bühnenweihfestspiel* as the essence of Wagner's whole mode of production: 'The aim of the *Gesamtkunstwerk* is not so much to express . . . a metaphysics as to produce it. A wholly profane outlook aspires to give birth to a sacred sphere from within itself; in this respect *Parsifal* merely makes conscious the tendency of the entire oeuvre' (p. 107).

CHAPTER FIFTEEN *Transformation music*

A recent commentary on Syberberg's film of *Parsifal* can be found in Marcia J. Citron, *Opera on Screen* (New Haven and London: Yale University Press, 2000). See also Jeremy Tambling, *Opera, Ideology, and Film* (Manchester: Manchester University Press, 1987). The film itself, of course, is one of the most striking and interesting commentaries on *Parsifal* yet produced; its treatment of the figures of Parsifal and Kundry in particular is remarkably sympathetic and suggestive (amid a generally hostile, or at least intensely sceptical, approach to the opera), and it is correspondingly attentive to the idea of transformation in general – an idea perhaps perfectly suited to the medium of film.

CHAPTER SIXTEEN   *The Grail*

For a properly theorized argument about the relation between Wagner's works and their production on stage, see Jean-Jacques Nattiez, ' "Fidelity" to Wagner: Reflections on the Centenary *Ring*', in Barry Millington and Stewart Spencer, eds, *Wagner in Performance* (New Haven and London: Yale University Press, 1992). The most complete guide to the visual history of Wagner's operas up to 1982 is Oswald Georg Bauer, *Richard Wagner: The Stage Designs and Productions from the Premieres to the Present* (1982; English ed., New York: Rizzoli, 1983). Bayreuth productions up to 1976 are exhaustively documented in Dietrich Mack, *Der Bayreuther Inszenierungsstil* (Munich: Prestel, 1976) (*The Bayreuth Production Style*) – even English readers can study the copious illustrations. Penelope Turing, *New Bayreuth* (London: Spearman, 1969) records the hugely influential postwar style of Wieland Wagner and his imitators and followers. The thoughts of an important early innovator in staging Wagner can be read in Adolphe Appia, *Staging Wagnerian Drama* (1895; English ed., Basel: Birkhäuser, 1982), along with the same author's *Music and the Art of the Theatre* (1899; English ed., Coral Gables, FL: University of Miami Press, 1962). See also Spotts's *Bayreuth* (see notes to chapter 14) for descriptions and illustrations of a number of productions in the Festspielhaus, as well as a very useful account of some of the major controversies they have provoked. The 1982 Bayreuth *Ring*, directed by Peter Hall, is the subject of Stephen Fay, *The Ring: Anatomy of an Opera* (London: Secker & Warburg, 1984), which gives an excellent idea of the production process as a whole. I will allow myself one excursion into Wagner literature outside the English-speaking world, since Jean-Jacques Nattiez, *Tétralogies – Wagner, Boulez, Chéreau* (Paris: Christian Bourgois, 1983) is the outstanding critical study of a single production (in this case, the 1976 *Ring* directed by Chéreau).

Index